Second Edition

Instructional Methods for Adolescents with Learning and Behavior Problems

Patrick J. Schloss
Bloomsburg University of Pennsylvania

Maureen A. Smith
State University College at Buffalo

Cynthia N. Schloss
Missouri Protection and Advocacy Services

Allyn and Bacon
Boston • London • Toronto • Sydney • Tokyo • Singapore

Series Editor: Ray Short
Editorial Assistant: Christine M. Shaw
Marketing Manager: Ellen Mann
Production Administrator: Annette Joseph
Production Coordinator: Holly Crawford
Editorial-Production Service: Ann Mohan, WordCrafters Editorial Services, Inc.
Composition Buyer: Linda Cox
Manufacturing Buyer: Megan Cochran
Cover Administrator: Linda Knowles
Cover Designer: Suzanne Harbison

Copyright © 1995, 1990 by Allyn & Bacon
A Simon & Schuster Company
Needham Heights, Mass. 02194

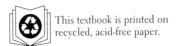

This textbook is printed on recycled, acid-free paper.

Library of Congress Cataloging-in-Publication Data

Schloss, Patrick J.
    Instructional methods for adolescents with learning and behavior problems / Patrick J. Schloss, Maureen A. Smith, Cynthia N. Schloss.
    — 2nd ed.
        p. cm.
    Includes bibliographical references and index.
    ISBN 0-205-16083-2
    1. Learning disabled youth—Education. 2. Handicapped youth—Education (Secondary) 3. Special education—Curricula. I. Smith, Maureen A. II. Schloss, Cynthia N. III. Title.
LC4704.S35 1995
371.9—dc20   94-23755
                                                               CIP

Printed in the United States of America

10 9 8 7 6 5 4 3 2   00 99 98 97 96

Contents

PART THREE   *Instruction in Basic and Functional Skills*

Foreword

What happens to special education students after they leave the educational system? Do they assimilate nicely into community life, find decent-paying jobs, and become happy and productive citizens? Or do the vast majority face a major struggle for survival? The answer is that most former students lead unproductive lives in all important life and work roles—employment, social relationships, recreation, independent living, community participation—and in self-esteem.

This is the sad state of affairs at present even though an army of professionals has been available to focus on the needs of these students for the past 20 years. Many pieces of significant legislation have been passed in the United States giving persons with disabilities the right to engage meaningfully in society—educationally, vocationally, and in the community. But, in most instances, the schools, agencies, organizations, employers, and the general public have not changed their attitudes and policies enough to permit these individuals to take their rightful place in society as contributing citizens and workers.

It is a tough world out there, especially if you have a disability! Whether children with disabilities will develop into competent adults who can meet the complex demands of society depends a great deal on educators and parents. It is widely believed that over 80% of all persons with disabilities could become independent adults with satisfying employment. Instead, up to 80% of persons with disabilities leaving educational programs end up as dependent and basically unemployed adults who lead miserable lives.

Educators must change their philosophies and practices substantially if students with disabilities are to enter mainstream society. No one would deny that children and adolescents with disabilities need to acquire basic academic skills during their education. But the curriculum must also focus on critical career/life skills. The educational program must have a "whole-person" orientation and through its scope and sequence must gradually teach the student how to engage in all the important roles he or she will be expected to cope with as an adult in the community.

The purpose of education is to help every student become a happy, productive, and independent adult. Before this goal can be achieved, substantial changes will have to take place in many school districts. Educational innovations come and go, but most of them—even the significant ones—have little impact because they are usually rejected. Yet changes must be made if students in special education are to be successful.

It is my hope that the readers of this book are ready to take the steps needed to permit students in special education to get the services they really need. That is the fundamental message of this text.

This excellent book can broaden your perspective and help you understand why the adolescent's educational program should cover not only basic academic skills, but also other areas of equal importance—work, leisure, and independent living. The book presents, in a logical manner, the wide range of considerations and resources that must be part of any educational program the goal of which is to meet all the important needs of adolescents and young adults with disabilities. I congratulate the authors on the extensive work they have done to make this publication a major contribution to changing the flow of educational practice to a more applied and systematic method of preparing the special student for successful life after school.

Donn E. Brolin
The University of Missouri—Columbia

Preface

The educational system in the United States was originally formed to provide for a well-educated citizenry. This country's founders believed that a democracy would operate effectively only if its citizens possessed the basic skills they needed to contribute to majority governance.

Early educational efforts emphasized essential communication and computational skills. Literacy was considered important for the efficient exchange of information between the policy makers and their constituents. Written language skills were thought to be equally useful for the efficient exchange of information. This was particularly true prior to the advent of advanced telecommunications. Short of personal appearances, handwritten letters were the only means by which a constituent could provide feedback to a distant legislator. The importance of spoken language is evidenced by legendary incidents in which public opinion on sensitive issues was swayed through carefully staged orations. Mathematics, in the form of measurement and computation, was considered to be important for the conduct of governmental and private business.

These basic skills were also deemed to be essential to the economic success of the country. The vast majority of trades required some basic skill in written language, spoken language, and mathematics. The professions required even greater skill in these areas. Even unskilled farm or industrial laborers benefited from basic academic skills.

Needless to say, the importance of basic academic skills has not diminished with time. In fact, the need for adequate academic skills has grown substantially in light of political and economic changes. With the recent advances in technology and society's increasing reliance on the service sector and on skilled professionals, there is a growing need for a well-educated citizenry. This trend has sparked an unprecedented increase in the number of students obtaining baccalaureate degrees.

Legislation over the past two decades has emphasized that public education should be made available to *all* citizens in the country, including those with disabilities. Special educators have become increasingly aware that public education has the potential to prepare even individuals with the most severe disabilities to contribute to society. Advances in educational technology and the increased availability of services have been partly responsible for lowering the barriers to community integration faced by individuals with disabilities.

Unfortunately, recent data suggest a guarded prognosis for individuals with even mild disabilities. Employment rates for persons with mild disabilities are substantially below those for the general population. Individuals who have disabilities are likely to spend several years finding stable employment. Only a small number of individuals with disabilities are entering skilled occupations, and once there are finding few opportunities for advancement. Clearly, public education as conceived by our founding fathers has not fulfilled its promise for individuals with disabilities.

Even so, public education *has* substantially improved the basic academic skills of individuals with disabilities. Children and youths previously excluded from academic programs and served only in custodial and compensatory programs are now progressing through elementary levels of mathematics, reading, and writing.

The problem is that a gap seems to exist between the acquisition of basic academic skills and the application of these skills in work, leisure, and independent living. This gap results in part from excessive reliance on methods generalized from elementary-aged populations to secondary-aged learners. This overreliance is exemplified by the frequent use of the term *disabled children*, where "children" includes individuals at intermediate and secondary levels. It is also exemplified by curricula having a developmental orientation that overlooks the functional application of basic skills. Furthermore, it is exemplified by the lack of attention given to the special problems of adolescence and adulthood in special education methods courses.

Instructional Methods for Adolescents with Learning and Behavior Problems was written to help fill this gap. It describes special education methods that are effective in promoting skills that may generalize to adult life. The book is similar in several ways to methods books concerned with elementary populations. First, it has an empirical orientation to special education. The basic teaching model described in the text can be used to evaluate learner characteristics, establish corresponding goals and objectives, implement educational strategies that have been demonstrated to be effective in applied research literature, evaluate the impact of the procedures with the individual learner, and modify educational interventions when sufficient progress is not noted.

The book is unique in its focus on the special needs of intermediate- and secondary-aged learners. It pays special attention to the following topics:

- the unique psychosocial problems of adolescents
- community resources available to young adults who have disabilities
- curriculum needs as related to basic skill development and community integration
- special social and interpersonal skill training priorities of young adults who have disabilities
- postsecondary educational, leisure, vocational, and residential opportunities
- validated learning strategies for adolescents and young adults who have disabilities
- classroom management and motivational strategies that reflect the personal characteristics associated with adolescence.

Upon completing the text, readers will be able to develop and implement educational programs suited to the special needs of adolescents and young adults who have disabilities.

Organization

The second edition of *Instructional Methods for Adolescents with Learning and Behavior Problems* is organized into three main parts. The first deals with educational perspectives characteristic of instructional services for youths who have disabilities. The chapters in this part of the book focus on the legislative and social foundations of secondary and postsecondary education, postsecondary service options, and special problems associated with adolescence and adulthood.

Part Two examines general instructional approaches that are effective in teaching secondary-level learners who have disabilities. It opens with a discussion of a comprehensive model that illustrates how to provide direct instruction for youths with disabilities. It is followed by an informal assessment of strategies that will ensure learner progress within the instructional model. The next chapter presents strategies for managing the learning environment. The concluding chapter of this part presents some consultative and resource functions of educators working with adolescents who have disabilities.

Part Three includes a description of special education methodologies at the secondary level and curricula within each of the major curriculum areas. Each chapter reviews specific curriculum concerns, educational approaches, assessment procedures, and instructional materials. One of the main themes here is that curriculum objectives should be based on the skills of the learner and the functional demands of the community. Also of importance is a new chapter in the second edition on teaching in the content areas.

The methodology in each of the specific curricular areas is based on the general instructional strategies presented in the preceding chapters. The final chapters cover some traditional topics such as listening and speaking, written language, reading, mathematics, science, and social studies. Also covered are nontraditional curricular areas that are particularly appropriate for adolescents making the transition to adult life, including leisure skill training, vocational education, and interpersonal skill development.

Features

We have included several distinctive features that are intended to enhance the value of *Instructional Methods for Adolescents with Learning and Behavior Problems* as both a course text and a reference.

- *DID YOU KNOW THAT. . . ?* The chapters begin with cognitive competencies. These statements outline the scope of the information contained in the chapter. Cognitive competencies are likely to be assessed by college instructors through class discussion and paper-and-pencil measures.
- *CAN YOU. . . ?* The chapters also begin with separate performance competencies. These statements identify specific strategies discussed in each chapter. Performance competencies are likely to be assessed by college instructors through direct observations in practical situations or through microteaching simulations.
- *ACTION PLANS.* These features occur throughout the individual chapters. They draw attention to performance by offering a step-by-step guide to implementing

educational strategies. In most cases, the action plans summarize activities presented in the text without repeating the underlying rationale.

- *CASES FOR ACTION.* The cases for action provide an opportunity for readers to study and resolve hypothetical instructional problems. They are typically open-ended vignettes that may be resolved through information contained in the text.
- *TECHNICAL WRITING.* Professionals in the discipline of special education employ technical terms to convey particular concepts. It would be inappropriate for a college text to exclude any such terms that are critical to a precise understanding of these concepts. Therefore, when appropriate, technical terms are included and defined. Jargon that does little to communicate the philosophy or strategies associated with secondary special education is excluded.

A Word of Thanks

We are grateful to the people who have made the writing of this text possible. Our appreciation is extended to Ray Short, editor at Allyn and Bacon. Ray has provided editorial leadership from the initial conception of this project through the final production. This leadership has ensured that the product is responsive to the needs of inservice and preservice training programs for secondary special educators. Similarly, we are indebted to Professors Gwendolyn Cartledge, of The Ohio State University, Iva Dean Cook, of West Virginia Graduate College, William H. Evans, of the University of West Florida, H. Earle Knowlton, of the University of Kansas, and Donald F. Maietta, of Boston University, for their extensive and insightful reviews of the initial prospectus and subsequent drafts.

We would also like to express our appreciation to Ann Mohan, of WordCrafters Editorial Services, for seeing the manuscript through production. We acknowledge the assistance of Nell Loraine Alexander for her careful reading of the manuscript and contributions of text features. Appreciation is also expressed to Shannon Ward, Robin Brueckner, Bette Stetzel, Virginia Tennill, and Eileen McBride for their clerical assistance. Our appreciation is also extended to Gae Arnold-Reid, Michael Aylward, and Sharon Aldrich for research assistance in updating this second edition.

Finally, we would like to acknowledge the extraordinarily fine work of our chapter contributors.

P. J. S.
M. A. S.
C. N. S.

$Chapter$ 1

Foundations of Secondary Special Education

Did you know that . . .

- Recent reports on the quality of education available in U.S. public schools do not mention special education?
- There are overlapping themes in legislation addressing special and vocational education?
- Of the secondary students receiving special education, 30% drop out of school?
- Employment rates of persons with mild disabilities leaving secondary schools range from 30% to 90%?
- Only a minority of individuals with disabilities will enter skilled occupations?
- Students with severe disabilities are less likely than those with mild disabilities to drop out of school?
- Many professionals believe the prevalence of elementary special education programs makes secondary programs unnecessary?
- Most teachers of secondary students with special needs were trained at the elementary level?
- Many special educators are certified but not qualified to teach at the secondary level?

Can you . . .

- Identify the court cases that contributed to the provisions of PL 94-142?
- List the provisions of PL 94-142?
- Define FAPE, LRE, and IEP?
- List the components of an IEP?
- Identify the instructional settings included in Deno's Cascade?
- State the purpose of Sections 503 and 504 of the Rehabilitation Act of 1973?

- Describe the provisions of the Americans with Disabilities Act of 1990?
- Describe the efforts by OSERS to remedy the deficiency in current educational services to persons with disabilities?
- Describe steps to ensure that learning is retained and skills are transferred to life situations beyond the school setting?
- Discuss six factors that hinder the development of secondary special education programs?
- Identify the goals of secondary special education?

The status of regular secondary education is a recurring theme in public and professional circles. Reports such as *A Nation at Risk* (National Commission on Excellence in Education, 1983) have focused on the quality of the educational services typically available to students and the impact of these services on their lives. Unfortunately, the picture is bleak.

It is interesting to note that reports such as *A Nation at Risk* fail to discuss the status of special education in general or secondary special education in particular. Although this omission may have the short-term advantage of avoiding public criticism over the current state of affairs, some negative publicity could be just what the doctor ordered. Widespread public recognition of the problems facing secondary special education might stir authorities to develop and implement comprehensive measures to increase the quality and quantity of services available to students.

As Wilcox and Bellamy (1982) have suggested, it would be nice to believe that the impact of elementary special education was so positive that it would enable the vast majority of secondary students with disabilities to enter the regular education classroom and perform at levels comparable to those of their nondisabled peers for the duration of their academic careers. Unfortunately, this has not been the case. Some students are likely to require some form of special education services the entire time they are eligible for public education. Furthermore, the quality and quantity of the special services available at the secondary level are likely to be inferior to those at the elementary level. Indeed, special services available to secondary students may be little more than a repetition or a continuation of elementary-level programs. Special education teachers who are not specifically trained for work at this level may use instructional strategies that have not been validated for use with secondary learners. In addition, the instructional materials frequently used at this level may have been intended either for elementary students with disabilities or for secondary students who are not disabled (Kokoszka & Drye, 1981; Miller, Sabatino, & Larsen, 1980; Sabatino, 1982; Warger, 1987; Wilcox & Bellamy, 1982; Wimmer, 1981).

The prognosis for young adults with mild disabilities has been summarized as follows with reference to career outcomes: (a) employment rates of persons with mild disabilities leaving secondary schools range from 30% to 90%; (b) individuals with mild disabilities are likely to change jobs three times during the two-year period following their high school graduation; (c) poor social skills are the most likely reason for unsuccessful employment; (d) the longer the individual is in the workforce, the more likely it is that he or she will obtain stable employment, (e) only a minority of individuals with disabilities will enter skilled occupations; (f) workers with disabilities are likely to be satisfied with their positions, but dissatisfied with the limited opportunities for advancement; and (g) the modal earning level of workers with disabilities is estimated to be only slightly higher than the minimum wage (McAfee, 1988).

The prognosis is equally unimpressive for civic outcomes. Individuals with disabilities are thought to commit a disproportionate number of crimes, vote less often (even though state mandates ensure voting rights for individuals with disabilities), and are unlikely to perform community service (McAfee, 1988). Individuals with disabilities are somewhat less likely to marry and have children. Participation in community leisure, social, and religious activities is more limited than it is among individuals who are not disabled. As pointed out by Madeline Will (U.S. Department of Labor, 1979; Will, 1984, p. 2), former assistant secretary of the Office of Special Education and Rehabilitative Services,

> *Youth with disabilities face an uncertain future when they leave the nation's public schools. Qualification for employment is an implied promise of American education, but between 50 and 80 percent of working age adults who report a disability are jobless. . . . Without employment, many individuals turn to community services only to find long waiting lists. Those adults with disabilities who do gain entry into public programs offering vocational services often experience low wages, slow movement to employment, and segregation from their nondisabled peers.*

Public education has in all probability substantially improved the basic skills of individuals with disabilities (Mangrum & Strichart, 1984). Individuals who in the past might have gained only a few domestic or manual skills are now progressing through elementary levels of mathematics, reading, and writing. Some individuals with mild disabilities even have a strong prognosis for success in postsecondary educational settings (Astin, Hemond, & Richardson, 1982; Lawrence, Kent, & Henson, 1981; Rogan & Hartman, 1976). The main obstacle to further improvement seems to lie in the transfer of training from social service and educational contexts to adult-living environments (Parmenter, 1986; Rusch & Mittaug, 1985). Individuals with disabilities may possess higher levels of basic academic skills, but they appear to be poorly prepared to apply these skills to the demands of community life.

The Office of Special Education and Rehabilitation Services (OSERS) has provided some guidelines on how to treat this deficiency of our current educational efforts. OSERS has defined transition as

- *A period that includes high school, the point of graduation, additional postsecondary education or adult services, and the initial years of employment.*
- *A process that requires sound preparation in the secondary school, adequate support at the point of school leaving.*
- *An effort that emphasizes shared responsibility of all involved parties for transition success, and extends beyond traditional notions of service coordina-*

tion to address the quality and appropriateness of each service area. (Will, 1984, p. 2)

The OSERS definition of transition has been criticized by some for being narrow in scope in that it focuses on employment as the major outcome of transition services (Halpern, 1985). This sentiment was reflected in the passage of the Individuals with Disabilities Education Act (Public Law 101-476) in 1990, which described transition outcomes in broader terms:

Transition services *means a coordinated set of activities for a student, designated within an outcome oriented process, which promotes movement from school to post-school activities, including post-secondary education, vocational training, integrated employment (including supported employment), continuing and adult education, adult services, independent living or community participation. (Section 300.18)*

This legislation calls for a multidimensional definition of transition outcomes, including physical and mental health, mobility and community access, leisure and recreation skills, citizenship, and a sense of general well-being (Halpern, 1993).

The purpose of this chapter is to review the foundations of secondary special education. We begin with the legislation mandating secondary special education services. Second, we identify the goals of secondary education for regular education students and students with disabilities. Next we examine factors that have prevented secondary learners with disabilities from attaining these goals. Finally, we identify some of the problems that must be addressed if a free appropriate education is to be made available to all students at the secondary level.

Legislative Foundations

For a long time, secondary special education was a neglected component of the education system (Heller, 1981; Miller et al., 1980). Fortunately, in the last 15 years several pieces of legislation have been enacted that provide the legal foundation for providing quality services to learners with special needs at the secondary level. These acts reflect federal commitments to special education and vocational education.

Special Education

The 1970s witnessed numerous landmark court decisions that affected the education of learners with disabilities. These cases are listed in Table 1.1. A consent agreement in *PARC, Bowman et al.* v. *Commonwealth of Pennsylvania* (1971) guaranteed the following to children who had mental retardation: (1) a free and appropriate public education, (2) education in the least restrictive environment, (3) periodic review and evaluation of the educational program, and (4) procedural due process. *Mills* v. *Board of Education of*

TABLE 1.1   Special Education Litigation Influencing Secondary Students

Litigation	Provisions
PARC; Bowman et al. v. Commonwealth of PA	Guaranteed to students with mental retardation 1. free appropriate public education 2. least restrictive environment 3. periodic review 4. procedural due process
Mills v. Board of Education of the District of Columbia	Provisions of PARC extend to all students with handicaps
Diana v. State Board of Education	Assessment must be in the student's native language
Wyatt v. Aderholt; Halderman v. Pennhurst	Right to adequate treatment
Armstrong v. Kline; Battle v. Commonwealth	Extended school year

the District of Columbia (1972) extended these rights to all children and youth with disabilities. *Diana* v. *State Board of Education* (1970) was a class action suit on behalf of Mexican-American students who had been labeled mentally retarded because of low scores on standardized intelligence tests. The court ruled that evaluation practices had to be modified to take into account a student's native language and to include periodic reevaluation. *Halderman* v. *Pennhurst State School and Hospital* (1977) reiterated an earlier decision made in *Wyatt* v. *Aderholt* (1971) by guaranteeing the rights of individuals with severe disabilities to adequate treatment. *Armstrong* v. *Kline* (1980) and *Battle* v. *Commonwealth* (1980) extended the length of the traditional school year for students who, by virtue of the severity of their disability, do not maintain their skill levels when school is not in session.

The spirit of these court decisions was reflected in Public Law 94-142, the Education for All Handicapped Children Act of 1975, the most comprehensive law ever enacted on behalf of children and youth with disabilities. PL 94-142 ordered states to provide a free appropriate public education (FAPE) to all children and youth between 5 and 21 years of age. States could, at their own discretion, provide services for children as young as 3 years of age.

PL 94-142 contains five broad measures. The first stipulates that an individualized education program (IEP) is to be developed under the guidance of a team of parents and professionals. The IEP is expected to cover seven major topics: current levels of performance; annual goals; short-term objectives; objective criteria, evaluation procedures, and schedules for annual assessment; degree of participation in regular education; special education and related services; and dates for initiating services and their expected duration.

The second measure requires that services be provided in the least restrictive environment (LRE). Service providers are obligated to make available a variety of educational alternatives to students with disabilities. Deno (1970) developed a "cascade of services" ranging from placement in the regular classroom to special schools and homebound instruction. This model is presented in Figure 1.1. In addition, Deno (1970) suggested that the needs of most learners with disabilities can best be met in less restrictive settings, that is, in settings at the top of the cascade. One ultimate goal of special education is to help the learner move toward the next less restrictive environment; however, educators are advised to closely monitor a student's performance and to promote such movement as needs dictate.

The third measure calls for nondiscriminatory testing and mandates that all contact with the learner, including evaluation, be conducted in that learner's native language. In

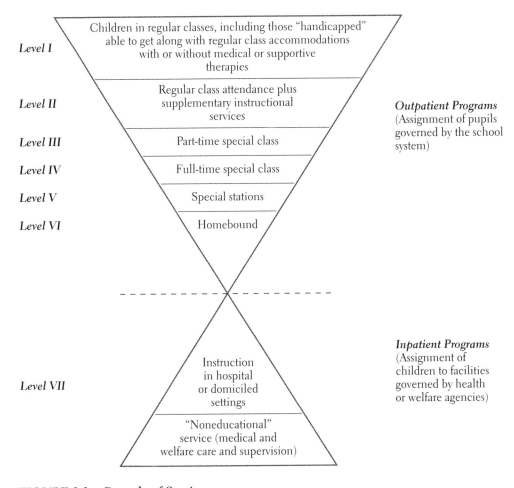

FIGURE 1.1   Cascade of Services

Source: From "Special Education as Developmental Capital" by E. Deno, *Exceptional Children, 37,* 1970, 229–237. Copyright 1970 by The Council for Exceptional Children. Reprinted with permission.

addition, educators must use the communication mode normally used by students who have sensory impairments or are unable to read and write.

The fourth measure provides for confidentiality. PL 94-142 guarantees students with disabilities and their parents the right to confidentiality of information and record keeping. Parents must be informed of their rights to (a) review their child's educational records, (b) amend content that is inaccurate or misleading or that violates their right to privacy, and (c) request a hearing to challenge the accuracy of information in the file.

The fifth measure pertains to due process. It guarantees that a learner will not be evaluated or the educational program altered until parent permission has been granted. Parents are entitled to a hearing if they and the educational agency disagree on the need for an evaluation or a change in the child's program.

In 1983, the Education of the Handicapped Amendments (PL 98-199) were enacted by Congress to address major education and employment transition difficulties experienced by youth with disabilities (Rusch & Phelps, 1987). Section 626 of this act, Secondary Education and Transition Services for Handicapped Youth, provides for funds for the development of training programs and related services. Section 626 has two main objectives: (1) to improve and develop secondary special education programs and (2) to facilitate the transition to postsecondary experiences through the careful coordination of education, training, and related services.

In 1986, PL 94-142 was amended by PL 99-457, Education of the Handicapped Amendments, which extended the rights enjoyed by students between the ages of 5 and 21 years to children between the ages of 3 and 5 years. PL 99-457 also contained provisions formulated specifically for secondary students with disabilities. Congress authorized the allocation of federal funds to activities that would (a) strengthen special education and related services that promote transition of secondary learners to postsecondary environments, (b) improve and develop secondary special education programs, and (c) enhance the vocational and life skills of students with disabilities.

In 1990, PL 101-476 mandated transition services for students with disabilities. It stated that services were to be tailored to the student's individual needs and interests. Such services included career planning, employment options, postsecondary training, financial assistance, community participation, advocacy/legal supports, leisure, transportation, self-advocacy, personal management, living arrangements, medical support, and insurance.

The mandate required that transition goals and objectives be developed no later than age 16 years, and earlier if appropriate. The school, therefore, became a key element in assuring that adult agencies were aware of particular students with disabilities.

PL 94-142, PL 98-199, PL 99-457, and PL 101-476 provide ample evidence of federal interest in the educational opportunities available to students with disabilities. Local education agencies are legally obligated to provide a free appropriate education to all students regardless of the nature or severity of their disability. Timely implementation of appropriate educational programs during the elementary grades may reduce the number of students requiring special education and related services at the secondary level. On the other hand, elementary programs may not be long enough to bring about the desired changes in student performance. Therefore, federal laws have mandated that special education and related services be provided at the secondary level for students who would benefit from them. Additional support for secondary special education programs is found in legislation addressing vocational education.

Vocational Education

Vocational education has been identified as the most realistic means of helping individuals make the transition between education and the world of work (Sarkees & Scott, 1985). Legislation in this area of education reiterates the themes contained in legislation designed to promote special education for individuals with disabilities. These also emphasize free appropriate educational programming, placement in the least restrictive environment, and cooperative planning by the various parties interested in the student's development (Gartland, 1988).

Sections 503 and 504 of the Rehabilitation Act of 1973 (PL 93-112) mandate that persons with disabilities be given equal access to training and employment opportunities. Section 503 requires employers receiving federal assistance of $2,500 or more to develop an affirmative action plan to recruit, hire, and train individuals with disabilities. This section also requires employers to provide reasonable accommodations for persons with disabilities such as ramps, curb cuts, and other modifications that make the work environment accessible. Section 504 guarantees that all individuals with disabilities will have equal access to programs, jobs, and housing. Agencies receiving federal funds could lose this support if they fail to provide individuals who have disabilities with services, benefits, and opportunities that are comparable to those afforded to nondisabled individuals. Therefore, students enrolled in secondary special education programs should have access to vocational instruction, counseling, prevocational services, and work–study and job placement programs. They should also be placed in regular education programs to the maximum extent possible.

The Americans with Disabilities Act of 1990 (PL 101-336) expanded the definitions and intent of the Vocational Rehabilitation Act of 1973 to include all public and private employers, services, and facilities. It prohibited private employers, state and local governments, employment agencies, and labor unions from discriminating against qualified individuals with disabilities in job application procedures; hiring, firing; advancement; compensation; job training; and other terms, conditions, and privileges of employment. A qualified employee or applicant with a disability was defined as any individual who, with or without reasonable accommodation, could perform the essential functions of the job in question. Reasonable accommodation included (a) making existing facilities used by employees readily accessible to and usable by persons with disabilities; (b) restructuring jobs, modifying work schedules, and reassigning to a vacant position; and (c) acquiring or modifying equipment or devices; adjusting or modifying examinations, training materials, or policies; and providing qualified readers or interpreters.

The law required employers to make an accommodation to the known disability of a qualified applicant or employee if it would not impose an "undue hardship" on the operation of the employer's business. *Undue hardship* was defined as an action requiring significant difficulty or expense when considered in light of factors such as an employer's size, financial resources, and the nature and structure of its operation. An employer was not required to lower the quality or production standards to make an accommodation, nor was an employer obligated to provide personal-use items such as glasses or hearing aids.

PL 93-380, the Education Amendments of 1974, had implications for individuals with disabilities. Specifically, the act stated that students should be adequately prepared to undertake employment and participate in society according to their abilities. In addition, state and local education agencies were authorized to provide secondary students with a career education program that maximized employment and participation opportunities. Career education should obviously begin early in all academic programs, but its importance for learners with disabilities cannot be overstated. Students with special needs should be exposed to all the opportunities available in employment and community settings from an early age. The secondary school is an ideal place to expand upon the foundations laid earlier and to prepare students with disabilities for the challenges that await them on the job and in the community.

Career education received further attention in PL 95-207, the Career Education Incentive Act of 1977. The purpose of this act was to increase career awareness and exploration and to improve career education planning and decision making. Many agencies, including school districts, were allocated funds to develop and implement career exploration and work experience programs, workshops for education personnel, and seminars for community leaders.

The Comprehensive Employment and Training Act of 1978 (CETA) enhanced the employability of youth who were disadvantaged or had disabilities. CETA allocated funds to local communities and school districts to disseminate occupational information, develop exploration activities, and provide summer and part-time work experiences. CETA was replaced by the Job Training Partnership Act (JTPA), known as PL 97-300, in 1982. The purpose of JTPA was to (a) establish programs that prepared youths and unskilled adults for entry into the job market and (b) provide training for individuals facing serious barriers to employment. Private Industry Councils (PICs) were established and charged with identifying the services to be made available in the service delivery area (SDA). The PIC includes representatives from local businesses, organized labor, rehabilitation, economic development agencies, and education. Individuals eligible for JTPA funds include those who have a mental or physical disability that presents a substantial barrier to employment. A number of services are available to individuals whose eligibility has been established, including job-search assistance, counseling, remedial education, and basic-skills training (Sarkees & Scott, 1985).

The Carl D. Perkins Vocational and Applied Technology Education Act of 1990 provided supplementary services that are essential for members of special populations to participate in vocational programs successfully. Special populations include (a) individuals with disabilities; (b) educationally and economically disadvantaged individuals; (c) individuals of limited English proficiency; (d) individuals who participate in programs designed to eliminate sex bias; and (e) individuals in correctional institutions.

Federal funds were allocated to states to provide information about vocational education, as well as provide support personnel to programs. Funds were also provided for instructional aides and devices, including interpreters for the deaf, bilingual interpreters and tutors, readers and notetakers, materials and supplies, equipment, and other services necessary for success.

Sections of the Perkins Act require that students enrolled in vocational education (a) be assessed to identify their interests, abilities, and special needs; (b) receive special services such as curricular adaptations, instruction, equipment, and facilities; (c) participate in counseling and career guidance activities; and (d) receive counseling to facilitate transition from school to postsecondary opportunities (Sarkees & Scott, 1985).

Implications of Special and Vocational Education Legislation

The preceding paragraphs have outlined the types of legislation designed to support secondary education for students with disabilities. As suggested earlier, acts addressing both special and vocational education have many goals in common. Ideally, secondary students with special needs should receive a free appropriate public education in the least restrictive environment. Assessment should be conducted in each student's native language and should take into account all aspects of the disability. Special education and related services should be tailored to each student's particular needs and should be included in an individualized education program (IEP). The IEP should include long-term goals and short-term objectives, which, when mastered, will prepare students to meet the challenges of those environments in which they are currently functioning as well as those they expect to enter in the near future.

A Transition Perspective

Identifying Goals and Objectives

Educators have traditionally emphasized a developmental orientation when prescribing educational objectives. Until recently, they assumed that skills within a given domain can be enumerated in a logical sequence; the sequence typically corresponds with the order in which skills are acquired by the general population. They also assumed that educational evaluation can identify the developmental level at which an individual is functioning within the domain. In addition, they argued that the goal of instruction should be to improve the skill in the developmental sequence in which the individual has not demonstrated mastery.

The developmental orientation is appropriate for the majority of students in U.S. public schools. Adherence to the model ensures that learners in general will acquire a logical sequence of competencies. Each competency model is built upon previously mastered skills and concepts. Upon graduating from high school, the students will have acquired advanced skills within the respective curricular domains. These advanced skills will by and large prepare the individual for future success in postsecondary educational, vocational, and community endeavors.

Children and youth with disabilities, however, have specific learning and behavioral characteristics that minimize the effectiveness of developmental curricula. Among these are slower rates of acquiring information and skills, deficits in the ability to generalize learned skills to other settings or conditions, and a lack of ability to retain learned material (Schloss & Sedlak, 1986). Therefore an adolescent with disabilities is likely to master far fewer skills and concepts by the end of formal schooling. Given the development orientation, the youth may have progressed only to the fourth- to seventh-grade level in basic academic skills. Consequently, the youth may not have been afforded the opportunity to develop specific vocational skills, leisure skills, independent living skills, and other functional competencies. As already mentioned, basic skills acquired in the classroom context may be less likely to generalize to community settings. This further compounds the problem.

Transfer of Training

Adolescents with disabilities do not maintain and generalize skills to the same extent as nondisabled learners. Further, youths with disabilities are more likely to have a variety of unsuccessful employment experiences before obtaining a relatively permanent position (Kidd, 1970; McAfee, 1988). Thus a primary goal of educational strategies should be to generalize skills from formal educational settings to community environments. A number of instructional procedures have been devised to promote this transfer (Greenan & Sitlington, 1987; Horner, McDonnell, & Bellamy, 1966). The transition orientation would apply these procedures in secondary special education programs.

Altering instructional conditions ensures that the student will do more than just acquire a restricted set of rote skills that cannot be applied beyond the instructional setting. In addition, artificial incentives should be replaced by naturally occurring reinforcers. Reinforcement procedures should be as unobtrusive as possible and yet be sufficiently strong to motivate performance. Finally, self-control skill development can be used to enhance generalization of skills from the classroom to community settings. Self-control is the ability to recognize and manage events that influence one's own behavior (Zarkowska & Clements, 1988).

Articulation of Services

Despite the care and attention that educators may pay to the technology required to promote the transfer of skills, it is unreasonable to expect all students to graduate from high school and enter productive careers. Longitudinal and comprehensive service delivery systems are the most effective means of ensuring that the youth will have skills and abilities needed to adjust to changing community demands (Beebe & Karan, 1986; Schloss, 1985).

One individual must be responsible for coordinating services. During the school years, the special educator usually acts as the case manager. After the student reaches the age of 18 or 21, a vocational rehabilitation counselor, mental health or mental retardation specialist, or the individual's parents may become the case manager.

The Goals of Secondary Special Education

In 1964, Rollins and Unruh reported that the five goals of American secondary schools were to give students an opportunity to

1. receive a twelfth-grade education
2. develop independent critical thinking skills
3. learn the traditions, ideas, and processes of U.S. democracy
4. develop an understanding and appreciation of the art, literature, history, science, customs, and people of the United States and other nations
5. prepare for the roles they will assume after graduation.

Experts have also identified goals for students enrolled in secondary special education (Deshler, Schumaker, & Lenz, 1984):

1. to be placed in the least restrictive environment
2. to earn a high school diploma, for which they may have to pass minimum competency exams
3. to develop independent learning skills that will enable them to acquire information in new environments
4. to demonstrate social competence so that they will be able to function in employment and other community settings
5. to prepare for a career.

Woodward and Peters (1985) limited their list to the following three goals:

1. full-time education with nondisabled peers
2. the opportunity to earn the credits required for a high school diploma
3. vocational training, functional skill development, and job placement for students with a poor prognosis for academic success.

Although these lists address separate populations, they have some points in common. First, students should be provided with the opportunity to maximize their potential. For some, this will mean obtaining a twelfth-grade education; for others, it will mean participating in an educational program that emphasizes the mastery of functional and vocational skills. Second, to the greatest extent possible, students should receive their education in close approximation to their peers. Third, students should become independent thinkers who are capable of acquiring information outside the school setting. Fourth, students should possess the skills necessary to locate and maintain suitable employment and to meet the challenges of community living. Unfortunately for learners with disabilities, the outcomes of secondary education programs may not match their goals (Deshler et al., 1984).

Services at the secondary level have been expanded as a result of the increased emphasis on transition and the need to preserve gains derived from previous education programs. Despite hopeful signs, an alarming number of secondary students with disabilities do not yet enjoy the benefits extended by special and vocational education legislation. Edgar (1987) estimated that 30% of the students enrolled in secondary special education programs drop out. Eighteen percent of the students identified as having mild retardation do not complete secondary programs. Students with learning or behavior disabilities experience a 42% dropout rate. Zigmond and Thornton (1985) reported that secondary students with learning disabilities have a dropout rate of 54%. Edgar (1987) suggested the rates would be higher if it were not for the fact that students with more severe disabilities—who account for approximately 20% of the secondary special education population—are captives of the system because they are transported to and from the educational facilities. It may be a moot point. Circumstances under which secondary students with special needs leave school appear to have little effect on how they adjust to community settings. Edgar (1987) reported that neither graduates nor dropouts find adequate employment opportunities. Despite federal mandates, secondary students with disabilities appear to be without appropriate programming (Gartland, 1988).

Factors Influencing the Development of Secondary Special Education Programs

The statistics cited by Edgar (1987) and Zigmond and Thornton (1985) suggest that many secondary students with disabilities do not take advantage of their rights to an educational program under current legislation. The high dropout rate may indicate that these students are actually receiving either poor services or no services at all. The professional literature identifies six problems in secondary programming. They are presented in Action Plan 1.1.

Attitude toward Secondary Special Education

Perhaps the biggest problem limiting the development of appropriate secondary programs is that many professionals do not think students with disabilities require much attention at the secondary level (Heller, 1981; Lerner, Evans, & Meyers, 1977; Wells, Schmid, Algozzine, & Maher, 1983). This attitude may reflect the amount of professional attention directed toward students receiving special education and related services at the elementary level. The importance of providing appropriate services during the elementary years cannot be overstated, as their effectiveness is maximized through early, consis-

---

Action Plan 1.1   Factors Undermining the Success of Secondary Special Education

Special educators should be aware of six factors that undermine the effectiveness of special education for secondary students:

1. Limited recognition of the need for services at this level.
2. The inflexible structure of regular secondary education.
3. Curricular emphasis of regular secondary education.
4. Inadequate teacher preparation.
5. Lack of theoretical and empirical support.
6. Lack of appropriate materials.

tent implementation (Scranton & Downs, 1975). Unfortunately, many professionals hold the misguided belief that elementary special education sufficiently addresses all the educational needs of all students. It is true that many students who complete an elementary special education program may return to regular classes, where they may function appropriately without additional services. Some students, however, will continue to require special education and related services for all or part of their high school careers.

Structure of Regular Secondary Education

At present, secondary schools are still organized along traditional lines based on departmental interests and subject matter (Heller, 1981; Kauffman & Nelson, 1976). Obviously, this model limits the use of self-contained classes, a popular service delivery format for special education. Because it is difficult to accommodate self contained classrooms in secondary schools, students with special needs may have to adapt to a preexisting format that does not fit their needs (Heller, 1981). The idea of keeping students in the regular class as much as possible is appealing and certainly within the spirit of PL 94-142; however, true benefits cannot be enjoyed in this setting unless regular education teachers are prepared to meet the unique needs of the students with disabilities who are placed in their care. The responsibilities assumed by regular education teachers in today's secondary programs are overwhelming, leaving them with little time and perhaps little inclination to deal with the educational demands of special needs students (Kokoszka & Drye, 1981; Lerner et al., 1977).

Curricular Emphasis

The movement promoting excellence in education has encouraged the public to put more emphasis on academic achievement and to make competency tests a graduation requirement (Edgar, 1987). Many students with special needs enter high school with deficits in background information, vocabulary, reading ability, and social skills (Deshler et al., 1984; Kokoszka & Drye, 1981). Without the prerequisite skills, they are not likely to master a rigorous high school curriculum. Thus, students may either be given credit for completing a watered-down version of the general curriculum or be placed in a vocationally oriented curriculum. These scenarios are inappropriate for at least three reasons. First, a watered-down curriculum may render students unable to pass any competency examinations required for graduation. Many students with disabilities fail to meet minimum competency standards even when tests are modified for them (Miller, 1983). Second, placement in a watered-down curriculum or in a vocational program should not constitute the entire range of programming alternatives available to secondary students with disabilities (Heller, 1981). Third, they are not in keeping with the intent of FAPE as stated in PL 94-142.

Alternatives or additions to traditional secondary curricula have been proposed in the professional literature. The learning strategies curriculum, in particular, is exerting a strong influence in education programs for secondary students with special needs (Alley & Deshler, 1979; Deshler & Schumaker, 1986; Schumaker, Deshler, Alley, & Warner, 1983). Also, social skills curricula are being developed that will enable secondary students to enhance their functioning in educational and vocational settings. Learning strategies and social skills are discussed in detail in subsequent chapters.

Teacher Preparation Programs

Another factor limiting the effectiveness of existing programs is the nature of the professional preparation program typically completed by secondary special education teachers (Kauffman & Nelson, 1976; Miller et al., 1980; Scranton & Downs, 1975; Wimmer, 1981). Despite the widespread recognition of the legal and social need for programming at this level, authorities have not developed enough secondary special education teacher preparation programs (Sabatino, 1982). Indeed, many professionals currently working at the secondary level have been trained under programs that emphasized elementary special education in both coursework and practicum experiences.

Moreover, graduates of regular education preparation programs usually receive certification at either the elementary or the secondary level. Many practitioners are certified to teach kindergarten through twelfth-grade special education classes, regardless of the emphasis of their training program (Heller, 1981). There is a big difference between being certified and being qualified to teach at the secondary level. Many secondary special education teachers do not have the background or training in various content areas necessary to adequately present subject matter to students with disabilities (Kokoszka & Drye, 1981). Although the interest and dedication of many secondary special education teachers are above reproach, whatever success their students experience may well be the result of the teaching skills acquired through trial and error rather than through the successful completion of preparation programs featuring appropriate course sequences and practicum experiences.

Insufficient Database

The ineffectiveness of existing programs can also be traced to a weak database. The secondary special education programs in existence lack strong theoretical and empirical foundations (Alley & Deshler, 1979; Miller, 1981; Scranton & Downs, 1975; Wilcox & Bellamy, 1982; Wimmer, 1981). Secondary-level teachers who graduated from preparation programs with an elementary emphasis may know little about the needs of secondary students who have disabilities or about the most successful methods of dealing with them. Furthermore, they may not be documenting the impact of their programs on the performance of secondary students. Therefore, it is likely that current secondary special education programs are not contributing systematically to a sound base of knowledge.

Lack of Appropriate Materials

Secondary special education programs are also plagued by a serious shortage of appropriate materials (Lerner et al., 1977; Wilcox & Bellamy, 1982; Wimmer, 1981). Two types of problems arise with the materials generally available to secondary teachers and students. First, the instructional material may have been intended for elementary students with special needs. Whether such materials are appropriate for older students is highly questionable. In any case, secondary learners will already have been exposed to these materials. Second, some material may have been originally designed for regular secondary education students. Therefore, it may not address relevant concepts, be written at an appropriate reading level, or provide the amount of practice required by secondary students with special needs.

Summary

The goals of secondary special education are to provide services that will enable students to acquire the skills they need to function successfully in employment and community settings. Numerous pieces of legislation address special and vocational education and provide ample support for the services needed by secondary students with disabilities. Unfortunately, there are not enough data to document the effectiveness of current endeavors. A number of significant problems appear to hamper the development and delivery of appropriate educational services to secondary students with special needs. Not all professionals recognize the need for special programming at this level. The structure and curricular emphasis of regular secondary education cannot easily be adapted for use with learners with special needs. Teachers whose skills are being developed and refined while on the job are working in programs with limited empirical support using materials not specifically designed and validated for secondary students with disabilities.

Some experts may consider problems of this magnitude to be insurmountable; however, there can be no debate over whether secondary special education services will be provided. Legal mandates and professional ethics will not allow us to abandon the cause. The question is "How can we best deliver such services?" (Wimmer, 1981, p. 610).

The transition perspective underlies the orientation to secondary special education advocated in this volume. If secondary special educators are to achieve lasting performance gains with their students, they must abandon the teaching of isolated skills that have little bearing on future adjustment. Instead, they should focus on educational activities that promote adaptation to future independent residential, work, and leisure settings. Educational objectives based on the developmental expectations of nondisabled youth must be evaluated against the criteria of the individual's potential for future adaptation. These criteria pertain to objectives that are most likely to be practiced and reinforced in home and work environments. Those that are least essential should be eliminated.

Emphasis should also be placed on the articulation of services from secondary to post secondary service providers. Individuals who have disabilities are not likely to adjust to the adult world without special assistance beyond the high school setting. Educational personnel must work with professionals in the fields of vocational rehabilitation, mental health and mental retardation, and other postsecondary service agencies. The result of this effort should be a smooth shift of services from the educational to the community environment.

The purpose of this book is to provide professionals and preservice educators with information that will help them develop appropriate programming for secondary learners with special needs.

References

Alley, G., & Deshler, D. (1979). *Teaching the learning disabled adolescent: Strategies and methods.* Denver, CO: Love.

Armstrong v. Kline, 476 F Supp. 583 (E.D. Pa. 1979) aff'd CA 78-0172 (3rd Cir. July 15, 1980).

Astin, A. W., Hemond, M. K., & Richardson, G. T. (1982). *The American freshmen: National norms for fall 1982.* Los Angeles: Higher Education Research Institute.

Battle v. Commonwealth, 79, 2158, 2188-90, 2568-70 (3rd Cir. July 18, 1980).

Beebe, P. D., & Karan, O. C. (1986). A methodology for a community-based vocational program for adults. In R. H. Horner, L. H. Meyer, & H. D. Fredericks (Eds.), *Education of learners with severe handicaps: Exemplary service strategies.* Baltimore, MD: Paul H. Brookes.

Deno, E. (1970). Special education as developmental capital. *Exceptional Children, 37,* 229–237.

Deshler, D. D., & Schumaker, J. B. (1986). Learning strategies: An instructional alternative for low achieving adolescents. *Exceptional Children, 52,* 583–590.

Deshler, D. D., Schumaker, J. B., & Lenz, B. K. (1984). Academic and cognitive interventions for LD adolescents: Part I. *Journal of Learning Disabilities, 17,* 108–117.

Diana v. State Board of Education, No. C-70-37 RFR (District Court of Northern California Feb. 1970).

Edgar, E. (1987). Secondary programs in special education: Are many of them justifiable? *Exceptional Children, 53,* 555–561.

Gartland, D. (1988). Educational service options. In P. J. Schloss, C. A. Hughes, & M. A. Smith (Eds.), *Mental retardation: Community transition* (pp. 57–113). San Diego, CA: College-Hill.

Greenan, J. P., & Sitlington, P. L. (1987). The role of generalizable skills in the vocational assessment of special needs learners. *Journal of Industrial Teacher Education, 25*(1), 52–59.

Halderman v. Pennhurst State School and Hospital, 446 F Supp. 1295 (E.D. Pa. 1977).

Halpern, A. (1985). Transition: A look at the foundations. *Exceptional Children, 51,* 479–486.

Halpern, A. (1993). Quality of life as a conceptual framework for evaluating transition outcomes. *Exceptional Children, 59,* 486–498.

Heller, H. W. (1981). Secondary education for handicapped students: In search of a solution. *Exceptional Children, 47,* 582–583.

Horner, R. H., McDonnell, J. J., & Bellamy, G. T. (1986). Teaching generalized skills: General case instruction in simulation and community settings. In R. H. Horner, L. H. Meyer, & H. D. Fredericks (Eds.), *Education of learners with severe handicaps: Exemplary service strategies.* Baltimore, MD: Paul H. Brookes.

Kauffman, J. M., & Nelson, C. M. (1976). Educational programming for secondary school age delinquent and maladjusted pupils. *Behavioral Disorders, 2,* 29–37.

Kidd, J. W. (1970). The "adultated" mentally retarded. *Education and Training of the Mentally Retarded, 5*(2), 71–72.

Kokoszka, R., & Drye, J. (1981). Toward the least restrictive environment: High school learning disabled students. *Journal of Learning Disabilities, 14,* 22–23.

Lawrence, J. K., Kent, L., & Henson, J. W. (1981). *The handicapped student in America's colleges: A longitudinal analysis.* Los Angeles: University of California at Los Angeles, Higher Education Research Institute. (ERIC Document Reproduction Service No. ED 215 625)

Lerner, J. W., Evans, M. A., & Meyers, G. (1977). LD programs at the secondary level: A survey. *Academic Therapy, 13,* 7–19.

McAfee, J. (1988). Adult adjustment of individuals with mental retardation. In P. J. Schloss, C. A. Hughes, & M. A. Smith (Eds.), *Mental retardation: Community transition.* Boston: Little, Brown.

Mangrum, C. T., & Strichart, S. S. (1984). *College and the learning disabled student: A guide to program selection development, and implementation.* Orlando, FL: Grune & Stratton.

Miller, K. (1983). *An analysis of the performance of LD students on the Kansas Minimal Competency Test.* Unpublished doctoral dissertation, University of Kansas, Lawrence.

Miller, S. A. (1981). A crisis in appropriate education: The dearth of data on programs for secondary handicapped adolescents. *Journal of Special Education, 15,* 351–370.

Miller, S. R., Sabatino, D. A., & Larsen, R. P. (1980). Issues in the professional preparation of secondary school special educators. *Exceptional Children, 46,* 344–350.

Mills v. Board of Education of the District of Columbia, 348 F. Supp. 866 (D.D.C. 1972).

National Commission on Excellence in Education. (1983). *A nation at risk.* Washington, DC: U.S. Government Printing Office.

PARC, Bowman et al. v. Commonwealth of Pennsylvania, 334 F. Supp. 279 (1971).

Parmenter, T. R. (1986). *Bridges from school to working life for handicapped youth: The view from Australia.* New York: World Rehabilitation Fund.

Rogan, L. L., & Hartman, L. D. (1976). *A follow-up study of learning disabled children as adults. Final report.* Washington, DC: Bureau of Education for the Handicapped. (ERIC Document Reproduction Service No. ED 163 728)

Rollins, S. P., & Unruh, A. (1964). *Introduction to secondary education.* Chicago: Rand-McNally.

Rusch, R. R. & Mittaug, D. E. (1985). Competitive employment in education. In K. C. Lakin & R. H. Bruininks (Eds.), *Strategies for achieving community integration of developmentally disabled citizens.* Baltimore, MD: Paul H. Brookes.

Rusch, F. R., & Phelps, L. A. (1987). Secondary special education and transition from school to work: A national priority. *Exceptional Children, 53,* 487–492.

Sabatino, D. A. (1982). Prescription for better secondary programming: A teacher-broker. *Academic Therapy, 17,* 289–296.

Sarkees, M. D., & Scott, J. L. (1985). *Vocational special needs.* Homewood, IL: American Technical Publishers.

Schloss, P. (1985). Postsecondary opportunities: The role of secondary educators in advocating handicapped young adults. *Journal for Vocational Special Needs Education, 7*(2), 15–21.

Schloss, P. J., & Sedlak, R. A. (1986). *Instructional methods for students with learning and behavioral problems.* Boston: Allyn & Bacon.

Schumaker, J. B., Deshler, D. D., Alley, G. R., & Warner, M. M. (1983). Toward the development of an intervention model for learning disabled adolescents: The University of Kansas Institute. *Exceptional Education Quarterly, 4,* 45–74.

Scranton, T. R., & Downs, M. L. (1975). Elementary and secondary LEA district programming in the U.S.: A survey. *Journal of Learning Disabilities, 8,* 394–399.

U.S. Department of Labor. (1979). *A study of handicapped clients in sheltered workshops.* Washington, DC: U.S. Government Printing Office.

U.S. Public Law 93-112 (Rehabilitation Act of 1973), Section 504, 29 U.S.C. 794.

Warger, C. (1987). Introduction to secondary special education programs. In C. L. Warger & B. B. Weiner (Eds.), *Secondary special education* (pp. 1–6). Reston, VA: The Council for Exceptional Children.

Wells, D., Schmid, R., Algozzine, B., & Maher, M. (1983). Teaching LD adolescents. *Teacher Education and Special Education, 6,* 227–234.

Wilcox, B., & Bellamy, G. T. (1982). *Design of high school programs for severely handicapped students.* Baltimore, MD: Paul H. Brookes.

Will, M. (1984). *Bridges from school to working life: OSERS programming for the transition of youth with disabilities.* Washington, DC: Office of Special Education and Rehabilitation Services, U.S. Department of Education.

Wimmer, D. (1981). Functional learning curricula in the secondary school. *Exceptional Children, 47,* 610–616.

Woodward, D. M., & Peters, D. J. (1985). *The learning disabled adolescent.* Rockville, MD: Aspen.

Wyatt v. Aderholt, 334 F. Supp. 1341 (1971).

Zarkowska, E., & Clements, J. (1988). *Problem behavior in people with severe learning disabilities: A practical guide to a constructional approach.* London: Croom Helm.

Zigmond, N., & Thornton, H. (1985). Follow-up of post-secondary age learning disabled graduates and dropouts. *Learning Disability Quarterly, 1,* 50–55.

Chapter 2

Postsecondary Service Options

Did you know that . . .

- PL 94–142 mandates appropriate educational services to individuals up to the age of 21?
- No single federal or state law articulates mandated services to adults with disabilities, beyond the age of 21?
- Aside from parents, educators are the primary source of assistance for individuals making the transition to postsecondary settings?
- Programs and services that meet the special needs of young adults with disabilities have proliferated in recent years?
- Rehabilitation programs place over 20,000 individuals with developmental disabilities in competitive employment each year?
- The number of academic support services available to students with disabilities at the college level is growing?
- The Rehabilitation Act of 1973 and its 1978 amendments state that no qualified individual with disabilities shall be denied benefits of or be subjected to discrimination under any program or activity receiving federal financial assistance?
- The Job Training Partnership Act authorizes support for educational services provided by technical schools, community colleges, and to a lesser extent, four-year institutions?
- Vocational rehabilitation services are authorized to assist individuals with disabilities in obtaining or sustaining gainful employment?

Can you . . .

- List the mandates of PL 94–142 regarding services to individuals with disabilities?
- Describe common postsecondary obstacles that young adults with disabilities face during the transition to successful employment?
- List the basic elements of the Individualized Written Rehabilitation Program (IWRP)?

- Describe how a Sheltered Rehabilitation Center functions to provide specialized training and work experience in a supportive environment?
- Describe the advantages of programming at enclaves in industry?
- Describe the advantage of programming at sheltered rehabilitation centers?
- Describe the elements of supported employment?

Educational services available prior to the age of 21 are mandated by state and federal legislation. Consequently, there is great uniformity in available services regardless of the school district or state that serves the individual. Specifically, prior to the age of 21 all learners with disabilities are assured of the following:

- A free public education that is appropriate to the learning and behavioral characteristics of the student
- Screening, in an effort to identify those individuals who will benefit from special education services
- Educational services in the least restrictive environment
- Free provision of related services (e.g., counseling, transportation, physical and occupational therapy, etc.) that will enhance the learner's ability to benefit from educational services
- Nondiscriminatory testing conducted in the dominant language of the learner
- Freedom of information for the learner and his or her parents or guardians
- Confidentiality of records
- Annual development and evaluation of an education plan designed to meet the individual needs of the learner
- Due process when disagreements arise regarding the nature of the educational program (Turnbull & Turnbull, 1990).

These mandates indicate what services are available to school-aged individuals with disabilities. During the time that youths with disabilities are in the educational system, they, their parents, and teachers have a clear understanding of the services to be provided in the immediate future. When disputes arise, specific protective safeguards exist to ensure that the best interests of the learner are served. These provisions allow educators to design current services in a way that will promote the learner's transition into future educational programs.

Unfortunately, the picture becomes clouded when the learner leaves the public school system. Outside elementary and secondary educational services, no single federal or state law spells out all the mandated services available to adults with disabilities (Bursuch, Rose, Cowen, & Yahaya, 1989; Hill, Seyfarth, Banks, Wehman, & Orelove, 1987). This situation has given rise to a number of problems.

- There is no mandate for enrolling young adults with disabilities into educational, residential or rehabilitation programs (McDonnell, Wilcox, & Boles, 1986).

- Many programs that do exist do little to prepare the individual for community work and living (Bellamy, Rhodes, Bourdeau, & Mank, 1986; Lakin & Bruininks, 1985).
- Agencies may deny services to young adults because of the severity of the individual's condition, the lack of resources, or the great demand for limited services, among other factors (McDonnell & Wilcox, 1983; Turnbull & Turnbull, 1985).
- Young adults with disabilities and their parents or guardians are required to identify appropriate services and pursue the proper course to enrollment (Hill et al., 1987).
- No individual or agency is required to speak on behalf of the young adult with disabilities; and the question of process is seldom raised among adult service providers (Schloss, 1985).
- Owing to confidentiality requirements, efforts of discrete agencies (e.g., Office of Vocational Rehabilitation, or Private Industry Council) are seldom coordinated, with the result that some services overlap and others are not provided (Schalock, 1985).
- Eligibility requirements and performance standards for adult service providers are seldom coordinated and often conflicting (Schalock, 1985).
- There is no systematic provision for reenrolling young adults with disabilities into supportive programs when attempts at independent living or work fail.

Aside from an individual's parents or guardians, educators are the primary source of assistance for individuals making the transition to postsecondary settings (Hill et al., 1987; Test, Keul, & Grossi, 1988). As mentioned earlier, this role may consist of two related functions. First, the teacher may provide direct educational experiences that prepare the learner for success in specific postsecondary settings. Second, the teacher may facilitate the young adult's transition to these settings. To perform in these roles, the educator must be familiar with postsecondary resources leading to independent life (Edgar, Horton, & Maddox, 1984). Therefore, the purpose of this chapter is to identify postsecondary services available to young adults with disabilities. The main topics covered are postsecondary educational programs, postsecondary technical programs, business and industry, vocational rehabilitation, and supported and independent living.

Postsecondary Educational Programs

Two-Year Colleges

The mission of two-year or community college programs has changed a great deal over the past decades. Initially, community colleges served as transfer programs. Students enrolled in these programs to meet the basic educational and liberal arts requirements for baccalaureate degree programs at other institutions. Some state systems of higher education, for example, restrict university enrollment to upper-division undergraduate students and graduate students. Entering freshmen and sophomores enroll in community colleges where credits will automatically transfer to state universities.

Recently, community colleges have developed a wide range of vocational and technical programs. Students completing these programs may be awarded special certificates and associate degrees. Some typical programs of study appropriate for many youth with mild disabilities are emergency medical technician; paraprofessional educator; food systems management; licensed practical nurse; auto mechanics; and clerical and bookkeeping training.

The structure of many certificate and associate degree programs is shaped by the employment opportunities in the geographic area surrounding the college. For example, community colleges in resort areas typically emphasize travel and hospitality programs. Those in mining regions include mineral engineering or mineral processing programs. And those in rural areas feature agricultural and wildlife management programs.

Two-year and community college programs usually receive considerable support from local, state, and federal taxes. Consequently, the cost of these programs is very low in comparison with the cost of four-year degree programs. At the national level, for example, the reauthorization of the Vocational Education Bill, HR 4164, allocates a portion of the basic state grants for postsecondary programs (most often community colleges) for youths who are economically disadvantaged or have disabilities.

Four-Year Colleges and Universities

Colleges and universities offer a wide range of degrees and certificates. Successful matriculation may yield a bachelor of arts or bachelor of science degree. Typical degree programs require two years of full-time equivalent study in the liberal arts (e.g., social sciences, mathematics, physical sciences, humanities, and fine arts). The remaining two years are devoted to specific programs of study such as consumer studies, criminal justice, information systems management, food science, journalism, broadcasting and speech, geosciences, psychology, and so on.

Programs and services that meet the special needs of young adults with disabilities have proliferated in recent years (see Scheiber & Talpers, 1987). The number of buildings accessible to individuals with physical disabilities has also increased (Burbach & Babbitt, 1988). Despite some evidence that college students with disabilities are unlikely to seek assistance (Cowen, 1988), a growing number of academic support services are now available. Many colleges and universities offer the following resources:

- Note-taking services
- Tutoring laboratories
- Special sections and course offerings
- Career-counseling centers
- Special advisement services
- Instructional resources in the areas of time management, study skills, campus mobility, etc.

The Rehabilitation Act of 1973 and its 1978 amendments have provided the impetus for a majority of these programs. Under the act, "No otherwise qualified handicapped individual in the United States . . . shall, solely by reason of his handicap, be excluded in participation, be denied benefits of, or be subjected to discrimination under any program or activity receiving Federal financial assistance" (p. 39).

Of course, much of the support received by public institutions of higher education comes from the federal government. Consequently, the Rehabilitation Act requires these institutions to provide equal opportunity to youths with disabilities. Action Plan 2.1 identifies standards that publicly supported colleges must meet in order to comply with the Rehabilitation Act. The cost of a four-year college education is likely to be substantially more than the cost of other postsecondary programs. Unfortunately, federal vocational education legislation excludes programs that award baccalaureate degrees from reimbursement for occupational and technical training. Consequently, community colleges and technical schools that are eligible for federal support may provide a better value.

Postsecondary Technical Programs

Technical schools are similar to community colleges in a number of ways. Both institutions are located in the community in which a majority of applicants reside. Also, both community colleges and technical schools are closer in size to area high schools than comprehensive universities. Both types of institutions offer a wide range of specialized training programs and certificates. Also, technical school programs, like the programs in community colleges, are by and large supported by federal, state, and local taxes. As a result, tuition and fee schedules are generally modest.

The main difference between technical schools and community colleges is the breadth of their program offerings. As already mentioned, community colleges offer a variety of academic, preprofessional, and technical programs. Students frequently use these programs to enter advanced training at other institutions.

Action Plan 2.1   Standards for Publicly Supported College and University Compliance with the Rehabilitation Act

---

The Rehabilitation Act requires publicly supported colleges and universities to comply with the following standards:

1. Admissions test cannot discriminate against qualified individuals who have disabilities.
2. Auxiliary aids must be provided when impaired sensory, manual, or speaking skills limit an individual's ability to adapt to collegiate programs.
3. Academic requirements must often be modified (e.g., deadlines extended, course formats adapted, alternative competency measures provided) to help individuals with disabilities succeed.
4. Alternative, but not necessarily segregated physical education programs must be provided to meet the needs of individuals with physical or sensory limitations.
5. Infirmary services must be provided that are comparable to those used by nondisabled young adults.

Technical programs generally specialize in vocational curricula to the exclusion of liberal arts courses leading to advanced degrees. This specialization is the principal advantage of technical schools over community colleges. Instruction in the applied fields can be provided by an experienced faculty, facilities can be well equipped, and instruction can be intense.

Support for the educational services of technical schools, community colleges, and to a lesser extent, four-year institutions is provided by the Job Training Partnership Act (JTPA). JTPA replaced a similar legislative mandate, the Comprehensive Employment and Training Act (CETA) in the fall of 1983. The main difference between the two bodies of legislation is that CETA provided substantial support for on-the-job training. JTPA severely restricts funds available for employment remuneration. If fact, 70% of available funds must be targeted for preservice and inservice training support. The remaining 30% is for support services and administrative expenses.

Because of the diffuse organizational structure provided by JTPA, it is not possible to describe the services provided in each community. Statewide services are controlled by the governor, who appoints representatives of service delivery areas (SDAs). These representatives appoint members of the private industry council (PIC). Members of the PIC are typically local businesspeople and educational administrators. These individuals make local policy decisions regarding the ways in which PIC funds are to be spent at the community level.

Under this system of decentralized control, the services provided to youth with disabilities by JTPA programs differ greatly from one locale to another. In general, PICs tend to support any vocational or technical program that is likely to result in gainful employment for trainees who are economically disadvantaged or have disabilities. PICs are therefore apt to request data that demonstrate the strong potential that employment (at a level substantially above the minimum wage) will be realized from support of the training program. The data may include assurances from employers that individuals who complete the training program will be hired, facts on a personnel shortage in the area in which training is being provided, and a history of successful placements attributed to the training program.

In a national project to help learners with disabilities participate in JTPA programs, approximately 600 private industry councils were asked to identify exemplary JTPA projects designed to help individuals with disabilities (Tindall & Hedberg, 1987). Of the 30 projects identified, two-thirds were based in public school special education depart-

---

Case for Action 2.1

In your role as guidance counselor for secondary students who have learning disabilities you have been asked to prepare a brochure describing postsecondary educational opportunities. Provide the essential content. Include a description of possible educational programs, funding sources, special accommodations, and possible employment outcomes.

ments and 10 were based in public school vocational education departments. The projects served over 1,500 young adults, and most projects enrolled over 50 students. Typical services included assessment, work experience, career exploration and job seeking, vocational training, job placement, and counseling. Over half of the young adults served entered competitive employment after completing the program. Close to 90% of all participants were considered positive terminations.

Business and Industry

More and more private companies are initiating their own intensive and specialized training programs. The large fast food companies, for example, provide advanced corporate training. The largest program of this type is McDonald's Restaurant Corporation's extensive training system, which leads to graduate degrees in *hamburgerology* at Hamburger University. Of course, this is not an actual academic degree. However, many colleges and universities will apply a limited number of credits from McDonald's program to associate or baccalaureate degree requirements.

Despite the effect of the Americans with Disabilities Act in enhancing access to the workplace, the strongest predictor of the extent to which opportunities are made available to individuals with disabilities may be the employer's attitude. For this reason, education and rehabilitation agency personnel have launched vigorous campaigns to encourage business and industry to employ adults with disabilities.

Vocational Rehabilitation

Vocational rehabilitation services are authorized by the Rehabilitation Service Administration of the U.S. Department of Education. These services are intended to help individuals with disabilities obtain or sustain gainful employment. Eligible individuals include persons with mental, physical, or learning problems that constitute a substantial obstacle to employment. An additional eligibility criterion is that the individual must demonstrate the potential to benefit from rehabilitation services to the extent that he or she can be gainfully employed in business or industry.

Specific rehabilitation services range from career information and exploration, to vocational evaluation and occupational training, on-the-job evaluation and training, and job placement. Rehabilitation services may also include psychological counseling; medical evaluation and treatment; support in independent living; transportation; licensing fees; and special therapeutic, prosthetic, or occupational equipment.

Federal law requires each state to identify one or more agencies to provide vocational rehabilitation programs for individuals with disabilities. Two typical designations for these agencies are *Office of Vocational Rehabilitation* and *Bureau of Vocational Rehabilitation*. The state agencies, in turn, establish regional offices that serve clients within the immediate area.

Regional offices are staffed by vocational rehabilitation counselors. These professionals are assigned to individual clients. Their basic responsibility is to develop and supervise an Individualized Written Rehabilitation Program (IWRP). The IWRP paral-

---

Action Plan 2.2   Elements of the Individualized Written Rehabilitation Program (IWRP)

The following are the basic elements of the IWRP:

1. A statement of the eligibility for either direct service or extended evaluation
2. The individual's rights and responsibilities under the rehabilitation program (these include the right to confidentiality, periodic evaluations of progress toward program goals, and annual reviews of the program)
3. Long-range goals and a justification for goal selection
4. Intermediate objectives, direct services to be provided, time limits, and a justification for how these procedures will resolve the vocational disability
5. The extent of participation and benefits
6. Responsibilities of the client in meeting his or her own rehabilitation goals.

---

lels the Individualized Education Program mandated by PL 94–142. It forms a written contract between the rehabilitation agency and the client. The basic elements of an IWRP are presented in Action Plan 2.2.

Any number of services may be made available to a young adult through the state vocational rehabilitation agency. In most cases, the actual services will not be provided by the rehabilitation counselor. The counselor is primarily a broker of services. For example, rather than actually providing on-the-job evaluation and training, the counselor may obtain the services through a contract with a private nonprofit agency, such as a chapter of the Association for Retarded Citizens or the United Cerebral Palsy. Occupational education services may be provided through contracts with a technical school or community college. Psychological and medical services may be provided through contracts with local clinics and hospitals. Two of the services most frequently contracted for are placement and training in sheltered rehabilitation centers and supported employment.

Sheltered Rehabilitation Centers

Rehabilitation facilities are staffed by individuals who offer specialized training and work experience in a supportive environment outside of the private workforce. Sheltered Rehabilitation Centers are best suited for individuals who are not able to succeed in competitive employment. However, many such centers are beginning to provide specialized training (e.g., simulations and on-the-job training) that will lead to competitive employment. Therefore, client goals may range from long-term adjustment as an employee of the center to short-term preparation for a placement in a private business or industry.

Most of the work in sheltered rehabilitation centers is provided through subcontracts from business and industry (U.S. Department of Labor, 1977). These contracts usually call for the assembly of small parts, repair, labeling, or packaging of units. Sheltered rehabilitation centers obtain contracts through a competitive bidding process. Sheltered rehabilitation centers may also enter into independent manufacture, service, or sales operations. For example, some centers employ clients to construct shipping pallets, picnic tables, storage sheds, or other products. Centers may also employ clients to clean and service automobiles, clean homes and businesses, launder linens and clothing, provide lawn and garden maintenance, and so on.

A more recent development is the provision of *enclaves in industry*, which serve sheltered rehabilitation clients within the facilities of private businesses or industries. The individual with disabilities is placed in an occupational setting with nondisabled competitively employed individuals. In most situations, the client remains under the general supervision of rehabilitation center personnel and is paid on the basis of the ratio of his or her productivity to that of an individual who does not have disabilities. Advantages of this approach are identified in Action Plan 2.3.

Most individuals with mild and moderate disabilities would find long-term placement in a sheltered work setting excessively restrictive. Consequently, most transition specialists agree that sheltered rehabilitation centers should act mainly as ancillary services and should provide general and special training programs. Ancillary services are generally designed to correct cognitive, social, or motor problems that interfere with work adjustment. They may consist of vocational and personal adjustment counseling, social services, occupational and physical therapy, mobility training, and speech and language training.

General training programs may prepare the participants to obtain and sustain employment. These training programs may include experiences that lead to career exploration and awareness, self-appraisal, employment application skills, interviewing skills, vocational-related social skills, community mobility skills, and the like.

Action Plan 2.3   Advantages of Enclaves in Industry

For the following reasons, we recommend the enclave-in-industry approach for many young adults who have disabilities. It offers several advantages, in contrast to services provided within a sheltered workshop.

1. The young adult is able to interact with nondisabled individuals within a fairly typical work environment. This opportunity may enable the individual to model appropriate work behaviors demonstrated by the competitive workers.
2. The individual who has disabilities may acquire the exact skills necessary for success in the competitive placement. He or she has the benefit of the same tools, work space, materials, and social expectations as nondisabled workers in the setting.
3. Once specific performance criteria are achieved, the young adult is more likely to be accepted as an employee of the specific business or a related business.
4. Young adults employed by a business or industry in which they worked in an enclave are less likely to have difficulty generalizing skills.

Special training programs may be similar to occupational training programs offered by community colleges or postsecondary technical schools. The main difference is that technical training provided by sheltered rehabilitation centers is conducted by rehabilitation and special education personnel. These professionals are skilled in adapting instruction to the needs of individuals with exceptional characteristics. Conversely, community college and technical school personnel are generally well qualified in a particular trade but may not be as skilled in the methodology of teaching young adults who have special needs.

Supported Employment Services

Advocacy groups, educational units, state developmental disabilities services, and sheltered rehabilitation programs are becoming increasingly interested in providing supported employment services. Rehabilitation programs place over 20,000 individuals with developmental disabilities in competitive employment each year (Kiernan & Ciborowski, 1985).

Professional efforts directly concerned with helping people achieve success in competitive employment are described as supported employment services. Supported employment is defined as employment within a business or industry that is under the direct supervision of the business's management staff and that receives normal compensation and benefits. Another characteristic of supported employment is that extraordinary guidance or assistance is offered to help individuals succeed in given positions. This may include the use of prosthetic devices, specialized training, or extra supervision.

A supported employment program that was recently described in the professional literature is PROGRESS, which is run by the Association for Retarded Citizens in State College, Pennsylvania. This program has a number of interesting features:

1. Individuals with disabilities are referred through the regional Office of Vocational Education, the County Office of Mental Health and Mental Retardation, and county school districts.

2. Participating employers are recruited through a media campaign, classified advertisements, and personal contacts.

3. An agreement is reached with cooperating employers on all important aspects of training and supervision responsibilities.

4. Training and evaluation materials are designed to ensure that the participant will succeed on the job. These materials include a job-station analysis and a performance checklist corresponding to the competencies identified in the job-station analysis.

5. Work assignments and the workstation are modified with the consent of the employer to better accommodate the characteristics of the young adult.

6. Prosthetics such as permanent props, special tools and equipment, and other aids are designed and provided for the young adult.

7. A job coach employed by the Association for Retarded Citizens works directly with the individual with disabilities. This assistance continues until the learner is able to perform the responsibilities of the position without extraordinary assistance.

Case for Action 2.2

You are responsible for developing a supported employment model for your secondary school students who have mild disabilities. Use PROGRESS as a guide in forming your own model.

8. As the youth gains increasing independence, the employer gradually assumes the standard supervisory responsibilities.

9. Follow-up observations and retraining occur periodically for the next year or two (Schloss, McEwen, Lang, & Schwab, 1986).

Postsecondary Service Selection

The preceding sections describe a range of postsecondary services that may be appropriate for learners who have disabilities. Actual services provided must match the needs and interests of the learner. Students with more severe disabilities are likely to require more restrictive services such as placement in sheltered rehabilitation centers. More capable learners may be served in less restrictive settings such as community colleges and technical schools.

To some extent, postsecondary services parallel educational services provided in grade schools and secondary schools. Similar to the Cascade of Services Model proposed by Deno (1970), these opportunities fall on a continuum based on restrictiveness. Figure 2.1 contains the Keystone of Postsecondary Placements Model adapted from Schloss (1985).

The keystone model demonstrates the relationship between these postsecondary offerings. Services identified in the keystone range from the most to least restrictive: sheltered work, enclaves in industry, competitive work supervised by the employer with specialized services (e.g., job coach), competitive work supervised by the employer with prosthetic assistance (e.g., calculator, color-coded operations, etc.), and competitive work supervised by the employer. It is likely that postsecondary educational services in the form of technical school, community college, and four-year college educational programs would be preparatory for placements at a higher level on the keystone.

The proportion of graduates with disabilities expected to be placed at any given position in the keystone is represented by the area within the cell. The largest percentage

Case for Action 2.3

You have been asked to prepare a policy statement indicating appropriate vocational options for students with varying disability levels. Use the Keystone of Postsecondary Placements Model to formulate your policy.

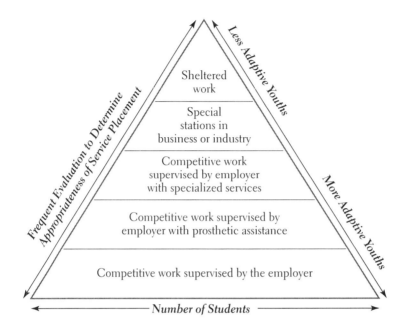

FIGURE 2.1   Keystone of Postsecondary Placements Model

Source: From "Postsecondary Opportunities: The Role of Secondary Educators in Advocating for Handicapped Young Adults," by Patrick J. Schloss, 1985, *The Journal of Vocational Special Needs Education*, 7(2), 18. Copyright 1985 by The National Association of Vocational Education Special Needs Personnel affiliated with The American Vocational Association.

of young adults with disabilities is expected to enter competitive work supervised by the employer. The smallest percentage with disabilities is expected to be served in sheltered rehabilitation settings.

Education and training opportunities that occur after young adults complete high school are likely to lead to a more restrictive placement and eventually to a less restrictive setting. This pattern is depicted by arrows on the side of the keystone.

Summary

The Keystone of Postsecondary Placements Model suggests a general orientation to the articulation of services for students graduating from secondary programs. Postsecondary services are not uniformly provided from one region of the country to another. Federal law does not provide for a comprehensive and logical array of resources for young adults who have disabilities. Consequently, new educational services must be identified within the context of the resources available in local communities.

References

Bellamy, G. T., Rhodes, L. E., Bourbeau, P., & Mank, D. (1986). Mental retardation services in sheltered workshops and day activity programs: Consumer outcomes and policy alternatives. In F. R. Rusch (Ed.), *Competitive employment issues and strategies* (pp. 257–271). Baltimore: Paul H. Brookes.

Burbach, H. J., & Babbitt, C. E. (1988). Physically disabled students on the college campus. *Remedial and Special Education*, 9(2), 12–19.

Bursuch, W. D., Rose, E., Cowen, S., & Yahaya, M. A. (1989). Nationwide survey of postsecondary education services for students with learning disabilities. *Exceptional Children*, 56, 46–265.

Cowen, S. E. (1988). Coping strategies of university students with learning disabilities. *Journal of Learning Disabilities*, 21(3), 161–164.

Deno, E. (1970). Special education as developmental capital. *Exceptional Children*, 37, 229–237.

Edgar, E., Horton, B., & Maddox, M. (1984). Post school placements: Planning for public school students with developmental disabilities. *Journal for Vocational Special Needs*, 6, 15–18.

Hill, J. W., Seyfarth, J., Banks, P. D., Wehman, P., & Orelove, F. (1987). Parent attitudes about working conditions of their adult mentally retarded sons and daughters, *Exceptional Children*, 54, 9–23.

Kiernan, W. E., & Ciborowski, J. (1985). *Employment survey for adults with developmental disabilities* (project no. 03DD0135/12). Washington, DC: U.S. Department of Health and Human Services, Administration on Developmental Disabilities.

Lakin, K. C., & Bruininks, R. H. (1985). Contemporary services for handicapped children and youth. In R. H. Bruininks & K. C. Lakin (Eds.), *Living and learning in the least restrictive environment*. Baltimore, MD: Paul H. Brookes.

McDonnell, J., & Wilcox, B. (1983). *Issues in the transition from school to adult services. A survey of parents of secondary students with severe handicaps*. Unpublished manuscript, University of Oregon.

McDonnell, J., Wilcox, B., & Boles, S. M. (1986). Do we know enough to plan for transition? A national survey of state agencies responsible for services to persons with severe handicaps. *Journal of the Association for Severe Handicaps*, 11(1), 53–60.

Schalock, R. L. (1985). Comprehensive community services: A plea for interagency collaboration. In R. H. Bruininks & K. C. Ukin (Eds.), *Living and learning in the least restrictive environment*. Baltimore, MD: Paul H. Brookes.

Scheiber, B., & Talpers, J. (1987). *Unlocking potential: College and other choices for learning disabled people. A step by step guide*. Bethesda, MD.: Adler & Adler.

Schloss, P. J. (1985). Postsecondary opportunities: The role of secondary educators in advocating handicapped young adults. *Journal for Vocational Special Needs*, 7, 15–19.

Schloss, P. J., McEwen, D., Lang, E., & Schwab, J. (1986). PROGRESS: A model program for promoting school to work transition. *Career Development for Exceptional Individuals*, 9(1), 16–23.

Test, D. W., Keul, P. K., & Grossi, T. (1988). Transitional services for mildly handicapped youth: A cooperative model. *Journal for Vocational Special Needs*, 10, 7–11.

Tindall, L. W., & Hedberg, S. B. (1987). Job Training Partnership Act. *Teaching Exceptional Children*, 19(1), 43–45.

Turnbull, H. R., & Turnbull, P. (1985) *Parents speak out: Then and now (2nd ed.)*. New York: Macmillan.

Turnbull, A. P., & Turnbull, H. R. III. (1990) *Families, professionals, and exceptionality: A special partnership* (2nd ed.). Columbus: Merrill.

U.S. Department of Labor. (1977). *Sheltered workshop study*. Washington, DC: U.S. Government Printing Office.

U.S. Department of Labor. (1982). *A study of accommodations provided to handicapped employees by federal contractors*. Washington, DC: U.S. Government Printing Office.

U.S. Public Law 93–112 (Rehabilitation Act of 1973), Section 504. 29 U.S.C. 794.

C h a p t e r **3**

Problems of Adolescence

ANJALI MISRA

Did you know that . . .

- More than 150,000 adolescents under the age of 22 are confined in correctional institutions and another 300,000 spend time in pretrial detention centers and jails?
- Individuals with disabilities are disproportionately overrepresented among the juvenile population?
- Very few juvenile offenders who have disabilities receive a legally mandated, appropriate special education program?
- Offenders who have mental retardation are likely to be incarcerated at an earlier age and for a longer period of time than nonretarded youths?
- Economically disadvantaged adolescents are more likely to be officially reported for delinquent acts than middle-class youths?
- The age at which delinquents commit their first unsocial act is related to future criminal activities?
- A high proportion of delinquents have been abused by their families?
- The juvenile justice system was established in 1899?
- About 4.3 million or 13% of 16- to 24-year-old students drop out of school?
- The dropout rate among students who are seriously emotionally disturbed is approximately 50%?
- School failure is the most common reason for leaving school?
- Only 51% of those who drop out of school are employed?
- The average age at which alcohol consumption begins is 12 years and 5 months?
- The most commonly used drugs are marijuana and alcohol?

Anjali Misra is an associate professor in the Department of Professional Studies, State University of New York at Potsdam, Potsdam, New York.

- Approximately two thousand 15 to 19 year olds commit suicide every year?
- Suicide is the third most common reason for death among adolescents?
- Females attempt suicide more often than males, but fewer females are successful?
- School failure is related to suicide attempts?
- Most students with disabilities are grossly uninformed or misinformed about sex?
- One in every ten women become pregnant premaritally?
- HIV/AIDS is the sixth leading cause of death among 15 to 24 year olds?
- Many teachers have little or no training in developing or implementing a sex education curriculum?
- Estimates of depression are higher for students with learning and/or behavioral problems than for nondisabled youth?

Can you . . .

- List problems in program implementation for adolescents with disabilities in correctional facilities?
- Identify acts that signify delinquent behaviors to isolate high-risk students?
- Develop a curriculum for use with delinquents?
- Highlight ways of obtaining parental involvement for rehabilitation of delinquent adolescents?
- Describe students who are likely to drop out of school?
- Plan school-based experiences to reduce dropout rates?
- Enlist parent support to increase school attendance?
- State different drug categories and their impact on behavior?
- Recognize signs of drug use among adolescents?
- Incorporate methods in your curriculum to reduce or prevent drug use?
- Spot distress signals indicative of suicidal thoughts?
- Create an environment that increases communication and prevents suicide?
- Provide sex education to adolescents with disabilities?
- Identify ways in which sex education may be provided through schools?
- Identify and correct myths associated with HIV/AIDS?

Adolescence is portrayed as the most turbulent period of human development. Events during this time influence the future personal and social growth of the individual. These changes occur in physical and social areas and place challenging demands on the adolescent's ability to make required adjustments. Despite these challenges, adolescents must make rational decisions regarding their future career prospects and life goals. A number of formidable obstacles threaten their ability to make appropriate decisions. These include delinquency, drug abuse, suicide, pregnancy, and dropping out. Adolescents with disabilities face similar obstacles; however, their ability to overcome difficulties may be hampered by their disabilities. Young individuals with disabilities require special assistance and education to enable them to select the most constructive course of action. This chapter describes some of the problems adolescents face and some steps that can be taken to remediate such problems.

Juvenile Delinquency

The legal definition of a juvenile delinquent is "a person under a specific age who violates any state or local law, or commits any act that would be considered a crime if committed by an adult" (Kvaraceus, 1971, pp. 7–8). Delinquent acts include crimes against a person, crimes against property, crimes against society, and status offenses.

Incidence

More than 450,000 adolescents under the age of 22 are confined in juvenile detention centers and state training schools in the United States for crimes such as larceny, theft, and aggravated assault (Leone, Rutherford, & Nelson, 1991). An additional 300,000 are in adult facilities, and 84,000 juveniles spend time in pretrial detention centers and jails. A disproportionate number of these youths (30%–60%), when compared to the prevalence of students with disabilities in public schools (6.5%–13.7%), require special education services (Pasternack & Lyon, 1982; Rutherford, Nelson, & Wolford, 1985; Sylvester, 1982).

Researchers who have studied the prevalence of specific disabilities among the delinquent population have found variable results. This variability can be attributed in part to inconsistencies in definitions of disabilities and also to discrepant criteria employed by states to classify individuals as "juvenile." Pervasive emotional or behavioral problems have been associated with most (Eisenmann, 1991) to all (Kauffman, 1989) delinquent youth. Estimates by administrators from 13 states regarding the prevalence of mental retardation among delinquents have ranged from 0 to 26% (Nelson & Rutherford, 1989). Estimates of prevalence of learning disabilities among juvenile offenders have ranged from 9 to 76% (Nelson & Rutherford, 1989).

Causes

Although juveniles comprise 20% of the total population, they commit over 40% of all violent crimes and nearly 50% of all property offenses (Snarr & Wolford, 1985). Several factors are associated with delinquency among adolescents. A disproportionate number of delinquent youths are African American or Hispanic and come from economically disadvantaged backgrounds (Farrington, 1980). One reason may be that economically disadvantaged adolescents are more likely to be officially reported and recorded, whereas middle-class youths are more likely to be bailed out by parents and not included in police records.

Adolescent males outnumber females in the rate of delinquent crimes committed (Cairns & Cairns, 1983). The peak ages for offenders are 15 to 17 years in both sexes. The offenses for which males and females are arrested vary. Females are more likely to be apprehended for running away from home, sexual behavior, or drug abuse, whereas males are arrested for crimes against property, theft, and vandalism.

Delinquency does not develop suddenly. Adolescent delinquents exhibit antisocial patterns during middle childhood, which typically do not disappear during later years (Loeber, 1982). Furthermore, the age at which delinquents commit their first unsocial act is related to future criminal activities (Cantwell, 1983). Early and frequent inappropriate activities persist over a longer time period.

Inadequate family and peer relationships also contribute to delinquency. Juvenile delinquents are more likely to come from broken homes (Nelson & Rutherford, 1990). Parents of delinquents do not provide support; they use punitive methods of discipline, reject their children, and may be emotionally disturbed themselves (Glueck & Glueck, 1962). A high proportion of delinquents have a history of having been abused by their families. Shanok (1981) reported that 75% of extremely violent children had, in the past, been severely abused by their families.

Repeated school failure may motivate delinquent activities, as is evident from figures indicating high representation of youths with disabilities among this population. Delinquents reportedly function two to four years behind grade level (Hill, Parker, Corbett, & Miano, 1980), experience repeated academic failure (Reiter, 1982), and often drop out of school (Bullock & Reilly, 1979). Keilitz and Dunivant (1986) found that adolescents with learning disabilities were 220% more likely to be adjudicated than other adolescents. Furthermore, it has been suggested that offenders who have mental retardation are likely to be incarcerated at an earlier age and for a longer period of time than nonretarded youths. Contributing factors include their inability to communicate; likelihood to plead guilty; and reduced chances for appeal, parole, or rehabilitation.

Participation in gangs also culminates in delinquent acts. Gangs exert a strong influence over members and provide the direction and reinforcement to engage in illegal actions. Adolescents with disabilities are especially susceptible to such pressures because of characteristics such as impulsivity, inability to foresee consequences, failure to recognize social cues, suggestibility to peer instigations, and poor decision-making skills. In addition, acceptance and participation in a peer group situation may provide much-desired social contact for a youth with a disability, who may be willing to engage in any activity to maintain this new-found acceptance.

Intervention Needs

The juvenile justice system originated in 1899 to help juveniles and prevent their entrance into the adult justice system. The goal of this system was to provide rehabilitation rather than punishment to young offenders. The underlying premise was that delinquents could be redirected to meaningful and responsible ways of fulfilling their needs.

The juvenile system often appears to be far from a blessing to the young offender. Problems such as presumption of guilt, presence of the traditional adversarial relationship between prosecutor and defender, and hasty procedural decisions create barriers to the original intentions of such an establishment. Within correctional institutions, youths with disabilities are more likely to be physically, sexually, and economically abused by other inmates (Snarr & Wolford, 1985). These problems, coupled with inadequate educational provisions, highlight the urgent need for a collaborative, interdisciplinary approach to intervention and follow-up of young offenders with disabilities.

In accordance with Public Law 94-142 and Section 504 of the Rehabilitation Act (1973), correctional programs are mandated to provide a free appropriate public education to adjudicated youths with disabilities. However, results of a national survey suggest that not all juvenile offenders with disabilities are being provided appropriate educational opportunities (Rutherford et al., 1985). Those in adult facilities are less likely to receive appropriate services than those in juvenile facilities. Other findings have suggested a student-to-teacher ratio of 17 to 1; lack of functional skills curricula in several programs; and a range of variations in the size, programs, and services of facilities.

Several programmatic failures in the development and implementation of educational plans for adolescents with disabilities in correctional facilities have been identified by Leone, Price, and Vitolo (1986). First, variability in state laws results in educational laws that exclude correctional and social service agencies. Second, lack of specific standards for curriculum and course content for incarcerated youths makes provision of a specialized program difficult. Third, adjudicated youths are frequently moved from one institution to another, which is a major impediment to continuity of educational programming. Fourth, there is not enough information on the educational background of adolescents, most of whom are placed in correctional institutions without IEPs. Assessment methods are not refined and are conducted in group testing situations by test administrators who are unfamiliar with issues governing assessment of youths who have disabilities. Fifth, most correctional facilities do not work in collaboration with the school district attended by the youth. Judges, court officers, and probation officers are not trained to recognize or provide for the special needs of adjudicated youth with disabilities. Finally, some ethical problems are associated with provision of special educational services to a particular group when other youths, although not labeled, evidence a definite need for similar services.

Different community agencies must collaborate to address these failures in programming and develop the most appropriate service delivery model for delinquent youths, keeping in mind their unique needs and circumstances. With the assistance of special education personnel, special programs need to be developed as preventive measures to deter delinquents from returning to criminal activities. Apart from basic academics, these programs must emphasize functional living skills, vocational education, behavior management, and family therapy. Education must be based on needs assessment and collaborative goal development. The Juvenile Corrections Interagency Transition Model (Webb, Maddox, & Edgar, 1985) provides a transition model to help local agencies integrate delinquent youths into public schools and reduce recidivism. This model assumes that there is a need for (a) accurate information about services available to these adolescents, (b) efficient transfer of records, (c) preplacement planning to avoid failure due to improper placement, and (d) clear communication between all involved in the process.

One method found to be successful with adjudicated youths in increasing on-task and cooperative behaviors is called team-assisted individualization (TAI; Salend & Washin, 1988). TAI involves heterogeneous groups of individuals who work cooperatively to master individualized assignments (Slavin, Leavey, & Madden, 1984). Rewards are based on team performance. Group-based activities are likely to be successful because peer-administered rewards are more reinforcing to adolescents and peer pressure exerts greater influence than adult direction. This method encourages group cohesiveness, which may stimulate a sense of responsibility and provide valuable success experiences to juvenile delinquents.

Teacher Responsibilities

Teachers must be willing to work with the juvenile justice system to provide an appropriate education to delinquents with disabilities. They must recognize their role is pivotal in preventing the recurrence of criminal actions among this population. To do so, teachers must acquire the skills required in working with the police, courts, correctional officers, and other agents of the criminal justice system. Visits to juvenile facilities, detention centers, group homes, and prisons must be an essential component of their training program. Leone and colleagues (1986) have suggested that in addition to professional competence, teachers need to be streetwise and politically savvy to work with adjudicated youths with disabilities. Specific efforts need to be directed toward the following areas.

Identifying the Problem.   Teachers must be cognizant of factors associated with delinquency and identify students who may succumb easily to the lures of negative influences. Teachers can work with these youths by channeling their energies toward positive and rewarding activities in and out of school. Teachers must also involve other staff members such as the counselor or school psychologist and work with them to develop suitable programs for these youngsters. Timely identification is especially important given that youths with behavior disorders are usually not welcome in school environments and are likely to go through school without remediation for their academic and social problems (Kauffman, 1989).

Preventing the Problem.   Programmatic efforts in the prevention of delinquency have only been partly successful, and there are no model programs that provide an absolute solution to this problem. Collaborative efforts among all agencies involved seem to be the key. Schools must adopt secondary curricula that are functional so that students can apply new skills in their immediate environments. Results of the Learning Disabilities-Juvenile Delinquency Project, conducted from 1976 to 1983 by the National Center for State Courts in Williamsburg, Virginia, showed that direct instruction techniques can improve student achievement and decrease future delinquent acts among adjudicated youth (Keilitz & Dunivant, 1986).

Within the classroom, teachers must attempt to make learning highly motivating, relevant, and successful for students. It is important to have a structured, clearly defined, noncompetitive environment that is positive and nonthreatening. Furthermore, teachers must be familiar with culture-specific behavioral patterns, values, and expectations. Lack of understanding of cultural differences in behavior may create conflict and further exacerbate discipline problems (Misra, 1994). A positive, successful learning environment that caters to individual student differences can be powerful in influencing change.

Crime-prevention curricula must be incorporated into the education of students with disabilities from elementary through secondary levels. Special education teachers could team up with police officers, lawyers, judges, and correctional facility personnel to provide instruction to students regarding crime, delinquency, consequences of delinquent acts, and other relevant information. Juvenile officers could be a useful resource, since they might be more familiar with the community than representatives from other agencies.

Parent Involvement.   Maintaining regular contact with parents is an effective means of preventing, troubleshooting, or solving various student-related problems. Parental contact also helps teachers understand family circumstances and may alert them to potential student misconduct and thus help them identify high-risk students.

Parents of delinquents may require school support for information about the legal system and their role in the process. School personnel must be ready to provide this service and encourage parents to take an active role in future proceedings regarding their child. Interested and involved parents could be an important asset in the rehabilitation of an adolescent with a disability.

Dropouts

Incidence

The U.S. General Accounting Office reported that in 1985, 4.3 million or 13% of 16- to 24-year-old students dropped out of school. Of these, 3.5 million were white, 700,000 were black, and 100,000 represented other groups.

The presence of some disabling conditions among adolescent dropouts has been studied on a limited basis. The dropout rate among youths with behavior disorders is over 40% (U.S. Department of Education, 1991). Of these, about one third are unemployed and do not attend any postsecondary training program (Neel, Medows, Levine, & Edgar, 1988). Levin, Zigmond, and Birch (1985) surveyed the progress of 52 adolescents with learning disabilities and reported a 47% dropout rate. Zigmond and Thornton (1985) reported that half of the LD students who began ninth grade left school before graduation. The dropout rate of students enrolled in programs for students with learning disabilities was twice as high as the dropout rate of the general program (Bartnick & Parkay, 1991). Other disabilities among dropouts have not been well documented.

Causes

Voss, Wendling, and Elliott (1966) differentiated among three types of dropouts. The first type is the involuntary dropout who has to leave school because of unavoidable circumstances such as a family emergency. Disadvantaged students are three times more likely to drop out involuntarily than advantaged students. The second type is the dropout with disabilities who leaves because he or she lacks certain skills. The third type is the capable dropout who voluntarily leaves school for other reasons.

School failure is the most common reason for leaving school (Gainer, 1987). This may explain the high incidence of disabilities among dropouts. Negative experiences filled with failure and academic problems, poor grades, or alienation from peers often contribute to dropping out. Such experiences may cause an aversion to school-related activities and may result in poor self-perception and lowered self-esteem. Researchers have found lower self-esteem and greater hostility among dropouts than among nondropouts (Bachman, Green, & Wirtanen, 1972).

Negative peer group influences and participation in antisocial activities with other dropouts may encourage dropout behaviors. A high correlation exists between delinquency and dropping out of school; however, which comes first is not entirely clear (Farrington, Gallagher, Morley, St. Ledger, & West, 1986). Marriage, pregnancy, and employment are other contributing variables. Unwed pregnant women and those who get married during adolescent years often drop out of school. Young men who find jobs often become entrapped by the economic benefits and consider further pursuit of education a waste of time.

The family environment also plays a significant role in determining who will graduate and who will leave school prior to completion. Families of dropouts have been characterized as having conflict, higher rates of divorce, poor supervision, and lack of communication (Garbarino, Wilson, & Garbarino, 1986).

Intervention Needs

Dropouts with disabilities face serious vocational and social difficulties. Because they drop out, they do not avail themselves of the vocational and life-skills educational opportunities available at the secondary level. They enter the community without the skills they need to support themselves and become self-sufficient. Research has also confirmed that job prospects for dropouts are poorer than for those who graduate (Levin et al., 1985). Similar findings were reported by Hasazi, Gordon, and Roe (1985), who conducted a follow-up study of 462 students with learning and behavioral disorders. They found that 60% of students who graduated from school were employed, compared with 51% of those who dropped out of school. Lack of employability skills poses a severe handicap, given that the opportunities for unskilled workers are steadily decreasing. Other reported consequences of dropping out include involvement with drugs and crime (Farrington, 1980).

Programming to prevent dropping out combines several components such as mentorships and sustained counseling, social services, individualized instruction and competency-based curricula, effective school/business collaboration for placement, incentives for completing high school, year-round schools and alternative schools, increased school accountability for dropout rates, and involvement of parents and community in dropout prevention (Hahn, 1987). A need exists to increase the number of counselors, establish health and family planning programs, develop infant care facilities for teenage mothers, provide remedial instruction, increase student employability skills, and work in collaboration with community social service agencies (Hahn, 1987). Programs must be initiated earlier than secondary levels, since patterns of truancy develop gradually and prior to high school.

Teacher Responsibilities

Teachers can play an important role in reducing dropout among students. They must take an active interest in this serious problem, because the goal of teaching is not simply to provide instruction to students present in the classroom, but also to ensure that everyone eligible is included in the educational system. Teachers must become familiar with the special problems associated with dropping out and with the methods and resources that can help students overcome such problems. Teachers can help in several ways.

Identifying the Problem.   Students who are likely to drop out are those who are behind their grade level and older than their classmates, exhibit poor academic performance, lack basic skills, and have been frequently suspended or given detention. Action Plan 3.1 identifies risk factors. Other students at risk for dropping out include pregnant women and students from economically disadvantaged single-parent families and families on welfare. If teachers can identify and respond to the needs of these youngsters at an early stage, prevention is a possibility.

Preventing the Problem.   To prevent dropping out, teachers need to establish positive school-attending habits. They can emphasize the importance of regular attendance and establish a reward system that encourages school attendance.

Teachers must be actively involved with students and aware of their problems. They should involve students in classroom and school activities and establish clear standards and rules. Teachers must also design a learning environment that is relevant, motivating, and encourages success among students with disabilities. Surveys show that the rate at

---

Action Plan 3.1   Risk Factors Associated with Dropping Out

Teachers need to be aware of factors that contribute to dropping out of school. They include:

School failure	Frequent suspension/detention
Poor grades	Pregnancy
Lack of basic skills	Single parent families
Older age than the average student	Lower socioeconomic status
Poor peer relationships	

which dropouts return to school is consistently related to test scores. Curricula for adolescents must focus on functional living needs in the workplace, in the community, at home, and within social settings. Isolated work experiences are not motivating enough to keep secondary students in school. Links need to be established among job skills taught, student interest, and community needs. Follow-up activities are needed to help in job search, placement, problem resolution, and support services.

Schloss, Kane, and Miller (1981) have offered some suggestions for teachers. First, make school experiences positive. This may be accomplished by increasing the likelihood of student success, intervening in peer relations to reduce peer problems, increasing the frequency of social reinforcement, and increasing communication with parents. Second, decrease student satisfaction associated with staying away from school. One way to ensure this is to have the social worker pay a home visit to all late arrivals and send homework to sick students. Furthermore, a student found to be well by the home visitor should be accompanied to school. Refusal to attend school should have consequences in some form of lost privileges. Third, teachers should target for development those skills that enable adolescents to benefit from school.

Parent Involvement.   Parent involvement from the initial stages of school truancy is very important. Schools should intervene before the student reaches high school, because a well-established pattern is more difficult to break. Parent involvement can be increased if teachers send positive and encouraging reports home about their students. Such reports may serve to motivate parents and may also result in positive feedback for the student. Finally, conferences focusing on both progress and problems should be scheduled on a regular basis. Such conferences should be scheduled at times that allow parent attendance and participation. It may also be extremely beneficial to have the youth present during these meetings. If both teachers and parents monitor student activities, dropout rates may be reduced.

Substance Abuse

Incidence

The United States has the highest rate of substance abuse among high school students and young adults of any industrialized nation in the world (Johnston, O'Malley, & Bachman, 1988). Approximately 36% of all high school seniors have used some illicit drug other than marijuana; approximately 37% of all seniors consume a series of five or more drinks during a two-week period; and about 19% smoke cigarettes daily. Research also shows that the average age at which alcohol consumption begins is 12 years and 5 months and that 23% of youngsters between ages 12 and 18 have serious drinking problems (Horton, 1985). Marijuana remains the most commonly used drug, followed by stimulants, inhalants, hallucinogens, sedatives, and tranquilizers.

Of all the studies and surveys conducted to gather information regarding drug use among adolescents, only a handful have focused on youths with disabilities. Furthermore, the technical adequacy of research targeting individuals with disabilities is questionable (Leone, 1991). In a recent survey, significantly more adolescents with learning disabilities were classified as chemically dependent than were non-learning-disabled peers based on the results of the Substance Abuse Subtle Screening Inventory (Karacostas & Fisher, 1993). Devlin and Elliot (1992) found that 51% of students with behavior disorders displayed patterns of drug use, while only 14% of nondisordered students showed similar drug use. Limited information has also suggested that the risk for substance abuse may be higher among individuals with behavioral disorders, spinal cord injury, and traumatic brain injury (Leone, 1991).

These figures represent a widespread problem of breathtaking magnitude. The problem is compounded when one realizes that the leading cause of death among adolescents is motor vehicle accidents, often alcohol related. In addition, delinquent behaviors such as property destruction and crimes are usually related to alcohol and drug abuse (Blane, 1979). Health problems including liver damage, heart disease, ulcers, malnutrition, cancers, and brain damage may be incurred through heavy drinking. Adolescents may be especially susceptible to acute alcohol poisoning due to reckless practices involving binges, competitions, and drink-"chugging" games.

Causes

There is no single or most common cause for substance abuse. Numerous factors play a role in the adolescent's use of alcohol and drugs. Family disorganization and stress (Stern, Northman, & Van-Slyck, 1984), lack of parental direction and supervision, the need to rebel against authority (Jessor & Jessor, 1980), or the desire to explore new experiences often lead adolescents to seek chemical solutions to problems. Adolescents are more likely to engage in drug- and alcohol-related activities if their peers and parents do so (Brook, Whiteman, & Gordon, 1983). Youths from low economic groups or different ethnic and minority groups may be introduced to drugs early in their lives as a consequence of community conditions, gang-type liaisons, and minimal parental supervision. Advertisements and media link alcohol with enjoyment and good living, conveying a strong message to impressionable adolescents and encouraging substance abuse (Gitlin, 1990)

Several researchers have found a strong link among substance abuse, school failure, and low commitment to school (Friedman, Glickman, & Utada, 1985). The association between substance abuse and juvenile delinquency has also been established through research (Clayton, 1981). Lack of social competence may also play a part in substance abuse (Wills & Schiffman, 1985). Drug use may provide the adolescent with confidence to participate and interact with others and lead to feelings of self-worth and belonging (Jardin & Ziebell, 1981).

Factors that put students with disabilities at risk for drug use include a history of peer rejection, school failure, low social competence, poor self-concept, and inadequate adult relationships. These youths may find that drug use opens up avenues for developing friendships and acceptance within a peer group.

Intervention Needs

A systematic, broad-based program perspective is necessary to address drug problems. The cooperation of community institutions such as courts, police, the juvenile justice system, mental health agencies, private organizations, and parents is imperative. All personnel must be well-informed and encouraged to work together.

Schools must develop drug and alcohol policies. These policies must focus on preventive programming, include students with disabilities, and provide resources to individuals working to help youths overcome drug and alcohol dependency (Leone, 1991). Schools must also have ongoing drug and alcohol education through which students receive honest and accurate information. Support services such as counseling for students and families, information dissemination, emergency centers, and parent groups must be established. Schools must establish firm rules and guidelines regarding the use, trade, or possession of illegal substances. These guidelines must be detailed and precise so that the consequences of drug-related activities are clear to all students and can be implemented consistently and effectively by all personnel. The consequences for the first offense may include suspension, notifying the parents, and reporting to the police (Jardin & Ziebell, 1981). Police involvement reinforces the illegal nature of the act and may serve as a deterrent to future occurrences. Collaboration with agencies mentioned earlier is critical to the success of school-based programs. The narrow focus of such programs—namely, targeting individual students rather than powerful environmental contingencies—has often been blamed for their ineffectiveness.

Teacher Responsibilities

Substance abuse has a direct and serious impact on student performance within the educational environment. Therefore, this is an area that requires teacher attention and involvement. Reports suggest that teachers are reluctant to get entangled in problems related to substance abuse among their students, especially if the students have disabilities (Shannon, 1986). Researchers, however, warn teachers that they contribute to these problems by ignoring them (Johnson, 1988). Furthermore, concern for the well-being and health of drug and alcohol users and concern for other students who share the same environment invite teacher input. Teachers may provide a valuable service by identifying current or potential substance users and obtaining support services for them.

Identifying the Problem. Action Plan 3.2 lists four major categories of drugs, each having different physiological and behavioral manifestations. These include stimulants, to increase alertness and reduce hunger; depressants, to reduce activity; hallucinogens, to alter the senses and personality and create mood variances; and narcotics, to relieve pain and increase euphoria. Teachers may be the first to notice the existence of a problem through changes in student behavior. These changes are listed in Action Plan 3.3. The student may exhibit unusual and unacceptable behaviors such as sleeping in class, mood swings, incomplete work, skipping class, and disrupting other students (Jardin & Ziebell,

Action Plan 3.2 Drug Categories and Their Effects

We suggest teachers become familiar with the effects of different classes of drugs.

Stimulants	Increase alertness Reduce hunger
Depressants	Reduce activity Induce relaxation and sleep
Hallucinogens	Create perceptual disorders Create mood variances
Narcotics	Relieve pain Increase euphoria

1981). Other signs the teacher must learn to recognize include a lack of interest in extracurricular activities, conflicts with authority figures, problems with peers, new peer relationships, depression, a lack of energy, a lack of concern about personal well-being and hygiene, and evidence of a troubled home life (Horton, 1985). Teachers must refer students displaying such behaviors for evaluation. Personnel conducting assessments must be trained to assess students for the possibility of substance abuse. An assessment protocol for use by school psychologists has been developed by Fisher and Harrison (1992).

Teachers of students with disabilities must be warned not to make hasty judgments on the basis of a few signs, since several students will probably be on medication that produces similar symptoms. Furthermore, many of these signs are characteristic of behavior variances evident among special populations. The teacher who suspects a serious problem may make a referral to the appropriate person in the school. Once the problem has been clearly defined, remedial steps may be initiated with the cooperation of the school system.

Action Plan 3.3 Signs of Drug Use

Horton (1985) recommends that teachers remain alert to the following signs of drug use:

1. Sleeping in class
2. Mood swings
3. Incomplete work
4. Truancy
5. Disruptive behavior
6. Lack of interest in extracurricular activities
7. Conflicts with authority figures
8. New peer relationships
9. Depression
10. Lack of energy
11. Poor hygiene
12. Negative family circumstances

Preventing the Problem.   The best way to prevent substance abuse is to inform students about drug and alcohol abuse, its consequences, and its harmful effects. Students must be active participants in lessons focusing on increasing drug awareness and drug-free living skills. Teachers can create awareness among adolescents by engaging them in problem-solving activities. For example, teachers may hold brainstorming sessions on the positive outcomes of quitting alcohol and drug use. Students may be presented with scenarios regarding death resulting from drunk driving and be required to appraise such situations. Such activities encourage thoughtful decisions and responsible behavior. Teachers must convey the idea that drug and alcohol use is not associated with adult status or glamour. Teaching students to ignore peer pressures and providing alternative coping strategies for stressful situations gives students a means of avoiding negative consequences. Teachers must identify the positive consequences students derive through drug use and teach acceptable alternatives for experiencing similar gratification. For example, drug use may provide a student with access to a peer group; however, the student could be taught positive social skills that would help develop relationships with peers.

Because peer influences are the primary motivational source during adolescence, some researchers have utilized peer counseling and peer group processes (Biase, 1984; Dembo, 1983). Such attempts have shown positive results. Teachers must include social competence training as part of their curriculum because research evidence indicates less drug use among students who receive such instruction (Pentz et al., 1989). Students with disabilities require intensive exposure to social competence training programs, given their severe deficits in this area. The Life Skills Training program developed by Botvin and Tortu (1988) has shown good results.

Considering the relationship between substance abuse and school failure, teachers have the responsibility of providing an enriching and positive classroom environment to all students. Teachers are advised to familiarize themselves with the agencies and curricula related to substance abuse prevention and treatment listed in Action Plan 3.4. Some curricular materials have been specifically developed for students with sensory impairments, mental retardation, learning disabilities, and behavior disorders. Teachers may seek additional assistance and information from the resources listed in Action Plan 3.5.

Parent Involvement.   Parent involvement is essential for successful drug rehabilitation efforts. Parents are an important source of information regarding family, neighborhood, and community dynamics that perpetuate drug use. School-based programs are unlikely to succeed without parent cooperation, given the strong influence of environmental influences in drug use. A clear, realistic, mutually agreed upon plan of action must be developed, and parental understanding of the process must be ensured. The adolescent's involvement throughout this process must be encouraged. Parents must be told of the importance of their support and of the availability of school assistance at all times. Parents need encouragement because they often perceive themselves as helpless or are completely frustrated in their attempts to resolve their child's problem. Parents also need information regarding the nature of their child's problem, treatment options, resources available, and monetary issues.

Action Plan 3.4 Sources of Substance Abuse Prevention Curricula for Students with Disabilities

Teachers may contact the following agencies for information about substance abuse and how to prevent or address it:

Addiction Intervention with the
    Disabled
Sociology Department
Kent State University
Kent, OH 44242
214-672-2440

James Stanfield Publishing Co.
P. O. Box 1995H
Santa Monica, CA 90406
800-421-6534

Milwaukee Council on Drug Abuse
1442 North Farwell Street
Suite 304
Milwaukee, WI 53202
414-276-8487

Project OZ
201 East Grove Street
Second Floor
Bloomington, IL 61701
309-827-0377

Substance Abuse Resources for
    Disabled Individuals
Wright State University School of
    Medicine
Dayton, OH 45435
513-873-3588

Substance and Alcohol Intervention
    Services for the Deaf
Rochester Institute of Technology
50 West Main Street
Sixth Floor
Rochester, NY 14614
716-475-4974

Depression

Incidence

Depression in the school-aged population has been estimated to range from 1.8% to 13.9% (Pfeffer, Zuckerman, Plutchik, & Mizruchi, 1984), with higher rates among adolescents. The prevalence of depression among youths with disabilities has not been well documented. However, depression has been identified as characteristic of youths with emotional problems (Cullinan, Schloss, & Epstein, 1987), learning disabilities, and mild mental retardation (Reynolds & Miller, 1985). Estimates of depression among youths with learning and/or behavior problems are higher than reported for nondisabled youth, ranging from 50% to 60% (Forness, 1988; Mattison, Humphrey, Kales, Hernit, & Finkenbinder, 1986). Females are more likely than males to experience severe depressive symptomatology (Maag & Behrens, 1989a).

Action Plan 3.5   Resources

Teachers interested in obtaining more information regarding the problems facing adolescents are advised to contact the following agencies:

National Institute on Drug Abuse
5600 Fishers Lane
Rockville, MD 20852

The Addiction Research Foundation
33 Russell Street
Toronto, Canada M5S 2S1

U.S. Department of Education, Alcohol
   and Drug Abuse Education Program
400 Maryland Avenue, SW
Washington, DC 20202

Families in Action
3854 North Druid Hills Road
Suite 300
Decatur, GA 30033

National Federation of Parents for a
   Drug Free Youth
8730 Georgia Avenue
Suite 200
Silver Spring, MD 20910

National Center for Youth with
   Disabilities
University of Minnesota
Box 721-UMHC, Harvard Street at East
   River Road
Minneapolis, MN 55455
612-626-2825

National Clearinghouse for Alcohol
   and Drug Information
6000 Executive Boulevard
Suite 402
Rockville, MD 20852
301-468-2600

Resource Center on Substance Abuse
   Prevention and Disability
1331 F Street, NW
Suite 800
Washington, DC 20004
202-783-2900

Causes

Depression may be associated with anxiety disorders, conduct disorders, oppositional defiant disorder, phobias, or substance abuse (American Psychiatric Association, 1987). Problems such as poor peer relationships, poor communication, and parent–child hostility have been found to coexist with depression. Depression may result from an inability to cope with excessive school demands among youths with learning disabilities (Pfeffer, 1986). Researchers have noted a relationship between cognitive deficits and depression (Brumback, Staton, & Wilson, 1980). Medical problems often cause profound stress and may place students at risk for depression (Kashani, Venske, & Millar, 1981).

Intervention Needs

The need for intervention for depression among adolescents is obvious. Adolescents who are depressed are caught in a self-debilitating situation that impacts them, their teachers and peers, and their families. Research linking depression with suicide highlights the need for immediate intervention by the schools and the community.

Teachers must be trained to recognized symptoms and be knowledgeable about intervention methods for depression. Preparation of teachers of students with disabilities must shift its focus from being primarily academic to including social skills and problem-solving strategies that provide coping mechanisms for depressed adolescents. School support staff such as counselors, social workers, and school psychologists must work in collaboration with each other and with teachers of students who are depressed.

Teacher Responsibilities

Depression can be severely debilitating, and it affects student learning. Teachers have the responsibility of identifying and referring students who need intervention in a timely manner. Teachers must also present themselves as approachable and concerned individuals who are willing to listen and offer support to their students. The likelihood of students seeking teacher assistance can be greatly influenced by how teachers communicate with their students. Teachers can help students by engaging in the activities discussed in the following paragraphs.

Identifying the Problem.   Teachers must be alert to symptoms of depression typically displayed by adolescents. According to the *Diagnostic and Statistical Manual (DSM-III-R)* of the American Psychiatric Association (1987), five of nine symptoms must be evident nearly every day for at least two weeks for the diagnosis of depression. The symptoms include (1) loss of interest in pleasurable activities, (2) depressed or irritable mood, (3) change in weight and eating habits, (4) sleeping problems, (5) psychomotor differences, (6) fatigue, (7) feelings of guilt and worthlessness, (8) poor concentration, and (9) recurrent suicidal thoughts. The *DSM-II-R* also describes behaviors of adolescents that may signal underlying depression. These behaviors are listed in Action Plan 3.6.

Teachers must pay particular attention to students who are at risk of being overlooked because they do not disrupt the classroom or bother others (Stark, 1990). Often students who are gifted or do not have conduct disorders and behavior problems (e.g., hyperactiv-

---

Action Plan 3.6 *DSM-III-R* **Features of Depressive Disorders Among Adolescents**

The following feelings and behaviors are characteristics of depression:

School difficulties	Inattention to personal appearance
Negativistic or antisocial behavior	Increased emotionality
Substance abuse	Feelings of wanting to leave home
Restlessness	Feelings of being misunderstood
Grouchiness	Feelings of not receiving approval
Refusal to cooperate in family ventures	Sulkiness
Withdrawal from social activities	Aggression
Sensitivity to rejection in love relationships	

ity, aggression) are not referred for assessment and services for depression. Teachers must also pay special attention to students who consistently fall behind in their schoolwork and are experiencing academic difficulties. Prompt action upon the detection of signs of depression by the teacher is imperative, because depression is linked to suicide. Teachers play a critical role in making referrals within the school and in securing assistance from support staff, and their input is required during assessment of depression. Teacher responsibilities also include classroom follow-up of referred students by practicing strategies to alleviate factors related to depression. Teachers may have to monitor the side effects of antidepressant drugs on behavior.

Preventing the Problem.   Depression and school failure often result in a vicious cycle that must be broken. Immediate intervention efforts focusing on providing success experiences to students may hinder the onset of depression. Because poor peer relationships are linked to depression, strategies promoting social competence must be an integral part of the curriculum. To maintain a positive classroom environment, teachers must avoid use of punishment techniques and use positive behavior management strategies. Programs that enhance skill acquisition and increase school success and self-concept are especially beneficial for adolescents with learning disabilities and behavior problems. Teachers may get further information from organizations listed in Action Plan 3.7.

Action Plan 3.7   Organizations Providing Information on Depression Among Youth

Teachers may contact the following agencies for information about depression:

American Academy of Child and
   Adolescent Psychiatry
3615 Wisconsin Avenue, NW
Washington, DC 20016
202-966-7300

American Psychological Association
750 First Street, NE
Washington, DC 20002
202-955-7660, 202-336-5500

The Council for Exceptional Children
1920 Association Drive
Reston, VA 22091-1589
703-620-3660

National Alliance for the Mentally Ill
2101 Wilson Boulevard
Suite 302
Arlington, VA 22201
800-950-NAMI) (Recording)
703-524-7600

National Depressive and Manic
   Depressive Association
730 North Franklin Street,
Suite 501
Chicago, IL 60610
312-642-0049
312-908-8100 (Crisis Hotline)

National Mental Health Association
1021 Prince Street
Alexandria, VA 22314-2971
800-969-6977

For students who are not responsive to such techniques, a referral to the counselor and/or social worker may be necessary for intensive remediation. The counselor may be invited to the classroom to conduct problem-solving sessions with all students. Too often depressed adolescents blame themselves for negative events in their lives. Students who are depressed must be made to believe that they have control over personal success and failure. Providing opportunities to discuss and generate alternatives within the classroom will make counseling more realistic to students at risk for depression and at the same time benefit all students.

Parent Involvement. Depression among adolescents may have its roots in impaired family dynamics. Harris and Ammerman (1986) suggested the presence of conflict, disorganization, and psychopathology in the families of depressed adolescents. Furthermore, there is evidence of significant correlation between parents' depression and depression in children (Billings & Moos, 1985; Forehand, McCombs, & Brody, 1987). Depressed parents may propagate depression in the home by reinforcing and modeling the behavior. Therefore, the family's role is critical in any attempts at remediation made by school personnel. The teacher may initiate a referral for family therapy after discussions with the family. Parents require support from school personnel, because living with a depressed adolescent can be emotionally stressful. Furthermore, parents may feel helpless in resolving their child's feelings because they blame themselves. Cooperation from the school during the time they are undergoing treatment is essential for accelerating the recovery process.

Suicide

Incidence

Over 5,000 youths commit suicide every year. There are as many as 500,000 to 1 million attempts each year (Moore, 1986), accounting for 10% of all emergency room visits (McKendry, Tishler, & Kelly, 1982). Females attempt suicide five times more frequently than males, yet males are more often successful (Centers for Disease Control, 1986). This is attributed to use by males of more effective methods such as shooting or hanging, compared to the drugs or poisons typically used by females. Adolescent suicide has increased at an alarming rate. It rose from the fourth leading cause of adolescent death in 1975 (Tooland, 1975) to the third leading cause in 1980, ranking below accidents and homicide (National Center for Health Statistics, 1989). This trend is expected to continue. The rate of suicide in 1987 was 12.9 per 100,000 adolescents, and projections for the year 2000 suggest a rate increase of 15.5 per 100,000 (Pfeifer, 1986).

These shocking statistics misrepresent the actual number of suicides, which may be two or three times greater (American Psychiatric Association, 1985). Some reasons for misreporting suicides as accidental deaths or attributing cause of death to undetermined factors include (a) avoidance of social stigma related to suicide; (b) belief that youngsters do not attempt to take their own life; and/or (c) religious beliefs of a group of people (Hawton, 1986).

There is scant information regarding suicide by youths with disabilities. Some evidence indicates a higher rate of suicide among adolescents who have learning disabilities than adolescents without disabilities (Maag & Behrens, 1989b; Ritter, 1989).

Causes

Suicidal youths usually have a past history of personal, familial, or medical difficulties. Children of parents who suffer from depression disorders and alcohol abuse appear to be at high risk for committing suicide. Physically abused adolescents are five times more likely to attempt suicide than those with no history of abuse (Riggs, Alario, & McHorney, 1990). Other family problems include poor communication, conflicting values, and insufficient affection and support (Dukes & Lorch, 1989). School adjustment problems and poor school performance have been found to be related to adolescent suicide attempts (Kosky, Silburn, & Zubrick, 1990).

A recent government report compiled by Davidson and Linnoila (1991) identified biochemical, psychological, and social risk factors linked to youth suicide. These factors include (a) substance abuse, (b) psychiatric disorders such as depression and schizophrenia, (c) family breakdown and parental death, (d) familial predisposition to affective illness, and (e) low concentration of certain essential acids in the cerebrospinal fluid.

It appears that suicide can be "contagious," because research shows that suicides often occur in clusters in terms of time or location. A possible reason for this occurrence is the media attention to suicide. Pfeffer (1989) summarized information presented at the American Association of Suicidology (AAS) regarding the link between suicide and media coverage. Factors such as location of the story in a newspaper (front page vs. inside page), specificity of news coverage, and romanticized descriptions of reasons for committing suicide appear to have a significant impact on the rate of suicide.

Intervention Needs

Procedures to prevent adolescent suicide require immediate and concerted attention, since the consequences of failure are drastic and irreversible. Suicide not only causes social and emotional damage to the immediate family but may deeply affect others who know the victim. Too often, after a suicide, we hear repentant parents and teachers wishing they had foreseen the event and taken preventive measures. Ways must be found to avoid such mistakes.

Teachers must prepare themselves through education, resources, and related literature to be ready to deal with crisis situations. They must remain alert to the emotional environment in their classroom and make the extra effort to further investigate irregularities in student behavior. Schools must be equipped with services to provide frequent student counseling and family therapy as needed. Information dissemination, emergency help, and formation of support groups are services that must be given serious consideration by every school.

Teacher Responsibilities

Suicide prevention and support for adolescents who display suicidal tendencies are areas in which teachers could make a positive difference. The teacher's role cannot be stressed enough, given that school problems often contribute to adolescent suicide. In the case of adolescents with disabilities, teachers may often be singled out as primary adult caretakers and may significantly influence adolescent actions. Some suggestions for teachers that may help them identify and prevent suicide are given in the following paragraph.

Identifying the Problem. It is not always apparent that a student is experiencing suicidal feelings or is displaying associated symptoms. It has been suggested that adolescent suicide attempts are not impulsive actions but occur after numerous appeals for help and support have been ignored (Weiner, 1980). Some warning signs are included in Action Plan 3.8. Teachers must be aware of distress signals that may be verbally expressed in statements such as "You'll be sorry when I'm gone" or "All this will not matter soon." Such verbalizations must not be ignored. Many depressed adolescents, harboring suicidal thoughts, may express themselves through excessive fatigue and hypochondria or through restless, unproductive activity (Capuzzi, 1986). Themes or preoccupations in thinking may be yet another indicator of suicidal thoughts—for example, a sudden interest in religion related to life after death or an undue absorption in a recent personal loss. It is possible that parents and teachers may attribute these signs to normal adolescent problems; however, warning signs must never be cursorily dismissed. Results of a Gallup Poll indicated that of 1,152 adolescents who had thought about suicide, 6% made suicide attempts.

Teachers must not take on counseling responsibilities, because they are not trained to prevent suicide. Their responsibility is to identify and make a referral. They may assist the student in contacting a mental health service and contact parents and other professionals to make them aware of the problem (Mitchell & Resnik, 1981).

Action Plan 3.8 Warning Signs of Suicide

Guetzloe (1989) summarized the most commonly cited warning signs of suicide as follows:

1. Extreme changes in behavior
2. Signs of depression
3. Suicidal threat or statement
4. Previous suicide attempt
5. Substance abuse
6. Presence of suicide plan
7. Actions related to making final arrangements (e.g., giving away possessions)
8. Signs of procuring the means (e.g., purchasing a weapon or pills)

Preventing the Problem.   One approach to prevention is to increase teacher knowledge and awareness of how to identify and intervene with suicidal adolescents. Involvement with suicide prevention centers and other similar community agencies increases awareness and may lead to the early recognition and resolution of a problem. Teachers will also become better equipped to handle emergency situations.

Within the educational setting, young individuals who are apprehensive or anxious often need support from peers so they can communicate and learn to cope with their feelings. Open communication may also promote feelings of commonality among peers experiencing similar problems and subvert fears related to feelings of personal differences. An important first step is the willingness to verbalize anxieties and discuss problems that may become dangerous if ignored. Discussions should not, however, directly revolve around issues related to suicide. Use of suicide curricula including presentation of materials on suicide has been discouraged by Shaffer and colleagues (1990) due to their "contagious" effects. These researchers found that talking about suicide may result in suicide attempts by youths who are at risk. Providing individual help to those who require it is preferable. However, information regarding suicide prevention agencies and emergency hotlines may be provided to students. See Action Plan 3.9 for a list of agencies that can help.

Action Plan 3.9   Organizations Providing Information on Suicide Among Youth

Teachers can obtain information about suicide from the following agencies:

American Academy of Child and
  Adolescent Psychiatry
Public Information Office
3615 Wisconsin Avenue, NW
Washington, DC 20016
202-966-0985

American Association of Suicidology
2459 South Ash Street
Denver, CO 80222
303-692-0985

Council for Children with Behavioral
  Disorders
A Division of The Council for
  Exceptional Children
1920 Association Drive
Reston, VA 22091-1589
703-620-3660

National Institute of Mental Health
Suicide Research Unit
5600 Fishers Lane
Room 10-85
Rockville, MD 20857
301-443-2403

Suicide Information and Education
  Center
1615 10th Avenue, SW
Suite 201
Calgary, Alberta, Canada T3COJ7
403-245-3900

Suicide Prevention Center, Inc.
184 Salem Avenue
Dayton, Ohio 45406
513-223-9096

Teachers must develop a nonthreatening classroom atmosphere that is conducive to student learning. Reducing anxiety associated with learning is crucial, given that school-related stress is one factor that can result in suicide. A curriculum that fosters self-esteem and increases social skills and communication among students can go a long way in preventing suicide. Teachers must build positive rapport and maintain open lines of communication with students. Teachers may want to communicate their concern and desire to help and inform students of their availability and willingness to listen at any time. They must take all problems seriously and directly tell their students that they care about what happens to them. Immediate action in notifying parents and others who may be able to help is crucial. Students must be shown how to obtain help in an emergency when they are not in school. The exact procedures of making a telephone call and giving information while seeking help may be practiced within the school setting. Such attempts may circumvent suicide attempts by providing an option to those who consider suicide as their only resort.

Special education teachers who work with youths who are emotionally disturbed must be prepared to provide support during crisis situations. Although they are not expected to provide counseling or intervention during such times, they could be instrumental in ensuring that such services are made available.

Parent Involvement.   Parents must become familiar with the signs of suicide and precipitating events, such as parents' prohibiting the adolescent from going out, the breakup of a relationship, school failure, family altercations, pregnancy, and so on. Teachers play an important role in parent education. Involvement with parents will not only enable teachers to become familiar with family circumstances and high-risk students but could also prevent tragedies from occurring. Parent counseling could be included in student IEPs.

Sexually Transmitted Diseases

Incidence

Approximately 2.5 million teenagers get sexually transmitted diseases (STDs) each year (Division of STDs, 1986). Action Plan 3.10 lists STDs including chlamydia, gonorrhea, herpes, human immunodeficiency virus (HIV), and syphilis. It gives information on how an individual gets the disease, when symptoms appear, and available treatments. STDs can lead to pelvic inflammatory diseases, infertility, heart disease, arthritis, brain damage, and even death if a timely cure is not available. The life-threatening characteristic of HIV, which causes AIDS, has resulted in a deluge of statistical information on that disease. These statistics are being updated daily. As many as 1 to 1.5 million Americans are currently infected with HIV. By 1992, 365,000 of these people will develop AIDS. One out of every five people with AIDS is 20 to 30 years old. Between 1986 and 1988, 335 cases of AIDS were reported among 13 to 19 year olds (Centers for Disease Control, 1989). These figures suggest that transmission of the virus occurred during adolescent years, because the HIV virus can remain undetected for 8 to 12 years (Flora & Thoresen,

Action Plan 3.10   Sexually Transmitted Diseases

Teachers should be aware of sexually transmitted diseases, how they are transmitted, when symptoms appear, and treatment options.

Disease	Mode of Transmission	Onset of Symptoms	Treatment
Chlamydia	Sexual intercourse Oral or anal sex During birth	Women have no early symptoms Men have symptoms in 1 to 3 weeks	Antibiotics
Gonorrhea	Sexual intercourse Oral or anal sex During birth	Women have no early symptoms Men have symptoms in 2 to 10 days	Antibiotics
Herpes	Sexual intercourse Oral or anal sex Kissing someone with herpes blister	4 days to 2 weeks	No cure; pills and creams reduce pain and sores
HIV	Sexual intercourse Anal sex Infected blood Babies in the womb During birth Breast milk Infected needles and syringes	Blood test shows virus 2 weeks to 6 months after infection No symptoms for years in some people	No cure
Syphilis	Sexual intercourse Oral or anal sex Babies in the womb During birth	10 to 90 days for first stage 6 weeks to 6 months for second stage Years for the third stage	Penicillin

Source: Adapted from *Sexually Transmitted Diseases*, Family Planning Council of Iowa (1991).

1988). Although other STDs are not life threatening in themselves, they can be potentially fatal because the risk of transmission of HIV increases if there are sores on the genitals such as those cause by herpes, syphilis, and chancroid.

Causes

STDs are transmitted to individuals through sexual encounters and can be passed to babies during birth. It is important to specifically focus on the cause and transmission of HIV. HIV prevents the body from fighting diseases and infections that may become life threatening. The virus is transmitted through sexual intercourse, either vaginal or rectal; bodily secretions; intervenous drug use; the placenta; and possibly through breast milk. The virus does not survive outside the human body for long and cannot be transmitted through air. Adolescents engage in several behaviors that put them at a high risk for contracting this virus. Surveys reveal that adolescents possess a high degree of HIV-related information, but they continue to engage in sexual behaviors without using protection (Boswell, Fox, Hubbard, & Coyle, 1992). A Planned Parenthood poll revealed that 57% of teenagers engage in sexual intercourse by age 17; however, only 47% of males and 25% of females reported using condoms (Harris & Associates Inc., 1986). Statistics on drug use indicate that 61% of adolescents have experimented with drugs by graduation (Bennett, 1986). Approximately .9% to 1.5% of high school seniors use heroin (Johnston, O'Malley, & Bachman, 1985). According to researchers, over 200,000 teenagers have tried injecting drugs (Brooks-Gunn, Boyer, & Hein, 1988), and countless others share needles for piercing ears, tattooing, and becoming blood brothers. Surveys also indicate that there exist differences in knowledge based on sex, religion, ethnicity, and socioeconomic status (Anderson & Christenson, 1991).

Intervention Needs

The AIDS epidemic dictates that school personnel act promptly in taking preventive measures before the current statistics become even more deplorable. Schools must work in conjunction with health agencies to increase awareness about AIDS and other STDs among staff, parents, and students. A need for education and information was clearly evident when the results of a survey given to school administrators indicated that many respondents believed that students who were HIV positive would be best served in homebound placements (Smith, 1991). Administrators lacked information on how to include these students in regular educational programs and were unaware of services that may be necessary at different stages of the disease. Schools must develop sound policies regarding their attempts to fight against this disease. Black and Jones (1988) provided criteria to judge a school's success at meeting the intervention needs of students with STDs. These include nondiscriminatory policies, adequately informed staff, educated peers, a high-quality support system, and confidentiality of medical records.

Training for secondary school health education teachers is essential. Teachers must keep up with current scientific information and base their teaching on accurate data rather than fear. Teacher training must include strategies for teaching adolescents with special needs. Students with disabilities are in greater need of useful sex education because they have less information and opportunities to learn sex-related facts. They are also at greater risk of exploitation due to lack of knowledge (Smigielski & Steinmann, 1981).

Teacher Responsibilities

Teachers are responsible for educating their students regarding the health risks associated with STDs, especially those related to AIDS. This is a formidable task, given current information on the consequences of being afflicted by AIDS. Teachers have to take this mission seriously and make purposeful efforts to prevent the spread of STDs among their students. Imparting factual information in an open, honest manner is imperative. Facts about HIV are given in Action Plan 3.11.

Action Plan 3.11 Some Facts about HIV and AIDS

Teachers must make sure students know the following facts about HIV and its implications:

- AIDS stands for acquired immunodeficiency syndrome.
- There is no cure for AIDS.
- The human immunodeficiency virus (HIV) causes AIDS.
- AIDS does not discriminate among sex, race, profession, geographic location, sexual orientation, or socioeconomic status.
- People infected with HIV look and feel healthy for years.
- HIV is transmitted through sexual intercourse, sharing syringes, blood transfusion, the placenta, and breast milk.
- It is possible, but not likely, to get HIV if infected blood enters the body through cuts, sores, or other breaks in the skin.
- There is no risk of transmission through contact with stool, nasal fluids, urine, or vomit unless these fluids contain visible blood.
- Simple first aid steps and cleaning of equipment provide protection against HIV.

Identifying the Problem.   There are no easily identifiable signs to alert the teacher that students need help for sexually transmitted diseases. If a student confides in the teacher that he or she has an STD, then the teacher must refer the student for testing, counseling, and treatment immediately. Teachers may refer students who use drugs or who they suspect of having drug-related problems. Teachers may recommend testing to students who appear to be at high risk due to their sexual behaviors. However, every effort must be maintained to ensure confidentiality. Identification and referral may be facilitated if teachers keep the lines of communication open so students feel comfortable in approaching them and seeking assistance.

Preventing the Problem.   Discussion must focus on HIV prevention because of its seriousness and because the same measures can prevent other STDs as well. Abstinence, mutual monogamy in uninfected couples, and no intravenous drug use are the only sure ways of preventing AIDS. This message, in conjunction with other relevant information, must be shared with adolescents to prevent the spread of STDs. Information on STDs and AIDS must be integrated into health or sex education programs. Teachers must familiarize themselves with curricula adopted by schools on these topics and share this knowledge with their students. Curricula may vary in coverage emphasizing sexual abstinence, and school district policies may dictate what information can be given to students.

Working within the guidelines of school policies, teachers must convey important information on STDs to their students. Teachers can aid in prevention of STDs by conducting classroom discussion on topics critical to issues surrounding sexual activities of adolescents. Teachers must work toward terminating irrational fears and rumors.

Misconceptions must be dispelled (see Action Plan 3.12). Other topics may include family and personal values, decision making, communication skills, self-esteem, peer pressure, drug use, and so on. Teachers must conduct social skills training sessions focusing on how to say no, negotiating mutually acceptable solutions, and making decisions regarding safe sex. Students will benefit from practice related to skills acquired in the classroom. They may be given assignments that involve purchasing a contraceptive and discussing birth control with a dating partner. Several curricular materials are available that describe how teachers may teach these skills. Agencies listed in Action Plan 3.13 may be useful. Teachers must encourage students to delay sexual activity and practice safe sex when they decide to become sexually active. Information regarding condom use may be provided, and negative attitudes regarding condom use may be dispelled. Distribution of condoms in schools is controversial. Some teachers may have to provide information on how to obtain condoms. AIDS must also be discussed in relation to homosexuality. Students must also be educated regarding sharing needles for drug use and procedures for cleaning equipment if they must share needles. Students need to know safe ways of handling blood and other body fluids.

Students with disabilities will require adaptations to procedures and activities. *Circles III: Safer Ways* is a multimedia curriculum for individuals with developmental disabilities (Walker-Hirsch & Champagne, 1988). Color-coded, concentric circles drawn on floor mats are used in role-playing situations. The circles represent gradual movement from activities and role playing requiring little contact, nonthreatening scenarios, and familiar themes to intimate contact, more serious diseases, and less familiar situations.

Teachers must examine their personal beliefs and values and impart information in a nonjudgmental manner. If sex-related issues are left undiscussed, the outcome is miseducation and misinformation.

Action Plan 3.12   Misconceptions Regarding Transmission of the AIDS Virus (HIV)

Students may believe that one can get the AIDS virus (HIV) through:

    Hugging, touching, cuddling, shaking hands
    Sneezing, coughing, sweat, and tears
    Sharing forks, knives, spoons
    Eating meals cooked and/or served by someone with AIDS
    Sharing toilet or shower facilities
    Swimming pools
    Telephones
    Sports equipment
    Chairs, computers, desks, or bus seats
    Mosquitos, bed bugs, lice, flies, or other insects
    Pets

Teachers must provide them with accurate information.

Action Plan 3.13   Resources for AIDS Education

Teachers may contact the following agencies for information regarding AIDS:

Hotlines

National AIDS Information Hot Line
800-342-AIDS
In Spanish
800-344-SIDA
TTY/TDD users
800-AIDS-TTY

Sexually Transmitted Diseases National
  Hotline
800-227-8922

Teen Tap Hotline
800-234-TEEN

AIDS Crisisline
800-221-7044

The Minority Task Force on AIDS
Information for women
212-563-8340

Agencies and Organizations

American Foundation for AIDS
  Research
1515 Broadway
Suite 3601
New York, NY 10036
212-719-0033

AIDS Resource Center/National PTA
700 North Rush Street
Chicago, IL 60611
312-787-0977

Publications

U.S. Center for Disease Control
  Publications
*Guidelines for School Health Education
  to Prevent the Spread of AIDS*
STD: A Guide for Today's Young Adults
AIDS: What Young Adults Should Know
Teens and AIDS: Playing It Safe

*Learning AIDS: An Information
  Resources Directory*
American Foundation for AIDS Research
1515 Broadway
Suite 3601
New York, NY 10036
212-719-0033

*MMWR Guidelines for Effective School
  Health Education to Prevent the
  Spread of AIDS*
Massachusetts Medical Society
C.S.P.O. Box 2120
Waltham, MA 02254

AIDS: What Young Adults Should Know
The American Alliance for Health,
  Physical Education, Recreation, and
  Dance
1900 Association Drive
Reston, VA 22091
800-321-0789

AIDS Education for the Deaf
8350 Santa Monica Boulevard
Suite 103
West Hollywood, CA 90069
213-654-5822 (TTD)

Database

U.S. Public Health Services Combined
  Health Information Database (CHID)
Vendor: BRS Information Technologies
          800-468-0908
Includes: AIDS resources bibliography
          School programs
          Policies
          Films, videotapes, audiotapes,
            books, journal articles
          Parent materials
          Teacher training programs
National Institute of Health
301-468-2162

Action Plan 3.13 Continued

Training Programs

Abstinence-Based Programs
Postponing Sexual Involvement
Grady Memorial Hospital
P. O. Box 26158
80 Butler Street, SE
Atlanta, GA 30335
404-616-3513

Reducing the Risks
ETR Associates Network Publications
P. O. Box 1830
Santa Cruz, CA 95061
800-321-4407

Books and Magazines

Jeanne Blake, *Risky Times: How to be AIDS-Smart and Stay Healthy.* New York: Workman, 1990.

Straight Talk
Magazine for Teenagers
Rodale Press
33 East Minor Street
Emmaus, PA 18098

K. Hein and T. F. DiGeronimo, *AIDS: Trading Fears for Facts: A Guide for Teens.* New York: Consumer Union of the United States, 1989.

E. M. Johnson. *What you can do to avoid AIDS.* New York: Random House, 1992.

Curricula

AIDS Instructional Guide, Grades K–12
New York State Education Department
State University of New York
Bureau of Curriculum Development
Albany, NY 12234

Instruction About AIDS in Wisconsin Schools
Wisconsin Department of Public Instruction
1255 South Webster Street
P. O. Box 7841
Madison, WI 53707

AIDS Education–Supplemental Teaching Guide
Columbus Health Department, AIDS Program
181 Washington Boulevard
Columbus, OH 43215

SAFE: Stopping AIDS through Functional Education
For adolescents with mental retardation
University Affiliated Programs
Oregon Health Sciences University
Child Development and Rehabilitation Center
Portland, OR 97203

Videos

Teen AIDS in Focus
San Francisco Study Center
P. O. Box 425646
San Francisco, CA 94142-5646
800-484-4173

It Can Happen to You: Adolescents and AIDS
Ohio Department of Health
35 East Chestnut Street
Columbus, OH 43215
614-644-1838

Saving a Generation: Successful Teaching Strategies for HIV Education in Grades 4–12
Select Media
74 Varick Street
Third Floor
New York, NY 10013
212-431-8923

Action Plan 3.13   Continued

| *Materials* | Wrap It Up! |

Materials

Effie Dolls
Anatomically correct cloth dolls
Judith Franning
4812 48th Avenue
Moline, IL 61265

Body Charts
Planned Parenthood of Minnesota
1965 Ford Parkway
St. Paul, MN 55116

Wrap It Up!
Rock and roll message for safer sex
Tulare County Children's Mental
    Health Services Consortium
3350 South Fairway
Suite A
Visalia, CA 93227
209-733-6944

Teachers must refrain from lecturing or moralizing. Students may not be willing to ask questions or communicate with a teacher who is judgmental or uncomfortable discussing these issues. Discussion and training sessions must develop from student needs and concerns or students may not find them beneficial. Teachers may consider conducting a survey to gather information on their students' most pressing worries. This may be done through interest inventories, needs assessments, student drop boxes, group or individual counseling sessions, or classroom discussions.

Parent Involvement.   Parents of all students need to know the facts related to STDs so they can make informed decisions. Teacher must understand parental fears and emotions when confronted by issues surrounding AIDS. Educating parents can go a long way in overcoming their initial reactions of discomfort. Miller and Downer (1988) demonstrated that a 50-minute training session significantly increased AIDS awareness and resulted in higher levels of tolerance and compassion for people with AIDS.

Parents may need advice on how to talk to their children. Most parents do not feel comfortable approaching the topic of sex and sexuality. Adolescents sometimes require explicit information. Cultural views regarding sexual issues and levels of comfort in discussing such issues must be studied and considered prior to discussion with parents. Teachers can refer parents to sources of information including the agencies, publications, and materials provided in Action Plan 3.13.

Pregnancy

Incidence

Statistics indicate that 1 in every 10 American adolescent women (over 1 million) become premaritally pregnant at least once (Zelnick, Kanter, & Ford, 1981). Among African-American teenagers, 90% of their first babies are born out of wedlock. A third of pregnant adolescents elect abortion; however, a large proportion give birth and raise the child while unmarried. Over 20% of live births in 1980 were to unmarried women and over 90, 000 babies were born to mothers under age 15 (U.S. Bureau of the Census, 1986). Although exact numbers on the pregnancy rate among teenagers with disabilities are not available, unwanted pregnancies among this population occur frequently (Kerr, Nelson, & Lambert, 1987).

Causes

Klein (1978) identified several factors contributing to teenage pregnancy, including societal attitudes that popularize sexual activity; the failure of sex and family education; and the failure to provide birth control, early pregnancy detection, and prenatal care. Some adolescents fulfill their need for love, attention, peer acceptance, and independence by sexual promiscuity. Rebellion against family norms, the need for recognition, or the lack of family control or direction are other contributing factors. Exploitation by strangers, acquaintances, or even family members or caretakers may be other factors, especially among adolescents with disabilities, who are more susceptible and less equipped to avoid such advances.

Numerous other factors contribute to improper sexual behavior. Several myths surround the sexuality of adolescents with disabilities that make it difficult to dissipate misconceptions and promote their education (Daniels, Chipouras, Cornelius, & Makas, 1979). One myth holds that individuals with disabilities are asexual and unable to experience sexual feelings. In contrast, another myth attributes oversexuality and uncontrollable sexual urges to individuals who have disabilities. Some parents and professionals believe that youngsters must be protected from sexual corruption since they are "children." Thus they must not be educated regarding sex because it may result in undesirable consequences such as marriage or pregnancy. Another myth propagates the notion that a disability is hereditary and people with disabilities should have sexual relations only with others who have disabilities. Segregation is thus justified, and the belief that individuals with disabilities prefer to associate with others like themselves is reinforced. Moreover, sexual problems may be attributed to the disability (which may be true for cerebral palsy and problems involving the spinal cord) instead of the societal attitudes or the lack of education, information, or opportunity.

There is an unspoken yet prevalent belief among nondisabled members of society that only physically fit, young, intelligent, vocationally able individuals are entitled to express sexual feelings (Thorn-Gray & Kern, 1983). Opportunities for sexual expression are severely limited among individuals with disabilities who lack interpersonal skill, physical attributes, financial resources, dating options, and contacts with potential partners. Furthermore, adolescents with disabilities have few if any occasions to observe sexual interchange among others and thus have no models of appropriate behavior.

Intervention Needs

Issues surrounding sexuality must be given careful consideration in programs for adolescents who have disabilities. Research indicates that failure to function in the community is often attributed to inappropriate sexual behavior (Floor, Baxter, Rosen, & Zisfein,

1975). Despite concerns and needs in this area, sex education is not routinely provided by schools to youngsters who have disabilities. Secondary students with mild mental retardation have been found to have different levels of knowledge about sexual issues (Brantlinger, 1984). Students have been taught that sex is "wrong" and most are grossly uninformed and/or seriously misinformed. These sexual attitudes and the lack of knowledge could lead to irresponsible sexual behavior.

Special education teachers do not receive instruction on how to provide sex education during their university programs (May, 1980). Fewer than half of the special education teachers responding to a survey included sex education in their curriculum, and the rest covered it cursorily (Brantlinger, 1984). At the same time, these teachers expressed concerns over problematic sexual information, sexual activity, and misinformation prevalent among their students.

Relevant education must be provided to avoid sexual ignorance among adolescents who have disabilities. Increased knowledge and safer practices will aid in the reduction of pregnancies among teenage females. Sex education is particularly important for those with disabilities, in light of the movement toward normalization and integration of these individuals in the community. A functional curriculum must prepare adolescents with disabilities to enter the mainstream of society in a responsible way and increase their likelihood of acceptance among peers.

Parents are often ambivalent and confused about the sexuality of their teenaged children (Wolf & Zafras, 1982). In addition, they feel inadequate when it comes to providing sexual information, although they agree, more frequently than parents of nondisabled youths, that their children should receive education in this area (Goodman, Budner, & Lesh, 1971; Haavik & Menninger, 1981). Parents are extremely anxious about the dangers their with disabilities children face and prefer that sexual instruction be provided outside the home (Goodman et al., 1971). Haavik and Menninger (1981) found that most parents who sought professional advice did so to help their adolescent with issues related to sexuality.

It appears that the responsibility for providing sex education falls on the schools. The weight of the school's responsibilities becomes even greater when one considers the academic and social restrictions that prevent adolescents with disabilities from obtaining information from other sources such as media or the community. A curriculum may include factual information plus role playing, films, simulations that teach how to respond in sexual situations, and opportunities for appropriate interactions with the opposite sex.

Another important and challenging task is how to educate nondisabled persons so as to alter their misconceptions and help them accept the sexuality of individuals with disabilities. Peer attitudes are hard to alter because of the strong positive values associated with appearance, specific behaviors, interests, and activities by the adolescent culture. Increasing contact between adolescents with disabilities and their nondisabled peers so that it is frequent enough to alter attitudes will not be accomplished easily. Attempts in this area must continue.

Sex education classes have been found to have minimal influence on the sexual behavior of adolescents (Spanier, 1976). Adolescents receive information on an informal basis from peers, and that may motivate sexual action to a greater degree than high school classes on this subject. School officials must become familiar with the reasons why school programs fail and must take steps to ensure success. Two such reasons are the failure to provide classes at an earlier age and a biological rather than psychological orientation toward sex education (Calderone, 1981). Issues that adolescents commonly face, such as moral and ethical behavior, birth control, sex drives, dating conduct, and how to say no, must be an integral part of school courses. Real issues and concerns, discussed in an open, honest, and straightforward manner, may be highly beneficial to youngsters who may be confused about certain aspects of intimacy. Frank discussions may bring forth shared concerns and reduce anxieties associated with personalized problems. Schinke, Gilchrist, and Small (1979) suggested that other components of an education program must help adolescents not only make informed decisions but develop behaviors necessary to implement those decisions in real-life situations.

It is also important to provide help for pregnant female adolescents. Under federal law, schools are required to allow pregnant teenagers to continue their education; however, many schools do not have the infrastructure to permit this. Other schools do provide for these teenagers through educational programs on child care and family management and by supporting the mother after the birth of the baby with follow-up services (Helmrich, 1981).

Teacher Responsibilities

Parents who hesitate to provide sex information for adolescents, as already mentioned, put the onus on teachers to include sex education in the curriculum. Teenage pregnancy has serious implications for the educational, financial, marital, and professional futures of young women. Pregnant women are more likely to drop out of school, have unstable employment, get divorced, and depend on welfare for income and support. Women who demonstrate the best outcomes are those who marry the father, continue their education, and delay having additional children. Babies resulting from teenage pregnancies are in a high-risk group due to prematurity, infant mortality, and impairments such as deafness and blindness (Schnike et al., 1979). Teachers must recognize that the only effective way of avoiding these negative outcomes for their teenage students is through education. The following paragraphs suggest some ways in which teachers may help students.

Identifying the Problem. Teachers must be sensitive to the interpersonal dynamics among students in the classroom. A display of interest and concern regarding sexuality may motivate students to seek help and advice. Students should feel free to discuss any problems, fears about diseases, anxieties about relationships, or undesirable experiences with an adult at school or home. This may ensure early intervention in cases requiring immediate medical attention and may also prevent possible emotional problems. Teachers must be prepared to help those who ask for assistance and direction without letting their moral opinions and values govern their actions. They must be ready to make arrangements for referral to health care agencies and counseling services. Special education teachers must be aware of the early signs of pregnancy and secure immediate medical intervention.

Preventing the Problem. Teachers may stress the following topics during sex education (Gordon, 1974). First, masturbation is normal at any age or with any frequency, provided it occurs in private. This issue is important as it may be the main channel of release among individuals with disabilities and, if ignored, may result in incidents in inappropriate settings. Second, students must be taught that pregnancy is always a possibility during the sexual act and birth control is mandatory. Third, adolescents may be taught that they do not have to engage in sexual acts if urged to do so by an adult and it is wrong to force someone else to perform sexual acts. The likelihood of legal consequences may be stressed. Fourth, students must be told not to accept offers of money or other goods in exchange for sexual favors. Fifth, students need information on STDs owing to the increasing risk of AIDS. AIDS must also be discussed in relation to homosexuality, which is likely among adolescents with disabilities who have restricted contact with the opposite sex. Role play situations, films, and demonstrations may be helpful in teaching adolescents how to react under certain circumstances. A social skills curriculum must include opportunities to interact with the opposite sex during social situations.

Teenage girls with disabilities may require extended education using instructional techniques and materials suited to their functional abilities. An assessment of their awareness of giving birth and raising a family must be conducted. Youths with disabilities may have misconceptions about the hardships involved in bringing up a child. They have to be given a realistic picture of different aspects of child rearing through films, role play, or simple questioning techniques. A visit to a nursery or a day care center where youths can observe or experience the daily care activities necessary for children of different age groups may make them more aware of their lack of skills and resources as parents.

Parent Involvement. Parent involvement is essential in educating adolescents and preventing inappropriate sexual activity. For example, it may be necessary to involve parents if the adolescent engages in socially unacceptable sexual behaviors such as masturbation in public. Parents' personal feelings and beliefs regarding such behavior and other sexual issues must be explored. Some parents may have misconceptions about certain behaviors and may react to the situation by meting out severe punishment that may be unnecessary or even potentially harmful. They may be referred to a counselor or therapist to help resolve the problem.

If teachers suspect that a student is pregnant, parents must be contacted and solutions identified to reflect the well-being of all involved. Teachers may make referrals to agencies that can consult with the teenager and parents on the best course of action. Several issues have to be addressed, including the young woman's ability to carry, give birth, and raise a child; economic factors; the possibility of adoption; parental support; and genetic factors. Parent participation is essential if these problems are to be resolved.

Summary

Adolescence places several challenging demands on youngsters who are faced with major decisions concerning their future. Societal and physiological demands requiring adaptations in personal development, social roles, and parental and peer expectations often result in confusion, loss of self-confidence, and frustration among adolescents. Most emerge from the experience with new skills and motivations; however, others are unable to cope as effectively and may undergo intense feelings of hopelessness, insecurity, and depression. Obstacles such as drugs and alcohol, pregnancy, suicide, or participation in delinquent acts further complicate their lives. Most adolescents are able to cope with potentially harmful influences, although young individuals with disabilities may require special help and guidance.

Incidence figures on juvenile delinquency, dropping out, substance abuse, suicide, and sexual behavior related to individuals with disabilities provide a dismal picture of the scope of these problems and highlight the immediate need for collaborative programmatic efforts. Teachers can help to identify and prevent these problems. In particular, they should learn to look for the specific signs of different problems, and how to minimize their impact on youths with disabilities.

References

American Psychiatric Association. (1985). *Facts about teen suicide.* Washington, DC: Author.

American Psychiatric Association. (1987). *Diagnostic and statistical manual of mental disorders* (3rd ed., rev.). Washington, DC: Author.

Anderson, D. M., & Christenson, G. M. (1991). Ethnic breakdown of AIDS related knowledge and attitudes from the national adolescent student health survey. *Journal of Health Education, 22*(1), 30–34.

Bachman, J. G., Green, S., & Wirtanen, I. (1972). *Dropping out: Problem or symptom?* Ann Arbor: University of Michigan, Institute for Social Research.

Bartnick, W. M., & Parkay, F. W. (1991). A comparative analysis of the "holding power" of general and exceptional programs. *Remedial and Special Education, 12*(5), 17–22.

Bennett, W. (1986). *What works; Schools without drugs.* Washington, DC: U.S. Department of Education.

Biase, D. (1984). A drug abuse prevention program developed within a therapeutic community. *Journal of Psychoactive Drugs, 16,* 63–68.

Billings, A. G., & Moos, R. H. (1985). Children of parents with unipolar depression: A controlled one year follow-up. *Journal of Adolescent and Child Psychology, 14,* 14–166.

Black, J. L., & Jones, L. H. (1988). HIV infection: Education programs and policies for school personnel. *Journal of School Health, 58*(8), 317–322.

Blane, H. (1979). Middle age alcoholics and young drinkers. In H. Blane and M. Chafetz (Eds.), *Youth, alcohol and social policy.* New York: Plenum.

Boswell, J., Fox, E., Hubbard, B., & Coyle, L. (1992). A comparison of HIV-related knowledge, attitudes, and behaviors among adolescents living in rural and urban areas of a southern state. *Journal of Health Education, 23*(4), 238–243.

Botvin, G. J., & Tortu, S. (1988). Preventing substance abuse through life skills training. In R. H. Price, E. L. Cowen, R. P. Lorion, & J. Ramos-McKay (Eds.), *Fourteen ounces of prevention: A casebook for practitioners* (pp. 245–273). Washington, DC: American Psychological Association.

Brantlinger, E. A. (1984). *Teachers' perceptions of the sexual attitudes and knowledge of their mildly mentally handicapped secondary students.* Unpublished manuscript.

Brook, J. S., Whiteman, M., & Gordon, A. S. (1985). Stages of drug use in adolescence: Personality, peer, and family correlates. *Developmental Psychology, 19,* 269–277.

Brooks-Gunn, J., Boyer, C. B., & Hein, K. (1988). Preventing HIV infection and AIDS in children and adolescents. *American Psychologist, 43,* 958–964.

Brumback, R. A., Staton, R. D., & Wilson, H. (1980). Neuropsychological study of children during and after remission of endogenous depressive episodes. *Perceptual and Motor Skills, 50,* 1163–1167.

Bullock, L. M., & Reilly, T. F (1979). A descriptive profile of the adjudicated adolescent: A status report. In R. B. Rutherford & A. G. Prieto (Eds.), *Monograph in behavioral disorders* (Vol. 2, pp. 153–161). Reston, VA: Council for Children with Behavioral Disorders.

Cairns, R. B., & Cairns, B. D. (1983). *Gender similarities and differences: A developmental perspective.* Paper presented at the Nag's Head Conferences, Nag's Head, North Carolina.

Calderone, M. (1981). From then to now—and where next? In L. Brown (Ed.), *Sex education in the eighties.* New York: Plenum.

Cantwell, M. (1983). The offender. In *Report to the nation on crime and justice: The data.* Washington, DC: U.S. Department of Justice, Bureau of Justice Statistics.

Capuzzi, D. (1986). Adolescent suicide: Prevention and intervention. *Counseling and Human Development, 19*(2), 1–9.

Centers for Disease Control. (1986). *Youth suicide in the United States, 1970–1980.* Atlanta: U.S. Department of Health and Human Services.

Centers for Disease Control. (1989). Update: Heterosexual transmission of acquired immunodeficiency virus infection—United States. *Morbidity and Mortality Weekly Report, 38,* 423–433.

Clayton, R. R. (1981). The delinquency and drug use relationship among adolescents: A critical review. In *Drug abuse and the American adolescent* (pp. 82–103). (NIDA Research Monograph No. 38). Washington, DC: U.S. Department of Health and Human Services. (DHHS Publication No. ADM 85-1166).

Cullinan, D., Schloss, P. J., & Epstein, M. H. (1987). Relative prevalence and correlates of depressive characteristics among seriously emotionally disturbed and nonhandicapped students. *Behavioral Disorders, 12,* 90–98.

Daniels, S. M., Chipouras, S., Cornelius, D. A., & Makas, E. (1979). *Who cares? A handbook on sex education and counseling services for disabled people.* Washington, DC: George Washington University Press.

Davidson, L., & Linnoila, M. (Eds.). (1991). *Risk factors for youth suicide.* New York: Hemisphere.

Dembo, R. (1983). Preferred resources for help with a drug problem among young living in different inner city neighborhood settings. *Advances in Alcohol and Substance Abuse, 2,* 57–75.

Devlin, S. D., & Elliot, R. N. (1992). Drug use patterns of adolescents with behavioral disorders. *Behavioral Disorders, 17,* 264–272.

Division of STDs (1986). *Annual report, FY 1986.* Centers for Disease Control, Center for Prevention Services.

Dukes, R. L., & Lorch, B. (1989). The effects of school, family, self-concept, and deviant behavior on adolescent suicide ideation. *Journal of Adolescence, 12,* 239–251.

Eisenmann, R. (1991). Conduct disordered youth: Insights from a prison treatment program. *Beyond Behavior, 2*(1), 3–4.

Farrington, D. P. (1980). Truancy, delinquency, the home, and the school. In L. Hersov & I. Berg (Eds.), *Out of school: Modern perspectives in school refusal and truancy.* New York: Wiley.

Farrington, D. P., Gallagher, B., Morley, L., St. Ledger, R. J., & West, D. J. (1986). Unemployment, school leaving, and crime. *British Journal of Criminology, 26,* 335–356.

Fisher, G. L., & Harrison, T. C. (1992). Assessment of alcohol and other drug abuse with referred adolescents. *Psychology in the Schools, 29,* 172–178.

Floor, L., Baxter, D., Rosen, M., & Zisfein, L. (1975). A survey of marriages among previously institutionalized retardates, *Mental Retardation, 13*(2), 33–37.

Flora, J. A., & Thoresen, C. E. (1988). Reducing the risk of AIDS in adolescents. *American Psychologist, 43,* 965–970.

Forehand, R., McCombs, A., & Brody, G. H. (1987). The relationship between parental depressive mood states and child functioning. *Advances in Behavior Research and Therapy, 9,* 1–20.

Forness, S. R. (1988). School characteristics of children and adolescents with depression. In R. B. Rutherford, C. M. Nelson, & S. R. Forness (Eds.), *Bases of severe behavioral disorders of children and youth* (pp. 177–204). Boston: Little, Brown.

Friedman, A. D., Glickman, N., & Utada, A. (1985). Does alcohol and drug use lead to failure to graduate from high school? *Journal of Drug Education, 15*, 353–364.

Gainer, W. J. (1987). *School dropouts: Survey of local programs.* (Report No. GAO/HRD-87-108). Washington, DC: U.S. General Accounting Office.

Garbarino, J., Wilson, J., & Garbarino, A. (1986). The adolescent runaway. In J. Garbarino, C. J. Schellenbach, J. M. Sebes, & Associates (Eds.), *Troubled youth, troubled families.* New York: Aldine.

Gitlin, T. (1990). On drugs and mass media in America's consumer society. In *Youth and drugs: Society's mixed messages* (pp. 31–52) (OSAP Monograph No. 6). Washington, DC: U.S. Department of Health and Human Services. (DHHS Publication No. ADM 90–1689).

Glueck, S., & Glueck, E. T. (1962). *Family environment and delinquency.* Boston: Houghton-Mifflin.

Goodman, L., Budner, S., & Lesh, B. (1971). The parent's role in sex education for the retarded. *Mental Retardation, 1*, 43–45.

Gordon, S. (1974). *Sexual rights for the people . . . Who happened to be handicapped.* (sixth in the series) *Notes from the Center.* Syracuse, NY: , Syracuse University, Center on Human Policy.

Guetzloe, E. C. (1989). *Youth suicide: What the educator should know.* Reston, VA: The Council for Exceptional Children.

Haavik, S., & Menninger, K. A., II. (1981). *Sexuality, law, and the developmentally disabled person.* Baltimore: Paul H. Brookes.

Hahn, A. (1987). Reaching out to America's dropouts: What to do? *Phi Delta Kappan, 69*(4), 256–263.

Harris, F. C., & Ammerman, R. T. (1986). Depression and suicide in children and adolescents. *Journal of Child and Adolescent Psychotherapy, 4*, 199–203.

Harris, L., & Associates Inc. (1986). *American teens speak: Sex, myths, TV, and birth control.* New York: Planned Parenthood Federation of America.

Hasazi, S. B., Gordon, L. R., & Roe, C. A. (1985). Factors associated with the employment of handicapped youth exiting high school from 1979–1983. *Exceptional Children, 51*, 455–469.

Hawton, K. (1986). *Suicide and attempted suicide among children and adolescents.* Beverly Hills, CA: Sage.

Helmrich, D. (1981). School programs for pregnant teenagers. *American Education, 17*(6), 26–27.

Hill, N. C., Parker, L. G., Corbett, A., & Miano, K. L. (1980). *Attending behavior Commonalities and differences among educable retarded, learning disabled, and emotionally handicapped juvenile delinquents,* (ERIC Document Reproduction Service No. ED 197 569).

Horton, L. (1985). *Adolescent alcohol abuse.* Bloomington, IN: Phi Delta Kappa Educational Foundation.

Jardin, R. A., & Ziebell, P. W. (1981). Adolescent drug and alcohol abuse. In G. Brown, R. L. McDowell, & J. Smith (Eds.), *Educating adolescents with behavior disorders,* Columbus, OH: Merrill.

Jessor, R., & Jessor, S. L. (1980). Adolescent development and the onset of drinking. In R. E. Muus (Ed.), *Adolescent behavior and society* (3rd ed.). New York: Random House.

Johnson, J. L. (1988). The challenge of substance abuse. *Teaching Exceptional Children, 20*(4), 29–31.

Johnston, J. L., O'Malley, P. M., & Bachman, J. G. (1985). *Drug use among high school students, college students and other young adults: National trends through 1985.* Bethesda, MD: National Institute on Drug Abuse.

Johnston, J. L., O'Malley, P. M., & Bachman, J. G. (1988). *Illicit drug use, smoking, and drinking by America's high school students, college students, and young adults, 1975–1987.* Rockville, MD: National Institute on Drug Abuse.

Karacostas, D. D., & Fisher, G. L. (1993). Chemical dependency in students with and without learning disabilities, *Journal of Learning Disabilities, 26*(7), 491–495.

Kashani, J. H., Venske, R., & Millar, E. A. (1981). Depression in children admitted to hospital for orthopedic procedures. *British Journal of Psychiatry, 138*, 21–25.

Kauffman, J. (1989). *Characteristics of children's behavior disorders* (4th ed.). Columbus, OH: Merrill.

Keilitz, I., & Dunivant, N. (1986). The learning disabled offender. In C. M. Nelson. R. B., Rutherford, & B. I. Wolford (Eds.), *Special education in the criminal justice system* (pp. 120–137). Columbus, OH: Merrill.

Kerr, M. M., Nelson, C. M., & Lambert, D. H. (1987). *Helping adolescents with learning and behavior problems.* Columbus, OH: Merrill.

Klein, L. (1978). Antecedents of teenage pregnancy. *Clinical Obstetrics and Gynecology, 21*(4), 1151–1159

Kosky, R., Silburn, S., & Zubrick, S. R. (1990). Are children and adolescents who have attempted suicidal thought different from those who attempt suicide? *The Journal of Nervous and Mental Disease, 178*(1), 38–43.

Kvaraceus, W. C. (1971). *Prevention and control of delinquency: The school counselor's role.* Hanover, NH: TSC.

Leone, P. E. (1991). *Alcohol and other drugs: Use, abuse, and disabilities.* Reston, VA: The Council for Exceptional Children.

Leone, P. E., Price, T., & Vitolo, R. K. (1986). Appropriate education for all incarcerated youth: Meeting the spirit of P. L. 94–142 in youth detention facilities. *Remedial and Special Education, 7*(4), 9–14.

Leone, P. E., Rutherford, R., & Nelson, M. (1991). *Special education in juvenile corrections.* Reston, VA: The Council for Exceptional Children.

Levin, E., Zigmond, N., & Birch, J. (1985). A follow-up study of 52 learning disabled students. *Journal of Learning Disabilities, 18*, 2–7.

Loeber, R. (1982). The stability of antisocial and delinquent child behavior: A review. *Child Development, 53*, 1431–1446.

Maag, J. W., & Behrens, J. T. (1989a). Depression and cognitive self-statements of learning disabled and seriously emotionally disturbed adolescents. *The Journal Special Education, 23*, 17–27.

Maag, J. W., & Behrens, J. T..(1989b). Epidemiologic data on seriously emotionally disturbed and learning disabled adolescents: Reporting extreme depressive symptomatology. *Behavioral Disorders, 15*(1), 21–27.

Mattison, R. E., Humphrey, J., Kales, S., Hernit, R., & Finkenbinder, R. (1986). Psychiatric background and diagnosis of children evaluated for special class placement. *Journal of Child Psychiatry, 25*, 514–520.

May, D. C. (1980). Survey of sex education coursework in special education programs. *Journal of Special Education, 14*, 107–109.

McKendry, P. D., Tishler, C. L., & Kelly, C. (1982). Adolescent suicide: A comparison of attempts and nonattempts in an emergency room population. *Clinical Pediatrics, 21*, 266–270.

Miller, L., & Downer, A. (1988). AIDS: What you and you friends need to know—A lesson plan for adolescents. *Journal of School Health, 58*(4), 137–141.

Misra, A. (1994). Partnership with multicultural families. In S. K. Alper, P. J. Schloss, & C. N. Schloss (Eds.), *Families of students with disabilities: Consultation and advocacy.* Boston: Allyn and Bacon.

Mitchell, J. T, & Resnik, H. L. P. (1981). *Emergency response to crisis.* Bowie, MD: Brady.

Moore, P. S. (1986). *Useful information on suicide.* (DHHS Publication No. ADM 86-1489). Rockville, MD: National Institute of Mental Health.

National Center for Health Statistics. (1989). Advance report of final mortality statistics, 1987. (*Monthly Vital Statistics Report*, 38[5], Supplementary DHHS Publication). Hyattsville, MD: U.S. Public Health Service.

Neel, R. S., Meadows, N., Levine, R., & Edgar, E. B. (1988). What happens after special education: A statewide follow-up study of secondary students who have behavioral disorders. *Behavior Disorders, 13*, 209–216.

Nelson, C. M., & Rutherford, R. B. (1989, September) *Impact on the Correctional Special Education Training (C/SET) Project in correctional special education.* Paper presented at the CED/CCBD National Topical Conference in Behavioral Disorders, Charlotte, North Carolina.

Nelson, C. M., & Rutherford, R. B. (1990). Troubled youth in the public schools: Emotionally disturbed or socially maladjusted? In P. E. Leone (Ed.), *Troubled and troubling youth* (pp. 38–60). Newbury Park, CA: Sage.

Pasternack, R., & Lyon, R. (1982). Clinical and empirical identification of learning disabled juvenile delinquents. *Journal of Correctional Education, 33*(2), 7–13.

Pentz, M. A., Dwyer, J. H., MacKinnon, D. P., Flay, B. R., Hansen, W. B., Wang, E. U. I., & Johnson, C. A. (1989). A multicommunity trial for primary prevention of adolescent drug abuse. *Journal of the American Medical Association, 261*, 3259–3266.

Pfeffer, C. R. (1986). *The suicidal child.* New York: Guilford.

Pfeffer, C. R. (1989). Studies of suicidal preadolescent and adolescent inpatients: A critique of research methods. *Suicides and Life-Threatening Behavior, 19(1),* 58–77.

Pfeffer, C. R., Zuckerman, S., Plutchik, R., & Mizruchi, M. S. (1984). Suicidal behavior in normal school children: A comparison with child psychiatric patients. *Journal of the American Academy of Child Psychiatry, 23(4),* 416–423.

Pfeifer, J. (1986). *Teenage suicides What can the schools do?* Bloomington, IN: Phi Delta Kappa Educational Foundation.

Reiter, M. (1982). *School achievement and juvenile delinquency: A review of the literature.* (ERIC Document Reproduction Service No. ED 221 009).

Reynolds, W. M., & Miller, K. L. (1985). Depression and learned helplessness in mentally retarded and nonmentally retarded adolescents: An initial investigation. *Applied Research in Mental Retardation, 6,* 295–306.

Riggs, S., Alario, A. J., & McHorney, C. A. (1990). Health risk behavior and attempted suicide in adolescents who report prior maltreatment. *Journal of Pediatrics, 116(5),* 815–820.

Ritter, D. R. (1989). Social competence and problem behavior and adolescent girls with learning disabilities, *Journal of Learning Disabilities, 22,* 460–461.

Rutherford, R. B., Nelson, C. M., & Wolford, B. I. (1985). Special education in the most restrictive environment: Correctional/special education. *Journal of Special Education, 19,* 59–71.

Salend, S. J., & Washin, B. (1988). Team-assisted individualization with handicapped adjudicated youth. *Exceptional Children, 55,* 174–180.

Schinke, S. P., Gilchrist, L. D., & Small, R. W. (1979). Preventing unwanted adolescent pregnancy: A cognitive behavioral approach. *American Journal of Orthopsychiatry, 49(1),* 81–88.

Schloss, P. J., Kane, M. S., & Miller, S. (1981). Truancy intervention with behaviorally disordered adolescents. *Behavioral Disorders, 6,* 175–179.

Shaffer, D., Vieland, V., Garland, A., Rojas, M., Underwood, M., & Busner, C. (1990). Adolescent suicide attempters: Response to suicide-prevention programs. *Journal of the American Medical Association, 264,* 3151–3155.

Shannon, J. (1986). In the classroom stoned. *Phi Delta Kappan, 66(1),* 60–62.

Shanok, S. S. (1981). Medical histories of abused delinquents. *Child Psychiatry and Human Development, 2,* 222–231.

Slavin, R. E., Leavey, M., & Madden, N. A. (1984). Combining cooperative learning and individualized instruction: Effects on student mathematics achievement, attitudes and behaviors. *Elementary School Journal, 84,* 409–422.

Smigielski, P. A., & Steinmann, M. J. (1981). Teaching sex education to multiply handicapped adolescents. *Journal of School Health, 51,* 238–241.

Smith, M. (1991). An investigation of school administrators' beliefs and the relationship between HIV and special education. *Journal of Health Education, 22(1),* 43–48.

Snarr, R. W, & Wolford, B. I. (1985). *Introduction to corrections.* Dubuque, IA: Brown.

Spanier, G. (1976). Formal and informal sex education as determinants of premarital sexual behavior. *Archives of Sexual Behavior, 5,* 39–67.

Stark, K. (1990). *Childhood depression: School-based intervention.* New York: Guilford.

Stern, M., Northman, J., & Van-Slyck, M. (1984). Father absence and adolescent "problem behaviors." Alcohol consumption, drug use and sexual activity. *Adolescence, 19,* 302–312.

Sylvester, B. T. (1982). Opportunities and barriers in interagency collaboration: Perspectives of a juvenile justice board member. In M. B. Santamour & P. S. Watson (Eds.), *The retarded offender* (pp. 491–495). New York: Praeger.

Thorn-Gray, B. E., & Kern, L. H. (1983). Sexual dysfunction associated with physical disability: A treatment guide for the rehabilitation practitioner. *Rehabilitation Literature, 44,* 138–144.

Tooland, J. (1975). Depression and suicide: Second leading death cause. *Journal of the American Medical Association, 257,* 3329–3330.

U.S. Bureau of the Census. (1986). *Statistical abstracts of the United States: 1982–83* (107th ed.). Washington, DC: U.S. Government Printing Office.

U.S. Department of Education. (1991). *To assure free appropriate public education to all handicapped children. Thirteenth annual report to Congress on the implementation of the Education of the Handicapped Act.* Washington, DC: Division of Educational Services, Special Education Programs.

Voss, H. L., Wendling, A., & Elliott, D. S. (1966). Some types of high-school dropouts. *Journal of Educational Research, 59,* 363–368.

Walker-Hirsch, L., & Champagne, M. P. (1988). *Circles III: Safer ways.* Santa Barbara, CA: Stanfield.

Webb, S. L., Maddox, M., & Edgar, E. B. (1985). *The juvenile corrections interagency transition model.* Seattle: University of Washington, Experimental Education Unit.

Weiner, I. (1980). Psychopathology in adolescence. In J. Adelson (Ed.), *Handbook of adolescent psychology.* New York: Wiley.

Wills, T. A., & Shiffman, S. (1985). Coping and substance abuse: A conceptual framework. In S. Shiffman & T. A. Wills (Eds.), *Coping and substance abuse* (pp. 3–24). New York: Academic Press.

Wolf, L., & Zafras, D. E. (1982). Parents' attitudes toward sterilization of their mentally retarded children. *American Journal of Mental Deficiency, 87,* 122–129.

Zelnick, M., Kanter, J., & Ford, K. (1981). *Sex and pregnancy in adolescence.* Beverly Hills, CA: Sage.

Zigmond, N., & Thornton, H. (1985). Follow-up of postsecondary age learning disabled graduates and drop-outs. *Learning Disabilities Research, 1*(1), 50–55.

Chapter 4

Instructional Methods for Secondary Learners with Disabilities

Did you know that . . .

- Learning strategies are used primarily with secondary students who have learning disabilities?
- Students with disabilities are more likely to forget recently acquired knowledge and skills?
- There are types of curricular orientations that should be considered when selecting goals for secondary students with disabilities?
- Age is a key factor in making the shift from a developmental to a functional orientation?
- Annual goals must be included on the IEP?
- Short-term objectives are derived from annual goals?
- A short-term objective has three components?
- Teachers rarely deviate from their written lesson plan?
- Including contingency plans increases teacher flexibility?
- Materials for secondary learners with disabilities are scarce?
- Specific teacher behaviors are associated with student achievement?
- Large and small group instruction can be individualized?
- There are six levels of prompts?
- Homework should only be given to strengthen knowledge or skills already presented in class?

Can you . . .

- Define direct instruction?
- Describe a learning strategy?

- Explain the goals of a learning-strategy curriculum?
- Differentiate between direct instruction and a learning strategy?
- Identify the similarities between direct instruction and learning strategies?
- Use learning strategies to teach reading comprehension?
- Write an annual goal?
- Derive short-term objectives from an annual goal?
- Develop a task sequence from a short-term goal?
- Differentiate between advance planning and contingency planning?
- Write a lesson plan that includes a contingency plan?
- Write a lesson plan that reflects guidelines for presenting new information?
- Develop prompting hierarchies for academic and motor skills?
- Determine how much time an eleventh grader should spend doing homework?
- Use techniques to increase maintenance and generalization of knowledge and skills by secondary students with disabilities?

For over a decade, resource room/pull-out services were the most common model for the delivery of educational programming for secondary students with learning disabilities (Ellett, 1993). However, proponents of the Regular Education Initiative recommend that all students with mild disabilities receive their education in regular settings (Will, 1986). Thus, secondary educators who previously were used to having students with disabilities served elsewhere now face the challenge of meeting their needs in the regular classroom. Increased numbers of secondary students with special needs will add to the responsibilities already shouldered by high school teachers in the regular classroom. They must select which instructional techniques can be used to facilitate skill development by students with disabilities and their nondisabled peers.

A major goal for adolescent learners is to acquire the tremendous amount of information presented in the secondary curriculum (Deshler, Putnam, & Bulgren, 1985). Several factors limit the extent to which secondary learners with disabilities can accomplish this task. These factors reflect general learning and behavioral characteristics of individuals with disabilities, which are presented in Action Plan 4.1. First, according to Schloss and Sedlak (1986), many of these learners acquire information and skills at a slower rate than their nondisabled peers. They simply require more time to learn things. Second, youths with disabilities are less likely to benefit from incidental information. Many of the skills mastered informally by their nondisabled peers, such as social skills and leisure skills, will have to be directly taught to them. Third, knowledge and skills mastered in one setting may not be used in other settings by students with disabilities. For example, the study skill taught by the resource specialist may not automatically be used by the youth with disabilities who is preparing for a biology test. Finally, students with disabilities are less likely to retain newly acquired information following instruction. Teachers will have to provide review and practice activities to make sure that these students maintain their skill levels.

As a result of these characteristics, secondary students with disabilities may not bring to the learning situation all the prerequisite skills necessary for success in the secondary

Action Plan 4.1　Learning and Behavioral Characteristics of Students with Disabilities

Teachers should be aware that the following characteristics can influence the knowledge and skills acquired by students with disabilities:

1. Information and skills are acquired at a slower rate.
2. Information and skills are less likely to be acquired through experiences incidental to the learning task.
3. Information and skills acquired in one setting are less likely to generalize to other settings or conditions.
4. Information and skills are less likely to be retained following instruction.

school; however, they do bring a long history of academic failure. It is not surprising that they are poorly motivated to engage in additional activities closely resembling those on which they have experienced frustration (Zigmond, Sansone, Miller, Donahoe, & Kohnke, 1986a). Further complicating the issue is the limited amount of time left in their academic careers (Deshler & Schumaker, 1986).

Fortunately, two instructional methods—learning strategies and direct instruction—are suitable for use with secondary students with special needs. Despite some basic differences, these two approaches are closely aligned, particularly in the technology developed to teach learning strategies and the methods suggested in various phases of the direct-instruction process. Thus, although this chapter is primarily concerned with direct instruction, learning strategies figure prominently in some sections, most notably the section on instructional technology.

Learning Strategies

Many secondary students with disabilities are mainstreamed into regular classes for a substantial part of the school day and are expected to master the same curriculum as their nondisabled peers (Lenz & Hughes, 1990). Their success in these settings may be hindered by limited reading and written language abilities. They may not be able to obtain information from textbooks, write an essay, take notes, or study for a test. An instructional method involving the use of learning strategies was developed in response to the needs of secondary students with disabilities, particularly learning disabilities.

Learning strategies have been defined as "techniques, principles, or rules that . . . facilitate the acquisition, manipulation, integration, storage, and retrieval of information across situations and settings" (Alley & Deshler, 1979, p. 13). Secondary learners with disabilities in particular can benefit from these strategies (Deshler & Schumaker, 1986). The ability to develop and apply learning strategies appears to be related to age, so they are appropriate for use with secondary learners. Furthermore, learning strategies force secondary learners to assume the major responsibility for their own learning and progress.

Supporters believe that when this approach is used at the secondary level, students learn new skills and are able to respond to rapidly changing information and conditions in the future.

Unlike direct instruction, which emphasizes the presentation of new content-related skills, learning strategies emphasize how to learn new information. For example, a practitioner using direct instruction to teach history presents students with actual history, whereas one using a learning-strategy approach presents students with an organizational strategy to help them identify and remember important historical concepts (Schumaker, Deshler, Alley, & Warner, 1983). In addition, a learning-strategies curriculum includes strands to help students acquire information from written material and express themselves appropriately in writing. Action Plan 4.2 presents different learning strategies from each of these strands. Chapters 9 and 10 provide several additional examples of learning strategies and how they can be used to enhance the reading and written language abilities or secondary students with disabilities.

The ultimate goal of a learning-strategies curriculum is to develop skills that will enable the individual to analyze and solve novel problems encountered in academic and nonacademic settings. Not only will the individual be able to meet the challenge presented by the immediate situation, but he or she will be able to generalize these skills to other situations over time. A number of steps involved in teaching a learning strategy follow (Schumaker et al., 1983).

The first step is to assess the current level of performance. For example, a teacher may elect to use a learning strategy known as RAP (Ellis & Lenz, 1987) to enhance students' comprehension skills. RAP stands for

R = Read a paragraph.
A = Ask yourself what were the main idea and two details.
P = Put the main idea and details into your own words.

Action Plan 4.3 lists the steps the teacher follows to teach this strategy to the students. First, the teacher assesses the students' current level of performance. Using the formal and informal assessment methods discussed in Chapter 5, the teacher determines the students' present level of comprehension. She may also develop a pretest based on the RAP strategy and supporting details. Second, the teacher develops and implements a lesson plan that begins with a description of the strategy the students are going to learn and the benefits the strategy has to offer them. Third, the teacher demonstrates the strategy. This demonstration should include several examples of the teacher "walking through" the strategy after reading various passages. Fourth, the students use self-instruction to practice the strategy. During this time, they may verbalize each step of the strategy as they are using it. During subsequent practice, the students may reduce the volume of their voices until they are using the strategy silently. Fifth, the teacher provides controlled practice. She selects reading material that the students encounter daily. If the teacher is a general secondary educator, she may select material that is representative of the academic course she is teaching. If the teacher is a resource specialist or a consultant, she may select material that represents content from all the courses in which the students are enrolled. This measure ensures that the students will generalize their use of RAP.

Sixth, the teacher provides the students with reinforcement for appropriate use of the strategy or corrective feedback to address any errors. Finally, the teacher administers a posttest to make sure the use of the strategy has been mastered.

Action Plan 4.2

Smith (1994) summarized several learning strategies useful for secondary students with disabilities:

RIDER is a strategy for enhancing reading comprehension.

R = Read the sentence.
I = Image in your mind.
D = Describe how the new image is different from the previous sentence.
E = Evaluate the image to make sure it is complete.
R = Repeat as you read the next sentence.

DEFENDS is a strategy for defending your position in writing.

D = Decide on an exact position.
E = Examine the reasons for the position.
F = Form a list of points that explains each position.
E = Expose your position in the first sentence.
N = Note your reasons and support points.
D = Drive home your position in the last sentence.
S = Search for errors and correct.

PREPARE is a strategy for preparing for class.

P = Plan locker visits.
R = Reflect on what you need to get.
E = Erase personal needs.
P = PSYCH yourself up.
　　P = Pause for an attitude check.
　　S = Say a personal goal related to the class.
　　Y = Yoke in negative thoughts.
　　C = Challenge yourself to a good performance.
A = Ask yourself where class has been and where class is going.
R = Review notes and any study guides.
E = Explore the meaning of the teacher's introduction.

Case for Action 4.1

You are the resource teacher in a secondary school. A regular educator is curious about the concepts of learning strategies and asks for an explanation. What will you tell her? How can you work with her to implement a learning-strategies curriculum?

Action Plan 4.3 Teaching a Learning Strategy

Schumaker and colleagues (1983) have recommended that teachers use the following steps to teach a learning strategy:

1. Assess the current performance level.
2. Describe the skill.
3. Demonstrate the strategy.
4. Allow students to self-instruct.
5. Provide controlled practice.
6. Provide reinforcement or corrective feedback.
7. Postassess.

Direct Instruction

The effectiveness of direct instruction has been well documented. Early studies involved regular elementary and intermediate students (Anderson, Evertson, & Brophy, 1979; Evertson et al., 1981; Fisher et al., 1978; Good & Grouws, 1979); the suitability of these techniques for elementary students with special needs has also been demonstrated (Chow, 1981; Leinhardt, Zigmond, & Cooley, 1981; Sindelar, Smith, Harriman, Hale, & Wilson, 1986) and extended to the secondary level (Stallings, Needles, & Stayrook, 1979). Direct instruction has been defined as the direct measurement of a student's performance on a learning task and the accompanying arrangement of instructional programs and procedures for each child (Haring & Gentry, 1976). Haring and Schiefel-busch (1976) identified the following phases of direct instruction:

1. Assessment of student characteristics
2. Establishment of instructional goals
3. Systematic planning of instruction
4. Use of instructional materials
5. Use of replicable instructional procedures
6. Use of motivating consequences
7. Monitoring of student progress.

Secondary teachers who use direct-instruction procedures target a specific body of objectives they believe the learner should master. Usually, these objectives correspond to academic skills. For example, a history unit on civic responsibilities may include the procedures for nominating and electing candidates for the office of president of the United States. Secondary special educators may also target another body of objectives addressing functional life skills such as establishing and maintaining a checking account. After students demonstrate mastery of each body of objectives, the teacher targets another set and the process is repeated.

In summary, direct instruction is a comprehensive set of instructional practices that requires the teacher to evaluate the learning environment, define objectives, select and implement teaching techniques that reflect student characteristics, and apply motivating consequences (Schloss & Sedlak, 1986). The next section discusses each phase of direct instruction in detail.

The Sequence of Direct-Instruction Activities

As suggested earlier, direct instruction has been used successfully with students of all ages who display various disabilities. A number of experts have developed graphic representations of the sequence of activities they followed. These activities have been incorporated into the Sequence of Instructional Activities by Schloss and Sedlak (1986). A copy of their sequence is presented in Figure 4.1. Note that the information in the rectangles on the left side of the figure refers to the steps the practitioner takes in developing and delivering instruction. The vertical arrows connecting the rectangles indicate that instructional planning and delivery are proceeding normally. When difficulties are encountered, the practitioner is directed by the horizontal lines to the questions in the diamonds. Rather than assume that problems are the result of student flaws, the practitioner focuses attention on how the instructional program can be modified when resumed. Once the goal has been achieved, the entire sequence is repeated. This section describes each step of the sequence, with illustrations from the secondary special education literature. Special attention is given to the technology of learning strategies.

Identify Learner Characteristics

The first step in the sequence is to identify the learner's characteristics. Practitioners need to conduct a thorough analysis of the strengths and weaknesses a student brings to the learning situation. Traditionally, this assessment is conducted by all members of the multidisciplinary team upon a student's entry into the special educational program.

Goodman and Mann (1976) identified two reasons why secondary learners are assessed. First, an inventory of a student's strengths, accomplishments, and weaknesses in all areas helps educators identify the levels of instruction the student is currently receiving. This is particularly important to have before placing the student in specific curricular programs. For example, practitioners who are implementing a learning-strategies curriculum need to test the secondary student to determine current habits with regard to a particular task (Schumaker et al., 1983). Such an assessment is also used to establish preintervention baselines against which subsequent achievement gains can be measured. Zigmond (1978) also suggested that secondary educators determine their students' motivation and reinforcement history in this way. This information will be valuable when selecting motivational techniques for use during the fourth step in this sequence.

Several formal and informal instruments are available to help practitioners assess secondary students (Zigmond, 1978; Zigmond et al., 1986a). Formal measures include norm-referenced devices with specific instructions for administration and scoring. Informal measures include teacher-made and commercially produced criterion-referenced tests, systematic observation, trial teaching, skill checklists, student interviews, and rating scales. Houck (1987) suggested secondary educators examine student records and inter-

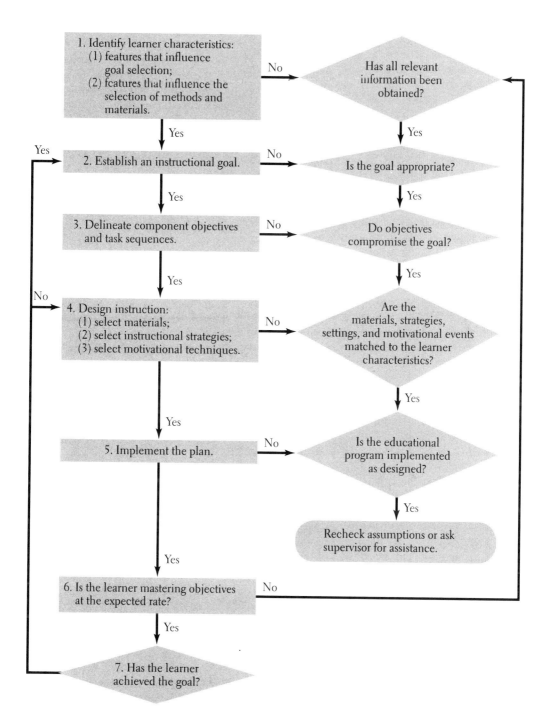

FIGURE 4.1   The Sequence of Instructional Activities

Source: From Patrick J. Schloss and Robert A. Sedlak, *Instructional Methods for Students with Learning and Behavior Disorders.* Copyright © 1986 by Allyn and Bacon. Reprinted with permission.

view significant others to determine the nature of previous educational interventions. Practitioners may be able to link student performance to specific instructional techniques and select for use techniques associated with achievement gains.

Assessment is essential if the student is to be properly placed in an instructional program and the effectiveness of that program is to be measured; however, a word of caution is in order. Secondary students with disabilities have a long and probably negative history of being tested. Test situations are frustrating because they highlight students' continuing inability to perform at expected levels. Practitioners are advised to avoid unnecessary testing. Appropriate methods of assessing secondary learners with disabilities are discussed elsewhere in this text.

Establish Goals

Public secondary schools have traditionally emphasized a developmental orientation when establishing instructional objectives. Educators assumed that skills within a given domain can be identified and arranged in a logical sequence. This sequence typically corresponds to the order in which skills are acquired by the general population. Educators also assumed that a traditional educational evaluation can identify the developmental level at which an individual is functioning in a given domain. Finally, educators have argued that the goal of instruction should be to improve the skills in the developmental sequence that have not been mastered by the students.

This developmental orientation is appropriate for the majority of students attending public high schools. Implementation of a developmental curriculum ensures that most students will acquire important competencies in a logical sequence. Each competency is built upon previously mastered skills and concepts. Upon graduating from high school, most students will by and large be prepared for the challenges they will face in educational, vocational, and community environments.

Unfortunately, the learning and behavioral characteristics demonstrated by students with disabilities, listed in Action Plan 4.1, make it likely that they will master far fewer skills and concepts by the end of high school. Basic academic skills may be limited, and these students may not have the opportunity to develop essential vocational, leisure, independent living, and social skills. Therefore, direct-instruction efforts should be directed toward the mastery of social, personal, academic, and vocational goals that prepare secondary students with disabilities for postsecondary environments.

Note that the traditional developmental approach is more suited to elementary students with disabilities. With adolescents, however, educators should consider IEP goals that reflect a functional orientation so that the students will develop skills necessary for successful functioning in adult settings.

Each student's IEP must target goals to be accomplished during the school year. These goals are established by the members of the student's multidisciplinary team and reflect the results of the assessment. Given the importance of carefully selecting goals for developmental and functional curricula, it is necessary to have the full cooperation of every member of the multidisciplinary team. Predictions about anticipated environments may be more accurate if all multidisciplinary team members concerned about the student provide input. In addition, it is advisable, and in some states mandated, that the secondary student be present during meetings in which goals are established. Although students have the right to attend multidisciplinary meetings, this right may not be exercised by younger or less able learners. Secondary students who attend relevant meetings have the opportunity to offer suggestions of their own and listen to the opinions and supporting evidence of others concerned about their welfare. Their participation may impress upon them the importance of the decisions being made and increase their commitment to the instructional program.

Two factors influence the nature and number of goals established by the multidisciplinary team. The first factor is the number and quality of skills currently in the student's academic and social repertoires. Students with milder disabilities may have more fully developed skill repertoires; therefore, they may have more goals that closely approximate those established for their nondisabled peers. A learning-strategies curriculum may be particularly appropriate for such learners. Goals for students with less well developed repertoires may be fewer in number and may have a more functional orientation. The second factor is the student's age, which suggests the number of years remaining in his or her academic career. Students just starting secondary school have more flexibility with respect to the goals selected. Goals for older students may address skills needed to function effectively in postsecondary environments such as higher education, employment, and community living.

Identify Objectives

Goals targeted during the multidisciplinary team meeting are broken down into instructional objectives. These objectives serve as the foundation for daily instruction. Each objective usually includes a statement of the conditions under which the student will perform, a description of the behavior to be displayed, and the criteria for acceptable performance. For example, the annual goal for a secondary learner may target the development of math skills needed for independent living. The practitioner then breaks this goal down into the following short-term objective: "Given 20 problems involving the addition of two numbers, the student will compute the answers with 100% accuracy by using a calculator." Related objectives could address the management of a checking account, management of a saving account, payment of utility bills, and computation of federal and state income tax returns.

Each of these objectives can be broken down even further into task sequences. For example, to use a calculator the student must do the following:

1. Locate a calculator.
2. Turn the calculator on.
3. Clear the calculator if necessary.
4. Enter the digits in the order in which the number is said aloud.
5. Identify the operation.
6. Press the operation button.
7. Enter the next digit.
8. Press the "=" button.
9. Read/record the answer.

Action Plan 4.4 Annual Goals and Related Instructional Objectives

Practitioners need to develop short-term goals from long-range objectives. The following example may be helpful.

Mark is a senior who is moderately retarded. Although he is living at home, he will be moving to a group home shortly after he graduates from high school. The multidisciplinary team has targeted the following goal:

Mark will develop independent living skills.

In addition, the team has decided Mark should be placed in a functional curriculum. His teacher has developed the following objectives:

Given a destination time and place, Mark will use public transportation to arrive in a timely manner without assistance.

Given a recipe, Mark will locate the ingredients and follow the directions to prepare a nutritious dinner with no assistance.

During free time, Mark will identify and engage in a recreational activity with the peer of his choice.

Case for Action 4.2

Bill is a senior with a mild learning disability. He has expressed an interest in attending a local community college to study hotel and restaurant management. Members of his multidisciplinary team have identified the following goal:

Bill will improve his written language.

Develop the short-term objectives.

Action Plan 4.4 presents objectives derived from annual goals established for secondary students with different abilities.

Design Instruction

Designing instruction for secondary learners with disabilities is a critical step in the sequence of instructional activities. During this stage, practitioners give careful thought to three factors that can influence the effectiveness of their instruction: materials, techniques, and motivation. These factors are frequently incorporated in a written lesson plan. The experienced practitioner also understands the value of combining advanced planning and contingency planning into a single lesson plan. During advanced planning, the practitioner analyzes students' characteristics, outlines the procedures that will be followed during the lesson, and identifies the materials that will be used to promote skill acquisition. A number of authors have identified components of an advanced written lesson plan (Academy for Effective Instruction, 1987; Cohen, 1986; Russell & Hunter, 1976). Action Plan 4.5 presents a lesson plan outline suitable for use with secondary learners.

During contingency planning, the practitioner reviews the advanced plan, identifies potential areas of student difficulty, and plans alternative instructional procedures. While this process increases the amount of time practitioners must commit to planning, it has the advantage of building flexibility into the lesson plan. The practitioner can better respond to student difficulty because he or she will already have preplanned instructional alternatives to implement. Figure 4.2 presents portions of a lesson plan that incorporate contingency plans.

As suggested earlier, effective lessons are those that pay attention to materials, techniques, and motivation. Although these factors are discussed separately, it is important to remember that they are related. For example, selecting age-appropriate materials for use during the body of the lesson may motivate students to participate in the activity.

Action Plan 4.5   Components of a Written Lesson Plan for Use with Secondary Learners with Disabilities

Practitioners developing a lesson plan for secondary students should include the following components:

1. Basic Information
    a. Curricular area and skill
    b. Nature of lesson (e.g., mathematics/subtraction; introduction)
2. Objective
    a. Conditions
    b. Behavior
    c. Criterion
3. Materials
4. Procedures
    a. Introduction: review previous material, motivate, establish purpose of current lesson
    b. Body: steps in the correct sequence, questions to ask students
    c. Conclusion: review, summarize main points
5. Evaluation
    a. Student performance: checklist, worksheet
    b. Teacher performance: strengths, weaknesses
6. Follow-up activities
    a. Review
    b. Extend
    c. Provide independent practice.

Objective

Given 10 word problems involving addition and subtraction, the student will use a calculator to compute the answer with 100% accuracy.

Procedures

1. Read a sample problem with the class. Determine the correct operation. Turn on the calculator. Show how to enter the first number, the operation sign, the second number, and the equal sign. Identify and record the answer.
2. Repeat with another problem requiring a different operation.
3. Show the class a third problem using a transparency on the overhead projector.
   a. Call on a student to read the problem out loud.
      Contingency: For a student unable to read parts of the problem, read it for him or her, then have the student repeat it.
   b. Determine the correct operation.
      Contingency: Students unable to determine the operation will be provided a list of key words and phrases that provide hints. For example, "how much more" indicates subtraction.
   c. Turn on the calculator.
      Contingency: Use a red marker to highlight the "on" button for students unable to locate it.
   d. Enter the first digit of the first number.
      Contingency 1: Students unable to determine which number should be entered first will be assisted in setting up the problem on paper first.
      Contingency 2: Students unable to determine which digit of a number should be entered first will be told to enter the digits as they are softly repeated out loud.
   e. Enter the operation sign.
      Contingency: Students unable to locate the operation sign will be referred to a sample problem on the board and asked to match the sign written on the board with the button on the calculator.
   f. Enter the equal sign.
      Contingency: Use a blue marker to highlight the "=" button for students unable to locate it.
   g. Record the answer.
4. Repeat with another problem presented to the entire group.
5. Provide a worksheet with 10 word problems to those who needed no assistance during the teacher-directed activity.
   Contingency: Continue to work in a small group with those who experienced difficulty.
6. If time permits, allow students who have mastered the skill to go "Christmas shopping" using a catalog from a department store. Tell them they have $200 to spend. They must keep track of their expenses.
   Contingency: Have students previously engaged in small-group instruction complete the worksheet containing 10 problems. Be available to provide assistance.

FIGURE 4.2   Contingency Plans Included in a Written Lesson Plan

Materials

As indicated in Chapter 1, educational programs for secondary students with special needs are seriously in need of suitable instructional materials. Although special education legislation has encouraged educators to produce more materials for learners with disabilities, the majority of commercially available material is designed for younger learners. Generally, secondary educators must choose between material that is intended for younger learners with disabilities and material for regular secondary students. The materials that accompany a learning-strategies curriculum are different. Typically, the packets of instructional material and procedures include whatever the teacher needs to implement the program.

Practitioners who are using a curriculum other than learning strategies will have to be cautious in their selection of suitable materials. The importance of using relevant, age-appropriate materials that are attractive and well organized has been emphasized by many authors (Gleason, 1983; Graham, 1985; Kutsick, 1982; Zigmond, 1978). Secondary teachers may need to look beyond traditional sources. For example, a few publishers offer high-interest low-vocabulary items that appeal to secondary students without overwhelming them (Kutsick, 1982); however, such materials may be expensive (Osterag & Rambeau, 1982). Before purchasing any new materials, practitioners are advised to identify what students have already been exposed to (Houck, 1987; Kutsick, 1982). This can be accomplished by reviewing the students' previous IEPs, checking with former teachers, and talking with the students themselves. In addition, practitioners are encouraged to consider nontraditional sources of material such as the newspaper, music trade magazines, computers, and the library (Kutsick, 1982). Practitioners who need to minimize reading as the primary vehicle for acquiring new information may consider audiotapes, videotapes, and talking books (Osterag & Rambeau, 1982). Chapter 6 presents additional information on the selection, adaptation, and development of appropriate materials for secondary students with disabilities.

Instructional Techniques

A substantial body of literature attests to the positive relationship between several instructional procedures and student achievement. Although the majority of these studies have involved younger learners (Anderson et al., 1979; Fisher et al., Good & Grouws, 1979), some have addressed the older student with disabilities (Stallings et al., 1979). More recently, a tremendous amount of data have appeared documenting the effectiveness of learning strategies for secondary students with learning disabilities (Deshler et al., 1985; Ellis & Lenz, 1987; Schumaker & Deshler, 1988; Schumaker et al., 1983). As already mentioned, a number of the techniques used to teach learning strategies are similar to the strategies that make up direct instruction. They fall into three categories: presentation of new information, guided practice, and independent practice. A fourth category, review and reteach, is also discussed.

Presenting the Information. The first phase of instruction consists of presenting new information and demonstrating a new skill. Although this seems to be a rather obvious step, a demonstration of the concept or skill students are expected to master is often omitted from the instructional activity or is poorly managed. Both the learning-strategies and direct-instruction literature have presented some guidelines for demonstrating the concept or skill. They are listed in Action Plan 4.6.

The first guideline states that it is important to cue the students that instruction is about to begin. Students may be distracted because they have just arrived and are settling

Action Plan 4.6   Guidelines for Presenting New Information

Practitioners should present new information using the following guidelines:

1. Use a discrete cue to gain student attention.
2. Motivate the learners to participate in the activity.
3. Teach to large and small groups.
4. Model the skill or concept.
5. Use precise language.
6. Ask questions frequently.
7. Provide feedback.
8. Review material.

down for the day or have just completed another activity. Practitioners need to use a consistent, discrete cue signaling that instruction is about to begin and, therefore, the students should pay attention. For example, practitioners may flicker the lights or they may consistently use a phrase as simple as "All eyes up front" or "We are ready to start working." Eventually, students will learn that instruction will not proceed until they are all paying attention to the teacher. Practitioners, particularly those using a learning-strategies curriculum, are also advised to teach their students to capitalize on attentional cues the teacher may use during the presentation of new information (Deshler et al., 1985; Kahn, 1980; Minskoff, 1982). These cues include changes in intonation, volume, or pitch or the use of pauses or common phrases (e.g., "Now listen...," "This is important..."). These cues should signal that the learner is expected to pay close attention and take notes because this information is particularly important.

The second guideline suggests that during the presentation of information the learners should be motivated to participate in the planned activity. Secondary educators can do this in a number of ways. For example, they can provide an advanced organizer (Deshler et al., 1985; Graham, 1985; Hudson, Lignugaris-Kraft, & Miller, 1993; Minskoff, 1982; Schumaker & Deshler, 1988; Zigmond, 1978). It might consist of the following items:

1. Checking homework
2. Reviewing information from the previous lesson
3. A preview of what the teacher intends to do
4. A rationale for the lesson, including an explanation of how it relates to previous material
5. An explanation of teacher expectations from the students.

The third guideline pertains to the size of the group being taught. Special educators have long held the belief that instruction is most effective when it is conducted on a one-to-one basis. Stevens and Rosenshine (1981) defined individualization from a different perspective. Rather than working one to one with a teacher, individualization refers to maximizing each student's success and confidence by providing activities that allow a high percentage of correct responses. Well-planned and carefully implemented group lessons can certainly accomplish this goal. Although some unique situations may warrant one-to-one instruction, it is generally not feasible for daily instruction in the secondary classroom.

Many secondary students with disabilities are included in regular classrooms; therefore, group size will reflect the number of students typically assigned to a regular high school class. In self-contained classrooms, it is possible that the teacher will be working with the entire group. In resource settings, it is likely that while the teacher is working exclusively with one youth, the other students will be assigned independent activities that they may or may not attend to and complete. Small or large groups during which teacher-led instruction is provided maximize the time on task and increase the number of opportunities for students to observe appropriate models and receive praise and corrective feedback (Stevens & Rosenshine, 1981; Stallings et al., 1979).

The fourth guideline states that practitioners should model the skill or concept to be mastered by the students (Howe, 1982; Schumaker & Deshler, 1988; Schumaker et al., 1983; Stevens & Rosenshine, 1981). Modeling allows students to observe the correct performance of a skill they are expected to acquire by the end of the lesson. If the skill can only be acquired through a number of steps, as is the case with a learning strategy, then the practitioner should model and verbally describe each component in sequence (Zigmond, Sansone, Miller, Donahoe, & Kohnke, 1986b). Several demonstrations or examples of the concept may have to be provided, depending on the learning characteristics of the students (Minskoff, 1982).

The fifth guideline for presenting new information calls for the use of precise language (Chilcoat, 1987). Students are confused by statements that are vague, uncertain, or include irrelevant language (Zigmond et al., 1986b). Teacher statements to the students should include the necessary vocabulary and should be clear, specific, and grammatically correct. They should provide students with the exact details needed to master the skill or concept.

Sixth, the practitioner should ask numerous questions while presenting information to determine the extent to which students are comprehending the material (Kahn, 1980). Asking frequent questions keeps students alert, accountable, and on task (Graham, 1985; McConnell, 1977). In addition, Stallings and colleagues (1979) recommended that questions be directed to specific students rather than to volunteers. Although volunteers usually raise their hands because they know the answer, their performance may not be representative of the entire group. Students' answers to questions allow the practitioner to detect and correct problems at an earlier stage, and thus help them avoid repeating errors (Zigmond et al., 1986b).

The seventh guideline states that feedback should be provided (Graham, 1985; Howe, 1982; Schumaker & Deshler, 1988; Schumaker et al., 1983; Stallings et al., 1979). Practitioners can enhance student performance by explaining what was correct and incorrect about their response (Deshler, Ferrel, & Kass, 1978). Feedback for a correct response can include a repetition of the answer and a compliment when appropriate (Zigmond et al., 1986b). In the event of an inaccurate response, the practitioner can use corrective feedback. The exact nature of corrective feedback can vary. Stallings and colleagues (1979) recommended that the teacher respond to an incorrect answer with guides and probing questions. Stevens and Rosenshine (1981) suggested that the practitioner provide a hint, a rule, or a process that will enable the student to respond correctly. Feedback helps not only the individual who is receiving it directly, but also other members of the instructional group (Zigmond et al., 1986b). Those who were not called upon but already knew the correct answer receive indirect confirmation of their response. Those who did not know the answer can benefit from the instruction being given to a peer.

Finally, practitioners should review material at the end of the lesson or as they move from one part of the lesson to the next (Kallison, 1980; Minskoff, 1982). This review highlights key points and helps students relate one part of the lesson to another.

The approach reflected in these eight guidelines has been shown to be effective with secondary learners with disabilities. It is suitable whether the students are enrolled in a traditional secondary curriculum, a functional curriculum, or a learning-strategies curriculum. General secondary educators who have students with disabilities included in their content area classes will find that direct instruction will benefit *all* of their students, not just those with disabilities. Instruction that adheres to these guidelines helps students acquire new information in a systematic, efficient way. Having mastered the material under close teacher supervision, they are now ready to proceed to the guided practice phase of direct instruction.

Guided Practice. As students become more proficient in a targeted skill, the teacher gradually shifts responsibility for learning to them (Palincsar & Brown, 1987). The purpose of guided practice is to allow the students to practice newly acquired skills under successively less structured conditions (Graham, 1985). Guided practice activities foster automaticity (Carnine, 1989), that is, the ability to access information and respond quickly. A student who can process information quickly can focus more of his or her attention on higher-order skills.

Specifically, the practitioner fades cues or prompts that may have been available to students during teacher-directed instruction (Zigmond, 1978). Prompts are events that help the student initiate a correct response. Schloss and Sedlak (1986) have arranged prompts in a hierarchy from least to most intrusive, as follows:

1. Cue: The teacher simply instructs the student to perform the behavior.
2. Graphic product: Students are shown an illustration of the product.
3. Graphic process: Students are shown an illustration of how a behavior is accomplished.
4. Oral: The teacher describes how a task is accomplished.

Case for Action 4.3

You are about to start a science lecture. How will you gain your students' attention?

Action Plan 4.7 A Prompting Hierarchy for an Academic Task

Prompts are more effective if their use is planned in advance, as in the following example.

The student is spelling words orally. The teacher has preplanned the following prompts:

1. *Cue:* Tell the student to spell the word "employer."
2. *Graphic product:* Present a flash card for the student to read.
3. *Modeling:* Say, "e-m-p-l-o-y-e-r."

5. Modeling: The teacher identifies the correct answer or shows the student how to perform the behavior.
6. Manual: The teacher physically guides the student through the task.

The nature of the task determines which prompts are available to students during guided practice. Action Plans 4.7 and 4.8 present prompting hierarchies for academic and motor tasks. Prompts can be made more effective if the teacher takes the following five steps (Schloss & Sedlak, 1986).

1. Preplan the use of prompts. Compare the hierarchies in Action Plan 4.7 and 4.8 to see the impact that the target behavior has on the prompts selected for use. For example, motor activities readily lend themselves to graphic-process prompts; therefore, the teacher who elects to use this level of prompt should have a bulletin board or illustration available for the student to look at.
2. Begin with the least intrusive prompt and move up the hierarchy only as student responses warrant. For example, the teacher cues a student to begin a science experiment

Action Plan 4.8 A Prompting Hierarchy for a Motor Skill

Prompts can be used to promote motor skills, as in the following example.

The student is laying out a pattern to make a pair of shorts. The teacher has preplanned the following prompts:

1. *Cue:* Lay out the pattern.
2. *Graphic product:* Show the student a bulletin board displaying a correctly laid out pattern.
3. *Graphic process:* Give the student a sheet listing the steps in order.
4. *Oral:* Describe how to lay out the pattern.
5. *Modeling:* Show the student how to lay out the pattern.
6. *Manual:* Physically guide the student's hands as the pattern is laid out.

and waits three seconds for the student to initiate a response. If the student does not respond, the teacher should provide an oral prompt, describing the task to the student. After three more seconds, if the student is still unable to respond, the teacher should model the task for the student.

3. Use only the least intrusive prompt necessary to ensure a high success rate. In the previous example, the teacher should stop progressing through the hierarchy if the modeling prompt is successful in producing the desired response. A manual prompt will undoubtedly be successful; however, its use may not be warranted.

4. Always pair intrusive prompts with less intrusive prompts to facilitate fading. For example, the teacher pairs oral and modeling prompts when he or she describes how to conduct the experiment while demonstrating it. Eventually, the student's behavior will be prompted by the use of the less restrictive verbal prompt.

5. Interrupt nontarget behaviors as soon as possible to reduce the amount of time students spend practicing errors. Schloss and Sedlak (1986) pointed out that if practice can strengthen appropriate behaviors, it can also strengthen inappropriate behaviors.

The hierarchy of prompts is a technique suitable for use in a variety of guided practice activities. Practitioners whose students are placed in a learning-strategies curriculum should design guided practice activities that closely resemble activities encountered in regular secondary classrooms (Schumaker & Deshler, 1988; Schumaker et al., 1983). For example, the steps of the CAN-DO strategy for learning content information (Ellis & Lenz, 1987) have been presented in a teacher-directed lesson. The practitioner may have the students apply the strategy to material from the history textbook used in the regular secondary classroom.

Other traditional activities used during guided practice include worksheets and games. Beattie and Algozzine (1982) compared the impact of worksheets and games on the mathematical ability of secondary students who had mental retardation. They concluded that the game format had a greater impact because it increased student participation and provided the opportunity to manipulate objects.

The basic point to remember is that guided practice activities allow students to have access to a teacher. Should they encounter any difficulty, the teacher is immediately available to interrupt and correct any errors using the appropriate prompt. When students no longer require a prompt to produce the correct response, they are ready to try the independent practice activities.

Independent Practice. At this phase of instruction, students can perform the skill correctly; however, they may need additional practice until the skill becomes automatic

---

Case for Action 4.4

You are planning a lesson on check completion. What prompts will you have pre-planned?

(Zigmond, 1978). Automaticity allows students to direct their efforts toward the acquisition of other concepts, skills, or strategies. Independent practice activities frequently involve the use of seatwork. Students complete drill sheets, workbooks, or chapter reviews. During school they may also use computer-assisted instruction, videotapes, audiotapes, and Language Masters (Schloss & Sedlak, 1986). Stevens and Rosenshine (1981) suggested that teachers remain available to students in the event they need assistance; however, they warned that teacher contact of more than 30 seconds could indicate that students are not ready for independent practice activities on this particular skill.

One of the most widely used independent practice activities is homework (Mims, Harper, Armstrong, & Savage, 1991). When teachers follow good policies, homework can be an effective learning tool, especially for students with disabilities (Epstein, Polloway, Foley, & Patton, 1993; Salend & Schliff, 1989). It is assigned only after the teacher is sure that knowledge or a skill has been learned with approximately 90% accuracy. Homework can be assigned by both general and special educators as a way to ensure mastery and retention of a newly learned skill and its application to new situations. However, Salend and Schliff (1989) surveyed 88 teachers of students with learning disabilities and reported that the biggest problem with homework assignments was that the students did not complete them. Obviously, students will not benefit from work they do not do. To increase the effectiveness of homework and the likelihood that students will complete it, Epstein and colleagues (1993), Hodapp and Hodapp (1992), Mims and colleagues (1991), and Oppenheim (1989) have recommended the following teacher guidelines:

1. Develop a method of record keeping such as a homework notebook.
2. Encourage students to build time for homework into their daily routines.
3. Make sure that homework assignments are a review of skills or knowledge that have been presented and practiced in class.
4. Make sure that homework assignments are relevant to special education students' long- and short-term goals.
5. When giving an assignment, state its purpose, review directions, provide a time estimate, give a deadline for its completion, and describe how it will be graded.
6. Give assignments that can be completed within a reasonable time frame. Epstein and colleagues (1993) noted that a minimum of two hours should be required from high school students. Oppenheim (1989) recommended ten minutes times the grade level as the amount of time a student should spend doing homework.
7. Evaluate all assignments so that students know they are accountable for the work. In addition, teachers can determine whether knowledge or a skill is being applied correctly.
8. Consider the attention span and functional level of the student when developing assignments. Less able students will require longer amounts of time to do less homework.

Review and Reteach. Experienced practitioners are familiar with the problems that secondary students with disabilities demonstrate in maintaining the level of skill or concept development. Concepts that are not immediately relevant to the students' needs or skills that are not frequently practiced may be lost after a period of time. Therefore it is important to carefully select the concepts and skills that will be targeted for development. It is also important to provide periodic reviews of previously mastered material. Schloss and Sedlak (1986) have recommended that newly acquired concepts be reviewed daily, then weekly, then monthly.

Motivational Techniques
The third factor that should be considered while practitioners are planning for instruction is motivation. Practitioners need to motivate secondary students to participate in activities similar to the ones in which they may have experienced little or no success. The previous sections have occasionally alluded to methods for accomplishing this task. First, teachers should select their goals and objectives with great care. These must reflect the students' interests and abilities. It was suggested earlier that secondary learners may be more motivated to participate in educational programs they have helped to develop; therefore, to the greatest extent possible, secondary students should attend and participate in multidisciplinary team meetings. Second, teachers are advised to explain the purpose of acquiring specific information or developing a skill. They should explain why this information or skill is important. Students who understand how knowledge or skills will contribute to their competence are more likely to participate in the instructional activity. Third, practitioners should pay close attention to the materials they incorporate into the lesson. Functional, age-appropriate materials that are bright, attractive, and novel will be more appealing to secondary learners with disabilities. Fourth, practitioners are advised to plan to use reinforcement when providing feedback for a correct response. This reinforcement may be a simple compliment or an elaborate contingency plan such as a token economy. Finally, at the end of a lesson, practitioners may need to reinforce student participation and achievement (see Chapter 6).

Implement Instruction

Having attended to materials, techniques, and motivation, the practitioner is now ready to implement the lesson plan. Brophy (1983) and Kounin (1970) have identified five behaviors displayed by effective teachers as they implement a lesson plan.

The first two behaviors are related: continuity and momentum. Continuity is displayed by the practitioner who builds one instructional sequence upon another without omitting information or steps in the skill. Momentum refers to the ability to make quick, smooth transitions from one phase of the lesson plan to the next. Teachers who display these behaviors during their lessons keep their students attentive and on task.

Third, effective teachers have the ability to "overlap." It has been suggested that teachers serve as "executive directors" of their classrooms (Graham, 1985). They must implement and monitor several activities simultaneously. For example, a practitioner who is directing a small-group lesson may also need to supervise two students engaged in peer tutoring. In addition, another student may be experiencing difficulty with seatwork while a fourth is completely off the task and teasing a peer. In a situation of this type, the practitioner has to teach, supervise, assist, and correct—all within a narrow time frame.

Fourth, effective implementation of the lesson plan also depends on the teacher's "with-it-ness," or the ability to anticipate problems and intervene before the situation gets out of hand. Consider the case of the secondary learner identified as behavior disordered who began to tap, then stomp his foot when a task became too frustrating. These warning signs were ignored, however, and the student progressed to even more disruptive behaviors. Of course, careful consideration of the nature of the independent task would have prevented the problem in the first place. In any case, attending to the student early in the chain of disruptive events minimizes its negative impact upon other students and the flow of the lesson. Practitioners can be more "with-it" by spending time developing contingency plans. They can also circulate among students engaged in guided and independent activities or, if directing a small-group lesson, they can frequently scan the room and observe student activity.

Fifth, effective teachers hold their students accountable for their own learning. They direct frequent questions to both specific students and volunteers to keep all learners interested and attentive.

Evaluate Mastery of the Objectives

At this point, the practitioner determines the extent to which the students have mastered the objectives established earlier in the direct-instruction sequence. While practitioners may choose from any number of assessment devices to make this determination, they are more likely to choose informal measures such as paper-and-pencil tests, checklists, and systematic observations. Ideally, these devices will indicate the effectiveness of the instructional program by documenting gains in student achievement, and thus allow the practitioner to move on to the next set of objectives. However, as the horizontal arrows on Figure 4.1 indicate, the students may not master the objectives at the anticipated rate. Practitioners are then directed back through the sequence to generate hypotheses about factors that may have contributed to student difficulty. For example, the goals may have been inappropriate or the instructional objectives out of sequence. Perhaps the materials failed to motivate. After examining and ranking these hypotheses, the practitioner systematically alters one condition at a time, implementing instruction again until the culprit is identified and modified. This process keeps practitioners from automatically blaming the student for his or her inability to learn. Of course, supervisor assistance should be obtained and a reconvening of the multidisciplinary team considered if the student does not achieve after all possible explanations have been ruled out.

Determine Whether the Goals Have Been Achieved

Consistent, appropriate use of the sequence of instructional activities should enable students to master the objectives derived from each annual goal. Students now possess a specific body of skills that previously eluded them. Practitioners have documented the effectiveness of a specific set of techniques that promote skill development. These techniques will be used in the future to help students with similar characteristics acquire new skills.

Transfer of Training

Use of direct-instruction techniques and learning strategies can increase the quantity of skills acquired by secondary students with disabilities. However, as noted at the beginning of this chapter, students with disabilities may not maintain a newly acquired skill to the same extent as their nondisabled peers. General secondary educators, resource specialists, consultant teachers, and the students themselves have invested too much time, resources, and energy to risk the loss of knowledge and skills. In addition, as noted earlier, students with disabilities may have difficulty generalizing knowledge and skills learned in one setting to another. Thus, it is possible that without additional effort on the part of all involved, students with disabilities may not use newly acquired skills and knowledge in postsecondary environments such as home, vocational, and community settings.

Educators need to take specific measures to ensure transfer of training, that is, to ensure that reasonably well developed basic skills are maintained and generalized to everyday life. A technology to promote maintenance and generalization has been developed (Stokes & Baer, 1977). One of the most effective and least troublesome ways to promote maintenance and generalization is to systematically alter instruction so that students are able to use the skills under a range of conditions. This outcome is important, because success in adult life depends on a person's ability to use appropriate responses throughout a range of vocational, consumer, and residential experiences. For example, a teacher using a functional orientation may teach a student to first pay utility bills, then consumer credit bills, then tax bills. A teacher using a learning-strategies curriculum may use RAP to enhance comprehension of newspaper articles, then stories from an English literature text, then science textbooks. In both instances, the students are doing more than learning a restricted set of rote skills that cannot be applied beyond the instructional setting. The students are encouraged to develop a flexibility that allows them to face a range of demands.

Another way to generalize skills to community settings is to replace artificial incentives with naturally occurring reinforcers. Educators must recognize that apart from a salary, there are few incentives. Behaviors that are supported by systematic reinforcement in educational settings may not be maintained in the community, where reinforcement contingencies no longer apply. It is important that reinforcement procedures be as nonintrusive as possible yet strong enough to motivate performance. Once a student consistently demonstrates target behaviors under initial reinforcement conditions, the teacher should begin fading to more natural conditions. The goal is that, upon completion of high school, the student's behavior will be maintained by the infrequent and variable reinforcers readily available in community settings.

Maintenance and generalization will also be enhanced by teachers who use multiple exemplars, that is, more than one example of a skill. The more exemplars the teacher uses, the more likely it is that students will be able to transfer their skills to the domain of skills. Multiple exemplars may be used in two ways. First, the teacher may encourage the students to demonstrate a skill in a series of related activities. A teacher using a functional orientation may arrange for students to participate in seven employment interviews rather than just one. A general secondary educator teaching a computer technology course may make sure that students are able to use a variety of word processing programs. Second, the teacher may select one or two activities that include a majority of the elements in the domain of related activities. Reflecting a functional curriculum, Smith and Schloss (1986) constructed an employment application that reflected 80% of all the questions and vocabulary used in 200 separate applications. A secondary science teacher using a developmental orientation may have students complete one or two experiments starting with setting up a hypothesis and finishing by writing and delivering a report. Completing all facets of a limited number of experiments may provide students with more information about and practice in using the scientific method than reading about a large number of experiments.

Self-management skill development is another technique for encouraging students to use newly acquired skills in community settings. Self-management refers to the ability to change or manage one's own behavior. Students are taught to set goals for themselves then monitor and evaluate situations that lead to inappropriate behavior, such as limiting one's intake of alcohol to avoid becoming rowdy. Self-management can also refer to arranging consequences that encourage appropriate behavior, such as treating oneself to a dinner and a movie after completing a big project. Chapter 6 provides more information about self-management.

Reasonable Accommodations

Secondary educators who use direct instruction and learning strategies can find that most students with disabilities can learn effectively in the regular classroom. Despite the

Action Plan 4.9   Reasonable Accommodations

Ellett (1993) reported that general secondary educators perceived the following instructional accommodations as reasonable:

1. Use supplemental resources. Teachers can use peer tutors or volunteers, introduce calculators and audio recordings of textbooks, and talk with the students' parents.
2. Simplify instructions. Give step-by-step instructions, or present the same information at a slower pace or in a different sequence.
3. Provide students with support and extra instructional cues. Use auditory and visual modes to present new information.
4. Use classroom management procedures. Establish specific consequences for appropriate and inappropriate behavior. Post grades and emphasize a student's good qualities.
5. Facilitate grade improvement. Develop alternative test-taking procedures such as open-book tests. Develop extra-credit assignments or allow students to retake tests.
6. Modify the learning environment. Change the room or the instructional materials.
7. Teach study skills. Help students get organized by setting up assignment notebooks. Teach students how to take notes and use their textbooks.

availability of these techniques and their record of success, however, secondary students with disabilities may occasionally experience difficulty. Teachers may need to make additional adaptations to promote academic, social, and behavior goals. Unfortunately, class size, pressure for content coverage, and lack of planning time may limit the amount of time secondary teachers have to develop and implement adaptations (Vaughn, Schumm, & Kouzekanani, 1993). Teachers will need to identify procedures they can reasonably implement, given the constraints on their resources. Ellett (1993) surveyed 85 secondary teachers and asked them to rate the reasonability of a series of instructional accommodations. Her suggestions are listed in Action Plan 4.9. It is recommended that the secondary teacher make at least two well-documented attempts to remediate any difficulty demonstrated by a student with disabilities. After that, the teacher may wish to pursue additional assistance form the resource specialist or the consultant teacher. Chapter 7 provides more information about these options.

Summary

Secondary students with disabilities will acquire important information and skills only through careful consideration, selection, and combination of curricular orientations. Appropriate goals and objectives can be mastered by students when their teachers use direct instruction and learning strategies. These teaching techniques are suitable for use by general secondary educators who are focusing on specific subject matter and by resource specialists and consultants who are providing direct and indirect services. All teachers must ensure, however, that knowledge and skills acquired by secondary students with disabilities are maintained over time and across settings.

In order to plan and implement appropriate instruction, practitioners must have at their disposal complete, relevant assessment data for each student. In addition, they need to be aware of and control factors that occur before, during, and after the plan is developed and implemented. This information is addressed in Chapters 5 and 6.

References

Academy for Effective Instruction. (1987). *Working with mildly handicapped students: Design and delivery of academic lessons.* Reston, VA: The Council for Exceptional Children.

Alley, G., & Deshler, D. D. (1979). *Teaching the learning disabled adolescent: Strategies and methods.* Denver: Love.

Anderson, L. M., Evertson, C. M., & Brophy, J. E. (1979). An experimental study of effective teaching in first grade reading groups. *Elementary School Journal, 79,* 193–223.

Beattie, J., & Algozzine, B. (1982). Improving basic academic skills of educable mentally retarded adolescents. *Education and Training of the Mentally Retarded, 17,* 255–258.

Brophy, J. E. (1983). Classroom organization and management. *Elementary School Journal, 83,* 265–287.

Carnine, D. (1989). Designing practice activities. *Journal of Learning Disabilities, 22,* 603–607.

Chilcoat, G. W. (1987). Teacher talk: Keep it clear! *Academic Therapy, 22,* 263–271.

Chow, S. H. L. (1981). *A study of academic learning time of mainstreamed learning disabled students.* San Francisco: Far West Educational Laboratory for Educational Research and Development.

Cohen, S. (1986). Teaching new material. *Exceptional Children, 20,* 50–51.

Deshler, D. D., Ferrel, W., & Kass, C. (1978). Error monitoring of schoolwork by learning disabled adolescents. *Journal of Learning Disabilities, 11,* 401–404.

Deshler, D. D., Putnam, M. L., & Bulgren, J. A. (1985). Academic accommodations for adolescents with behavior and learning problems. In S. Braaten, R. B. Rutherford, & W. Evans (Eds.), *Programming for adolescents with behavioral disorders (Vol. 2,* pp. 20–30). Reston, VA: The Council for Exceptional Children.

Deshler, D. D., & Schumaker, J. B. (1986): Learning strategies: An instructional alternative for low achieving adolescents. *Exceptional Children, 52,* 583–590.

Ellett, L. (1993). Instructional practices in mainstreamed secondary classrooms. *Journal of Learning Disabilities, 26,* 57–64.

Ellis, E. S., & Lenz, B. K. (1987). A component analysis of effective learning strategies for LD students. *Learning Disabilities Focus, 2,* 94–107.

Epstein, M. H., Polloway, E. A., Foley, R. M., & Patton, J. R. (1993). Homework: A comparison of teachers' and parents' perceptions of the problems experienced by students identified as having behavioral disorders, learning disabilities, and no disabilities. *Remedial and Special Education, 14(5),* 40–50.

Evertson, C. M., Emmer, E. T., Clements, B., Sanford, J., Worsham, M., & Williams, E. (1981). *Organizing and managing the elementary school classroom.* Austin: University of Texas, Research and Development Center for Education.

Fisher, C. W., Berliner, D. C., Filby, N. N., Marliave, R., Cahen, L. S., Dishaw, M. M., & Moore, J. E. (1978). *Teaching behaviors, academic learning time, and student achievement: Final report of Phase III-B Beginning Teacher Evaluation Study.* San Francisco: Far West Educational Laboratory for Educational Research and Development.

Gleason, J. J. (1983). ABCDs of motivating adolescent LD students. *Academic Therapy, 19,* 53–55.

Good, T. L., & Grouws, D. A. (1979). The Missouri Mathematics Effectiveness Project. *Journal of Educational Psychology, 71,* 355–362.

Goodman, L., & Mann, L. (1976). *Learning disabilities in the secondary school: Issues and practices.* New York: Grune and Stratton.

Graham, S. (1985). Teaching basic academic skills to learning disabled students: A model of the teaching-learning process. *Journal of Learning Disabilities, 18,* 528–534.

Haring, N. C., & Gentry, N. D. (1976). Direct and individualized instructional Procedures. In N. G. Haring & R. L. Schiefelbusch (Eds.), *Teaching special children.* New York: McGraw-Hill.

Haring, N. G., & Schiefelbusch, R. L. (1976). *Teaching special children.* New York: McGraw-Hill.

Hodapp, A. F., & Hodapp, J. B. (1992). Homework: Making it work. *Intervention in School and Clinic, 24,* 233–235.

Houck, C. (1987). Teaching LD adolescents to read. *Academic Therapy, 22,* 229–237.

Howe, B. (1982). A language skills program for secondary LD students. *Journal of Learning Disabilities, 15,* 541–544.

Hudson, P., Lignugaris-Kraft, B., & Miller, T. (1993). Using content enhancements to improve the performance of adolescents with learning disabilities in content classes. *Learning Disabilities Research and Practice, 8,* 106–126.

Kahn, M. S. (1980). Learning problems of the secondary and junior college learning disabled students: Suggested remedies. *Journal of Learning Disabilities, 13,* 445–449.

Kallison, J. (1980). *Organization of the lesson as it affects student achievement.* Unpublished doctoral dissertation, University of Texas.

Kounin, J. (1970). *Discipline and group management in classrooms.* New York: Holt, Rinehart, & Winston.

Kutsick, K. (1982). Remedial strategies for learning disabled adolescents. *Academic Therapy, 17,* 329–335.

Leinhardt, G., Zigmond, N., & Cooley, W. W. (1981). Reading instruction and its effects. *American Educational Research Journal, 18,* 343–361.

Lenz, B. K., & Hughes, C. A. (1990). A word identification strategy for adolescents with hearing disabilities. *Journal of Learning Disabilities, 23,* 149–158, 163.

McConnell, J. (1977, April). *Relationships between selected teacher behaviors and attitudes/achievement of algebra classes.* Paper presented at the annual meeting of the American Educational Research Association, New York, New York.

Mims, A., Harper, C., Armstrong, S. W., & Savage, S. (1991). Effective homework instruction for students with disabilities. *Teaching Exceptional Children, 24*(1), 42–44.

Minskoff, E. H. (1982). Sharpening language skills in secondary learning disabled students. *Academic Therapy, 18*, 53–57.

Oppenheim, J. (1989). *The elementary school journal: Making the most of your child's education.* New York: Pantheon.

Osterag, B. A., & Rambeau, J. (1982). Reading success through rewriting for secondary LD students. *Academic Therapy, 18*, 27–32.

Palincsar, A. S., & Brown, D. A. (1987). Enhancing instructional time through attention to metacognition. *Journal of Learning Disabilities, 20*, 66–71.

Russell, D., & Hunter, M. (1976). Planning for effective instruction: Lesson design. In *Increasing your teaching effectiveness* (pp. 63–68). Palo Alto, CA: Learning Institute (Pitman Learning).

Salend, S. J., & Schliff, J. (1989). An examination of the homework practices of teachers of students with learning disabilities. *Journal of Learning Disabilities, 22*, 621–623.

Schloss, P. J., & Sedlak, R. A. (1986). *Instructional methods for students with learning and behavior problems.* Boston: Allyn and Bacon.

Schumaker, J. B., & Deshler, D. D. (1988). Implementing the regular education initiative in the secondary schools: A different ballgame. *Journal of Learning Disabilities, 21*, 36–42.

Schumaker, J. B., Deshler, D. D., Alley, G. R., & Warner, M. M. (1983). Toward the development of an intervention model for learning disabled adolescents: The University of Kansas Institute. *Exceptional Education Quarterly, 4*, 45–74.

Sindelar, P. T., Smith, M. A., Harriman, N. E., Hale, R. L., & Wilson, R. J. (1986). Teacher effectiveness in special education programs. *Journal of Special Education, 20*, 195–207.

Smith, C. R. (1994). *Learning disabilities: The interaction of learner, task, and setting* (3rd ed.). Boston: Allyn and Bacon.

Smith, M. A., & Schloss, P. J. (1986). A "superform" for enhancing competence in completing employment applications. *Teaching Exceptional Children, 18*(4), 277–280.

Stallings, J. A., Needles, M., & Stayrook, N. (1979). *How to change the process of teaching basic reading skills in secondary schools.* Menlo Park, CA: SRI International.

Stevens, R., & Rosenshine, B. (1981). Advances in research on teaching. *Exceptional Education Quarterly, 2*, 1–9.

Stokes, T. F., & Baer, D. M. (1977). An implicit technology of generalization. *Journal of Applied Behavior Analysis, 10*, 349–367.

Vaughn, S., Schumm, J. S., & Kouzekanani, K. (1993). What do students with learning disabilities think when their general education teachers make adaptations? *Journal of Learning Disabilities, 26*, 545–555.

Will, M. (1986). Educating children with learning problems: A shared responsibility. *Exceptional Children, 52*, 411–416.

Zigmond, N. (1978). A prototype of comprehensive services for secondary students with learning disabilities. *Learning Disabilities Quarterly, 1*, 39–49.

Zigmond, N., Sansone, J., Miller, S. E., Donahoe, K. A., & Kohnke, R. (1986a). *Teaching learning disabled students at the secondary school level.* Reston, VA: The Council for Exceptional Children.

Zigmond, N., Sansone, J., Miller, S. E., Donahoe, K. A., & Kohnke, R. (1986b). Teaching learning disabled students at the secondary school level: What research says to teachers. *Learning Disabilities Focus, 1*, 108–115.

Chapter 5

Assessment for Placement
and Instruction

Did you know that . . .

- The quality of an educational program depends largely on the accuracy of educators' instructional decisions?
- Norm-referenced tests provide little information from which to design, conduct, or evaluate educational interventions?
- Many norm-referenced tests discriminate against minority students?
- Criterion-referenced tests are useful not only for identifying skills that adolescents have acquired, but also for measuring the efficiency and effectiveness of instructional procedures?
- Special behavioral objectives should serve as the basis for constructing criterion-referenced tests?
- Direct-observation procedures must be consistent with the behavioral objective being evaluated?

Can you . . .

- List the steps required to implement instruction for adolescents with disabilities?
- Describe the characteristics of the two general types of assessment procedures?
- Describe the limitations of norm-referenced tests in the assessment of students with disabilities?
- Describe the two principal uses for norm-referenced tests?
- Describe the two principal uses for criterion-referenced tests?
- List the seven steps used to develop criterion-referenced tests?
- Describe the factors that influence the reliability and validity of a test?
- List three criteria for judging the consistency of the observation procedure and behavioral objective?

The direct instructional sequence recommended in Chapter 4 for adolescents who have disabilities depends on the characteristics of the students involved (see Action Plan 5.1). The initial step in the sequence is to identify instructional goals. Norm-referenced and criterion-referenced test data ensure that these goals will be matched to the learning and behavioral characteristics of the student. That is to say, student performance data are used to set the goals.

The second step, which is to establish component objectives, also depends on student characteristics. These characteristics should be assessed by procedures that will ensure that the objectives are attainable by the student within a reasonable period of time. Overly simple objectives will inhibit progress because of the limited expectations held for the learner. Overly ambitious objectives may be equally harmful, for they will expose the student to unattainable demands, and the end result will be frustration and failure.

The third step, designing instruction, relies on student performance data to identify effective, efficient individualized instructional strategies. Test data may indicate variations, with consistently stronger performance under one set of conditions as opposed to others. This information may lead the teacher to use the more effective instructional procedure.

Action Plan 5.1   Assessment Procedures in the Direct-Instruction Model

Identifying instructional goals
   Norm- and criterion-referenced tests are used to match instructional goals to the learning and behavioral characteristics of the student.
Establishing component objectives
   Norm- and criterion-referenced tests are used to determine that objectives can be attained by the student in a reasonable period of time.
Designing instruction
   Criterion-referenced tests are used to identify or refine efficient individualized instructional strategies.
Maintaining accountability during instruction
   Criterion-referenced assessment probes are used during instruction to keep the student accountable for the mastery of information and skills.
Evaluating instruction
   Criterion-referenced assessment data are collected during instruction to ensure that adequate progress will be made toward objectives.
Revising the instructional plan
   Criterion-referenced assessment data are used to alter the instructional plan when satisfactory progress is not noted.
Determining that the goals and objectives have been achieved
   Norm-referenced and criterion-referenced data are used to summarize the student's progress.

During the fourth step, in which instruction is implemented, the teacher is encouraged to maintain student accountability. This procedure ensures that students are benefiting from the instruction that is taking place and that they are being kept alert. Students who expect to be called upon during a lesson are much more likely to pay attention than those who do not expect to be held accountable.

The fifth step, in which instruction is evaluated, relies on assessment data in particular. Formative assessment data, data collected frequently during instruction, should be used to ensure that adequate progress is being made toward the objective. Assessment data may be used to address several questions pertaining to instruction. The most basic question is whether the student is achieving the objective. Another is what specific performance problems are preventing the student from reaching the objective.

Data from each of the preceding steps are used in the sixth step—during which the instructional plan is revised. Evidence that the student is not making adequate progress toward the instructional objective and goal should prompt a review of all assessment data. Specific questions should be raised about all of the preceding steps. Is the goal appropriate for the learner? Are the objectives complete, logically sequenced, and matched to the learner's ability? Are the most efficient and effective educational procedures being used? Are students engaged in planned activities and are they accountable for satisfactory performance during the lesson? Finally, are all aspects of the objective being mastered?

During the final step, the educator tries to determine whether all component objectives and the ultimate goal have been achieved. Assessment data are used to summarize the student's progress over an extended period of instruction. The anticipated outcome is that the student has attained the goal and is ready to progress to a more rigorous goal.

It should be apparent that assessment occupies a central role in the direct-instruction sequence. The quality of an educational program depends largely on the accuracy of educators' instructional decisions. The most effective way to ensure accurate decision making is to base judgments on reliable observations of student performance. The purpose of this chapter is to describe assessment procedures that can serve this function.

Two general types of assessment procedures are discussed. The first, norm-referenced assessment, compares a student's performance on a standardized instrument to the performance of a large group of students. Recent studies have drawn attention to the limitations of norm-referenced tests in the instruction of youths with disabilities. Therefore, norm-referenced testing is only touched on in this chapter. The second, criterion-referenced or performance-based assessment, compares a student's performance to a specific performance standard or objective. This approach has been demonstrated to be highly useful in guiding direct instruction. Therefore, this chapter focuses on the development, application, and interpretation of the instruments used in criterion-referenced assessment.

Norm-Referenced Testing

As already mentioned, norm-referenced tests allow an examiner to compare the performance of an individual to the performance of a group of individuals. The norm-referenced test evaluates interindividual differences, or differences between learners. A norm-referenced achievement test may indicate that a student's mathematics performance is superior to 57% of the students in the standardization sample or reference group. An intelligence test may indicate that a student's IQ is two standard deviations below the mean established by the standardization sample. This also indicates that approximately 2% of the students taking the test obtained IQ scores lower than the given student.

Characteristics

Well-designed norm-referenced tests have several characteristics in common. First, the test procedures are standardized so that there is one and only one way to administer and complete the test. Obviously, valid comparisons could not be made between students if the nature of the evaluation task was different.

Second, test items are designed so that a wide range of scores are obtained from individuals in the standardization sample. A test that produced comparable scores from one individual to the next would not be effective in accentuating individual differences.

Third, a student's performance on a test item is a function of his or her competence relative to the attribute being assessed rather than to other factors. There should be only one legitimate interpretation of a student's final score. This explanation should relate to the student's ability in the area being studied. Alternative explanations (e.g., the student was unable to understand the directions, he or she did not fill in the answer sheet correctly, etc.) should be ruled out by the administration procedure.

Fourth, members of the standardization sample and the individual taking the test have similar characteristics. It is illogical to make comparisons between a student and the standardization sample if differences exist beyond those under study (e.g., dominant language, age, sex, ethnicity, specific disabilities, etc.).

Finally, the results of the test must correspond with other evidence of the student's capability in the area being studied. Low scores on a norm-referenced reading achievement test should correspond with poor performance in daily reading activities. Similarly, high career preference data in manual skills should be supported by evidence that others with similar scores eventually assumed positions in manual trades.

Unfortunately, the same characteristics that make norm-referenced measures appealing in general often detract from their usefulness for people with disabilities. Foremost, while it may be useful to know a student's relative standing in a group, we are often better served by the data referencing a student's abilities to community standards. Norm-referenced math scores, for example, do not indicate the extent to which a student can balance a checkbook, shop at a supermarket, or work as a shipping clerk. Norm-referenced reading scores give no idea of whether a student can use classified ads, participate in table games, or shelve books in a library.

Norm-referenced tests also provide little information that can be used to design, conduct, or evaluate educational interventions. Most of the early research studies that attempted to base instructional decisions on norm-referenced test data produced unimpressive results (Sedlak & Weener, 1973). Because it is important to follow the standard test administration procedures, teachers cannot modify the test to evaluate instructional hypotheses (e.g., Would a student's math performance improve if a horizontal format were used rather than a vertical format? Can a student's difficulties with word problems be explained by reading-comprehension deficits rather than math-skill deficits?). Moreover, if a norm-referenced test were administered several times a year, as would be required to evaluate the effectiveness of instruction, the results would be invalid. One would not know whether the student's performance improved because the items had become familiar or because skills had developed.

As mentioned earlier, the student being tested must be represented in the standardization sample. Unfortunately, many standardized tests fail to include a representative number of individuals who have disabilities or are bilingual or educationally disadvantaged in their standardization sample (McLoughlin & Lewis, 1990). It is therefore inappropriate to use normative data when interpreting their scores.

Still another drawback is that many norm-referenced tests discriminate against minority students (Taylor, 1993). A student's cultural background, rather than learning or behavioral problems, may account for low performance. For example, the American Indian culture values cooperative and careful work while rejecting independent and fast production. Thus students raised in this culture may be at a disadvantage when taking timed tests requiring solitary effort.

Placement and Summative Evaluations

The limitations outlined in the preceding section have led some authors to call for the total abolition of norm-referenced testing (for a comprehensive discussion, see Reynolds & Brown, 1984). In addition, recent litigation (*Larry P. v. Riles*, 1972; *Lora v. Board of Education of City of New York*, 1984; *Matti T. v. Holladay*, 1979) has placed strict controls on the use and reporting of norm-referenced tests. There is a similar impetus for states to draft legislation restricting norm-referenced testing. One example is New York's "truth-in-testing" legislation.

Nonetheless, many authors believe that norm-referenced tests can serve a valuable but limited function in educational programs for adolescents with disabilities (Meehan & Hodell, 1986; Peterson, 1986; Stodden, 1986). In particular, they can be used as tools of placement evaluation and summative evaluation (Taylor, 1993).

Placement Evaluation. Well-developed aptitude tests, achievement tests, intelligence tests, and other norm-referenced tests produce scores that have universal meaning. For example, a report may indicate that a student obtained scores above the mean on all subtests of the Peabody Individual Achievement Test, with the exception of the mathematics subtest, in which he scored significantly below the mean. The same report may reveal that the student's score on the Wechsler Intelligence Scale for Children—Revised (WISC—R; Wechsler, 1974) is within the normal range. Because the PIAT and WISC—R involve standardized application procedures with uniform norms and scoring, the data can be interpreted by any qualified professional across the country.

More important, because the tests compare the student to a group of individuals, the tests, coupled with other information, may provide strong evidence regarding the potential for success when placed with particular students in a given curriculum (McLoughlin & Lewis, 1990). It is important to note that many placement classifications are tied by state law to performance on norm-referenced tests. The learning disabilities classification

Case for Action 5.1

You have been asked by your superintendent to chair a committee on the use of norm-referenced assessment devices in your district. What are the main questions that your committee needs to address? Provide an outline for the final report that your group will submit.

and placement, for example, is tied to performance on intelligence and achievement tests (Mercer, 1991); mental retardation is tied to performance on intelligence tests and adaptive behavior scales (Cartwright, Cartwright, & Ward, 1989); visual impairment is tied to performance on the Snellen chart (Hatfield, 1975).

Summative Evaluation. Norm-referenced tests are also widely used to evaluate the long-term performance of a student (Bloom, Hastings, & Madaus, 1971). To serve this purpose, the test items must be matched to the curriculum content. A geography achievement test that includes items pertaining to all inhabited continents will produce little evidence of student performance in a geography course focusing on North America. Similarly, an adaptive behavior scale that includes social, independent living, vocational, communication, and academic adjustment domains will produce only a vague reflection of gains in a curriculum designed to increase self-control skills.

Similarly, norm-referenced tests used for summative evaluation purposes should be used only to sample skills in a broader curriculum domain. It is not appropriate to identify specific items on a test and provide instruction only on those discrete items. This approach would not provide an accurate reflection of competence in the general subject, but would only reflect one's ability to successfully complete the specific items.

Criterion-Referenced Testing

Criterion-referenced tests provide the type of data needed to reach decisions on most daily instructional questions. They are distinguished from norm-referenced tests in that rather than comparing a student's performance to the performance of a norm group, a student's performance is compared to an objective standard. The standard is typically the short-term objective of a specific lesson or group of lessons. Criterion-referenced tests are used primarily in formative and diagnostic evaluations.

Formative Evaluation

The instruction model described in the previous chapter emphasizes the direct and continuous measurement of progress toward objectives. This evaluation function is referred to as formative evaluation.

Formative data are used to determine the rate at which new skills are presented. The direct-instruction model suggests that the major objective be broken down into logically sequenced subskills. The subskills are presented in order, from the last to the first (backward chaining) or from the first to the last (forward chaining), until all of the subskills are mastered. Formative evaluation during instruction in each subskill indicates whether or not mastery has occurred. Instruction should progress to the next subskill only when mastery is demonstrated. If the student moves too quickly, "holes" are likely to develop in his or her repertoire. These deficiencies will limit the extent to which the objective is achieved. Conversely, if instruction continues on a subskill that has been mastered, less instructional time will be available for subsequent skill development at a more advanced level.

Diagnostic Evaluation

Educators need information not only on whether subskills have been mastered, but also on what specific aspects of a subskill are causing the learner difficulty. A criterion-referenced test may indicate that the student has not mastered multiplication with two-digit multipliers. Diagnostic evaluation may determine that the student has difficulty with replacement, zero as a place holder, specific math facts, and so on. Subsequent instruction addressing the subskill may focus on the specific errors uncovered in the diagnostic evaluation.

Diagnostic evaluation may also indicate what instructional methods are best suited for an individual learner. The teacher may note that the student performs better on criterion-referenced tests that follow instruction with a high ratio of guided-to-independent practice. Similarly, criterion-referenced test data may indicate that morning instruction is more effective than afternoon instruction. This information may lead the teacher to reschedule the day so that essential academic skills can be developed during morning periods.

Action Plan 5.2 outlines the main reasons for engaging in criterion- and norm-referenced testing.

Selection of Criterion-Referenced Instruments

We have defined a criterion-referenced test as any instrument that compares a student's performance to an objective standard. Consequently, criterion-referenced tests may vary greatly in form. For example, a paper-and-pencil test may compare a student's spelling ability with an objective indicating mastery of words commonly found on employment application forms. A task analytic assessment may compare a student's actual performance in wiring an electrical circuit with an objective indicating that each step of the process will be completed without error. Observational assessment may indicate that a student will increase the amount of time spent on academic tasks. Duration data may be used to measure the amount of time a student spends in seatwork. This may be compared with a standard indicating that the learner will be engaged in academic activities for 30 minutes during a 45-minute period.

It has been emphasized that the behavioral objective establishes the standard by which a learner's performance is judged. The objective also provides information that is used to select or design the testing instrument. Any statement regarding a student's

Action Plan 5.2   Uses of Criterion- and Norm-Referenced Tests

We recommend the following uses for each general assessment approach:

Norm-Referenced Tests

Provide information that contributes to placement decisions
Assist in determining a student's current performance level
Determine the long-term progress of a student.

Criterion-Referenced Tests

Select the most efficient and effective instructional procedure for an individual
    student
Provide a formative assessment of progress toward objectives during instruction
Identify specific performance problems during instruction
Maintain student accountability for skill and concept mastery.

---

performance level must be qualified by the conditions under which the measure of performance was obtained. For example, a statement indicating that a student was able to identify five European countries cannot be interpreted unless the testing conditions are known. Did the student fill in the names on an unlabeled map? Did the student match the five names with the five countries? Did the student provide the name of a country on the basis of a description of each country's culture?

As a general rule, objectives indicating that a student will identify, describe, or select can be assessed using paper-and-pencil (or verbal report) measures. Objectives indicating that a student will construct, perform, or demonstrate can be assessed using observational procedures. The manner in which these tests are designed and administered varies greatly.

Developing Paper-and-Pencil Tests

Schloss and Sedlak (1986) have suggested six steps that are used to develop criterion-referenced tests. These steps are included in Action Plan 5.3. They are also described in this section.

Step 1: Develop the Performance Objective

The obvious first step in developing a criterion-referenced test is to establish the standard by which the student's performance will be judged. As indicated in the preceding chapters, the adolescent's multidisciplinary team is responsible for establishing annual goals. We have argued that goal selection must be based on a comprehensive analysis of the learning and behavioral characteristics of the youth. It is also important to take into

Action Plan 5.3

We recommend the following procedure for constructing a criterion-referenced test:

1. Develop the performance objective.
2. Enumerate subskills.
3. Describe the question-and-answer format.
4. Prepare instructions for the test.
5. Prepare test items.
6. Establish scoring procedures.

account future environments in which the learner is expected to participate. In short, goals selected for a youth with disabilities should prepare the individual to participate in future community settings (e.g., work, leisure, social, and independent living).

The objectives are logically sequenced subsets of each goal. The goal "increase participation in community recreational activities" may include the following objectives:

Given a specially designed map and time schedule, Bill will be able to use the bus without error to go to three recreational settings.

Without assistance, Bill will be able to pay for community recreational events without miscalculating the cost or change expected.

Bill will be able to bowl one of three games over 80 points at the public lanes with the assistance of a friend only for scoring and no other assistance for selecting shoes, ball, lane assignment, etc.

Bill will be able to play three video games without assistance to the level of competence that he passes the initial screen.

Bill will be able to perform all tasks necessary without error to use a mechanical batting cage without assistance.

The behavioral objectives include four elements that have considerable bearing on the design of criterion-referenced tests:

1. *The student's name.* The direct-instruction approach emphasized in this text matches instruction to the characteristics and needs of individual learners. Including the student's name in the behavioral objective serves notice that instruction is designed for the individual adolescent.

2. *The actual skill or skills to be demonstrated by the student.* The target response portion of the objective indicates the response features to be included in the criterion-referenced test. An objective may indicate that Eddie will be able to state in writing the consequences that result from drinking and driving. To be consistent, the criterion-referenced test must provide an opportunity for Eddie to write down the consequences associated with drinking and driving. Similarly, an objective may state that Eddie will be

able to select the fastening device most frequently used in home construction. The word "select" indicates that Eddie must be provided the opportunity to choose the correct response from a set of options.

3. *The conditions under which the student is expected to demonstrate the target skills.* The condition statement indicates the context in which performance is expected to occur. An objective may indicate that Philip will write the correct answer to all one-digit math facts. The condition statement may include phrases such as "given an untimed math facts worksheet," or "given three seconds to respond verbally to math facts flash cards." Another objective may be that Philip will be able to plan menus for a week. The condition statement may be, "given a set of foods representing each of the basic food groups."

4. *The performance criteria.* This element of the behavioral objective sets the actual performance standard expected, given the preceding response and condition statement. The criteria may indicate quantitative aspects of the youth's performance such as, "Richard will accurately complete 8 of 10 math facts." It may also indicate qualitative aspects of performance such as, "sufficiently loud to be heard at a distance of 20 feet." It should be clear that changes in any of the components of the objective may substantially alter what is expected of the student. For this reason, careful attention must be given to defining specifications for all aspects of the objective.

Step 2: Enumerate Subskills

Just as performance objectives constitute the annual goal, subskills are logically sequenced subsets of the performance objective. Performance objectives are typically too broad to produce useful formative and diagnostic data. Knowing that Bill was unable to use the bus to go to three recreational settings provides little information that is of direct instructional value. It would be important to have additional information. To what settings, if any, was he able to go? What common mistakes did he make on the way to each setting? Was he early or late for the bus? Was he able to locate the initial and terminal bus stops? Was he able to signal the bus driver to stop? Did he use the appropriate change?

To provide a more refined analysis of the student's performance, the initial objective is broken down into its component subskills. The criterion-referenced test then indicates a student's competence in each of the subskills. For example, one objective may be that Wanda will be able to prepare a personal résumé. The subskills for résumé preparation include the ability to report personal information, educational history, employment history, and employment objectives. Test data may reveal adequate performance in each of the subskills except for reporting employment objectives. Of course, this information is far more useful than simply knowing that Wanda has failed to meet the criteria expected for preparing a résumé.

Step 3: Describe the Question-and-Answer Format

The teacher should produce a blueprint for the test before actually preparing items for it. This blueprint should follow the question-and-answer format for the test. Careful attention must be given to matching the question-and-answer format with the initial objective and subskills to ensure that the assessment results are valid.

Question formats can include the following measures:

- *Construct* objects to demonstrate important aspects of the instructions or questions. An objective that includes the condition "given a demonstration of mouth-to-mouth resuscitation" should be tested with items that include the construct dimension.
- *Present* a fixed visual display of instructions or questions. An objective that includes the condition "given a picture of a deciduous forest" should be tested with items that include the present dimension.
- *Put* questions or instructions in written or spoken language. An objective that includes the condition "given written questions" should be tested with items that include the stated dimension.
- *Graphically symbolize* questions or instructions. An objective that includes the condition "given a topographical map of the region" should be tested with items that include the graphically symbolized dimension.

Step 4: Prepare Instructions for the Test

The test should include clear and complete instructions, which should be detailed enough to ensure that there is only one explanation for poor performance. The explanation should be that the learner does not possess the required skills, not that he or she did not understand the directions. One additional safeguard is to provide completed and incomplete sample problems. The completed sample problems model the response format to the student. The incomplete sample problems provide the learner with an opportunity to demonstrate his or her understanding of the directions before beginning the actual test. These problems should have obvious answers, so that the difficulties in understanding directions can be distinguished from skill deficits.

Step 5: Prepare Test Items

As is indicated above, test items are developed directly on the preceding steps. The objective and subskills are used to determine the scope of the test. The test question format indicates the nature of each item. The answer format also indicates the nature of the response expected from the student. If these considerations are addressed in item development, the test results will be valid. *Validity* is the extent to which the test measures what it is intended to measure. Items that are well matched to all aspects of the performance objective are likely to produce accurate (valid) information regarding an individual's performance toward the objective.

One additional element that influences the validity of a criterion-referenced test is the reliability of the measurement. *Reliability* is the extent to which a test item produces consistent results over time. It is also the extent to which items on the test that measure the same skill produce comparable results. A test is said to have high reliability if it produces the same results each time it is administered (given that no actual change in learner competence has occurred). Of course, a test that produces inconsistent results will be ineffective in measuring what it was intended to measure. Consequently, reliability is a prerequisite to validity.

Aside from consistency between the test questions or responses and the elements of the performance objective, five additional factors influence the reliability and validity of a test. First, *the test should evaluate a sufficiently small number of subskills so that the learner's performance can be easily interpreted.* At the very most, a test should evaluate performance on all of the subskills that make up one objective. Depending on the breadth of the objective, only a subset of the subskills may be evaluated on one test.

Second, *the test should provide the learner with multiple opportunities to demonstrate his or her competence in each subskill.* The more opportunities that a student has to perform a subskill, the more reliable the measurement will be. Most sports competitions are judged on the basis of numerous opportunities for the athletes to demonstrate their skills. For example, baseball teams may play 9 innings, golfers may play 18 holes, and tennis players may go through 5 sets. If only one inning in baseball, one hole in golf, or one set in tennis were played, the actual outcome might be influenced by a range of extraneous factors other than the players' actual skills. These might include gusts of wind, tension, familiarity with the course or stadium, and the like. By providing multiple opportunities to perform, these factors are minimized.

Third, *test questions should be clear and unambiguous.* Vague questions or questions with incomplete qualifying information may fail to reveal conceptual or skill deficits. Negative statements and "all or none of the above" answers in multiple-choice questions should be avoided because they are often misconstrued for reasons other than conceptual deficits. Similarly, true or false questions should call on the student to judge the accuracy of only one concept at a time. Again, our goal is to obtain information on the student's level of mastery. Our goal is not to determine the extent to which a student can interpret poorly worded test items.

Fourth, *the vocabulary and syntax of test questions should be matched to the adolescent's language ability.* For example, a building trades examination may be designed to measure competence in the principles of home construction. If the student fails to comprehend the test questions, his or her score may suffer. The resulting score may be a more accurate reflection of language ability than skill in the building trades.

Finally, *test items should not include embedded clues.* These clues may allow sophisticated test takers to do well on the item even though they do not understand the concept. As emphasized previously, the item should test a student's knowledge of the concept and not his or her ability to take tests.

Step 6: Establish Scoring Procedures

Recording and scoring procedures should do more than indicate that the youth has mastered the overall objective. As emphasized previously, data obtained from the test should aid in the identification of specific errors. These errors may then become the focus of future instruction.

Preliminary planning of the criterion-referenced test can help to reduce the time and effort spent in analyzing errors. One of the first steps in constructing a test is to delineate the subskills that form the objective. A subsequent procedure is to develop 5 to 20 test

Case for Action 5.2

You are teaching a modern history unit on the presidents of the past three decades. Identify the goal of your unit. Identify six component objectives. Prepare five test items that assess each of the component objectives. Develop a diagnostic scoring procedure to use with your test. What instructional decisions can be made from your test data?

items that correspond with the subskills. Students are likely to perform well on most items that represent mastered subskills. They are likely to perform poorly on most items that represent deficiency subskills. The initial step in error analysis, then, is to record the rate of errors within each subskill. A subsequent step is to study each subskill error to obtain further information on the error patterns that may influence instruction.

Criterion-referenced paper-and-pencil tests are used for diagnostic and formative assessment purposes. That is, they can be used to identify skills that adolescents have acquired, the efficiency with which the skills were mastered, instructional procedures that were most effective in promoting the skills, specific impediments to skill development, and the speed with which new skills can be introduced. The effectiveness with which a teacher uses criterion-referenced measures can be judged using the criteria presented in Action Plan 5.4.

In the next section we turn to systematic observation, another criterion-referenced measurement strategy. This approach is appropriate for evaluating progress toward objectives indicating that a student will construct, perform, or demonstrate specific skills.

Observation Procedures

A number of methods for monitoring overt behavior of adolescents have been described in the literature. These strategies have three elements in common. First, the monitoring

Action Plan 5.4   Criteria for Evaluating a Criterion-Referenced Test

The following criteria are recommended for evaluating the reliability, validity, and usability of a criterion-referenced test:

1. Did a behavioral objective serve as the basis for the construction of the criterion-referenced test?
2. Were the subskills that make up the objective identified?
3. Were 5 to 20 items used to evaluate mastery of each subskill?
4. Were the test items matched to the condition statement, the target behavior, and performance criteria of the initial objective?
5. Did the recording and scoring procedure allow the teacher to identify specific subskill deficiencies?

procedures must be objective. The feelings of the observer or other factors must not influence data that result from the observation. Second, observations must result in valid statements about the learner's performance. That is, the teacher must provide a direct report of performance without unsupported inferences about motive or internal causation. Finally, monitoring procedures must be reliable. A reliable monitoring system produces the same results, regardless of who makes the observations.

Selection of Monitoring Procedures

Like paper-and-pencil measures, direct observation procedures must be consistent with the behavioral objective being evaluated. The consistency of the observation procedure and behavioral objective is bridged using three criteria. First, *the setting and conditions under which the observations are conducted must match the condition statement of the behavioral objective.* The condition statement indicates the situation in which the target behavior is expected to occur (or not occur). To be consistent, the observation must be conducted under the same conditions that are specified in the objective. If an objective indicates that the student will identify the shortest route from New York City to Los Angeles using a road atlas, pencil, paper, and ruler, observations must be conducted while the learner is using these instruments. If an objective indicates a youth will rebuild a two-cycle engine using a repair manual, mechanic's tool set, and working model, these same elements should be available during observation.

The second principle for ensuring consistency is that *the target behavior statement of the objective should correspond with the precise behavior being observed.* An objective indicating that a youth will remain in his seat for a 40-minute period must correspond with observation of the time spent in seat. An objective indicating that the youth will be punctual for class each morning must be measured through observations of the time the student arrives at class each day.

The third principle is that *the level of performance expected following intervention corresponds with the measure of behavior strength used in the observation procedure.* An objective that indicates the learner will increase the time on task by 50% must involve the use of rate data. An objective that indicates a youth will reduce the number of verbal attacks must involve the use of a frequency measure. The final sections of this chapter review five observational measures that correspond to most criterion statements: (1) frequency and rate, (2) permanent product, (3) task analysis, (4) duration and latency, and (5) interval. Before discussing observation methods, we should review the procedures for defining the behaviors being observed.

Observation Methods

Frequency recording requires the least amount of time and is often the most useful of the observation methods. The frequency of a student's behavior is established by tallying each occurrence of the target behavior over a specified period of time. Frequency recording is appropriate when several conditions are met.

First, the response must have a distinct start time and stop time. If the onset and termination of the response are unclear, the recorder may not be able to distinguish between an episode and a series of episodes. For example, it may not be clear whether a student was unhappy for one period lasting over an hour or was unhappy a number of times within the hour.

Second, the response must have a relatively consistent duration. A behavior that lasts from one second to over an hour (e.g., walking, crying, or writing) cannot be measured accurately with frequency recording. One walking tally may not be comparable to another because the actual time spent walking was substantially different.

Third, the time during which observations occurred must be consistent. A youth may be observed for three class periods one day and only one class period the next. Frequency data may indicate that the youth was aggressive three times each day. Because he was observed for different periods of time, it would be misleading to indicate that he was equally aggressive on the two days.

To take into account varying observation periods, frequency counts may be converted to rate data. This is accomplished by dividing the frequency tally by the amount of time in which the individual was observed. For example, if William wrote 12 sentences in a period of 30 minutes, the rate of sentence writing would be computed by dividing the frequency of occurrences (12) by the amount of time observed (30). The resulting rate would be four-tenths of a sentence per minute, or 24 sentences per hour. Figure 5.1 shows a standard form for collecting frequency and rate data.

Permanent product recording means evaluating the tangible result of a student's behavior. Permanent product recording may be appropriate for monitoring homework completion, property damage resulting from aggression, or production units assembled. Permanent product recording is very similar to frequency and rate recording, except that the observer tallies products of the behavior rather than the actual behavior.

As with frequency data, several conditions must apply if the recording method is to produce accurate information. First, the task or setting demands must be relatively constant from one observation to the next. For example, data on the number of assignments completed accurately are useful if the assignments are equally difficult. Second, the amount of time during which the permanent products are created must be constant. If this condition is not met, permanent product data can be transformed to "products over time." Finally, the standards for judging whether the product was completed must be clear and complete. Writing assignments, for example, may be considered completed only if certain standards are achieved. These may include the quality of penmanship, spelling, sentence structure, and so on.

Task-analytic measurement is a natural adjunct to task-analytic instruction. Earlier in this book, we described task analysis as a strategy for dividing complex behaviors into their component parts. Once the first skill is mastered by the student, the second skill is introduced. Once the youth masters the second skill, the third skill is taught. This process continues until all skills making up the complex behavior are mastered.

To be effective, task-analytic instruction must be linked to the teacher's ability to recognize when the youth has mastered a given skill. If the teacher moves to the next skill too quickly, the learner may become frustrated, or "gaps" in learning may develop and

Adolescent _____   Instructor _____

Setting(s) _____

_____

Response and definition _____

_____

_____

DATE	FREQUENCY	PERIOD OBSERVED			RATE
		Beginning	*End*	*Total*	

FIGURE 5.1   Standard Form for Recording Frequency and Rate Data

the complex skill may not be adequately mastered. Moving too slowly wastes instructional time and increases the chances that the student will become bored and lose motivation. Task-analytic assessment ensures that new skills will be introduced only when the preceding skill is mastered.

Figure 5.2 illustrates a sample task-analytic recording sheet. The short-term objective is written on the top of the sheet. This is the complex behavior that the student is expected to master following instruction. The component skills are listed from the first

Adolescent _____   Date _____

Instructor _____

Objective _____

_____

_____

Prompts: self-initiated; *verbal; model; physical*
or
Quality: excellent; good; *poor*

TASK	TRIAL									
	1	*2*	*3*	*4*	*5*	*6*	*7*	*8*	*9*	*10*
1										
2										
3										
4										
5										
6										
7										
8										
9										
10										

FIGURE 5.2   Standard Form for Recording Task Analytic Data

to the last down the left side of the sheet. These skills must be stated in behavioral terms so that there can be full agreement on the quality of their performance. Spaces are provided on the right side of the sheet for recording the level of performance on each component skill during each trial.

Note that task-analytic assessment is a dynamic process. Data collected during one lesson should reflect several opportunities to perform the skill. Demonstrating the number of component skills that are mastered over a number of trials may be as important as demonstrating the level of performance upon completion.

Each component skill may be scored in several different ways. The simplest approach is to record that the student did or did not perform the skill at an acceptable level. A more elaborate and useful approach is to record the level of prompt required for the student to perform the subskill. Recording prompt levels allows the teacher to monitor his or her level of involvement with the learner. Ideally, the teacher should see a reduction in assistance (e.g., from frequent manual guidance or verbal instruction to frequent independent performance) as the students become more competent.

Data obtained through task-analytic recording are typically summarized by reporting the number of component skills performed independently on the final trial of instruction. Unfortunately, this summary approach eliminates much of the useful data. The teacher should preserve the entire record of task-analytic assessment so that the following information can be used: (a) level of performance in each component skill; (b) level of prompt required for skills that are not performed independently; and (c) the number of trials required to develop each component skill.

Duration and latency measurement is useful for determining the amount of time a youth spends in an activity. It is also useful for determining the amount of time that elapses between an event and the initiation of a response. A teacher may use duration recording to determine the amount of time that a student spends cleaning the shop. Duration recording may also be used to monitor the amount of time spent practicing specific skills. Latency recording may be used to determine the amount of time that a student is tardy. It can also be used to determine the amount of time required for a student to comply with specific instructions.

Duration and latency recording are appropriate when several conditions are met. First, as in frequency recording, the response must have a distinct start time and stop time. If the start and stop times are not clear, the recorder will not know when to begin or stop timing. Second, the overall period of time during which observations occurred must be consistent. A student may appear to have been more productive on one certain day. However, in fact, he or she may have simply had more time to work during the first day. As with other recording methods, varying times available for observation can be accounted for by computing a rate. That is, the number of minutes that the student was observed engaging in the behavior is divided by the amount of time available.

Duration and latency data may be difficult to collect in most instructional situations. Not only must the teacher watch the student to determine the start and stop time for responses, he or she must also keep an eye on a clock or stopwatch. It would be very difficult for the teacher to do this while conducting a lesson. Consequently, many teachers select other measures of behavior that can be used more efficiently.

Figure 5.3 illustrates a form that can be used to collect duration data. The teacher records the day of the observations in the left column, and then records the times that the behavior begins and ends next to the day. The duration for each episode is added for the day and entered in the far right column. This form may be altered to collect latency data by changing the center columns to read "time of cue" and "time of student response." The far right column would be changed to read "latency from cue to response."

Interval measurement avoids many of the special conditions required for frequency, latency, and duration measurement. Responses measured with interval recording need not have a discrete start and stop time. In addition, interval recording standardizes the amount of time available for observation. Interval data accurately reflect the strength of behaviors that are of variable duration. Interval data are obtained by sampling a student's behavior within a portion of the school day. Behavior that occurs in a seven-hour day may be observed during three 10-minute intervals. These 10-minute periods may be divided

Adolescent _____   Instructor _____

Setting(s) _____

_____

Response and definition _____

_____

_____

DATE	TIME		DURATION/LATENCY
	Begin	*End*	

FIGURE 5.3   Standard Form for Recording Duration or Latency Data

into twenty 30-second intervals. A response is scored as occurring or not occurring throughout each interval. The resulting measure is the percentage of intervals that contained the uninterrupted occurrence of the target behavior.

Interval data can be collected using three types of procedures. The first, *whole-interval*, requires the behavior to occur throughout the interval (e.g., 30 seconds of writing during a 30-second period). The second, *partial-interval*, requires the behavior to occur any time during the interval (e.g., an amount of writing during the 30-second period). The third, *momentary-interval recording*, requires the behavior to occur at the precise time the interval begins or ends (e.g., writing during the start of the interval).

Figure 5.4 depicts a form that may be used to collect interval data. The teacher marks a + or – to signify that the behavior occurred or failed to occur during the interval (partial interval), throughout the entire interval (whole interval), or at the start of the interval (momentary interval). Data are translated to the percentage of intervals in which the behavior occurred by dividing the number of occurrences by the number of intervals.

Interobserver Agreement

The preceding methods of observation are useful only to the extent that they produce accurate reflections of the learner's actual behavior. Interobserver agreement is usually the preferred method for determining the accuracy of observational data. Interobserver agreement is the extent to which two independent observers agree or disagree that the responses occurred. The procedure for determining the level of agreement differs for each of the observation methods.

Frequency and rate reliability are judged by two individuals observing a student over the same period of time. The lowest tally reported by the two observers is divided by the highest to produce the reliability coefficient.

Permanent product reliability is judged by two individuals independently judging the same products. The smaller score is divided by the larger score to produce the reliability coefficient.

Task-analytic reliability is computed by two independent observers monitoring a student's performance through a number of trials in each of the subskills. The level of agreement for each subskill is the number of trials in which the observers agreed divided by the total number observed. The overall reliability of the task-analytic assessment is determined by computing the number of trials in which the two observers agreed by the number that they disagreed for all component skills.

Duration and latency reliability is determined by dividing the shorter time by the longer time reported by the independent observers.

Interval reliability is established by dividing the number of intervals in which both observers agreed on the occurrence or nonoccurrence of the behavior by the total number of intervals observed. Intervals in which both observers scored a nonoccurrence may be excluded from the analysis to produce a more conservative measure.

A reliability check should be conducted before initiating a formal baseline. Reliability should also be evaluated periodically throughout baseline and each intervention phase. Fewer reliability checks may be made when high reliability levels are obtained (e.g., 0.95 to 1.0). Low but adequate reliability levels (e.g., 0.75 to 0.80) should signal the need for more frequent checks.

The criteria for adequate reliability levels are based on target behavior, the observation method, and the purpose for which data are being collected. Affective behaviors may necessarily yield lower reliability levels. Conversely, permanent product data should yield high levels of reliability. Reliability of data gathered by independent observers who do not have instructional responsibilities should be higher than data collected by indi-

Adolescent _____ Instructor _____

Setting(s) _____

_____

Response and definition _____

_____

_____

Interval length _____

+ = occurrence
− = nonoccurrence

DATE	TIME	1	2	3	4	5	6	7	8	9	10	% SCORED +

FIGURE 5.4   Standard Form for Recording Interval Data

viduals implementing instructions. Finally, data used for minor instructional/behavior management decisions may be less reliable than data used for placement decisions. In general, reliability levels exceeding 0. 75 can be considered to be acceptable for most instructional purposes.

When it is necessary to obtain higher reliability coefficients, the teacher should consider the following: Is the target behavior clearly and completely defined? Is the definition unambiguous? Are the observers well trained? Do they understand the definition and use the observation method accurately? Would another observation method produce more reliable data?

Graphing Observational Data

Data obtained on recording sheets are transferred to a line graph so that comparisons may be made over a period of time. As demonstrated in Figure 5.5 and summarized in Action Plan 5.5, there are five major conventions for graphing observational data. First, the horizontal axis should record the period of each observation. This may be in days, weeks, sessions, periods, and so on. Second, the vertical axis indicates the measure of behavior strength. This may include frequency, rate, and permanent product. Third, vertical lines in the graph represent the onset of intervention or changes in the program. These lines should be accompanied by a brief description of the program change (e.g., addition of a response cost, use of an extraordinary aide, etc.). Fourth, solid points are used to denote

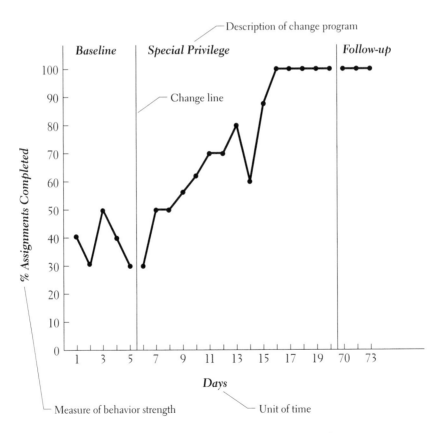

FIGURE 5.5   Sample Graph Illustrating Conventions for Reporting Observational Data

Action Plan 5.5   Major Conventions for Graphing Observational Data

The following elements are usually included in graphic reports of observational data:

A horizontal axis reports the period of each observation.

A vertical axis indicates the measure of behavior strength.

Vertical lines in the graph represent the onset of intervention or changes in the program.

Solid points are used to denote behavior strength in each observation.

Solid lines join individual observations, except when separated by missing observations or phase changes.

Missing observations are denoted by connecting points on either side of the missing observation with a broken line.

the level of behavioral strength in each observation. These points are joined by a solid line, except when separated by missing observations or phase changes. Finally, missing observations are denoted by connecting available points on either side of the missing observation with a broken line.

Interpreting Graphs

Four principal criteria are used to analyze observational data: mean, level, latency, and trend (Kazdin, 1982). Although we discuss these criteria separately, it is important to recognize that they are best used in combination when judging the effectiveness of an intervention.

Mean.   This is the average measure of behavior during a baseline or program phase. The mean is determined by adding the measures of behavior strength for each of the sessions in the baseline or intervention period. This sum is then divided by the number of measures added together.

Demonstrating a mean increase from 15 words written per minute for the baseline to 28 for intervention suggests that the instructional procedure was effective. Similarly, demonstrating a mean decrease from 12 aggressive acts per week when planned ignoring was used to 3 aggressive acts per week when a response cost was used suggests the effectiveness of the response cost over planned ignoring.

Level.   Next to mean, level may be the most frequently used criterion for evaluating program effectiveness. Level is determined by comparing measures of behavior strength for observations immediately before and after the phase change. Level differs from mean in that mean uses all of the data in the phase whereas level uses only the data points near or adjacent to phase changes.

Case for Action 5.3

You have collected observational data that indicate a substantial improvement in the social behavior displayed by one of your students while in a work placement. Some of your colleagues question whether so much attention should be placed on his interpersonal skills. How can you use social validation techniques to support your focus on social skills?

The level may shift from 4 and 5 assignments completed before using a token economy to 8 and 12 assignments completed immediately after using the token economy. This suggests that the token economy had an immediate and direct effect on assignment completion.

Trend.   This criterion indicates the extent to which the behavior was improving, stable, or deteriorating before and after intervention. One would expect the behavior to be stable or deteriorating during baseline. One would also expect the behavior to improve following intervention. The more drastic the change in slope from baseline to intervention, the more effective the educational or behavior management procedure.

Suppose, for example, that during a typical class period a teacher observes a youth respond when called upon from 0 to 10% of the time. This level remains constant over a period of weeks. One week after counseling begins, the rate moves to 20%. As the youth gains increased insight into the importance of the class, his performance increases to 40%, 60%, and eventually 100%. This performance pattern suggests that counseling has gradually modified the student's response.

Latency.   This is the period of time between the start of intervention and the time that the adolescent's behavior begins to change. Direct and intrusive procedures such as punishment, physical management, and some reinforcement procedures result in little or no latency. When told that a youth will be fined $20 for parking his car illegally, the youth may immediately discontinue this activity. Less direct and intrusive procedures such as counseling and instruction may produce a longer latency period. For example, progressive muscle relaxation may have actually begun a month before one actually sees an improvement in the youth's ability to remain calm during the testing situation.

Summary

Assessment data are used to establish placements, diagnose instructional difficulties, monitor the short-term effectiveness of instruction, and establish the long-term effectiveness of instruction.

There are two main types of assessment. One is norm-referenced assessment, which is an evaluation procedure that compares an individual's performance on a standardized instrument with the performance of a group of individuals. Norm-referenced assessment is considered to be most appropriate for supporting placement decisions and for determining the long-term effectiveness of instruction. The other is criterion-referenced assessment, which includes both paper-and-pencil and observational measures; it compares an individual's performance with an objective standard. Criterion-referenced measures are most appropriate for conducting diagnostic evaluations and establishing the short-term effectiveness of instruction.

Criterion-referenced measures are used in many direct instructional activities. There are two main types of criterion-referenced procedures: paper-and-pencil measures and observational techniques.

In conclusion, all aspects of educational service for adolescents with disabilities depend on the careful analysis of learner characteristics. Placement decisions, specific goals and objectives, the instructional procedures, and the method used to determine the effectiveness of instruction hinge on the secondary educator's ability to evaluate youth.

References

Cartwright, G. P., Cartwright, C. A., & Ward, M. E. (1989). *Educating special learners* (3rd ed.). Belmont, CA: Wadsworth.

Hatfield, E. M. (1975). Why are they blind? *Sight Saving Review*, 45(1), 3–22.

Kazdin, A. E. (1982). *Single-case research designs: Methods for clinical and applied settings.* New York: Oxford University Press.

Larry P. v. Riles, 343 F Supp. 1306 (N.D. Cal. 1972), 502 F. 2d 963 (9th Cir. 1974), 495 F. Supp. 926 (N. D. Cal. 1979), aff'd. 9th Cir., Jan. 2 3 (EHLR 555: 304, Feb. 3, 1984).

Lora v. Board of Education of City of New York, 456 F. Supp. 1211 (E.D. N.Y. 1978), 623 F. 2d. 248 (2d Cir. 1980), 587 F. Supp. 1572 (E.D. N.Y. 1984).

McLoughlin, J. A., & Lewis, R. B. (1990). *Assessing special students* (3rd ed.). New York: Macmillan.

Mattie T. v. Holladay, No. DC-75-31 (N.D. Miss. Jan. 26, 1979) (EHLR 551-109, Apr. 1, 1979).

Meehan, K. A., & Hodell, S. (1986). Measuring the impact of vocational assessment activities upon program decisions. *Career Development for Exceptional Individuals*, 9, 106–112.

Mercer, C. D. (1991). *Students with learning disabilities* (3rd ed.). New York: Macmillan.

Peterson, M. (1986). Work and performance samples for vocational assessment of special students: A critical review. *Career Development for Exceptional Individuals*, 9, 69–76.

Reynolds, C. R., & Brown, R. T. (1984). *Perspectives on bias in mental testing.* New York: John Wiley & Sons.

Schloss, P. J., & Sedlak, R. A. (1986). *Instructional methods for students with learning and behavioral problems.* Boston: Allyn and Bacon.

Sedlak, R. A., & Weener, P. (1973). Review of research on the Illinois Test of Psycholinguistic Abilities. In L. Mann & D. A. Sabatino (Eds.), *The first review of special education.* Philadelphia: Journal of Special Education Press.

Stodden, R. A. (1986). Vocational assessment: An introduction. *Career Development for Exceptional Individuals*, 9, 67–68.

Taylor, R. L. (1993). *Assessment of exceptional students: Educational and psychological procedures* (3rd ed.). Boston: Allyn and Bacon.

Wechsler, D. (1974). *Manual for Wechsler Intelligence Scale for Children—Revised.* New York: Psychological Corporation.

Chapter 6

Managing the Learning Environment

Did you know that . . .

- Student learning is maximized by an effective classroom management system?
- PL 94–142 increased the production of materials for students with special needs?
- Only a few publishing companies sell materials suitable for secondary students with disabilities?
- There are three alternatives to purchasing instructional material?
- Arrangement of the classroom can influence student behavior?
- The school day is generally broken into four categories of time?
- Antecedents precede a behavior and influence the probability of future occurrences?
- Consequences can be arranged on a continuum that reflects their intrusiveness?
- Token reinforcers are more appropriate for secondary learners with more severe disabilities?
- Punishment techniques should never be used in isolation?
- There are different forms of time-out?
- Students with disabilities cannot be suspended or expelled for demonstrating behaviors related to their disabilities?
- There are few data documenting the effectiveness of suspension and expulsion, despite the fact that these techniques are used frequently?
- In-school suspension was developed to circumvent the problems associated with out-of-school suspension?

Can you . . .

- Identify the steps required to obtain and validate new materials?
- Modify a complicated set of directions for secondary learners with special needs?
- Explain the importance of a seating chart?

- Identify basic equipment for the secondary classroom?
- Explain the importance of minimizing transition time?
- Describe how to minimize transition time?
- Describe how to maximize engaged time during teacher-directed and guided practice activities?
- Explain why some antecedent control techniques must be faded?
- Set up rules for a secondary special education classroom?
- Devise a schedule for secondary students with special needs?
- Develop a systematic desensitization hierarchy?
- Arrange consequent techniques on a continuum?
- Deliver appropriate reprimands?
- Distinguish between detention and in-school suspension?
- Identify inappropriate behaviors that warrant detention, in-school suspension, out-of-school suspension, and expulsion?
- Identify the disadvantages associated with suspension and expulsion?
- Develop a self-management program?

The learning environment must be managed effectively if the teaching process is to meet its objectives. The practitioner can invest precious time and effort assessing student characteristics. He or she can plan interesting lessons to demonstrate new concepts and provide students with creative practice activities. Yet, for reasons unrelated to the lesson itself, students may fail to master the targeted skill or they may not learn at the anticipated rate. These outcomes indicate that other factors must be addressed before, during, and after the lesson. When these factors are taken into account, less time is spent on activities not directly related to the learning process. Ultimately, teacher efficiency is maximized and student learning is enhanced. This chapter presents techniques that contribute to effective management of the secondary classroom environment.

Time Management

Classroom management techniques cannot be discussed without some explanation of how teachers use the time available to them during the school day. In general, time can be assigned to one of four categories: allocated time, engaged time, academic learning time, and transition time. The amount of time spent in these categories influences student achievement. The classroom management techniques presented later in the chapter can help practitioners use time that contributes to achievement more efficiently and minimize time spent performing tasks not related to achievement.

Allocated Time

Learning will not occur if sufficient time is not allocated to instruction (Graham, 1985). Allocated time refers to periods during the school day in which specific activities are scheduled. Each period reflects the maximum amount of time for which students will be receiving instruction in a subject area. Unlike their colleagues at the elementary school level, secondary educators may have little or no flexibility in scheduling the length of instructional periods as these may be dictated by administrative concerns. Practitioners may simply be told that they will have eight 40-minute instructional periods each day, for a total of 40 per week. Similarly, state regulations may dictate that minimum amounts of time are to be devoted to instruction in specific areas such as health or physical education. It is the practitioner's responsibility to ensure that the time allocated to instruction at the secondary level reflect state requirements and goal areas included on students' IEPs.

Secondary educators can allocate time within an instructional period. As discussed in Chapter 4, instruction consists of four stages: the presentation of new information, guided practice, independent practice, and review/reteach. Practitioners may use the students' characteristics to develop and implement lesson plans that allocate time to more than one of these phases during the same instructional period. Conversely, depending on the students' skill levels, a secondary educator may elect to devote an entire lesson to just one of these phases.

Engaged Time

The rate at which students acquire knowledge and skills depends on how effectively their teachers use the time that has been allocated to instructional areas. Time in which students are allowed to daydream, repeat errors, or interact with inappropriate materials does not contribute to their academic success (Graham, 1985). Engaged time refers to the time students are on task, performing the work that has been assigned to them. Bettencourt, Gillet, Gall, and Hull (1983) and Wilson and Wesson (1986) identified the teacher behaviors that maximize students' engaged time during teacher-directed and guided practice activities. During teacher-directed activities, practitioners can select and prepare materials and instructional techniques in advance of the lesson. They can reduce seatwork by increasing the number of teacher-led groups. Instructions can be delivered

---

Action Plan 6.1   Effective Use of Time during Teacher-Directed Activities

The following behaviors can increase engaged time during teacher-directed activities:

1. Be prepared. Have instructional materials and techniques planned in advance.
2. Create more teacher-led groups.
3. Increase the amount of demonstration, feedback, and review.
4. Reduce the number of seatwork activities. Make sure that the activities assigned are relevant.
5. Use more teacher questions.
6. Increase teacher enthusiasm through varied vocal delivery, frequent demonstrative gestures, facial expression, and acceptance of students' ideas and feelings.

Action Plan 6.2   Effective Use of Time during Guided Practice

Teachers can maximize students' engaged time during guided practice activities by following these practices:

1. Use novel activities that motivate the students.
2. Give precise instructions for completing the task.
3. Reward correct responses with praise and other forms of reinforcement.
4. Monitor the time required to answer students' questions or explain errors. If it takes more than 30 seconds, the activity may be too difficult.
5. Organize practice activities so that students who finish earlier than anticipated know they should engage in another activity such as silent reading, peer tutoring, or computerized instruction.

by means of questions and appropriate gestures and expressions. During guided practice activities, teachers can provide specific instructions for completing interesting and challenging activities. They can also monitor student performance to ensure that students are not practicing errors. These and other suggestions are included in Action Plans 6.1 and 6.2.

Academic Learning Time

Students in classrooms can often be found completing a worksheet or writing answers to questions in a chapter review; however, their work is likely to contain several errors. Practitioners need to avoid this scenario by presenting instructional activities that challenge students without frustrating them. Academic learning time refers to the time in which students are engaged in an instructional activity and are experiencing a high rate of success. Teachers can increase academic learning time by presenting information in small steps, giving frequent feedback, and providing practice on materials that will be used on a test.

Transition Time

Transition time includes the time in which secondary practitioners and students prepare for an assignment, straighten up after a lesson, and change classes (Zigmond, Sansone, Miller, Donahoe, & Kohnke, 1986b). Additional time may be spent locating materials and supplies and performing classroom routines. Practitioners should reduce the amount of time spent making transitions because it does not contribute to students' academic success. Schloss and Sedlak (1986) and Wilson and Wesson (1986) have suggested a number of techniques for reducing transition time (see Action Plan 6.3), such as establishing student schedules and classroom routines, developing an appropriate floor plan, and using discrete cues to signal the beginning and end of an activity.

Action Plan 6.3   Techniques for Reducing Transition Time

Practitioners can control the amount of time lost to transition by doing the following:

1. Prepare folders of additional activities related to each subject area for use when students complete an assignment earlier than anticipated.
2. Develop and teach routine classroom procedures for getting assistance, obtaining a hall pass, distributing materials, and so on.
3. Cue the beginning and end of an activity.
4. Develop student schedules.
5. Develop a floor plan that facilitates passage from one area of the room to another.
6. Shorten free time.

Case for Action 6.1

You notice that the students in your secondary class are noisy and late coming to your class. They frequently forget items and return to their lockers, disrupting your lesson with questions about the location of their materials. What can you do to improve the situation?

Components of Effective Management

Although students are the focal point for most classroom activities, it is the teacher who serves as the executive director (Graham, 1985). The practitioner is responsible for the selection, arrangement, and implementation of materials and strategies that enable students to acquire knowledge and improve their skills. Attention should be given to the following areas: classroom organization, antecedent control, related personal characteristics, and consequence control.

Classroom Organization

Classroom organization refers to the way in which the physical environment is managed. Practitioners and students will benefit if the classroom is organized so that appropriate instructional materials are readily available, there is enough space to work in, and routine procedures for using materials and moving from one place to the next are clearly delineated.

Instructional Materials.   As discussed in Chapter 1, secondary education for students with disabilities is currently hampered by the lack of appropriate instructional materials. The materials found in secondary special education classrooms may have been intended for either elementary students with disabilities or regular secondary students. Although materials designed for elementary students may emphasize skills that the secondary student should master, their format may be highly unsuitable for this level. For example, they may feature large illustrations or cartoon characters that appeal to younger learners but embarrass older learners. Materials designed for regular secondary students also present a variety of problems. First, the material is more difficult to read because of the vocabulary level and the use of complex sentences. Textbooks may also lack transition words and cues (such as italics, boldface print, and introductory and summary paragraphs) to highlight key concepts (Deshler, Putnam, & Bulgren, 1985). Second, the material in some textbooks may require the student to have a knowledge base that secondary students with special needs do not possess. Third, the concepts presented in regular secondary materials may not be functionally related to the needs of youths with disabilities. For example, a text on consumerism that devotes a chapter to the law of supply and demand may not be relevant to a student who is having trouble managing checking and savings accounts. Fourth, even if regular secondary materials do address concepts relevant to students with special needs, they may not provide sufficient practice to ensure that they will master the concept. Although the consumerism text may mention checking and savings accounts, for example, it may provide only one or two practice activities.

Laws such as PL 94–142 have made it possible to increase the amount of commercial material suitable for students with disabilities. Although most of this material has focused on elementary students, some publishing companies are now supplying items that are suitable for older students who have disabilities. Some of these companies are listed in Action Plan 6.4. Practitioners are advised to familiarize themselves with these companies and consult their catalogs before purchasing new materials for their secondary classrooms. In addition, practitioners may consider writing to publishers and asking to be kept

Action Plan 6.4   Publishers of Materials Suitable for Use with Secondary Students with Disabilities

Teachers seeking materials suitable for secondary learners with special needs may contact the following companies:

Barnell Loft and Dexter Westbrook
  Publications
958 Church Street
Baldwin, NY 11510

Edmark Associates
13241 Northup Way
Bellevue, WA 98005

Educational Design
47 West 13th Street
New York, NY 10011

Fearon-Pitman Publishers, Inc.
6 Davis Drive
Belmont, CA 94002

Frank E. Richards Publishing Company
P. O. Box 66
Phoenix, NY 13135

Janus Book Publishers
2510 Industrial Parkway West
Hayward, CA 94545

Steck-Vaughn Company
P. O. Box 2028
Austin, TX 78768.

informed about any new materials suitable for secondary students with disabilities. Such requests may sensitize publishers to the need for more materials in this area.

Secondary special educators could also serve on committees established to review and purchase materials for the secondary school (Deshler et al., 1985). Colleagues in regular education who have been sensitized to the unique needs of secondary students with disabilities can make more thoughtful, appropriate decisions. Practitioners should take the following steps if the opportunity to purchase new materials for the secondary classroom arises (Mercer & Mercer, 1989; Wiederholt & McNutt, 1977). First, identify all the curricular areas in which new materials are needed. Second, rank the curricular areas in terms of priority. Third, identify affordable materials in the curricular area(s) receiving the highest priority. Fourth, obtain and evaluate the material using the criteria included in Action Plan 6.5. Publishers may send specimen sets for practitioners to examine. Nearby resource or curriculum materials center may have the item in its collection.

Of particular concern is the textbook selected for use in secondary content classes (Schumm & Strickler, 1991). In most instances, teachers do not have the opportunity to select a textbook; rather, they chose texts from brief lists of district- or state-adopted books. These books may not meet the needs of secondary students with disabilities. Armbruster and Anderson (1988) identified steps teachers can take to choose the most "considerate" text from those that are available. The recommendations include looking for books that are well structured, coherent, and appropriate for the audience. Specific strategies for carrying out these recommendations are included in Action Plan 6.6.

Some practitioners may elect to not purchase any new materials because those available do not meet their students' needs. Instead, they may try to adapt existing materials to their needs, use material from nontraditional sources, or make their own materials.

When adapting materials for learners with special needs, the teacher usually has to modify the reading level, format, pace, or directions. The reading level can be modified in a variety of ways. Students can be encouraged to develop and maintain their own glossaries of vocabulary words. Practitioners can highlight essential information in a text or block out extraneous information by covering parts of a page and then copying it. They can also provide students with an outline, an overview, study questions, and a summary.

A paraprofessional or a volunteer can record the book on tape (Meese, 1992). Recorded segments should be short and clear. The reader may also provide a preview before beginning the section, provide signals indicating page location, and stop occasionally to summarize important information. A secondary educator can also design a graphic organizer, which is a diagram depicting relationships in text material. This diagram provides students with a visual overview of reading material before they actually read it (Horton, Lovitt, & Bergerud, 1990; Meese, 1992). Chapter 16 includes more information on how graphic organizers can be used to teach secondary students with disabilities who are included in content area classes.

A more complex method of modifying the reading level is to rewrite the text (Osterag & Rambeau, 1982). Some guidelines to assist the secondary educator who elects to rewrite materials are presented in Action Plan 6.7. Bear in mind that rewritten material

Action Plan 6.5   Criteria for Evaluating Instructional Materials

The following guidelines help teachers measure the suitability of commercial materials. Positive answers to the following questions support the appropriateness of commercial materials being considered for use with secondary learners:

A. General Information

1. *Publisher*
    Is it a reputable company that you or your colleagues have successfully dealt with in the past?
2. *Major Skill Area*
    a. Does this material represent a neglected skill area in your classroom?
    b. Can the major goals of the material be easily identified?
    c. Is the material relevant to your students' current or anticipated needs?
3. *Cost and Durability*
    a. Is the cost of the material within the budget?
    b. Are supplemental materials inexpensive and easily obtainable?
    c. Is the material well constructed and built to last?
4. *Target Age*
    a. How old are your students?
    b. Was this material designed for students of a similar age?
5. *Research and Field Test Data*
    Are data available to support the effectiveness of this material with secondary students with special needs?

B. Characteristics Related to Teaching

1. *Sequence of Skills*
    a. Is the sequence complete?
    b. Is it logically arranged?
    c. Do students have the necessary background experiences?
2. *Directions*
    a. Are directions to the teacher complete and clear?
    b. Are directions to the student complete and clear?
3. *Task Levels*
    a. Does the material contain activities for students who are at concrete or abstract levels of ability?
    b. Is the reading level appropriate for secondary students with special needs?
    c. Is the language level appropriate?
4. *Stimulus–Response Modality*
    a. Are a variety of modalities used to present new information?
    b. Can students respond to activities using a variety of formats (written responses, motoric responses)?
    c. Can the material be used without disrupting peers?

Action Plan 6.5   Continued

    5. *Pace*
        a. Is the rate at which information is presented appropriate?
        b. Is there frequent review of key concepts?
        c. Is there a sufficient number of practice activities?
    6. *Motivation*
        Will the materials increase the students' desire to learn the subject matter?

C. Characteristics Relating to Classroom Management

    1. *Evaluation and Record Keeping*
        a. Are methods for measuring student progress included?
        b. Are data sheets included?
        c. Can students or peers measure and record progress?
    2. *Space Requirements*
        Can the material be stored easily?
    3. *Time Requirements*
        Can the material be set up and taken down quickly?
    4. *Teacher Involvement*
        After initial instruction, can the material be used independently?
    5. *Interest Level*
        Will secondary learners enjoy using this material?

will be longer than the original work, and therefore may seem threatening to an insecure reader. Practitioners who do rewrite are advised to allocate more sessions to instructional units in which rewritten materials are incorporated.

A confusing format can be improved by "cutting and pasting." The practitioner can arrange materials in a more reasonable sequence, insert new headings, and eliminate distractors. The pace of instructional materials can be adjusted by providing additional practice in the form of games, peer teaching, and computer technology. In addition, the practitioner can modify the directions accompanying instructional material by pairing oral and written instructions, defining and explaining terms, giving one or two directions at a time, or asking students to repeat directions.

A secondary educator may also want to consider using high-interest low-vocabulary materials. Many of these materials are available from the publishers listed in Action Plan 6.4. Educators are encouraged to review these materials to make sure they have proper content coverage (Mercer & Mercer, 1989).

If materials cannot be purchased or modified, practitioners may need to use items from nontraditional sources. Community settings in which secondary students are functioning or expected to function should contain a variety of materials suitable for use in the classroom. Items from nontraditional sources include newspapers, catalogs, bills, receipts, phone bills, magazines, food labels, and employment applications. Nontradi-

Action Plan 6.6   Choosing a "Considerate" Textbook

Armbruster and Anderson (1988) have suggested the following guidelines for identifying a considerate textbook:

1. *Look for structure.*
   a. Make an outline of the headings and subheadings. How reasonable is the structure that is revealed? Does it reflect your understanding of the content?
   b. Look for signals. Are the headings and subheadings informative? Are there marginal notations, graphic aids, boldface, italics, or underlining? Are there signal words that designate patterns of organization, such as "on the other hand" or "first, . . . , second, . . , third, . . ."?
2. *Look for coherence.*
   a. Are pronoun referents clear?
   b. Are there too many vague quantifiers such as "some," "many," or "few"?
   c. Are transition statements used?
   d. Is there a chronological sequence that is easy to follow?
   e. Are the graphic aids important, clearly referenced to the text, easy to read and interpret, and clearly labeled?
3. *Is it appropriate for the target audience?*
   a. How adequate are explanations? Select a topic you know well and then read about it in the book. Determine whether its treatment was too light or too heavy.
   b. Check for the salience of main ideas. Are topic sentences the first sentences of the paragraphs? Does the text provide previews or summary statements? Are main ideas underlined, italicized, boldfaced, or highlighted in any other way?

---

tional materials might even contribute to the maintenance and generalization of students' skills because of their functional relevance.

Practitioners may also find it necessary to develop their own materials to supplement or replace items that cannot be purchased, adapted, or located in nontraditional sources. Practitioners may need these materials to motivate students, emphasize important concepts, or provide additional practice. Such items include worksheets, games, flash cards, drill sheets, and self-correcting activities.

Locating nontraditional materials or adapting materials requires a time commitment from a secondary educator who is already busy. Teachers who are unsure of how to proceed and who need assistance should contact a special education resource specialist or a consulting teacher. Chapter 7 provides information on working effectively with these professionals.

Physical Arrangement.   Most general secondary teachers are assigned one classroom in which they conduct their lessons or a few classrooms they move to throughout the day. Similarly, secondary special education teachers, whether self-contained or resource, have little control over the location of their classrooms. However, where possible they should

Action Plan 6.7   Rewriting Materials

We recommend the following suggestions made by Osterag and Rambeau (1982) for rewriting materials for secondary special needs students.

1. Identify the current readability level.
2. Try to retain most of the material. Keep essential facts.
3. Reorganize the original sequence of ideas only if it is unnecessarily complex.
4. Rewrite materials that will be used again.
5. Shorten sentences by dividing them and deleting adjectives or adverbs.
6. Reduce the number of difficult words.
7. Use action verbs as much as possible.
8. Team up with other teachers to reduce the workload.
9. Read the revised story to someone else and revise as needed.

try to obtain a classroom located near rooms for regular secondary students to promote mainstreaming and peer tutoring (Fimian, Zoback, & D'Alonzo, 1983; Zigmond, Sansone, Miller, Donahoe, & Kohnke, 1986a). The room should also have easy access to the main office, the guidance counselor's office, and restrooms.

Having obtained or been assigned a classroom, general secondary teachers and special education teachers should arrange it in a manner that is conducive to student learning. Fimian and colleagues (1983) have recommended that the following equipment be standard items in secondary classrooms:

1. A desk for each student
2. A large, rectangular table suitable for games and activities involving a large number of people
3. Tables of various sizes and shapes for group lessons and learning centers
4. Extra chairs
5. Bookcases of various sizes suitable for storage
6. Partitions to separate instructional areas
7. Cabinets that can be locked to protect files and valuable pieces of equipment
8. Bulletin boards
9. Chalkboards
10. Wastebaskets.

Left to arrange their own seating, students of similar ability may cluster together. More able students tend to sit in the front, where they receive more attention from the teacher. Less able learners tend to cluster together in the back of the room, where they are easily overlooked by the teacher. Practitioners are encouraged to avoid these "action zones" by developing and implementing a seating plan that mingles students of varying ability levels. (See Weinstein, 1979, for more information on the physical arrangement of the secondary classroom.)

Case for Action 6.2

A new student refuses to use the supplemental reading series you have in your classroom. He says his other teacher used it in his other classroom and he hated every minute of it. What can you do?

Classroom Routines.   Practitioners and students will save time and effort if events that occur frequently are identified and routines for managing them are established and taught early in the school year. It is difficult to develop a set of all-encompassing guidelines for establishing routine procedures because they will vary from class to class, depending on student characteristics. For example, practitioners dealing with secondary students with mild disabilities may follow standard procedures for obtaining a hall pass or using the restroom. On the other hand, students with more severe disabilities may require more structure. Practitioners are advised to consider routines related to academic and nonacademic business. Academic business requires teachers to develop routines for setting up and taking down lessons, obtaining assistance with an independent assignment, and using a learning center. Nonacademic business includes obtaining permission to use the restroom; getting a hall pass; distributing, using, and returning supplies such as the dictionary and pencil sharpener; and socializing.

Antecedent Control

The term *antecedent* is synonymous with prevention (Schloss & Smith, 1994). It precedes a behavior and influences the probability of future occurrences. In addition, an antecedent can cue either appropriate or disruptive behaviors. For example, a student who enjoys math will smile and quickly prepare for the lesson when instructed to do so by the teacher. A student who dislikes math may procrastinate or become disruptive upon hearing the teacher's directive.

Antecedents that cue student behaviors vary with the characteristics of the students in the class. Some are predictable—most students are pleased by good grades and are upset by low grades. Other antecedents are unique, as in the case of a secondary student diagnosed as emotionally disturbed who engaged in both self-abuse and physical aggression against others whenever he was told "no," "don't," "stop," can't," or "won't."

Antecedents that prompt appropriate and inappropriate behaviors should be identified and controlled by practitioners; however, a word of caution is in order. It is important to realize that some antecedents to disruptive behavior should always be eliminated or controlled by the teacher because to do so is simply good teaching. For example, good teachers provide their students with schedules and establish procedures for completing routine events in the classroom. These antecedent control techniques will remain intact throughout the school year. Other antecedent control techniques, however, should be in place only for a short time and should be used in combination with techniques that address related personal characteristics and consequences. For example, exposure to words with negative connotations was minimized for the student described earlier. At the

Case for Action 6.3

It is September and your principal has advised the faculty that all students will be required to carry hall passes except when classes are changing. What procedure for obtaining passes will you develop and teach to your secondary students?

same time, the student was participating in carefully structured social skill lessons that enhanced his ability to respond appropriately to critical remarks. The frequency of his exposure to negative words increased as his social skills improved. In the long run, it would have been unethical to shield the student from negative words. It is unnatural to have an environment in which every wish is granted and there are no disappointments. The authors could not guarantee similar treatment in future environments; indeed, it is extremely likely the student would not have moved to a less restrictive setting at all if he was unable to respond appropriately to critical remarks from peers and authority figures.

Ten useful antecedent control techniques are listed in Action Plan 6.8. Each is discussed separately.

Rate of Success. If students experience a rate of success that is too high, they may become bored and disinterested in the task. If the assignment is too difficult, they may become frustrated. In both cases, students may engage in behaviors that are disruptive to the rest of the class. Schloss and Sedlak (1986) identified four levels of mastery to guide practitioners in the selection of student assignments.

Tasks that have been completed with 100% accuracy have been mastered and should only be reviewed occasionally. Tasks that lend themselves to paper-and-pencil activities can be kept in review folder for use when students complete other activities ahead of schedule. These activities should be interesting in nature, not simply a review. For

Action Plan 6.8 Antecedent Control Techniques

Attention to the following areas can minimize classroom disruption:

1. Rate of success
2. Teacher-student interactions
3. Rules
4. Student schedules
5. Routine classroom procedures
6. Functional, age-appropriate activities
7. Systematic instruction
8. Review of the educational program
9. Interaction with nonhandicapped peers.
10. Modeling

example, a student who has mastered calculator skills could be assigned a worksheet that requires her to simulate purchase of catalog items necessary to attend the prom.

Tasks completed with 90% to 99% accuracy are considered learned, although the student occasionally makes an error. The teacher needs to provide guided practice activities such as games and drill and practice sheets. As noted in Chapter 4, homework assignments may be given for material learned to this level of accuracy.

Students completing activities with 70% to 90% accuracy should still be receiving teacher-directed instruction. Left to their own devices, they will make and practice errors. Instruction should occur in large or small groups and should be characterized by teacher behaviors that include a discrete cue, a logical sequence, minimal digressions, several examples, and many teacher questions (see chapter 4).

Performance that is less than 70% accurate indicates the student is working at the frustration level. Practitioners are advised to break the instructional objective into smaller steps and teach them using the techniques suggested earlier. These activities should never be assigned as independent work, because they will lead to frustration and disruptive student behaviors. As noted in Chapter 4 and repeated in Chapter 7, the secondary teacher needs to make at least two well-documented attempts to assist the learner with special needs who is having difficulty. If a problem still persists, the teacher is encouraged to contact either a resource specialist or the consulting teacher.

Teacher–Student Interactions.   Secondary learners with severe disabilities frequently approach academic tasks with some degree of trepidation because they have experienced limited or no success in earlier endeavors (Houck, 1987). Practitioners can minimize this anxiety by developing positive, stable relationships that provide students with encouragement and warmth and increase their comfort in learning situations (Graham, 1985; Houck, 1987). The following guidelines proposed by Schloss and Sedlack (1986) indicate how to enhance teacher–student interactions:

1. Speak in concrete terms. Students with disabilities may be confused by frequent references to past or future events. Practitioners are advised to speak about concerns of immediate importance, using vocabulary and syntax that are sensitive to their students' level of comprehension.

2. Talk with students in a manner that indicates respect for their age and abilities. Although it may be necessary to modify vocabulary and syntax to accommodate the language characteristics of some learners, avoid talking down to them. Secondary students may resent the teacher who uses intonation patterns, facial expressions, or postures that are appropriate for conversations with much younger children.

3. Balance praise with corrective feedback. Secondary students with disabilities may display a number of problem behaviors that make them easy targets for criticism from their teachers. It may be necessary to limit critical remarks to a short list of inappropriate student behaviors. Additional behaviors can be added as old behaviors improve and are displayed less often. Practitioners are also encouraged to identify and comment on any positive behaviors that students display.

4. Provide objective feedback. Praise or criticism that is immediate and specific can enhance student performance. Practitioners need to get the student's attention and

deliver a complimentary or critical remark in objective terms. Feedback of this nature helps students identify precise aspects of their performance that should be repeated or modified.

5. Encourage students to develop their own solutions to problems. Students are more likely to assume responsibility for changing problem behaviors if they identify appropriate alternatives. Practitioners are advised that not all students with special needs will be able to identify appropriate solutions.

6. Redirect irrational or dysfunctional lines of thought. Sometimes students may not have all the information they need to identify valid explanations for, and suitable alternatives to, inappropriate behaviors. Practitioners may need to challenge and question the statements students make or identify reasonable alternatives for them.

Rules.   Being able to follow a set of rules is one key to a successful secondary experience (Schumaker & Deshler, 1984). Developing and posting classroom rules can minimize behavior problems and disruptions because students will know exactly what will and will not be tolerated and the consequences of inappropriate behavior. There are six guidelines for rule development for the secondary student (Schloss & Smith, 1994). First, keep the number small. There should be no more than seven rules, and they should include only those that are absolutely necessary. Second, make sure the classroom list reflects school policies. For example, administrators trying to minimize confusion during the times classes change may only allow students to go to their lockers immediately before and after lunch. This regulation should be on the list developed for the class. Third, depending on the nature of the students, consider soliciting student opinion regarding the specific rules to be established. At times, however, student input results in more rules or more serious consequences for violations than the practitioner had originally intended. Fourth, state the rules operationally. Students may have their own interpretation of what it means to "be polite," and it may not reflect the practitioner's perceptions. A rule such as "Use please and thank you" leaves little room for misinterpretation. Fifth, state rules positively. Students may be well aware of inappropriate behavior and could benefit from a positively stated alternative. Sixth, identify the consequences for rule violations. Planning them in advance allows the teacher to make a fair, unemotional decision regarding the exact nature of a response to an infraction.

It is not enough to simply establish classroom rules. They must be permanently on display in a prominent place in the room. They need to be taught the same way subject matter is taught to ensure that students know and understand them. Practitioners need to monitor adherence. A student who continuously breaks rules may be in need of a special program beyond the scope of the one already in place. Furthermore, consequences need to be implemented for rule infractions. Rules have been clearly posted, taught, and frequently reviewed; therefore, consequences should come as no surprise. It is vital that consequences be implemented immediately and consistently, preferably by the individual who witnessed the infraction. Students will test, but they need to learn that violations will not be tolerated.

Student Schedules.   Another factor contributing to a successful secondary experience is the ability to follow a schedule (Zigmond et al., 1986a). A schedule can be considered a set of instructional activities that delineates the organization of every school day (Wilcox & Bellamy, 1982). There are two advantages to developing a student schedule. First, it allows the practitioner to translate IEP goals and objectives into practice. Ideally, there should be an exact correspondence between goal areas stated on the IEP and the subject matter included in the students' schedules. This practice ensures that sufficient attention is being given to all prioritized areas. Second, a schedule permits the student, the teacher, and ancillary personnel to predict what will happen during the school day, In some cases, predictability will minimize disruptions. For example, a thoughtfully planned schedule will help the student who dislikes science to maintain an appropriate attitude because he knows exactly how long the lesson will last. In other cases, a schedule allows staff members to anticipate and prepare for student difficulty. The teacher can arrange for other staff members to provide management assistance for a student who has a history of becoming disruptive just before gym class.

Schloss and Smith (1994) also identified eight guidelines for schedule development:

1. When possible, seek student input. General secondary education students will probably receive a completed schedule the first day of class. Schedules of secondary students with special needs may be more flexible if they include both some content area instruction and resource room assistance. While some items, such as lunch or gym, may have already been scheduled, a list of negotiable items can be presented to students for discussion.

2. Schedules should be available for quick reference. The schedule, like rules, should be on permanent display in a format that is consistent with the age and ability of the students. Some students may tape their schedule inside textbooks or carry them in appointment books.

3. Use the Premack principle. Students are more likely to engage in a less preferred activity when they expect it to be followed by an activity they do enjoy. Anticipation of something pleasant produces a positive mood that may sustain students through a disliked activity. For example, a secondary student with special needs who is included in a challenging math class may need a change of pace. If possible, schedule math first, then gym or resource room assistance.

4. The duration of the activity should reflect students' abilities. Older, more able students should engage in activities for lengths of time that correspond to those found in classrooms for nondisabled students.

Secondary schools typically have instructional periods that last 40 minutes. Students with special needs who are included in content area classes should be able to participate for this length of time. If a student has difficulty maintaining attention this long, the teacher can break the period into chunks of time during which the student is doing different things. For example, the teacher can review homework, discuss the purpose of the lesson, demonstrate a skill, ask questions, and allow students to practice the skill in a variety of novel ways. All students, not just those with special needs, will benefit from this format. As the student's attention span develops, the teacher can gradually lengthen the amount of time the class is participating in any one activity.

5. Avoid revision. Inform students of holidays, staff personal days, assemblies, and field trips as soon as possible. Some secondary school officials vary the time when assemblies or other special events occur so that the same time period is not always lost. Other officials keep the time of special events constant, but shave off five minutes from each instructional period. This allows all students to complete each item on their schedule while leaving sufficient time for the special event.

Do not disrupt the schedule any more than necessary, because revisions undermine the students' ability to anticipate pleasant activities. In addition, a student may use disruptive behaviors to avoid or escape a scheduled activity. As soon as the student is ready to resume work, he or she should reenter the schedule at the point of disruption. The student will learn that manipulation of the schedule through inappropriate behaviors will not be tolerated.

6. Motivate students. Occasionally, students will complete an activity earlier than expected. Practitioners should have a variety of related activities available so that students are appropriately engaged for the time scheduled.

7. Reinforce effort. Occasionally, the practitioner may overplan and assign more work than can be finished in the time allocated to instruction. Reinforce effort as well as task completion.

8. Include parents. Send a copy of the schedule home to parents. In addition, schedules may be placed in students' permanent files.

Functional, Age-Appropriate Activities. Practitioners need to plan and implement lessons that are appropriate and motivating for students. Activities that are too difficult, too easy, or not relevant to the students' needs may result in disruptive behavior. Activities should be functional, that is, there should be a direct relationship between the skills acquired and the demands of the environment in which students must function. For example, students who need to practice their addition and subtraction skills would find it more appropriate to work on balancing a checking account than on completing drill sheets. Activities should also be age appropriate. Secondary students with special needs should be reading newspapers rather than books from an elementary basal reading series. Practitioners are advised to design activities and locate materials that reflect their students' chronological age. Resource specialists and consultant teachers can assist with this task. Practitioners working with students with special needs in the regular classroom are advised to use the introductory phase of a lesson to emphasize the relationship between the target objective and environmental demands.

Routine Procedures. As noted earlier, routine classroom procedures are a key component of general classroom organization. They also serve as an antecedent control device because they enable students to use appropriate rather than disruptive behavior to obtain assistance or materials.

Systematic Instruction. Classroom disruptions are minimized or prevented when students are actively engaged in teacher-directed lessons. (See Chapter 4 for a review of teacher behaviors that contribute to student achievement.)

Review of the Educational Program.   Ideally, practitioners should provide their secondary students with information and activities that facilitate mastery of IEP goals and objectives. An educational program can become out of date sooner than anticipated. *Legally, IEPs must be reviewed once a year; however, practitioners are advised to review them on a more frequent, informal basis. This will ensure that goals and objectives are still appropriate and are being met at the expected rate.* Practitioners experiencing concerns over existing programs can arrange for a meeting with all interested parties to formally review and update students' educational programs.

Interaction with Nondisabled Peers.   Where appropriate, secondary students with disabilities should be included with their peers in regular education. Interaction with nondisabled secondary learners provides learners who have special needs with opportunities to observe competent models of how to meet academic and social challenges in an appropriate manner. The nature and extent of participation are a reflection of the degree of a student's disability. A student with a highly developed skill repertoire may be included for most or all academic areas. A student with a less developed repertoire may be with peers only for nonacademic areas at the beginning of the year. Carefully sequenced instruction and the use of resource specialists and consulting teachers can increase the amount of time that secondary students with more severe disabilities are included in the regular program.

Modeling.   Modeling can have a powerful effect on secondary students with disabilities. Most teachers are models for their students whether they plan to be or not. The ways a teacher acts, addresses others, dresses, or even wears his or her hair can influence these same aspects of student behavior. Bearing this in mind, it is important that secondary teachers model acceptable standards of behavior at all times.

Teachers can do more than just rely on incidental modeling to influence the likelihood that their students will demonstrate appropriate behavior. More proactive measures can draw students' attention to appropriate models and increase their desire to emulate them. Secondary teachers who have students with disabilities included in their content area classes have an ideal opportunity to use modeling to motivate use of

---

Case for Action 6.4

Identify antecedents and antecedent control techniques for the student described below.

Louis is a 17 year old who has been dually diagnosed as having moderate mental retardation and serious emotional disturbance. He becomes frustrated when confronted with academic tasks he cannot do. This frustration leads to object aggression on his part. Louis becomes physically aggressive toward anyone who attempts to halt his object aggression. Recently, Louis has been allowed to leave the room when feeling upset. This has been followed by one-to-one informal counseling by the teacher in the hall. This procedure has decreased the number of aggressive outbursts, but Louis continues to do poorly on his academic work.

acceptable behavior. Some suggestions for using modeling appropriately follow. First, since motivation to perform a skill is an essential but not sufficient condition for modeling to succeed (Schloss & Smith, 1994), make sure that the student with a disability is able to perform the targeted skill. Second, identify students in class who are admired and respected by their peers. Choose carefully, some students are admired for the wrong reasons. Third, praise these students for appropriate behavior in the presence of others. (It is assumed that these models do not object to overt teacher praise.) Fourth, make sure that praise statements specify the appropriate behavior and its consequences, thereby highlighting the connection between the behavior and the reward. Finally, be sure to praise the student with disabilities when he or she demonstrates the desired behavior.

Related Personal Characteristics

As suggested earlier, practitioners must use antecedent control techniques carefully. They must decide which techniques should be permanent and which should be used only until students develop skills that will enable them to respond appropriately to previously provoking events. Related personal characteristics refer to those skills that enable students to behave appropriately. Schloss and Smith (1994) defined them as the observed and inferred characteristics of the individual that influence the target behavior. Once developed, these skills mediate between a provoking antecedent and a disruptive response. Previously, students may have acted inappropriately because it was the only response they had in their skill repertoires. After appropriate instruction, students no longer need to be disruptive; they will have in their repertoires a number of socially acceptable alternatives. Three strategies are available for improving students' related personal characteristics (for a more detailed discussion, see Schloss & Smith, 1994). They can be classified under academic skills, social skills, and emotional learning.

Academic Skills. Certainly many secondary students with disabilities display inappropriate behaviors when requested to participate in academic activities. This is not surprising given the frustration and anger they must feel after experiencing years of poor achievement. Practitioners will probably have to examine the secondary curriculum carefully or develop a functional curriculum from which to select skills that will have an immediate and positive impact on students' functioning. Secondary students with disabilities are more likely to respond appropriately to academic demands if the content is relevant and they believe they can master it. (See Chapter 4 for information on how to select and teach academic skills to secondary students with disabilities.)

Social Skills. Many secondary students with disabilities use disruptive behaviors in social settings because they are unaware of the socially appropriate methods for attaining their goals. Suppose that an individual receives a paycheck that is less than expected because of a clerical error. He proceeds to the payroll office, locates a clerk, and, using abusive language, demands a new check. He probably will get a new check; however, it is equally likely that he will get a reprimand from his employer criticizing his behavior and warning him that the firm will not tolerate similar outbursts in the future.

The difficulties that individuals with disabilities encounter in employment and community settings may be as much a function of social skill deficits as of the lack of academic or vocational competence (Schloss & Schloss, 1988). Consequently, it is important to include social skills training in educational programs developed for secondary students with disabilities. Social skills may need to be taught in separate small groups by a speech/language pathologist, the resource specialist, or the consultant teacher. However, it is essential that these skills be practiced in regular settings. Including students with disabilities in regular secondary programs will give them the opportunity to use newly acquired social skills and experience the reinforcement that occurs naturally as a result of their use. Inclusion will also expose them to appropriate models of socially skillful behavior. (See Chapter 14 for a detailed discussion of social skill development.)

Emotional Learning.   Emotional learning techniques are based on respondent learning in which the environment acts on an individual to produce an uncontrollable emotional response. For example, a pop quiz produces anxiety, a good grade produces happiness, and a sarcastic remark produces anger. Students who have been exposed to supportive environments in which they have observed and participated in satisfactory relationships acquire and demonstrate appropriate emotional behaviors. In contrast, students who have been exposed to unpleasant events or who have interacted with punitive adults may acquire and display less desirable emotional characteristics (Gardner, 1977). Unfortunately, many secondary students with disabilities fall into the latter category. Their teachers may have to develop and implement techniques that promote positive emotional development.

A new emotional response can be developed through pairing. The practitioner (a) identifies the event that fails to produce a positive response, (b) identifies an event that does produce the positive response, and (c) pairs the two events. For example, Ann may not display positive responses during interactions with peers. Her teacher, knowing how much she enjoys going to the mall, may arrange a field trip for Ann and some of her peers. A new emotional response may also be developed through vicarious conditioning. The practitioner (a) identifies the event that fails to produce a positive response, (b) identifies situations in which other individuals display the response, and (c) arranges for the learner to observe these situations. A student who is afraid to raise his hand in class needs to see other students being reinforced for doing so.

Emotional learning can also assist practitioners in reducing excessive responses demonstrated by their students. Counterconditioning can be conducted by (a) identifying the event that produces the excessive response, (b) identifying an event that produces a stronger response, and (c) pairing them. For example, students who are anxious about taking an exam can eat homemade chocolate chip cookies at the same time. Another technique for reducing excessive emotionality is desensitization. All the events related to an excessive response are identified and listed in order, from least to most provoking. An incompatible response is identified and repeatedly paired with the least provoking event until the individual no longer exhibits the response. Gradually, more provoking events from the hierarchy are introduced. An example of a desensitization hierarchy is presented in Action Plan 6.9.

Action Plan 6.9 A Systematic Desensitization Hierarchy

Eric becomes extremely agitated when his peers tease him. He and his teacher have developed a plan to help Eric control his feelings. They believe that his peers will stop after they see that their teasing no longer affects him.

Eric loves the beach. Therefore, while his teacher describes a peer who is teasing him, Eric will pretend to be relaxing on the sand, basking in the warmth of the sun. Eric and his teacher have developed the following hierarchy:

1. A peer is at the end of a long hall.
2. A peer is at the end of a long hall and is teasing Eric in a quiet voice.
3. A peer is about one-third of the way down the hall.
4. A peer is about one-third of the way down the hall and is teasing Eric in a voice at normal volume.
5. A peer is two-thirds of the way down the hall.
6. A peer is two-thirds of the way down the hall and is teasing Eric in a loud voice.
7. A peer is standing next to Eric.
8. A peer is standing next to Eric and is shouting teasing remarks.

Of course, an incompatible response may not be in the student's repertoire and therefore may have to be developed before a systematic desensitization program can be implemented. Bernstein and Borkovec (1973) suggested a progressive muscle relaxation technique that requires the systematic tensing and relaxing of major muscle groups including the arms, neck and shoulders, face, and legs. As each muscle is relaxed, the learner is asked to focus on the contrast between relaxed and tensed muscles. (For more information on progressive muscle relaxation, see Bernstein & Borkovec, 1973; Schloss & Smith, 1994.)

Consequence Control

A consequence is an event that follows a behavior and influences the probability of future occurrences. A behavior has been reinforced if it increases in strength or frequency; similarly, it has been punished if its strength or frequency decreases. Consequent control techniques have received a great deal of professional attention; indeed, entire books have been devoted to the topic. The following section highlights some of the techniques suitable for secondary learners with disabilities. (For more elaborate discussions, see Alberto & Troutman, 1991; Sulzer-Azaroff & Mayer, 1991.)

Consequent control techniques exist on a continuum. This continuum is presented in Figure 6.1. On the left end are techniques that enhance the development of new behaviors. On the right end are techniques that reduce or eliminate inappropriate behaviors. Movement from the left end to the right end represents a shift away from positive techniques that are fairly common in educational practice toward techniques that are less natural and used cautiously only after less intrusive procedures have failed

Primary Reinforcers			Secondary Reinforcers				Extinction		Punishment						
Food	Drinks		Social	Activity	Token	Contracts		Planned ignoring		Reprimands	Response cost	Time-out	Detention	In-school suspension	Suspension	Expulsion

FIGURE 6.1 The Continuum of Consequence Control Techniques

to produce desired results. The main points on the continuum are discussed in the following subsections.

Positive Reinforcers

Positive reinforcers are administered contingently and immediately upon the display of the desired response, and they increase the probability that the response will be repeated in the future. They are used to shape the development of a skill and to increase or maintain the use of a skill already in the learner's repertoire. There are two types of positive reinforcers: primary and secondary. Primary reinforcers are biologically important to the individual and include food and liquid. In classrooms, they are typically used with younger, less able learners because they are highly motivating and quickly affect behavior.

Secondary reinforcers are not biologically important—students have learned to appreciate their value. There are four types of secondary reinforcers, and all are suitable for use with high school students. The first type is the social reinforcer, which includes many techniques practitioners use almost unconsciously, such as praise, facial expressions, hugs, body gestures, and teacher proximity. Social reinforcers have many advantages. They take little of the practitioner's time and effort; they occur frequently in the natural environment; they can be paired with other techniques; and their use with one student may have a positive impact on the behavior of peers.

A word of caution is in order when using social reinforcement with secondary students. Some students perceive teacher attention, even when positive, as unpleasant because it makes them look like the teacher's pet. A teacher who uses overt praise may

Case for Action 6.5

What related personal characteristics would you target for development by Louis? How would you develop them?

in fact be punishing the very student he or she intended to reinforce. The teacher may find the behavior decreasing rather than increasing in occurrence. In such cases, the teacher is advised to use facial expressions (such as a smile), a nod of the head, or a gesture (such as a thumbs-up sign). These examples of social reinforcers communicate to students, albeit very subtly, that their work or behavior is appropriate.

The second type of secondary reinforcer is the activity reinforcer. It is based on the Premack principle, which was discussed previously with regard to schedule development. The practitioner can use any activity in which a student voluntarily engages to reinforce participation in an activity in which the student is reluctant to engage. A variety of activities are reinforcing to secondary students. They include free time and time to play computer games or listen to a portable stereo.

A secondary reinforcer appropriate for high school students with more severe disabilities is the token reinforcer. A token reinforcer is comparable to money in that it can be exchanged for something considered valuable by the students. As with all reinforcers, a token is delivered immediately and contingently upon the display of the target behavior. Typically, it is small, portable, durable, and easy to handle. Practitioners may use poker chips, buttons, or play money; however, they are cautioned against using objects that students can easily obtain elsewhere. "Counterfeit" tokens will undermine the effectiveness of a token economy. Tokens are exchanged at predetermined intervals for any one of a variety of items that are age appropriate for secondary learners. Examples of appropriate items include coupons for fast food restaurants, cosmetics, movie passes, key chains, and comic books.

The fourth secondary reinforcer is a contingency contract. A contract is a written document developed and signed by the teacher and a student that identifies the relationship between specific behaviors and consequences. Consider the case of Mike, a secondary learner who displayed high rates of physical aggression against authority figures. Figure 6.2 presents the contract used to bring Mike's behavior under control. Mike's contract contains the components of a good contract. First, it was the result of mutual negotiation. Second, it clearly described the behaviors being targeted for development and reduction. Third, it identified the pleasant consequence for displaying appropriate behavior for a specific period of time. Fourth, it also identified the consequences for not living up to the agreement. Fifth, it required the signatures of Mike and his teacher.

The consequent control techniques just described are all designed to promote the development of new skills or to increase the use of skills already in the learner's repertoire. In all likelihood, secondary special educators will not only have to develop new skills; they will also have to reduce or eliminate inappropriate behaviors. Other points on the continuum assist practitioners with this task.

Extinction

The next point on the continuum of consequent control techniques is extinction. Extinction has been referred to as planned ignoring. An inappropriate behavior is extinguished by removing the positive reinforcement that maintained it. For example, Jim uses profanity every time the practitioner announces a homework assignment. The practitioner reprimands Jim, not realizing he is using this language to get her attention and possibly postpone the assignment. By no longer taking notice of it, the teacher can extinguish

Name: Mike S.   Date: September 8, 1987

Teacher: Mrs. Klein

Part A

Mike must pay attention to the teacher. He must follow her directions. When the teacher gives a direction, Mike will

1. look at her and listen;
2. begin following the direction within 10 seconds; and
3. finish the task on time.

Part B

Mike will follow every teacher's direction for three days. On September 11, Mike and his teacher will go to McDonald's for lunch.

Part C

When the teacher gives a direction, Mike will not

1. swear or shout;
2. refuse to comply;
3. try to leave the room; or
4. try to hit the teacher.

If these behaviors occur, Mike will

1. not go out to lunch;
2. lose points for noncompliance; and
3. go to the time-out room if necessary.

_____   _____
Student signature   Date   Teacher signature   Date

FIGURE 6.2   A Contingency Contract for a Secondary Student with Severe Behavior Disabilities

Jim's swearing. Unfortunately, this is not as easy as it sounds. There could be an extinction burst—that is, Jim's behavior might escalate as he swears more vehemently to get his teacher's attention. In addition, he might find the laughter of his peers reinforcing. Nonetheless, Jim's behavior will eventually subside as the teacher continues to ignore him and praise other students for their cooperation.

Punishment

The third major point on the continuum is punishment. It is defined as an event delivered immediately and contingently upon the display of a targeted behavior that reduces the probability of future occurrences. The use of punishment has distinct advantages. First, it is quick; that is, there should be an immediate change in the student's behavior. Second, it facilitates learning by providing a clear discrimination between behaviors that are and are not acceptable. Third, it illustrates for other students the consequences of displaying the behavior. Punishment procedures also have their drawbacks. First, the student who is being punished may escalate his or her behavior. For example, the student who is being punished for swearing may become physically aggressive. Second, it is possible that the student who has been punished may withdraw. Secondary students may "get sick," cut class, or even drop out of school. Third, a student being punished may try to escape the situation. Fourth, the teacher who punishes may serve as a model for other students in the class. Finally, the use of some punishment procedures has been challenged in the courts (*Gary W.* v. *Louisiana*, 1976; *Ingraham* v. *Wright*, 1977; *Romeo* v. *Youngberg*, 1982; *Wood* v. *Strickland*, 1975). Practitioners who use aversive behavior management techniques risk legal complications if they are unfamiliar with their conceptual bases, correct applications, and legal implications. These disadvantages show how important it is to adhere to the guidelines presented in Action Plan 6.10 when developing a punishment program.

Reprimand.   One of the least intrusive techniques a secondary teacher can use to stop inappropriate behavior is a reprimand. Reprimands are used frequently in all public school classrooms, but teachers can increase their effectiveness by following the guidelines established by Misra (1991). These guidelines are listed in Action Plan 6.11. First, make the reprimand a brief and specific statement, focusing on one behavior at a time. Identify the student by name, pinpoint the target behavior, briefly explain why the behavior is not acceptable, then describe an alternative. Using statements rather than questions clearly identifies what the student should be doing yet minimizes the likelihood that the student will talk back or try to answer sarcastically. Second, avoid judgmental words such as "bad" or "stupid." Such language has no place in the classroom. Third, use

Action Plan 6.10   Guidelines for Using Punishment Techniques

Secondary special educators are advised to use punishment techniques cautiously. The following guidelines may be useful:

1. Use the procedure only in extreme instances such as for behavior that is of a long-standing nature or that threatens personal safety.
2. Document the ineffectiveness of less intrusive consequent control techniques.
3. Obtain the permission of parents or legal guardians.
4. Observe safety guidelines.
5. Use the procedure at an intensity expected to be effective. Do not let the student develop a tolerance for it.
6. Deliver the punisher consistently, immediately, and in a nonemotional, matter-of-fact manner.
7. Target the development of appropriate alternatives and reinforce their use.
8. Document the effectiveness of the punisher. Its effects should be immediately noticeable and should be maintained over a period of time.

Action Plan 6.11   Reprimanding

Misra (1991) offered the following guidelines for using reprimands:

1. Be brief and specific.
2. Avoid judgmental language.
3. Use concrete terms and appropriate vocabulary and syntax.
4. Do not repeat ineffective reprimands.
5. Be courteous.

concrete terms that reflect age-appropriate vocabulary and syntax. As suggested earlier in this chapter, students with disabilities may have difficulty understanding abstract vocabulary and complex syntactic structures. Concrete, measurable terms increase the likelihood that students will follow through with the suggestions provided in a reprimand. Fourth, do not repeat a reprimand that has failed to produce desired changes in student behaviors. Repetition does not increase the likelihood that students will comply. Students may in fact learn that they can stall the teacher and prolong the delivery of more intrusive consequences. Fifth, be courteous and talk in an age-appropriate manner. A teacher's tone of voice and facial expression should always convey respect for students, even when they are misbehaving. Action Plan 6.12 provides sample reprimands.

Action Plan 6.12   Appropriate versus Inappropriate Reprimands

Fifteen-year-old Kate is in health class, staring out the window rather than watching the filmstrip.

Appropriate:

"Kate, don't look out the window. You are missing the filmstrip. You need to watch carefully."

Inappropriate:

"Kate, stop looking outside." (Lacks specificity; does not provide an appropriate alternative)

"Kate, how many times do I have to tell you to pay attention?" (Asks a question; does not provide an appropriate alternative)

"Kate, how many times do I have to tell you to pay attention? You are always looking out the window. You will be really sorry when it's time to take the quiz. All of your answers will be dumb." (Asks a question; does not provide an appropriate alternative; is too long and judgmental)

Response Cost.   Response cost procedures involve the immediate removal of a reinforcer contingent upon the display of an inappropriate behavior. Secondary learners may already be familiar with the concept of response cost. For example, they may have paid a fine for keeping a library book past the due date. They may have been docked a portion of their allowance for not complying with a parental request. The fact that response costs occur frequently in the natural environment makes them particularly useful in the classroom. Unfortunately, they have their disadvantages as well. Response cost procedures don't necessarily motivate students to use appropriate behavior. As a result, response cost procedures must be used in conjunction with reinforcement techniques that promote skill development and use. Another disadvantage is that a response cost may produce a negative emotional reaction that leads to more disruptive behavior. A student who is upset because he lost points for refusing to open his textbook may throw the book across the room. Practitioners who need to develop a response cost system for their students should follow the procedures listed in Action Plan 6.13.

Time-Out.   Time-out denies students the opportunity to receive reinforcers for a specific period of time. There are different forms of time-out: contingent observation, exclusion, and seclusion (Yell, 1990). Contingent observation involves the removal of the disruptive student to some peripheral area of the classroom. The student can still observe activities occurring in the classroom; however, he or she can not participate for a period of time. During exclusion time-out, the student is removed from the immediate setting for a period of time. For example, the student is removed to a corner of the room sectioned off by partitions or to the hall. This form of time-out is less drastic that total seclusion, and it protects the rights and interests of other students in the classroom. Seclusion time-out requires the removal of the student from the classroom to an isolation room. This form of time-out ensures the safety of others in the classroom and affords the disruptive student the opportunity to learn and practice more appropriate behavior. Procedures for using seclusion time-out are listed in Action Plan 6.14. Be advised that the room used for seclusion time-out must adhere to certain standards (Alberto & Troutman, 1991). These

---

Action Plan 6.13   Steps in Developing a Response Cost System

Secondary special educators should follow these steps when developing a response cost system:

1. Target the behavior to be reduced.
2. Identify the type and amount of reinforcer to be withdrawn contingent upon the display of the targeted behavior.
3. Teach and reinforce the use of appropriate alternatives to the targeted behavior.
4. Explain the response cost procedures to the students.
5. Document the effectiveness of the program.
6. Prepare a backup procedure in the event that a disruptive behavior escalates.

Action Plan 6.14   Using Seclusion Time-Out

School officials who elect to use seclusion time-out should adhere to the following guidelines:

1. Determine disruptive behaviors that will result in seclusion time-out in advance and clearly explain them to all students.
2. Develop procedures for being released from seclusion time-out and explain them to all students. These include the demonstration of appropriate, nondisruptive behavior for a specified period of time, restitution for destroyed property, identifying and role-playing alternatives to disruptive behavior, and a return to the activity during which the disruptive behavior occurred.
3. Attempt other, less intrusive procedures first.
4. Use seclusion time-out in conjunction with positive procedures such as social reinforcement of appropriate behavior.
5. Minimize all verbal communication with the disruptive student. Only encourage him or her to calm down.
6. Document its use.
7. Evaluate its effectiveness.
8. Become familiar with any district policies regarding the use of seclusion time-out.
9. Ensure that time-out room meets specifications.

include using a room that measures at least 6 feet by 6 feet, has adequate lighting and ventilation, and does not contain any potentially harmful objects. In addition, the room may not be locked, and it must be monitored by staff members when in use. Central to all forms of time-out is the premise that the secondary classroom and the activities occurring in it are appropriate and interesting. Time-out will not be an effective punishment technique if time-in does not have any reinforcing properties.

Detention.   Detention refers to a period of time before of after school during which students report to a separate room because they have committed rule infractions. Kerr and Nelson (1989) indicated that this time period can range from 30 to 90 minutes. They also recommended that school officials carefully plan a detention policy using guidelines presented in Action Plan 6.15.

First, develop a schedule for staff who will be responsible for monitoring the detention room. School officials may consider having a coordinator who is responsible for scheduling detention and contacting parents. Second, clearly specify the behaviors that will result in detention and share them with staff, students, and parents. These behaviors should be less serious than those that would result in in-school suspension. Third, consider transportation options. For example, parents may be contacted and asked to make transportation arrangements; however, the need for most parents to work may undermine their ability to transport their children to and from school. Therefore, a late bus may be arranged for students who are transported to and from school. Fourth, set

Action Plan 6.15 Using Detention

Kerr and Nelson (1989) recommended several guidelines for developing and implementing a detention policy:

1. Assign staff to monitor the detention room.
2. Clearly specify behaviors that will result in detention.
3. Consider transportation options.
4. Schedule detention for certain days and times.
5. Assign detention in writing.
6. Notify parents.
7. Have assignments ready.
8. Establish, post, and review rules for the detention room.
9. Evaluate the effectiveness of detention.

aside certain days and times for detention days. For example, detention may be scheduled for every Tuesday, Wednesday, and Thursday. This guideline has the disadvantage of postponing the delivery of punitive consequences, which could undermine its effectiveness. However, scheduling detention in this manner makes it more enforceable. It allows time for parents to be informed and for transportation arrangements to be made. In addition, such advanced notice enables school staff to make adjustments to their schedules to cover detention duty. Finally, regularly scheduled detention days should provide teachers and students with sufficient time to identify and prepare appropriate independent assignments. Fifth, assign detention in writing. A detention slip, preferably several carbonless copies, should note the rule violation, the date of detention, and the name and phone number of a school official parents can contact if they have any questions. Sixth, notify parents in writing that their son or daughter has been assigned to detention. Adjustments can be made to accommodate any reasonable, verifiable excuses for absences (such as a doctor's appointment). Seventh, have teacher-made assignments ready in the detention room for students to complete. Students who fail to bring their own assignments, having previously been instructed to do so, should be given another detention. Eighth, establish, post, and review firm rules for behavior in the detention room. Finally, regularly review the impact of detention on student behavior. School officials may want to keep track of repeat offenders, the nature of their offenses, and which teachers are abusing the system.

In-School Suspension.   More intrusive than detention is the use of in-school suspension (ISS). It is being used more frequently in public schools as an alternative to the disadvantages associated with out-of-school suspension and expulsion, which will be discussed shortly (Yell, 1990). Kerr and Nelson (1989) identified three assumptions in effective in-school suspension programs. First, like time-out, it is assumed that the setting from which the student is removed is reinforcing. Second, it is assumed that the ISS room is nonreinforcing. Third, it is assumed that the student moves to and from in-school suspension on the basis of carefully constructed contingencies. Used correctly, ISS offers many advantages to secondary school officials. Disruptive students are separated from the rest of the school population yet are still in school, rather than roaming about the community unsupervised. In addition, ISS does not deprive students of their right to an appropriate education (Yell, 1990).

Kerr and Nelson (1989) identified specific guidelines to increase the effectiveness of in-school suspension. These guidelines are listed in Action Plan 6.16. First, school officials can either select one individual to assume ISS responsibilities on a permanent basis or rotate this responsibility among different staff members. Regardless of which option is chosen, those who assume this responsibility must be able to manage disruptive behavior. Second, students can enter ISS only at the beginning of the school day. Those who arrive late or during the day may create additional problems by being disruptive. Third, students assigned to ISS should meet in a central location at the beginning of the school day. At this location, they can be reminded of both their offenses and the rules governing the ISS room. Fourth, the staff member in charge of ISS should already have students' assignments prepared. These assignments should come from teachers whose courses will be missed as a result of being sent to ISS. It is most helpful if classroom teachers provide work that students can complete independently or with minimal assistance. This will minimize the likelihood that the inappropriate behavior that resulted in ISS is inadvertently reinforced by teacher attention. Fifth, there should be only limited opportunities for students to leave the ISS room. For example, only one or two students should be allowed to use the restroom at a time. Also, students should eat their lunch in the ISS room to minimize disruptive behavior in the cafeteria. Sixth, additional days should be assigned to students who violate rules governing behavior in the ISS room. Seventh, when the student has completed ISS time, the staff member in charge should review appropriate alternatives to the behavior that resulted in being sent to ISS. Eighth, the staff member in charge of ISS should ensure that the teacher who requested ISS placement is aware of how the student behaved during this time.

Action Plan 6.16 Guidelines for ISS

The following guidelines for ISS were adapted from Kerr and Nelson (1989):

1. The staff member in charge of ISS should be a skilled behavior manager.
2. Students must enter ISS at the beginning of the school day.
3. Prior to entering ISS, students should meet at a central location where their offenses and ISS rules are discussed.
4. Assignments should be ready at the beginning of ISS.
5. Opportunities to leave the ISS room should be minimized.
6. Additional ISS days should be required for students who violate rules in the ISS room.
7. At the end of ISS, alternatives to inappropriate behavior should be reviewed.
8. Teachers should be kept advised of student behavior during ISS.

The major advantage of ISS is that it allows for the provision of instructional time and support services to students whose behavior is disruptive to teachers and classmates. Kerr and Nelson (1989) warned that ISS could be easily misused and recommended several troubleshooting ideas, which are listed in Action Plan 6.17. First, they suggested that ISS rules be shared with all staff, students, and parents. Yell (1990) advised establishing a written ISS policy. Second, any violation of these rules should result in firm negative consequences. Third, parents must be informed on each occasion that their son or daughter has been assigned to ISS. Fourth, disruptive behaviors that will result in ISS assignment must be considered carefully. They should be behaviors of a more serious nature that require more severe consequences than time-out or detention. For example, Rose (1988) reported that ISS was used with students with disabilities who were disruptive, fighting, displaying repeated violations of a behavior code, late for or cutting classes or detention, using profanity, smoking, or stealing. These behaviors should be clearly defined and thoroughly explained to staff, students, and parents at the beginning of the school year. Such specificity and clarity keep the ISS room from being overrun by students who have committed minor rule violations. Fifth, student assignments to ISS should be monitored to ensure that a teacher is not making unnecessary referrals. Finally, as is true for any intervention program, ISS should be monitored and reviewed to ensure that it is effective. Staff, students, and parents should be informed of any revisions.

Suspension and Expulsion. Other disciplinary techniques that may be available to secondary school officials include suspension and expulsion. Suspension is a short-term exclusion from school for a period of time, usually between 1 and 10 days. Expulsion is exclusion from school for an indeterminate amount of time. Suspension and expulsion are the most frequently litigated punishment procedures used with students who have disabilities (Yell, 1990).

The rulings resulting from these court cases have clarified the use of out-of-school suspension for students with disabilities (*Board of Education* of Peoria v. *Illinois State Board of Education*, 1982; *Goss* v. *Lopez*, 1975; *Honig* v. *Doe*, 1988). Learners with

---

Action Plan 6.17   Troubleshooting ISS Procedures

Kerr and Nelson (1989) identified the following ways school officials can reduce misuse of the ISS room:

1. Share ISS policies with staff, students, and parents.
2. Establish firm consequences for violating rules in ISS.
3. Inform parents when their children are assigned to ISS.
4. Clearly define those behaviors that warrant a referral to ISS.
5. Monitor referrals to ISS.
6. Evaluate the impact of ISS and make necessary revisions.

disabilities may be suspended for up to 10 days, using the same procedures as those used for nondisabled learners. These short-term suspensions are not viewed as changing the learner's educational placement (Rose, 1988; Yell, 1989). Out-of-school suspensions for more than 10 days may be used if the student with disabilities is posing a danger to himself or herself or others. Rose (1988) reported that students were suspended for being disruptive, fighting, repeatedly violating a behavior code, being late, cutting classes or detention, showing a lack of respect, using profanity, smoking, stealing, using weapons, hitting an adult, committing a felony, and abusing drugs or alcohol. A student can be suspended only after the multidisciplinary team has determined (a) whether the behavior was related to the student's disability and (b) that due process rights have been protected. These suspensions provide school officials with time to conduct additional evaluations and consider alternative placements. If it has been determined that the offense was not a function of the students disability, then he or she can be treated as a typical student (Bartlett, 1989).

Rose (1988) reported that students were expelled for fighting, repeatedly violating a code of behavior, showing a lack of respect, using weapons, hitting an adult, committing a felony, or abusing drugs or alcohol. Thus, there is a great deal of variability and overlap in the nature of offenses that result in ISS, suspension, and expulsion.

Yell (1989, 1990) stated that the decision in *Honig* v. *Doe* clearly indicated that students with disabilities cannot be expelled from public schools. To do so constitutes a change in the student's educational placement, something that can only be done with parent permission or with the permission of the courts. School officials have at their disposal other methods, such as the use of time-out, detention, and restriction of privileges. An emergency suspension of up to 10 days can be used to temporarily remove a student who is dangerous and whose parents refuse to agree to a change of placement. This 10-day period can be used by school officials to identify alternative placements or seek court permission to remove the student from school for an extended period (Bartlett, 1989).

No longer can school officials automatically use expulsion to deal with secondary students with special needs who display dangerous or extremely disruptive behavior. Bartlett (1989) recommended that the following procedures be followed with these students. First, parents must be notified in writing. Second, there must be a meeting of the multidisciplinary team to determine whether the student's conduct was related to his or her disability and whether the current placement is appropriate. Team members must be trained and knowledgeable about the student's disabling condition. Third, the student's educational needs must be evaluated. Fourth, parents must be informed of their rights to demand an impartial hearing. Finally, if parents and school officials disagree regarding placement, the student must remain in the current placement until administrative and judicial reviews have been completed.

There are disadvantages associated with both out-of-school suspension and expulsion. They include the loss of instructional time, isolation from peers, encouragement of dropping out, a loss of parent and community support, a loss of state aid if based on average daily attendance, and an increase in daytime juvenile delinquency (Rose, 1988). In addition, some students may prefer being away from school and all of its demands; thus, suspension and expulsion may reinforce inappropriate behavior rather than deter it.

Finally, it should be noted that procedures such as detention, ISS, suspension, and expulsion are used in many schools; however, there are few data supporting their efficacy. School officials who use these procedures are reminded to evaluate the effect they have on the frequency and severity of disruptive behavior. Practices that do not contribute to the development and use of appropriate behaviors should be modified or discontinued in favor of those that do.

Self-Management

Self-management refers to an individual's ability to maintain or change his or her own behavior. It includes several behaviors such as self-determination of criteria, self-determination of reinforcement, self-evaluation, self-instruction, self-monitoring, self-punishment, self-reinforcement, and self-scheduling (Carter, 1993; Schloss & Smith, 1994). Self-management offers several advantages over traditional externally managed systems of reinforcement. It increases students' independence by making them accountable for their own behavior. It allows the teacher more time to deal with other school matters. It can easily be adapted to meet a wide variety of students' behavioral needs across a range of settings. Finally, self-management is a powerful tool for promoting generalization and transfer of training of newly acquired knowledge and skills. These advantages make self-management ideal for use by students in the secondary school.

Most students with disabilities will need to be taught to self-manage their behavior. Generally, teachers will have used externally managed systems such as token economies and response cost to gain control over student behavior. Having established this control, teachers can now rely on the set of procedures listed in Action Plan 6.18 to turn the reins over to the students. First, the teacher needs to review the target behavior, providing representative examples and nonexamples. Next, the teacher should explain the purpose and benefits of self-management. Third, the students should determine the nature and amount of reinforcement they should award themselves for achieving their goals. Fourth, the teacher must develop and teach the students a system for monitoring and recording their behavior. The teacher can adapt the informal systematic observation methods described in Chapter 5. Fifth, the teacher and students should practice monitoring and

---

Action Plan 6.18   Self-Management

Use the following steps to teach students how to manage their own behavior:

1. Define target behaviors.
2. Explain the purpose and benefits of self-management.
3. Determine which reinforcers will be earned.
4. Develop a system for recording behavior.
5. Role play.
6. Implement the system with occasional reliability checks.
7. Self-reinforce.

Case for Action 6.6

What consequence control techniques would you select for use with Louis? How would you reinforce appropriate behaviors? How would you punish inappropriate behaviors?

recording target behaviors using role play. Sixth, both the teacher and the students should monitor behavior separately. Occasional comparisons with the teacher's records should provide students with feedback regarding the accuracy of their recording. The frequency of these comparisons can be faded as the students become more proficient. Finally, the students should be encouraged to reinforce themselves less frequently and to use items and activities found in typical secondary schools.

Summary

The four components of effective classroom management are classroom organization, antecedent control techniques, related personal characteristics, and consequence control techniques. Practitioners are advised to implement these components simultaneously. Using effective classroom management techniques in conjunction with the systematic instruction procedures described in Chapter 4, it is possible to improve the quality of secondary programming for students with disabilities.

References

Alberto, P., & Troutman, A. (1991). *Applied behavior analysis for teachers* (3rd ed.). Columbus, OH: Merrill.

Armbruster, B. B., & Anderson, T. H. (1988). On selecting "considerate" content area textbooks. *Remedial and Special Education*, 9(1), 47–52.

Bartlett, L. (1989). Disciplining handicapped students: Legal issues in light of *Honig v. Doe. Exceptional Children*, 55, 357–366.

Bernstein, D. A., & Borkovec, T. D. (1973). *Progressive relaxation training*: A *manual for the helping professions*. Champaign, IL: Research Press.

Bettencourt, E., Gillet, M., Gall, M., & Hull, R. (1983). Effects of teacher enthusiasm training on student on-task behavior and achievement. *American Educational Research Journal*, 20, 435–450.

Board of Education of Peoria v. Illinois State Board of Education, 1531 F. Supp. 56 148 (C. D. ILL. 1982).

Carter, J. F. (1993). Self-management: Education's ultimate goal. *Teaching Exceptional Children*, 25(3), 28–32.

Deshler, D. D., Putnam, M. L., & Bulgren, J. A. (1985). Academic accommodations for adolescents with behavior and learning problems. In S. Braaten, R. B. Rutherford, & W. Evans (Eds.), *Programming for adolescents with behavioral disorders* (Vol. 2, pp. 20–30). Reston, VA: The Council for Exceptional Children.

Fimian, M. J., Zoback, M. S., & D'Alonzo, B. J. (1983). Classroom organization and synthesization. In B. J. D'Alonzo (Ed.), *Educating adolescents with learning and behavior problems* (pp. 123–151). Rockville, MD: Aspen Systems.

Gardner, W. I. (1977). *Learning and behavior characteristics of exceptional children and youth*: A *humanistic behavioral approach*. Boston: Allyn and Bacon.

Gary W. v. Louisiana, 437 F. Supp. 1209 (E. D. La. 1976).

Goss v. Lopez, 419 U.S. 565, 95 S. Ct. 729, 42 L. Ed. 2d 725 (1975).

Graham, S. (1985). Teaching basic academic skills to learning disabled students: A model of the teaching-learning process. *Journal of Learning Disabilities, 18,* 528–534.

Honig v. Doe, 108 S. CL 592 (1988).

Horton, S. V., Lovitt, T. C., & Bergerud, D. (1990). The effectiveness of graphic organizers for three classification of secondary students in content area classes. *Journal of Learning Disabilities, 23,* 12–22, 29.

Houck, C. K. (1987). Teaching LD adolescents to read. *Academic Therapy, 22,* 229–237.

Ingraham v. Wright, 430 U S. 651 (1977).

Kerr, M. M., & Nelson, C. M. (1989). *Strategies for managing behavior problems in the classroom* (2nd ed.). Columbus, OH: Merrill.

Meese, R. L. (1992). Adapting textbooks for children with learning disabilities in mainstreamed classrooms. *Teaching Exceptional Children, 24*(3), 49–51.

Mercer, C. D., & Mercer, A. R. (1989). *Teaching, students with learning problems* (3rd ed.). Columbus, OH: Merrill.

Misra, A. (1 99 1). Behavior management: The importance of communication. *LD Forum, 11,* 26–28.

Osterag, B. A., & Rambeau, J. (1982). Reading success through rewriting for secondary LD students. *Academic Therapy, 18,* 27–32.

Romeo v. Youngberg, 451 U.S. 982 (1982).

Rose, T. L. (1988). Current discipline practices with handicapped students: Suspensions and expulsions. *Exceptional Children, 55,* 230–239.

Schloss, P. J., & Schloss, C. N. (1988). A critical review of social skills research in mental retardation. In J. L. Matson & R. P. Barrett (Eds.), *Advances in mental retardation and developmental disabilities: A research annual* (pp. 107–151). Greenwich, CT: JAI Press.

Schloss, P. J., & Sediak, R. A. (1986). *Instructional methods for students with learning and behavior problems.* Boston: Allyn and Bacon.

Schloss, P. J., & Smith, M. A. (1994). *Applied behavior analysis for teachers.* Boston: Allyn and Bacon.

Schumaker, J. B., & Deshler, D. D. (1984). Setting demand variables: A major factor in program planning for the LD adolescent. *Topics in Language Disorders, 4,* 22–40.

Schumm, J. S., & Strickler, K. (1991). Guidelines for adapting content area textbooks: Keeping teachers and students content. *Intervention in School, 27,* 798–84.

Sulzer-Azaroff, B., & Mayer, G. R. (1991). *Behavior analysis for lasting change.* Ft. Worth: Holt, Rinehart & Winston.

Weinstein, C. (1979). The physical environment of the school: A review of the research. *Review of Educational Research, 49,* 577–610.

Wiederholt, J. L., & McNutt, G., (1977). Evaluating materials for handicapped adolescents. *Journal of Learning Disabilities, 10,* 11–19.

Wilcox, B., & Bellamy, G. T. (1982). *Design of high school programs for severely handicapped students.* Baltimore, MD: Paul H. Brookes.

Wilson, S., & Wesson, C. (1986). Making every minute count: Academic learning time in LD classrooms. *Learning Disabilities Focus, 2,* 13–19.

Wood v. Stricland, 420 U.S. 308 (1975)

Yell, M. L. (1989). *Honig v. Doe:* The suspension and expulsion of handicapped students. *Exceptional Children, 56,* 60–69.

Yell, M. L. (1990). The use of corporal punishment, suspension, expulsion, and time-out with behaviorally disordered students in public schools: Legal considerations. *Behavioral Disorders, 15,* 100–109.

Zigmond, N., Sansone, J., Miller, S. E., Donahoe, K. A., & Kohkne, R. (1986a). *Teaching learning disabled students at the secondary school level.* Reston, VA: The Council for Exceptional Children.

Zigmond, N., Sansone, J., Miller, S. E., Donahoe, K. A., & Kohnke, R. (1986b). Teaching learning disabled students at the secondary school level: What research says to teachers. *Learning Disabilities Focus, 1,* 108–115.

C h a p t e r 7

Resource Room and Consultative Functions

Did you know that . . .

- The Regular Education Initiative (REI) could increase the number of students with special needs who are enrolled in regular classrooms?
- Resource rooms are the most used and abused forms of service delivery?
- Effective use of a resource room requires the cooperation of the resource room teacher and the regular educator?
- The responsibilities of resource teachers are not uniform across school districts?
- The resource teacher's job description may be developed without the cooperation of the teacher?
- There are many similarities between the responsibilities of resource teachers and those of consulting teachers?
- Consultation, in its strictest sense, involves indirect services to students?
- Many factors must be considered when developing a consultant teacher program?
- The caseload for a consultant teacher should be no more than 35 students?
- Many regular educators may be hesitant to use the services of a consultant teacher?

Can you . . .

- Define the Regular Education Initiative?
- Identify three barriers to the implementation of REI in secondary schools?
- Describe the advantages of placement in a resource room?
- Explain why the resource room teacher "wears many hats"?
- List the responsibilities of the resource teacher?
- Set up a schedule for a secondary resource room?
- Define consultation?

- Identify the advantages of consultation?
- Describe the process of consultation?
- Identify factors that undermine the effectiveness of the consulting teacher?
- Identify ways to decrease the resistance of regular educators to participating in the consulting process?

In the past, special education was perceived as a vehicle by which specific academic deficits were remediated and the negative impact of a disability reduced. Special education professionals believed their primary responsibility was to develop and provide direct services for children with disabilities. Traditionally, instructional objectives were selected from a separate curriculum and occurred in settings other than those utilized by regular education personnel. In essence, regular and special education were perceived as mutually exclusive categories, with little or no interaction at either the professional or the student level (Lilly & Givens-Ogle, 1981).

Fortunately, times have changed. Legislation such as PL 94–142 and Sections 503 and 504 of the Vocational Rehabilitation Act of 1973 have mandated that students with special needs should receive appropriate educational services in the least restrictive environment (Huefner, 1988). As a result, a greater number of students with disabilities are spending all or part of their instructional day in the regular classroom; there is less emphasis on a separate curriculum. Instead, educators are focusing on the development of skills that will enhance functioning in the regular class. Researchers in the area of direct instruction have documented the suitability of a single set of instructional principles for use with children and youth, regardless of the presence or absence of a disabling condition.

These factors have signaled a gradual change in the focus of special education (Lilly & Givens-Ogle, 1981); however, a more recent development—known as the Regular Education Initiative (REI)—has provided additional momentum (Will, 1986). The REI is a partnership formed by regular and special educators to better serve children and youth who fail to learn. REI has generated intensive debate among professionals. The question at the center of these discussions is to what extent and how regular education should be involved in addressing the problems of underachieving children and youth (Huefner, 1988).

Several proposals for implementing the concept of REI have been offered; many call for comprehensive and complex changes in the delivery of educational services to students with mild disabilities. Schumaker and Deshler (1988) advised that these proposals be evaluated within the constraints imposed by regular education settings. Regular secondary education programs present three barriers to the implementation of REI. First, secondary students with disabilities traditionally enter high school without the skills necessary to ensure success in this setting. The gap between their skill levels and the skills needed in the secondary environment widens as students progress through the curriculum. Second, the tremendous workload already demanded of regular secondary educators may leave them with little time and motivation to provide the intensive, empirically based, small-group instruction required to overcome skill deficits. Third, major reforms may be difficult to initiate because of secondary education organizational structures such as teacher centered didactic instruction, limited teacher–student contact time, and autonomous curriculum planning.

Professionals at the secondary level need to develop and implement methods of service delivery to secondary students with special needs that can circumvent these barriers. They need to do so as soon as possible. Currently, the majority of students with disabilities receive most of their education in the regular classroom. Secondary educators need to be prepared for the possibility that implementation of the Regular Education Initiative could increase this number substantially. Two alternatives are particularly well suited to the characteristics of the secondary education setting: resource rooms and consultation. This chapter describes each of these alternatives.

Resource Rooms

The resource room is the most common method of service delivery for secondary students with mild disabilities (Ellett, 1993). It is also the most abused. However, properly organized and implemented, it can assist regular and special educators in meeting the educational needs of secondary students with disabilities (D'Alonzo, 1983).

Defining the Resource Room

Friend and McNutt (1984) have defined a resource room as a structural arrangement in which students with disabilities receive some instructional assistance, although most of their educational program takes place in the regular classroom setting. A resource room is most frequently multicategorical; therefore, it can accommodate students displaying mild or moderate disabilities. The time each student spends in the resource room is based on his or her needs and usually ranges from three hours per week to half of the school day. Traditionally, instruction focuses on academic areas in which students display severe skill deficits; however, Schumaker and Deshler (1988) have suggested that nonacademic areas be addressed, including social skills, job finding and maintenance, and appropriate use of leisure time. Regardless of the skill being addressed, instruction will be more effective if it reflects the cooperative efforts of regular and special educators (D'Alonzo, 1983; Sargeant, 1981).

Advantages of Resource Room Placement

The resource room has six advantages in particular for secondary students with disabilities (Sargeant, 1981; Weiderholt, Hammill, & Brown, 1983). First, most students who receive resource room services remain integrated with their nondisabled peers for most of the school day. This is less stigmatizing than placement in a self-contained secondary special education classroom. Second, more students can receive special education assistance. Indeed, some students who need assistance may not be getting it because their problems are not severe enough to warrant a more intrusive form of service delivery. Yet, they remain in the regular secondary class with a teacher who may have neither the time nor the skills to adequately address their needs. A resource room may be a viable option for these students. Third, some students assigned to full-time special classes might be included in less restrictive settings if resource support were available. They could be included in a regular secondary class for select subjects and receive resource room assistance where necessary. Thus, self-contained secondary special education classrooms would be reserved for those students who truly needed them. This may have the added benefit of keeping students with disabilities in their neighborhood schools. Fourth, the flexible scheduling that is characteristic of the resource room enables resource personnel to quickly meet the changing needs of students and their teachers. Fifth, in addition to providing direct services for students, resource room personnel can assist other professionals. For example, resource teachers can keep their colleagues apprised of the latest developments in curricula, materials, effective teaching, and classroom management. Sixth, placement in a resource room may be more acceptable to parents of secondary students with disabilities.

Action Plan 7.1 summarizes the advantages of a resource room placement. It appears that students and professionals can benefit from a carefully planned and utilized resource room.

The Resource Room Teacher

The success of resource rooms depends to a large extent on the professionals who serve as resource room teachers. To be fully effective, these individuals must be able to wear many hats (Weiderholt et al., 1983). Of course, resource room teachers must be teachers. Much of their time is devoted to providing direct services to students with mild and moderate disabilities. As such, they must be skilled in the use of teaching strategies that

---

Action Plan 7.1   The Advantages of Resource Room Placement

Secondary students who receive resource room services may benefit in the following ways:

1. They may remain in the classroom with their nondisabled peers.
2. They may receive services unavailable to them in the regular classroom.
3. They may avoid being placed in a self-contained class.
4. New problems may be more easily addressed because of flexible scheduling.
5. Their regular education teachers may receive assistance.
6. They may receive increased parental support.

Case for Action 7.1

You are at a multidisciplinary meeting where a secondary student's placement is being discussed. The parents have expressed concern about scheduling resource room services for their child. They would prefer a self-contained setting. How will you argue for resource room services?

enhance student competence in a variety of domains. Unlike their elementary counterparts, secondary resource teachers may also need to be highly skilled in the content areas. Students assigned to the resource room may display deficits in subject areas as discrete as algebra, geometry, biology, or chemistry. A solid background in one or more content areas improves the effectiveness of secondary resource teachers.

Secondary resource teachers must also be curriculum specialists. They must be thoroughly familiar with all aspects of the curricula being used in the secondary school. In addition, they need to be aware of and able to locate alternative curricula for students who need them. For example, a student may not he benefiting from the home economics curriculum being implemented in the school. Therefore, the resource teacher may need to locate a curriculum with a more functional orientation. On a related note, resource teachers must be skilled in curriculum development. They may need to assume leadership roles in the development of a functional curriculum in the event that an appropriate one cannot be located.

In their added role of technician, resource teachers are required to have extensive knowledge all the tools of the trade. They must be familiar with the latest developments in educational materials, be able to locate and demonstrate them for their colleagues, and provide guidelines for evaluation. Their task is complicated by the number of content areas addressed by the secondary school curriculum. An even greater challenge is presented by computer technology, which has grown tremendously with respect to both the availability and complexity of hardware and software.

Resource teachers must also be competent administrators. They are responsible for processing referrals, writing reports, maintaining records, arranging schedules, ordering materials, attending meetings, and organizing and managing the learning environment.

Resource teachers may also need to be counselors. In addition to academic difficulties, or perhaps as a result of them, secondary students with disabilities frequently experience problems in their relationships with peers and authority figures. They may also demonstrate limited confidence in their ability to achieve academic, interpersonal, or vocational goals. In addition, colleagues may need to vent their frustrations or be reassured that they are capable of handling challenging students and unique situations. Resource teachers should be skilled in counseling techniques suitable for use with both of these groups.

Furthermore, resource teachers need to be public and human relations experts. They are in frequent contact with administrators, colleagues, students, parents, public officials, and representatives of outside agencies. They may be called upon to teach, explain, confront, counsel, request, or advocate. Regardless of the nature of the interaction, they must conduct themselves in a professional manner.

Case for Action 7.2

You have been asked by your principal to consider a professional reassignment to a resource room from a self-contained classroom for secondary special needs students. What skills should you possess to assume such responsibilities?

Responsibilities of Resource Teachers

Although resource teachers are known to have a great many responsibilities, the exact nature of these responsibilities remains open to debate, despite the numerous studies conducted in this area (Davis, 1983; Friend & McNutt, 1987). To complicate matters, at times school officials develop job descriptions outlining the resource teacher's responsibilities without consulting the professional involved (D'Alonzo & Wiseman, 1978). Respondents to surveys of resource room practitioners (D'Alonzo & Wiseman, 1978; Davis, 1983; Friend & McNutt, 1987) have identified several key areas of responsibility.

Program Planning.   Resource room personnel are responsible for developing programs that meet the needs of secondary students and their teachers. They need to consider several factors early in the establishment of a secondary resource room. When possible, resource teachers should begin by securing a room that is located in close proximity to regular education classrooms (Elman, 1981). Such a location will have two advantages. First, it may reduce the negative feelings and stigma students and other educators attach to a "special" room. It is more likely to be used if it is viewed as an integral part of the regular education setting. The second advantage is convenience. An accessible location minimizes the amount of the student's instructional day that is lost in transition time. Related to the location of the room is its name. "Resource room" or "learning lab" are titles appropriate for use in the secondary school (Elman, 1981).

The resource teacher also needs to consider the physical design of the room. It should resemble other secondary classrooms in the high school as much as possible. Allocation of space should reflect the various skill levels students may display within academic and social domains. For example, desks can be arranged to provide room for small-group instruction and, when necessary, one-to-one instruction. Study carrels are ideal for independent work. Part of the room can be carpeted, furnished with comfortable chairs, and reserved for use during counseling sessions or social skill development.

When planning a program, resource teachers should locate materials that are suitable for secondary learners. Chapters 1 and 4 pointed out how difficult it can be for secondary special educators to obtain appropriate materials. Chapter 6 presented techniques for purchasing, adapting, and modifying materials. Practitioners are again reminded of the importance of obtaining and using relevant, age-appropriate materials with secondary students with disabilities. In addition to being more appropriate to the students' skill levels, these materials may encourage them to enter and use the resource room.

Program planning also involves the complex task of scheduling. The structure of secondary school may pose a challenge to resource teachers. Not only do they have to schedule time in the resource room, they may also have to accommodate secondary students with disabilities who are included in regular classes. Resource teachers should consider five factors when choosing regular classes (Elman, 1981). They are listed in Action Plan 7.2.

A fourth aspect of program planning is public relations. Setting up shop in close proximity to regular secondary classrooms may be an ineffective way of advertising the room and its functions. Elman (1981) has suggested that secondary resource teachers publicize resource room services in a school bulletin. Informal invitations to administra-

Action Plan 7.2   Tips for Scheduling for Secondary Resource Teachers

We recommend that resource teachers follow Elman's (1981) suggestions for arranging schedules for students with disabilities:

1. Examine the composition of the regular education class. Students with special needs may be more difficult to place in heterogeneously grouped classes.
2. Examine the teaching style of the regular educator. Some special needs students may benefit from a highly structured approach.
3. Check to see whether other special education students are placed in the class. More than three or four may overburden the regular educator.
4. Examine the course requirements and make sure that the student with special needs can keep pace. Modify where possible.
5. Gain the cooperation of the regular educator.

tors, colleagues, students, and parents to visit the room would allow the teacher to explain the program and establish rapport. In addition, resource teachers should be highly visible and should assume duties assigned to regular educators, such as supervising the cafeteria, the detention room, and after-school activities.

Program planning should also be concerned with establishing routine classroom procedures. Ideally, services available through the resource room will attract a great many students and colleagues. This puts pressure on the resource teacher to devise ways of making assistance and information readily available to those who need them. Resource teachers need to develop rules for the resource room and procedures for managing materials and audiovisual equipment, providing assistance, and monitoring independent work. (See Chapter 6 for a more elaborate discussion of routine classroom procedures.)

Direct Service.   Secondary teachers who use the instruction techniques described in Chapter 4 will probably find that most of their students with disabilities are progressing toward the goals that have been established for them. However, if an instructional difficulty persists after two well-documented attempts have been made to resolve them, secondary educators may seek outside assistance. This assistance may take the form of either direct or indirect services.

Much of the resource teacher's day is spent providing direct service to secondary students with disabilities. Instruction may address any of the academic content areas typically encountered in the secondary school curriculum. For some students, especially those with mild learning disabilities, instruction may focus on the development of learning strategies. In addition, resource teachers may try to help some secondary students develop social skills.

The approach to direct instruction should follow the guidelines presented in Chapter 4. Specifically, a resource teacher should be a member of the multidisciplinary team that assesses aspects of a student's behavior relating to the suspected disability. This means the resource teacher must be a skilled diagnostician, thoroughly trained in the administration and interpretation of formal and informal assessment devices. Assessment data must be translated into carefully prioritized annual goals and correctly sequenced instructional objectives that reflect the current and anticipated demands of the environment. Next, the resource teacher must develop and implement lesson plans that incorporate the instructional techniques, materials, and motivation necessary to promote student achievement. The effectiveness of the lessons in facilitating mastery of short-term objectives is evaluated and progress toward achievement of the annual goal is determined. Adherence to these guidelines should increase the number of skills present in students' repertoires. Ideally, continued progress will lead to the termination of resource room services for a particular student and full-time inclusion in regular secondary education classes. However, it is important to conduct follow-up observations to ensure that students are maintaining and generalizing new skills and are functioning effectively in the regular class.

Indirect Service.   For a variety of reasons, the secondary resource teacher is likely to provide indirect services to regular education personnel on a daily or weekly basis. These services are indirect in the sense that direct work with regular education colleagues indirectly benefits secondary students with special needs. For example, a regular education teacher may report that a student with disabilities is experiencing difficulties mastering the goals of a particular instructional unit. Assistance from the resource teacher can assume a variety of forms. He or she may examine the goals of the unit and make suggestions for modifications that more closely approximate the student's needs. Additional materials can be located and utilized. The resource teacher can also observe the classroom during the scheduled activity and identify strategies that will facilitate student learning. The resource teacher may even offer to conduct a sample lesson for the group of which the special needs student is a member.

 Behavior management is another area that may require the cooperative effort of regular and resource educators. A regular educator may seek the assistance of the resource teacher in managing a problem that quantitatively or qualitatively exceeds the norm typical of secondary classrooms. The resource educator can assist in defining the behavior; identifying current antecedents and consequences; gathering baseline data; and designing, implementing, and evaluating an intervention program.

 There are two advantages to providing indirect services to regular education teachers. First, regular education teachers can give students with disabilities the assistance they need to maintain the academic and behavioral standards of the mainstream classroom, and thus eliminate the need for a more restrictive placement. Second, regular education

---

Case for Action 7.3

A mainstream teacher is experiencing difficulty in getting a student with special needs to complete her homework and to hand it in on time. She asks for your advice. What will you suggest?

Case for Action 7.4

You are establishing a resource room program in a secondary school where no such program has ever been available. Your principal has asked that you provide four 30-minute inservice sessions for the faculty. Identify your topics and outline the content of each.

teachers may acquire or fine-tune specific techniques for teaching academic skills and managing behavior that may prove useful in other situations with other students.

Inservice Education. Closely related to indirect services are the inservice sessions that can be conducted occasionally by resource room personnel. Regular education teachers in a particular building may have a common need for specific information or skills. The resource room teacher can organize and present an inservice solution to this problem. Topics of potential interest include recent legislation, current research regarding the characteristics and educational needs of students with disabilities, technological developments, behavior management techniques, and learning strategies. Inservice time should be reserved for presenting new information or demonstrating new materials or techniques, with sufficient time budgeted for discussing the implications for the regular educator.

Parent Education. The secondary resource educator frequently comes into contact with parents. This may occur on a regular basis as a result of multidisciplinary team meetings. In addition, the resource teacher may need to schedule informal meetings with parents for a discussion of their child's progress. Before the conference, the resource teacher should prepare a list of points to be covered and locate student work samples to share. The meeting should begin with a discussion of the student's positive points. Obviously, negative points must also be discussed; however, they can be framed in a way that highlights what can be done to assist the student. Parents should be encouraged to share any insights, concerns, or suggestions they have regarding their child's educational program. The resource teacher may also suggest or demonstrate techniques parents can use at home to make their child's educational program more effective (Elman, 1981).

Administration. Secondary resource teachers have a number of administrative responsibilities. They develop and monitor IEPs, arrange and participate in multidisciplinary team meetings, keep records, process referrals, schedule inservice sessions, and maintain contact with other public and private agencies serving students with disabilities.

It appears that resource room programs play a valuable role in the delivery of educational services to students with disabilities. Their most notable advantage is that they keep students in a less restrictive environment without compromising the integrity of their educational programs. The success of a resource room obviously depends on the skills of the practitioner assigned to this setting. The roles and responsibilities in this setting can only be carried out by a well-trained, dedicated professional.

Closely related to the resource teacher is the consultant teacher, whose role in delivering educational programs to students with disabilities is described next.

The Consultant Teacher

The use of consultation in special education has become increasingly popular in the last 10 to 15 years (Johnson, Pugach, & Hammitte, 1988). The services of the consultant teacher are in keeping with the spirit of the Regular Education Initiative. Specifically, they enable some students with disabilities to function effectively in the mainstream classroom. The consultant teacher may also be extremely helpful to those providing educational services in nontraditional settings such as correctional facilities and hospitals. In some respects, the teacher who provides resource room assistance is similar to the teacher who acts as a consultant.

Definition

According to Idol (1988), special education is a process for providing special education services for students with special needs who are enrolled in general education classes. This process involves many professionals, including special educators, regular educators, ancillary professionals, and parents. These individuals cooperatively plan, implement, and evaluate instruction conducted in the regular classrooms so that educational problems can be prevented or remediated.

This definition emphasizes a collaborative relationship that is based on mutual consent and commitment to a goal, joint development of an intervention plan, and shared responsibility for the implementation and evaluation of that plan (West & Idol, 1987). Idol, Paolucci-Whitcomb, and Nevin (1986) developed the following, broad definition of consultation:

> *Collaborative consultation is an interactive process that enables teams of people with diverse expertise to generate creative solutions to mutually defined problems. The outcome is enhanced, altered, and produces solutions that are different from those that the individual team member would have produced independently. (p. 1)*

Consultation has two goals. The first goal is to maximize the interaction between students with disabilities and their peers through the development and implementation of comprehensive, effective educational programs (Idol et al., 1986). The second goal is to enhance the teacher's skills to facilitate subsequent problem solving (Haight, 1984).

Advantages of Consulting

Consultation is said to have several advantages, some of which resemble those of resource rooms (Haight, 1984; Huefner, 1988; Idol, 1988; Paolucci-Whitcomb & Nevin, 1985).

First, outcome effectiveness data summarized by Idol (1988) have indicated that consultation is an effective means of increasing the skill levels of students with disabilities. Second, the teamwork promoted by effective consultation makes regular and special educators more effective because their combined impact is greater for students than special education services alone. Third, the title "consultant teacher" dissociates students from the label *disabled*. In its purest sense, consultation offers indirect services to students through their teachers; therefore, students remain in their regular education classrooms and participate in intervention programs implemented by the regular teacher. Fourth, the regular classroom provides appropriate peer role models to be emulated by students with disabilities. Fifth, nondisabled peers have the opportunity to understand and appreciate students with disabilities. Sixth, consultation enhances the skill repertoires of the regular educator by providing on-the-job training in areas such as task analysis, behavior management, diagnostic assessment, curricular adaptation, and continuous measurement. Other students in the class not known to be experiencing specific difficulties may benefit from enhanced teacher performance. Seventh, consulting teachers can reduce the cost of special education services. Students can remain in regular classes in their neighborhood schools, thus reducing the costs associated with both busing and the establishment and maintenance of more restrictive educational alternatives. Cost effectiveness is also enhanced when potential academic and behavior problems are prevented, thereby reducing the number of referrals to special education. Eighth, the communication required to implement the consultant model can dispel the mystique associated with special education. Regular and special educators can develop a better understanding of and appreciation for the talents each brings to an educational program. Ninth, the consultant model is uniquely suited to the secondary school. Tenth, use of consultation facilitates the identification of staff development needs that can be address through inservice education.

Consultant teachers can assist secondary content area teachers with the modifications necessary to ensure the success of students with special needs enrolled in the regular classroom. Action Plan 7.3 summarizes these advantages.

Developing a Consultant Teacher Program

Careful consideration must be given to several factors if a consultant teacher program is to provide the benefits previously identified (Idol, 1988). First, it must be carefully funded. Second, preferral and referral strategies must be formulated and should include making a request of consultation and conducting observations and conferences. Third, performance standards should be established for the individual who will serve as the consultant teacher. Idol (1988) has recommended that this individual have at least three years of experience as either a regular or a special educator and possess a credential or certification. Fourth, an appropriate caseload for consultant teachers should be determined. The pupil–teacher ratio should reflect the responsibilities of the consultant. For example, consultant teachers who provide some direct services should have a lower ratio than those who assume only indirect responsibilities. Idol (1988) has recommended a maximum load of no more than 35 students. Fifth, a workload schedule must be developed that allows the consultant teacher to meet all the responsibilities of direct and

Action Plan 7.3   Advantages of the Consulting Teacher

The following advantages are associated with the use of the consulting teacher:

1. Increases students' skill level.
2. Promotes teamwork.
3. Minimizes the need to label students.
4. Provides access to peer models.
5. Nondisabled students can develop an understanding of and appreciation for students with disabilities.
6. Regular educators get on-the-job training.
7. Reduces the cost of special education.
8. Dispels the mystique surrounding special education.
9. Is especially suited to the secondary school.
10. Identifies suitable topics for inservice education.

indirect services. Sixth, an evaluation program must be designed and implemented to ensure that the consultation program is having the desired impact on students and their teachers.

Characteristics of the Consultant Teacher

A consultant can be an expert recruited from somewhere outside the school district, but several problems arise with this practice (McGlothin, 1981). School districts may lack the funds necessary to engage an outside consultant. Districts with sufficient funds may find the efforts of the consultant undermined by the lack of faculty support for proposed changes. Moreover, outside consultants may not be available frequently enough to provide teachers the support they need to initiate change. They may only have time to suggest solutions to teachers who may require an inservice session with follow-up classroom observations and evaluation.

It has been suggested that the person most suited to serve as a consultant is the resource teacher (Evans, 1980). In fact, many resource teachers, by virtue of providing indirect services to regular educators, are already consulting. Haight (1984) and McGlothin (1981) noted that the line separating the resource teacher and the consultant teacher is becoming less distinct. More school districts have included consulting in the job descriptions of resource teachers to meet the needs of the growing number of students with special needs placed in mainstream classes. McGlothin (1981) warned that this may not be the most appropriate alternative, because many resource teachers may lack the training they need to be effective consultants. Haight (1984) suggested a training program that includes coursework, research, and extensive practicum experiences in applied behavior analysis, monitoring procedures, teacher and parent training techniques, and the design and evaluation of suitable materials and intervention programs.

Several authors have identified the qualifications needed to be a consultant (D'Alonzo, 1983; Friend, 1985; Gable, Hendrickson, & Algozzine, 1987; Haight, 1984; Huefner, 1988; Tindall, Shinn, & Rodden-Nord, 1990; West & Idol, 1987). These qualifications, listed in Action Plan 7.4, illustrate the specialized training and skills that go into consultation. First, consultants must be excellent teachers, highly skilled in diagnosis, prescription, and evaluation. Second, they must be able to communicate effectively. That is, they must be able to paraphrase, negotiate, conduct an interview that elicits information and actions, identify and empathize with the perspectives of others, interpret nonverbal communication, give and receive feedback, and minimize the use of jargon. Third, they must be able to solve problems. This means consultants must be able to identify learning and adjustment problems accurately and precisely, including antecedents and consequences; and to develop, implement, evaluate, and revise an appropriate intervention plan and coordinate the efforts of contributing professionals. Fourth, consultants must be experts in systematic observation procedures. They must be able to choose and use the procedure most sensitive to the nature of the learning or adjustment problem. Fifth, they must make every endeavor to follow through on interactions with staff and students. This could be as simple as following up on a suggestion made during an initial interview or as complex as conducting periodic checks on the success of a maintenance and generalization program. Sixth, consultants must manage time efficiently. They are dealing with a variety of teacher and student schedules and must be able to accommodate their needs in a timely manner. Seventh, consultants must be skilled at planning and implementing inservice training that enhances the skill level of their colleagues. Inservice sessions can be designed to provide content information or practice with a new skill. Eighth, they must possess administrative skills. They will be involved in student referrals, multidisciplinary team meetings, IEP development, and record keep-

---

Action Plan 7.4   The Qualifications of the Consulting Teacher

Consulting teachers need to demonstrate the following skills:

1. Be an excellent teacher
2. Be a good communicator
3. Solve problems
4. Utilize systematic observation procedures
5. Follow through on interactions
6. Manage time efficiently
7. Provide in-service training
8. Possess administrative skills.

Case for Action 7.5

You have just received a bachelor's degree in special education and are considering applying for a position as a consultant. What factors should figure in your decision?

ing. Consulting is also likely to take them to different agencies or other school districts; therefore, a working knowledge of the policies of each setting is essential.

Professionals serving as consultants to secondary programs must demonstrate high levels of expertise in several areas in order to perform their duties adequately. The work of consultants is discussed in the next section.

Responsibilities of Consultants

Consultants may need to address any number of issues, including academic problems, individualized instruction, large- and small-group instruction, classroom management, resequencing curriculum materials, large-group management problems, and inservice training (Idol-Maestas, 1981). The consulting process is said to consist of several steps (Cipani, 1985; Kerr & Nelson, 1983; Knight, Meyers, Paolucci-Whitcomb, Hasazi, & Nevin, 1981), as outlined in Figure 7.1.

Referral. The consultant accepts a written referral, signed by the teacher and the principal, describing the student's problem. It is also helpful if the referring teacher describes the problem in detail and identifies any remedial steps already attempted.

Parent Permission. The team of the consultant and the teacher informs the parents of the referral and obtain written permission to assess the student. Of course, parent permission is required by law, but early involvement may enhance the success of future endeavors.

Identification of Problem Behavior. Having reviewed the referral, the consultant should already have some indication of the nature of the problem. Additional information can be obtained from a comprehensive assessment of all areas believed to be related to the student's problem. Assessment may involve formal and informal measures such as norm- and criterion-referenced tests and systematic observations of student behavior in the classroom. Additional observations and interviews can be scheduled with the teacher, the student, and peers (Reisberg & Wolf, 1988). Current levels of performance are measured and factors contributing to the development and maintenance of the problem are identified. Next, the consultant and teacher determine the standard for acceptable performance. They may sample the behavior or skill levels of other students in the class to establish minimal standards of acceptable performance. By comparing the target student's performance with that of his or her peers, they will get an idea of the seriousness of the problem. In the event that there is more than one problem, the team will have to rank the issues in terms of intervention priority. These priorities may be reflected in the goals included on an IEP and should be established in cooperation with parents.

Establish Objectives. The team needs to translate goals into short-term objectives that clearly define both the targeted behavior in measurable terms and the criterion for acceptable performance.

Design an Intervention Program. The consultant and teacher next design an intervention program that addresses the targeted skill and that can be implemented by the regular

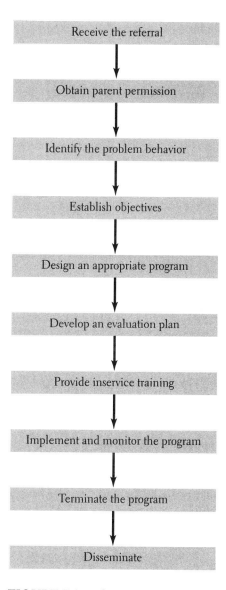

**FIGURE 7.1   The Steps in the
Consultation Process**

educator in the mainstream classroom. Whether the problem is academic or social, the consultant is advised to describe all aspects of the intervention program in technological terms, that is, in terms that allow a knowledgeable reader to apply the procedures with few or no questions. (See Chapter 4 for a description of the sequence of instructional activities that promotes the development of academic skills and Chapter 6 for suitable techniques for a behavior management program.)

Develop an Evaluation Plan. The team needs to consider how the impact of the program will be measured. This step ensures that all necessary sets of data are gathered.

Provide Inservice Training. It is possible that the individual(s) responsible for daily implementation of the intervention program may require training. The consultant may need to provide a demonstration lesson or opportunities to roleplay.

Implement and Monitor the Program. After sufficient practice during inservice training, the teacher implements the program and monitors it on a daily basis. Monitoring is extremely important for two reasons. First, the team needs to ensure that the program is being consistently implemented in the manner intended so that any discrepancies or confusion can be addressed in a timely manner. Second, the team needs to measure the impact of the program on student behavior and make adjustments accordingly.

Terminate the Program. After the student has met the criterion, the program may be faded and eventually dismantled. A team member should conduct periodic follow-up to ensure that new skill levels are being maintained.

Disseminate Results. All relevant parties should be notified of the results of the intervention program. Secondary students may find progress reports motivating, and this response may serve to enhance generalization and maintenance. In keeping with the law, parents should be informed of their child's performance throughout the program. Other professional staff members should be notified of results. They can watch for and reinforce the student's new appropriate academic and social behavior. In addition, it may be politically savvy to make others aware of the positive impact of the consultation program.

This sequence of consulting activities has two advantages. First, the student has acquired a skill that was previously unfamiliar. Furthermore, this was accomplished without removing the student from the regular class. Second, the teacher has also acquired new skills that may benefit either the same student or his or her peers at some future date.

Unfortunately, consultation may not proceed as smoothly as the preceding discussion suggests. A number of factors can adversely influence the effectiveness of the consulting teacher (Haight, 1984; Huefner, 1988; Idol, 1986; Idol & West, 1987; Lilly, 1977; McGlothin, 1981). These factors are presented in Action Plan 7.5 and include case overload, misunderstanding of the consultant's responsibilities, and the lack of appropriate training.

Overcoming Resistance

Consultants have the potential for making a positive impact on secondary students with disabilities and their teachers. Despite this potential, some secondary educators are reluctant to avail themselves of a consultant teacher's services. It is possible that some secondary educators would simply rather have students with special needs served elsewhere. It is also likely that the autonomous nature of secondary educators keeps them

Action Plan 7.5   Factors Undermining the Effectiveness of the Consulting Teacher

The following factors can limit the effectiveness of the consulting teacher:

1. Heavy caseload of more than 35 students
2. Role primarily that of tutor/aide
3. Unrealistic administrative expectations
4. Regular educators who resent having a troubled student removed from the room for a reduced time
5. Too much time spent in direct service
6. Lack of appropriate training.

Case for Action 7.6

A school district is considering implementing a consultant teacher program. What arguments in favor of this move would you offer to the superintendent?

from requesting assistance. While the desire to solve problems with a minimum amount of fuss is commendable, working cooperatively with a consultant teacher can result in problems being solved easily and more quickly, leaving the busy secondary educator more time to deal with other responsibilities.

Consultant teachers must prepare to deal with some resistance as they go about performing their duties. Margolis and McGettigan (1988) offered some specific suggestions consultant teachers can use to increase the possibility that reluctant teachers will work cooperatively to implement programs that increase student success. These suggestions are listed in Action Plan 7.6.

First, the consultant teacher is advised to involved the regular educator as much as possible in all facets of the consultation process. As directly stated in the definition offered earlier, consultation requires cooperation. Just as students are more likely to follow a plan they helped create, so too are secondary educators more likely to support a decision in which they had input. Therefore, it is essential that secondary educators be present and have influence at meetings in which programming decisions are made. Another suggestion is to make sure that the consultant teacher recommends instructional modifications that are practical, concrete, easy to use, minimally disruptive, and likely to yield positive results. On a related note, the secondary educator may need assurances that the recommendation can work. A teacher who does not expect a course of action to succeed is not likely to invest valuable time and energy implementing it. A teacher who is unsure of the effectiveness of a modification can be encouraged to use it provisionally. If it works, it can be implemented as long as needed. If it does not produce anticipated results, adjustments can be made. In addition, it is essential that the secondary educator believe that he or she is receiving adequate support. Thus, the consultant teacher must provide whatever assistance is necessary to implement an instructional modification. Next, a consultant teacher should listen carefully to the secondary educator's personal

Action Plan 7.6   Overcoming Resistance

Margolis and McGettigan (1988) identified steps a consultant teacher can take to increase the likelihood that secondary educators will participate fully in the consultation process:

1. Get the teacher involved.
2. Recommend instructional modifications that are practical, concrete, easy to use, minimally disruptive, and likely to yield positive results.
3. Assure the teacher that the recommended program can work.
4. Implement the program provisionally.
5. Provide adequate support during implementation of any instructional modifications.
6. Be a good listener.
7. Involve the teacher in collecting instructionally relevant information.

concerns and perceptions. Finally, the consultant teacher can involve the secondary teacher in gathering instructionally useful information. Such information can increase his or her knowledge of the problem and ability to identify possible solutions. This information may also foster the secondary educator's perception that his or her knowledge is comparable to that of the consultant teacher, thus increasing confidence and the willingness to participate in the consultation process.

Summary

The Regular Education Initiative has provided the impetus for putting secondary students with disabilities in classrooms for nondisabled learners. The movement has demonstrated the importance of obtaining the cooperation of regular and special educators in the delivery of services to these learners. Two alternatives currently available include the resource room and consultation. Properly implemented, both of these alternatives offer substantial advantages to mainstream educators and secondary students with disabilities.

References

Cipani, E. (1985). The three phases of behavioral consultation. *Teacher Education and Special Education, 8,* 144–152.

D'Alonzo, B. J. (1983). *Educating adolescents with learning and behavior problems.* Rockville, MD: Aspen Systems.

D'Alonzo, B. J., & Wiseman, D. E. (1978). Actual and desired roles of the high school learning disabled resource teacher. *Journal of Learning Disabilities, 11,* 390–397.

Davis, W. E. (1983). Competencies and skills required to be an effective resource teacher. *Journal of Learning Disabilities, 16,* 596–598.

Ellett, L. (1993). Instructional practices in mainstreamed secondary classrooms. *Journal of Learning Disabilities, 26,* 57–64.

Elman, N. M. (1981). *The resource room primer.* Englewood Cliffs, NJ: Prentice-Hall.

Evans, S. (1980). The consultant role of the resource teacher. *Exceptional Children, 46,* 402–404.

Friend, M. (1985). Training special educators to be consultants: Considerations for developing programs. *Teacher Education and Special Education, 8,* 115–120.

Friend, M., & McNutt, G. (1984). Resource room programs: Where are we now? *Exceptional Children, 51,* 150–155.

Friend, M., & McNutt, G. (1987). A comparative study of resource teacher job descriptions and administrators' perceptions of resource teacher responsibilities. *Journal of Learning Disabilities, 20,* 224–228.

Gable, R. A., Hendrickson, J. M., & Algozzine, B. (1987). Correlates of successful mainstreaming of behaviorally disordered adolescents. In S. Braaten, R. B. Rutherford, & J. Maag (Eds.), *Programming for adolescents with behavioral disorders* (pp. 16–26). Reston, VA: The Council for Exceptional Children.

Haight, S. L. (1984). Special education teacher consultant: Idealism v. realism. *Exceptional Children, 50,* 507–515.

Huefner, D. S. (1988). The consulting teacher model: Risks and opportunities. *Exceptional Children, 54,* 403–414.

Idol, L. (1986). *Collaborative school consultation.* (Report of the National Task Force on School Consultation). Reston, VA: The Council for Exceptional Children, Teacher Education Division.

Idol, L. (1988). A rationale and guidelines for establishing special education consultation programs. *Remedial and Special Education, 9*(6), 48–58.

Idol, L., Paolucci-Whitcomb, P., & Nevin, A. (1986). *Collaborative consultation.* Rockville, MD: Aspen Systems.

Idol, L., & West, J. F., (1987). Consultation in special education (Part II): Training and practice. *Journal of Learning Disabilities, 20,* 474–494.

Idol-Maestas, L. (1981). A teacher training model: The resource/consulting teacher. *Behavioral Disorders, 6,* 108–121.

Johnson, L. J., Pugach, M. C., & Hammitte, D. J. (1988). Barriers to effective special education consultation. *Remedial and Special Education, 9*(6), 41–47.

Kerr, M. M., & Nelson, C. M. (1983). *Strategies for managing behavior problems in the classroom.* Columbus, OH: Merrill.

Knight, M. F., Meyers, H. W., Paolucci-Whitcomb, P., Hasazi, S. E., & Nevin, A. (1981). A four year evaluation of consulting teacher service. *Behavioral Disorders, 6,* 921–100.

Lilly, M. S. (1977). The merger categories: Are we finally ready? *Journal of Learning Disabilities, 10,* 115–121.

Lilly, M. S., & Givens-Ogle, L. B. (1981). Teacher consultation: Present, past, and future. *Behavioral Disorders, 6,* 73–77.

Margolis, H., & McGettin, J. (1988). Managing resistance to instructional modifications in mainstreamed environments. *Remedial and Special Education, 9*(4), 15–21.

McGlothin, J. E. (1981). The school consultation committee: An approach to implementing the teacher consultation model. *Behavioral Disabilities, 6,* 101–107.

Paolucci-Whitcomb, P., & Nevin, A. (1985). Preparing consulting teachers through a collaborative approach between university faculty and field based consulting teachers. *Teacher Education and Special Education, 8,* 132–143.

Reisberg, L., & Wolf, R. (1988). Instructional strategies for special education consultants. *Remedial and Special Education, 9*(6), 29–40.

Sargeant, L. (1981). Resource teacher time utilization: An observational study. *Exceptional Children, 47,* 420–425.

Schumaker, J. B., & Deshler, D. D. (1988). Implementing the Regular Education Initiative in secondary schools: A different ballgame. *Journal of Learning Disabilities, 21,* 36–42.

Tindall, G., Shinn, M.R., & Rodden-Nord, K. (1990). Contextually based school consultation: Influential variables. *Exceptional Children, 56,* 324–336.

Weiderholt, J., Hammill, D., & Brown, V. (1983). *The resource teacher: A guide to effective practices* (2nd ed.). Austin, TX: Pro-Ed.

West, J. F., & Cannon, C. S. (1988). Essential collaborative consultation competencies for regular and special educators. *Journal of Learning Disabilities, 21,* 56–63.

West, J. F., & Idol, L. (1987). School consultation (Part I): An interdisciplinary perspective on theory, models, and research. *Journal of Learning Disabilities, 20,* 388–408.

Will, M. (1986). Educating children with learning problems: A shared responsibility, *Exceptional Children, 52,* 411–416.

Chapter 8

Listening and Speaking

DANIEL C. TULLOS

Did you know that . . .

- We spend approximately 75% of our time speaking and listening?
- The primary goal of listening is understanding?
- All speakers are occasionally dysfluent?
- There are 43 phonemes in American English?
- All phonemes are acquired by 8 years of age?
- Semantics may be the most important aspect of language functioning?
- Social skills and pragmatics are similar?
- Listening is best assessed through informal measures?
- Syntax is most effectively evaluated by a language sample?
- Listening instruction should be infused into other curricular areas?
- Instruction in spoken-language skills needs to be provided separately and infused into other curricular areas?
- Techniques for assessing and teaching pragmatic skills resemble those used to assess and teach social skills?

Can you . . .

- Define language?
- Identify the components of language?
- Identify four types of voice disorders?

Daniel C. Tullos is a professor and director of the Communication Disorders Program at Harding University, Searcy, Arkansas.

- Differentiate between two types of phonological problems?
- Identify morphological endings that pose difficulties for secondary students?
- Develop a listening skills assessment?
- Construct sentences to informally assess morphological skills?

If asked to list all the activities in which they participated during a given day, most individuals would neglect to mention communication. However, a careful consideration of these activities would reveal that two dimensions of communication—namely, speaking and listening—are important characteristics of most activities. Researchers have found that people spend between 33% (Weinrauch & Swanda, 1975) and 55% of their time listening (Werner, 1975) and around 26% of their time speaking (Weinrauch & Swanda, 1975). This means that individuals may spend up to 75% of their time in speaking and listening.

This chapter examines some of the basic characteristics of speaking and listening necessary for normal interaction within a secondary program. Emphasis is on the testing of speaking and listening skills as well as the remediation of speaking and listening deficits among secondary students who have disabilities. Note that many of the skills involved in successful speaking and listening are mastered before and during the elementary school years. Therefore, the age at which specified skills are usually mastered is presented. The goal of primary school speech, language, and hearing screening programs is to identify and provide remediation for deficits in normally acquired communication skills before a student participates in a secondary program. Also included in this chapter are sections on bidialectism and bilingualism. No discussion of speaking and listening would be complete without an awareness of issues inherent in our multicultural society.

Additional information regarding the application of these speaking and listening skills to social environments such as employment settings is presented in Chapter 14.

Listening

Listening is a selective process that involves both the reception of auditory cues and the interpretation of information contained in those cues. Listening is effective only when the listener is participating actively in the listening process and the primary objective is understanding. Listening is particularly important for secondary students with disabilities (Alley & Deshler, 1979). First, these students can gain a great deal of information through the auditory channel. Second, new information and a variety of leisure activities become accessible via devices that require listening skills, such as television, radios, and telephones. Third, employment and social situations demand efficient listening skills.

A student who seems to be having listening problems may actually have one of several basic disabilities: a hearing problem, an attention deficit, or a language comprehension deficit. In order to rule out a hearing problem, the student should be referred to an audiologist for a hearing screening or an audiological evaluation. If a school does not have an audiologist, the speech-language pathologist may screen the hearing of the student and, if necessary, refer him or her to a local audiologist for a more extensive assessment. If no hearing problems are indicated, then an attention or a language comprehension deficit should be suspected.

Attention deficits are often caused by mental and physical distractions. Physical distractions draw the student's attention away from the teacher and the information/instructions being presented to the class. Physical distractions can often be identified. Some examples are football practice outside the window, fish in a classroom aquarium, or a blinking neon light. Mental distractions are more difficult to identify. The student may be planning a party, rehearsing how to ask "Mr. or Miss Perfect" out on a date, or thinking about what the teacher would look like without any hair. In any case, the information communicated by the teacher is not received by the student. Note, however, that it is difficult to separate an attention deficit from an interfering language-comprehension problem.

Speech

In the past, an effort was made to clearly differentiate aspects of communication related to speech and those related to language. *Speech* was taken to mean the production of the sounds of language (articulation), and the quality (voice) and smoothness (fluency) with which those sounds are produced. Articulation and phonology are no longer as clearly differentiated. Researchers (e.g., McReynolds & Elbert, 1981; Weiner, 1981, 1986; Weiner & Wacker, 1982) have indicated that some sound production or articulation errors that have been labeled speech problems actually have to do with the rules governing how speech sounds are produced or combined (phonology). In this chapter we do not attempt to differentiate rule-governed or phonological errors from sound production errors caused by other factors. For the sake of convenience, all errors of sound production are discussed under phonology/articulation. However, the few sound production errors noted in a secondary classroom environment would probably not be rule-based errors.

A person is said to be "dysfluent" if the rhythm or smoothness of his or her communication is abnormally disrupted. This difficulty is frequently referred to as *stuttering*. Stuttering is often considered a "disorder of childhood" (Bloodstein, 1984, p. 104), although some students continue to be dysfluent during their secondary school and adult years. If a student appears to be struggling to say something, expresses concern about blocks or repetitions, or is criticized by his peers for abnormal rate or rhythm of communication, then he should be referred to the speech-language pathologist. The speech-language pathologist will observe the student in various speaking situations and compare his fluency to that of his peers. It should be noted that all speakers are dysfluent, depending on the circumstances, and only dysfluent speakers who fall outside the range of normal need therapy. The speech-language pathologist then meets with the teacher to discuss ways in which the pressures surrounding communication for the student may be reduced. The causes of and most effective treatment programs for fluency disorders continue to be widely debated.

Voice disorders may be divided into four types: pitch, loudness, quality, and duration. A secondary teacher would be most likely to observe students with disorders of voice quality, such as the hoarseness caused by vocal nodules. Unfortunately, many students with such nodules are never referred for proper management. If a student has persistent hoarseness and continuously sounds as though he or she has a cold, then a referral should be made to an otolaryngologist for a visual inspection of the vocal cords to determine whether nodules are present. The school speech-language pathologist can assist with the consultation and referral. Another voice disorder is hypernasality (nasal-sounding voice). The speech-language pathologist can evaluate and determine possible causes, and then either provide therapy or refer the student to someone for appropriate medical intervention.

Language

Language has been defined as "a code whereby ideas about the world are represented through a conventional system of arbitrary signals for communication" (Bloom & Lahey, 1978, p. 4). The words used to communicate are arbitrary signals in that they possess no inherent meaning. That is to say, their meanings have been arbitrarily assigned by the members of that language community. For communication to take place, the person sending the message must place the idea into code form (encode) and transmit that code to another person, who will translate that code into an idea (decode).

Language is rule governed in that it is predictable and, to a large extent, consistent throughout a language community. The system of rules governing a language can be divided into phonology, morphology, semantics, syntax, and pragmatics. Although these concepts may be defined and discussed separately, in the speaking process they are all combined.

Phonology/Articulation

Every language can be divided into a specific number of sounds. When combined, they form the words of that language. These small, distinctive, individual units of sound are called *phonemes*, and the system of rules that govern their combination or sequencing is termed *phonology*. Although the English alphabet contains only 26 letters, the sound system of American English contains approximately 43 phonemes, 25 of which are consonants and the remaining 18 vowels (Calvert, 1986). By the age of 3, a child can produce many of these sounds, especially the vowel sounds, in the standard way accepted by the community. Native English speakers do not usually have difficulty producing English vowel sounds unless they have a hearing loss (Mowrer & Case, 1982). Most individuals have acquired all 43 phonemes by the age of 8. Certainly, by the time an individual has reached a secondary program, no abnormalities in sound production should be noted.

Errors in producing or articulating the phonemes of American English fall into three main categories: substitution, distortion, and omission. When a student uses another recognizable American English sound for the target sound, a substitution has occurred. For example, a student who labels an object flying in the sky as a "tite" instead of "kite" is making a substitution error. A distortion error occurs when a student uses a sound not considered an English sound or not an American English sound for the target sound. For example, a student who forces air out of one side of her mouth when producing an "s" is distorting the sound. In an omission error, a student simply omits the target sound in words, as in "bo" for "boat" and "o" for "toe."

Other errors in sound production may be rule based (phonological). For example, a student may exhibit final consonant deletion. She can produce /t/, /b/, and /s/ and says words such as "tea," "bee," and "stay." However, all consonants occurring at the end of words are dropped. Thus, she says "e" for "eat," "ca" for "cab," and "pa" for "pass." The difference between rule-based phonological errors and the errors of articulation is that the former involves systematic application of rules governing sounds the student can produce; for example, the student above can produce all the consonants but does not use them if they appear at the end of a word. Articulation disorders render a student unable to produce a particular sound regardless of where it appears in the word.

Morphology

Morphology refers to the way the sounds of American English are combined into meaningful units and to the rules governing this process. The smallest meaningful units produced as a result of this combination of sounds are called *morphemes*. Root words, as well as prefixes, suffixes, and both parts of compound words are classified as individual morphemes. The word *cars*, for example, contains two morphemes. "Car" is called the root, and the "s" the marker of plurality. The types of morphemes that occur in English and the order in which they would normally be acquired are presented in Action Plan 8.1 (see Cole & Cole, 1989). Students who have experienced developmental delays, as well as students from "poor" language environments may have difficulty with morphological constructs. For example, a teacher, asking whether anyone has seen Mary and Sue, may receive a reply such as, "I seed them," instead of the acceptable "I saw them." Or consider the student who described a picture in which a dog is obviously pregnant by saying "Her's having puppies."

Semantics

The aspect of language that has to do with the meaning of words is referred to as *semantics*. Semantics is considered to be extremely important because "the communication of meaning is the central function of language" (Crystal, 1981, p. 131). Children learn through experience that whatever occurs around them can be described or controlled by using words. They hear significant individuals within their environment use certain words, and they begin to associate those words with specific objects, actions, and events. Understanding the meaning of a word (reception) precedes the use of that word (expression). At the age of 8 a child can understand approximately 8,000 words but will use approximately 2,218 words (Berry, 1969). This pattern, with isolated exceptions, continues throughout life.

Two aspects of semantics have great bearing on secondary education. The first is the type of words used by the student. Weiss and Lillywhite (1976) have stated that word acquisition normally follows this sequence:

nouns–verbs–adjectives–pronouns–adverbs
prepositions articles conjunctions interjections.

By the time students enter a secondary program, they should be using all of these types with the same frequency as their peers. Since vocabulary is so closely linked with experience, and experiences vary from location to location, as well as from person to person, the vocabulary used in an individual school should be a primary consideration for secondary educators.

Semantics also has to do with the way words are combined in sentences to convey complex meaning. A student must be aware of the meaning of words in order to be able to combine them into meaningful sentences. The significant classes of words in semantics are not the same as those in syntax discussed in the following section. Semantically, words are grouped into specific areas or fields of meaning. In a limited study of adults, Crystal (1981) found that 12 classes accounted for 55% of the words used by the sample group: time, leisure, possession, people, cognitive activity, quantity, location, coming and going, sensory perception, animals, foods and meals, and house and furniture. In the agent–action–object sentence, "The _____ sees the _____," semantic rules dictate that

Action Plan 8.1 The Development of Morphemes

Morphemes in Order of Acquisition

Morphemes	*Examples*
1. Present progressive form of verb	*is* eating
2–3. Prepositions in, on	*in* chair, *on* table
4. Plural (regular)	cats, dogs, witches
5. Past irregular tense verbs	*went, came, fell*
6. Possessives	*boy* coat, *Daddy* hat
7. Uncontractible copula	Here I *am*, there it *is*, here we *are*, I *be* good.
8. Articles	*a* ball, *the* doggie
9. Past regular tense verbs	*jumped, poured, waded*
10. Third-person regular verbs	Daddy *drives.*
11. Third-person irregular verbs	Debbie *does*, Mommy *has.*
12. Uncontractible auxiliary verb	I *am* working; boy *is* running; girls *are* jumping; they *be* working.
13. Contractible copula	He's boy; we're happy; she's a mommy; I'm good boy.
14. Contractible auxiliary (contraction form of an auxiliary verb)	I'm working; he's running; she's sewing; we're playing.

Source: Reprinted from *Effective Intervention with the Language Impaired Child*, 2nd ed., by M. T. Cole and J. T. Cole, p. 13, with permission of Aspen Publishers, Inc., © 1989.

only words from the people or animal class may fill the agent position, whereas words from additional classes such as foods and meals may be used in the object position. Semantic rules also dictate that the words chosen to fill specific positions must match the actual situation. In the sentence, "The *tall* man is eating the apple," the word *short* could not be used even though it would still produce an acceptable sentence. In this context, the meaning of the word *short* does not describe the 6-foot man eating the apple.

Vocabulary development is an ongoing process. People normally continue to add words to their receptive and expressive vocabularies on the basis of their experiences. Students participating in a science experiment, for example, may first learn the meaning of the word *reaction* when the teacher talks about and demonstrates a chemical reaction. The students begin to notice and understand *reaction* as the word is used in different situations. Gradually, *reaction* begins to appear in the students' expressive vocabulary as they describe specific situations. Words may also disappear from expressive vocabularies as experiences change. Remember that words do not have inherent meaning. The meaning of a word depends on how the word is used by the majority of people within a specific environment or by the communicator and receiver. Words may have a denotative or dictionary meaning, as well as a connotative or personalized meaning. The word *bad*, for example, has a negative denotative meaning but is frequently used with a positive connotative meaning. The sentence, "That music was bad!" could have two totally opposite meanings when expressed by a teacher and a student in Grade 10. Teachers must be aware of this potential problem in semantics.

Syntax

The rules of syntax determine the way in which words are put together to form phrases and sentences. What is commonly referred to as *grammar* is actually a combination of the rules of syntax and morphology. Listeners may not be able to list English syntactic rules, but they can detect when one has been violated. Developmentally, syntax becomes a factor in communication at around 18 months of age, when an infant begins to combine single words into two-word phrases. Initially, these phrases are made up of functional words and are telegraphic in nature (telegraphic speech). Gradually, these phrases and sentences become more complex until a child is able to master all patterns of sentence structure, usually about the age of 7 or 8.

Syntactic rules are grasped through repeated exposure to language. Children are surrounded by adults and older siblings who are using language to control their environment through interaction. These children begin to notice that words are always placed in a certain sequence. In an English-speaking environment, they notice that the subject usually precedes the verb, and the verb usually precedes the object. When they begin to produce two- and three-word combinations, these combinations follow the rules picked up from their environment in a progressive sequence.

After learning to construct simple or kernel sentences, children begin to transform them into more complex sentences. A transformation is the rule-based altering of a sentence. For example, the active construction, "The boy hit the ball" may be transformed into a passive construction, "The ball was hit by the boy." Another type of transformation involves embedded sentences. This type of sentence consists of two kernel sentences that have been combined in such a way that one depends on the other. The former is called the *dependent clause* and the latter the *independent clause*. As a general rule, students in a secondary program should understand and be able to generate all types of complex and embedded sentences. However, this area of syntax is most likely to present difficulties for secondary students who have experienced developmental delays or disorders.

Pragmatics

The rules underlying the functional use of language are collectively referred to as *pragmatics*. The social context in which language is produced and the way in which that context affects meaning are closely tied to pragmatic rules. An individual exhibiting problems with the pragmatics of language would also be exhibiting social skill deficits. Pragmatics takes in several aspects of communication, including nonverbal codes, discourse, and shifts in style.

A nonverbal code may be any form of communication that does not consist of words. Gestures, facial expressions, tone of voice, and even clothing can be considered pragmatic factors in communication. A student sent to the principal's office for fighting may say, "I will never cause any more trouble." However, if she is slouched in a chair in the office, has a bored look on her face, and is using a sarcastic tone of voice, the message that is being sent is the opposite of the words used. The message that the principal receives is "I will fight if I want to." Clothing, too, can influence the message transmitted. An individual who wears torn blue jeans and a dirty T-shirt to an interview for a summer job at a local clothing store is communicating that this job is not important. The fact that he really wants the job is not the message being conveyed.

Discourse refers to conversation in which individuals function as both speakers and listeners. To participate in a conversation, students need to be skilled in taking turns; initiating, maintaining, and terminating conversations; and making repairs in the event of a communication breakdown.

To communicate successfully, a person must be able to evaluate a specific speaking situation and determine the style of language that would be most effective or appropriate at that time. For example, a student offering a peer a candy bar may say, "Here, pig out on this." However, the same student offering the candy bar to a teacher needs to change the style to "Would you like this candy bar?" Some students with learning disabilities have difficulty recognizing the situational factors (pragmatics) necessary to shift to the appropriate style.

Assessment of Listening Skills

Listening skills may be assessed formally or informally. In a formal assessment, one measures the student's ability to retain and comprehend information presented auditorily. Few formal measures have been developed to assess listening skills alone; therefore, the teacher will have to use subtests of more comprehensive language assessment techniques. The Clinical Evaluation of Language Functions (CELF) (Wiig & Semel, 1980a) has sections that test students' abilities to process oral directions and spoken paragraphs.

The teacher may find informal assessment a more appropriate method for measuring the listening skills of secondary learners with disabilities. Wallace, Cohen, and Polloway (1987) described two methods of informal assessment: teacher checklists and skills assessment. A teacher checklist is used to document listening skills in areas that occur frequently and naturally throughout the day. A sample checklist is presented in Figure 8.1. This technique offers two advantages. First, it is easily adapted to other settings. For

Name: _____   Date: _____

Observer: _____   Setting: _____

Listening Skill	*S #1*	*S #2*	*S #3*	*S #4*	*S #5*
1. Responds to discrete cue signaling the beginning of instruction.					
2. Responds to bells signaling the end of class.					
3. Attends to announcements over the public address system.					
4. Participates in class discussions.					
5. Sequences events.					
6. Participates in informal conversations with peers.					
7. Appears to be listening: e.g., watches teacher and establishes eye contact, looks at maps, etc.					
8. Answers questions.					

FIGURE 8.1   A Teacher Checklist for Measuring Secondary Students' Listening Skills

example, the teacher may develop separate lists for mainstream and special-class environments. Second, teacher checklists are easy to use and interpret.

A skill assessment is a more structured method of measuring listening abilities. Rather than waiting for opportunities to occur in the natural environment, the teacher structures situations in which the student must respond. A skill assessment may be conducted to measure discrimination, recall, and comprehension skills. For example, the teacher may notice that a student frequently mispronounces common words. She develops a skill assessment to measure how well a student can discriminate sounds. She establishes a criterion level, pronounces one item at a time from material within the student's listening comprehension, has the student repeat it, and records the accuracy of the response. For a thorough evaluation of sound discrimination skills, the student should be referred to a speech-language pathologist (see Locke, 1980). Although this method requires more preparation time, it does allow the teacher to identify listening skills that need to be developed.

Assessment of Speaking Skills

The skills necessary for age-appropriate speaking are assessed according to the five components of language: phonology, morphology, semantics, syntax, and pragmatics. There are methods to evaluate skills in each of these areas; however, as indicated earlier, all of these components must work together to produce effective and appropriate communication. These components may be assessed by formal and informal measures, both of which provide valuable information for the remediation process.

Formal measures of language functioning are designed to assess language skills in designated area(s) and are usually purchased by the teacher or speech-language pathologist. These tests sample skills by examining specific items that research and standardization studies have shown to be typical of the performance of peers in the designated area(s). Formal language assessment measures focus attention on specific deficit areas, but do not describe the language system used by the student.

Unfortunately, a student may have no problems with the items sampled on a formal test, but still exhibit significant problems in that particular area. The Peabody Picture Vocabulary Test—Revised (Dunn & Dunn, 1981), for example, presents 175 vocabulary items and provides an age-equivalency score based on the number of items correctly identified. A student may obtain an appropriate age score because he is familiar with many of the items on the test, but still have a significant receptive/expressive vocabulary (semantic) problem. The reverse is also true. A student may obtain a low age-equivalent score because she is unfamiliar with the vocabulary items included on the test; however, she may have no difficulty with the vocabulary used in her home and educational environments.

Informal measures of language functioning usually consist of structured or unstructured observations. Suppose the teacher becomes concerned about a student who has trouble participating in class discussions. When he does respond, he uses several short, simple sentences rather than a complex sentence more typical of the responses from other students. The teacher has an aide make a list of all of this student's verbal utterances during a specified period of time. This observation will produce a better and clearer picture of how this student is forming sentences (syntax) and more specific information for developing a treatment program. Informal testing can provide ample information regarding the phonological, morphological, semantic, syntactic, and pragmatic rules that are being used by a student.

There is a place for both formal and informal spoken language assessment in secondary programs. Many of the formal tests of speech and language functioning are administered by the speech-language pathologist within each school. A teacher who suspects that a student is having difficulty with speaking should refer that student to the speech-language pathologist. A speech and language evaluation, which usually includes formal and informal measures, would then be conducted and the results discussed with the student, parents, and teacher. Note, however, that the classroom teacher is usually in a better position to conduct informal observations. He or she is around the students and can observe their verbal and nonverbal interactions more successfully than the speech-language pathologist (see Chapter 5). The speech-language pathologist may help the teacher identify specific behaviors that need to be observed and thus may enhance the teacher's contribution to the assessment process.

As already pointed out, it would be impossible to cover all of the assessment procedures that are used, or that are necessary for a thorough evaluation of speech and language functioning. We can only suggest some ways that each component of language may be assessed. Again, the specific areas of language will be considered individually, although in reality each must be considered within the framework of all the others. It is strongly recommended that students exhibiting any speech or language difficulties be referred to a speech-language pathologist for a complete evaluation of functional skills. Additional sources (see, e.g., Bloodstein, 1984; Cole & Cole, 1989; Owens, 1992; Reich, 1986; Shames & Wiig, 1982; Warren & Rogers-Warren, 1985) should also be consulted for complete information on normal and abnormal speech and language.

Phonology/Articulation

A secondary student who is exhibiting any sound production errors should be referred to a speech-language pathologist. One speech-language pathologist in a university program receives several referrals of incoming freshmen each year who are exhibiting sound production errors. The majority of these students have never received therapy, and report that they have never been informed that their articulation is abnormal. A disservice is done to these students if they have not been referred for services that are routinely provided within elementary and secondary school programs.

The speech-language pathologist will conduct an inventory of all sounds used in American English and determine any sound that a student is having difficulty with and whether there are any organic causes such as a hearing loss or poorly aligned teeth. Organic problems will be referred for appropriate management, perhaps to a dentist, or a treatment plan will be developed to remediate the errors in sound production.

Morphology

Few commercial measures are available to diagnose morphological difficulties. There-fore, information regarding morphological functioning must be based on informal obser-vation and testing. A teacher should take note of those students who seem to be having trouble with these endings (see Action Plan 8.1) and compare them with the other students in the class or school program. Morphological prefixes such as "de-," "ex-," and "un-" are more likely to present problems at the secondary level. A written or oral exercise would be one way for a teacher to evaluate a student's use of prefixes. This exercise could include a list of prefixes (see Wiig & Semel, 1980b, p. 41) with instructions for the students to describe the meaning and give an example of words containing certain prefixes.

Semantics

Semantic development can also be assessed informally. The most effective informal evaluation of semantic functioning works from a sample of the student's language in specific contexts. Semantic concepts are linked with experiences; therefore, the language that is used to relate characteristics of an experience should reflect ongoing semantic development. Ask each student to share a recent experience, such as a concert, with the class for about five minutes. Make a list of the concepts and vocabulary items expressed. Then generate a discussion and compare the vocabulary items and concepts to those used by the rest of the class. Introduce new semantic concepts to the class and note whether or not those concepts were understood and used by the students participating in the group. This same approach may be used in semantic training.

Syntax

There are few formal measures of syntactic ability available for secondary students. The Detroit Tests of Learning Aptitude—Auditory Attention Span for Related Syllables subtest (Baker & Leland, 1967) requires the student to verbally repeat increasingly complex and lengthy sentences. This test is designed for individuals between 3 and 19 years of age. As with any formal test, the results assist a teacher in identifying deficit areas that need to be assessed informally.

A spontaneously produced sample of oral language is again the most effective way of assessing syntactic functioning. A large sample of spontaneous language should be collected along with the context in which the sentences were produced. The number of sentences in this sample would range from at least 50 to well over 100 utterances. This record of the oral sample may then be analyzed according to the type of sentence used, such as noun + copula + noun/adjective simple sentences (The boy is very sick) and complex adverbial embedded sentences (You don't mind if I eat this apple). Some syntactic problems will be obvious, such as inappropriate word order and lack of agree-ment between subject and verb. A deeper analysis may indicate that a student is using very few complex sentences or is producing incorrect compound sentences. Although a language sample yields a great deal of useful information, it takes a great deal of time and substantial skill to collect and analyze. Time constraints may limit its use by secondary teachers; however, a speech-language pathologist may elect to use this procedure.

Pragmatics

Most pragmatic measures that are currently available look at the skills of children. Little is currently available for the assessment of adolescent pragmatic functioning. Following are some examples of pragmatic difficulties that would be noticeable in secondary students:

1. Utterances that lack adequate referential clarity and therefore confuse or mislead the listener
2. Difficulty in initiating topics, maintaining topic relevance, switching and returning to the main issue or topic, and terminating a conversation
3. Frequently impolite interrupting points in the conversation.

Schloss and Sedlak (1986) have stated that what speech-language pathologists refer to as *pragmatics*, special educators refer to as *social skills*. A review of social skills literature provides a variety of formal and informal techniques for measuring this aspect of spoken language. These techniques are reviewed in detail in Chapter 14.

Strategies to Improve Listening Skills

Although teachers cannot confer on students the ability to listen, they can provide experiences that will help them listen more effectively (Wallace et al., 1987). In other words, listening skills can be taught. Individuals should listen for a purpose. Teachers are advised to instruct their students to listen *for* something rather than listen *to* something. Rather than treat listening skills separately, one should develop them through activities conducted during instruction in other curricular areas.

Wallace and colleagues (1987) identified five general categories of listening that can be addressed throughout the curriculum: distinguishing nonlanguage sounds, discriminating voices, following directions, remembering what is heard, and organizing material. The last three categories are relevant to secondary students with disabilities. Wallace and colleagues (1987) also described a number of activities to promote listening skills in each of these categories.

Following Directions

The following activities can be useful in helping secondary students follow directions.

1. Assign a partner to each student. Give one student a picture to describe to his or her partner. The description should be a set of directions. The partner must draw the picture without asking any questions.
2. Explain the potential uses of a new piece of equipment and provide directions for its use to one student. Have that student explain to a peer how to operate the device.

3. Give students working on map skills a set of directions that takes them on a special trip.

Remembering What Is Heard

Being able to remember what is heard is vital if the secondary learner is to experience success in school and in community environments. Wallace and colleagues (1987) suggested the following activities to strengthen listening skills:

1. During class discussion, have students summarize the comments made by the individual who spoke immediately before them. They may follow up with their own comments.
2. Read an article from the newspaper aloud and instruct students to remember as many of the details as possible.
3. Give comprehension questions just before students listen to a selection from a social studies or science textbook.
4. Have students listen to a radio news broadcast. Ask each student to write a headline for every story remembered.

Taking Notes

Note taking is a necessary skill for effective participation in secondary education. Students who have trouble taking notes usually try to write too much, thereby missing many of the important points. Students should be encouraged to write down only key words and phrases. Usually the important information in a sentence could be captured by writing only the subject and verb. As the important words or phrases are written down, they should be organized in some way. Notes about the Civil War could take the following form in a student's notes, with the major subject mentioned first and related information indented.

Civil War
     -1861–1865
     -Union/Confederacy

Secondary teachers could develop note-taking activities for the entire class. Most students could use some assistance in this area.

Organizing Material

Teachers can use the following activities to help secondary students organize the information they acquire by listening.

1. Have students predict the outcome of historical accounts and scientific experiments.
2. Use the cloze technique. Read a series of sentences from which key words have occasionally been omitted. Students must decide which words can be inserted appropriately.

Case for Action 8.1

A secondary teacher working with a student with special needs in social studies reports that the learner has difficulty following directions. The student never appears to be on the correct page, does not follow along during oral reading, and frequently turns in the wrong homework assignment. What suggestions can you make?

3. Develop a timeline for a series of historical events or the events described in a story.
4. Prequestion students before an oral presentation. Students should be instructed to listen for the answers and take notes on what they are hearing.
5. Have students develop an outline to organize important information.

Finally, secondary teachers are advised to capitalize on opportunities for listening instruction that occur in real-life situations. These include listening to music on the radio or stereo headphones, watching a movie, talking with friends, and using the telephone.

Effective Questioning

Another important listening skill involves asking effective questions. Many secondary students may hesitate to ask questions, even if important information has been missed. Students should be encouraged to ask questions. A checklist of questions can be developed that would include "who," "is doing or did what," "where," "when."

A classroom activity can be developed that will assist students in asking questions. Students may be divided into groups of five, and one student in each group presented with a short story by the teacher. The rest of the group must obtain information only by asking questions. Each student must write down the question before it is asked and then write down the answer. Following a specified period of time, the teacher randomly selects students from each group to recreate the story. The group that recreates the story then presents their sequence of questions to the class. These questions are then analyzed to determine why they yielded the most information.

Strategies to Improve Spoken-Language Skills

Wallace and colleagues (1987) identified some guidelines for providing instruction in spoken-language skills. First, although students may display weaknesses in the reception or expression of one component of language, intervention techniques should highlight the integration of all components at both receptive and expressive levels. Second, language intervention should be scheduled and taught on a regular basis. Teachers should remember, however, to expect and reinforce newly acquired skills when they are demonstrated during the course of the school day. Third, teachers should always serve as models for the appropriate use of language.

Phonology/Articulation

Secondary students who make errors in sound production should be referred to the speech-language pathologist for a complete phonological/articulation evaluation. This evaluation will produce a complete inventory of the sound production errors exhibited by the student. In addition, the speech-language pathologist will attempt to determine whether the sound production errors are caused by an abnormality in the oral structure, confusion with phonological rules, or some other factor. This information is used to develop a remediation program. Generally, the speech-language pathologist provides therapy and identifies specific approaches that can be taken by the teacher in the classroom. A thorough discussion of the cause, identification, and remediation of sound production errors is available in other sources (see Bankson, 1981; Mowrer & Case, 1982; Weiner, 1986).

Although the speech-language pathologist provides direct intervention in the area of sound production, classroom teachers will continue to interact with students in their classrooms and will have many opportunities to assist with the therapy process. With this in mind, Sedlak and Sedlak (1985) have suggested several behaviors for a classroom teacher.

1. Do not embarrass or reprimand the learner for speaking poorly, because such negative behavior could be modeled by classmates. Do establish an atmosphere in which students feel free to experiment with speech.

2. Do become a good speech model, but do not overarticulate, because such behavior will call undue attention to the student's speech problems.

3. Do set aside time in the schedule for specific practice in speech development. Tape recorders, the Language Master, telephones, TalkBack, and similar types of materials and devices can be used for these periods.

Morphology and Semantics

Students exhibiting difficulties in the areas of morphology and semantics may profit from participating in a communicative environment. This type of environment is created when classroom material is presented in a discussion or interactive format. A teacher makes a list of vocabulary words that relate to a specific experience such as a classroom science experiment. The list includes not only the scientific words, but also the words related to the topic. The teacher conducts the lesson by stating what he or she is doing or has done and then asking students specific questions. For example, "First I dropped the red dye in the test tube, then shook it vigorously. Mary, what happened?" This type

---

Case for Action 8.2

A student in your class has speech that is very garbled. You and his peers find it difficult to understand him. You have to ask him to repeat things frequently, which you suspect causes him a great deal of embarrassment. What can you do to help?

of interaction allows the teacher to direct the responses of the students and even correct their responses without appearing to concentrate on the errors. Other activities include oral reports, informal class presentations, and role playing. In each of these situations, the teacher selects the topic or helps the student do so. Emphasis is placed on morphological endings and prefixes, as well as vocabulary and semantic placement of vocabulary words.

The following strategies could be applied to the previously presented activities after a list of key vocabulary words is developed:

1. Present the object or action in combination with the vocabulary item (e.g., dye).
2. Each student should repeat the word in combination with an observation. (The dye is red. The dye is a powder.)
3. Each student should ask a question using the new vocabulary word. (What would happen if you put less dye in the water?)

A thorough analysis of semantics and its role in communication is available in other sources (e.g., Crystal, 1981; Lucas, 1980; Wiig & Semel, 1980b).

Wallace and colleagues (1987) also suggested that revision be used to enhance semantic skills. The teacher provides students with a sentence or group of sentences and asks them to restate it/them in their own words. "Mary will not ride with Tom because he drives too fast" could be a revision of the following: "Mary will not ride with Tom. Tom likes to drive his car very fast. Mary will not ride with anyone who drives fast."

Teachers at the secondary level are also advised to make their students aware of the multiple meanings of some words. For example, the word *run* can refer to a motor act, competition for political office, a snag in a pair of panty hose, the operation of machinery, and a host of other meanings. Teachers may wish to screen reading material and present various meanings of words students may encounter. On a related note, teachers may need to familiarize students with the meaning of idioms such as "You can't tell a book by its cover."

Teachers can capitalize on sentences students produce throughout the school day. For example, during a social studies activity, a student may correctly answer a teacher's question by saying, "Columbus discover America in 1492." The teacher may respond, "Yes, Columbus discovered America in 1492," an expansion that reinforces the student's correct answer but also provides a model of appropriate language by including the verb marker. This technique is also useful for promoting syntax skills.

Syntax

If a student is exhibiting a serious problem with sentence structure, it is helpful to illustrate the appropriate ordering of the words within sentences graphically. The Fitzgerald key, developed by Fitzgerald (1954), is used to illustrate some types of appropriate sentence structure. It is illustrated in Figure 8.2. The Fitzgerald key shows the standard location of particular words in a sentence. This key can be displayed somewhere in the class for students who need visual aids.

The *Fokes Sentence Builder* (Fokes, 1976) is a commercially developed program for training students to recognize acceptable sentence structure. This program is designed to

What or Who	Verb	Whom or What	Where	When

FIGURE 8.2   The Fitzgerald Key

teach "grammatical rules, such as the inclusion of articles, auxiliary verbs, and preposi-tions" (p. 3) and to help students understand "different types of sentence constructions" (p. 3). Although it is designed for younger students, it may be useful for secondary students with significant syntactic difficulties.

Teachers may also help students improve their syntax skills by using the combination approach. Students are presented with a series of short sentences that they must combine into longer, more complex sentences. For example, a set of sentences may include "Sue had $20. She went to the store. She bought a new blouse. The blouse is for her mother. It is her birthday." The students can combine these sentences to produce "Sue went to the store with $20. She bought her mother a blouse because it was her birthday." It should be pointed out that there is no "correct" way to combine these elements into a more complex sentence. Several of the alternative methods of combining these simple sentences into more complex sentences should be discussed.

Pragmatics

An excellent resource is currently available for pragmatic training. Marquis (1990) developed *Pragmatic-Language Trivia for Thinking Skills,* a pragmatic interaction game for older children and adolescents. This gain approaches these skills in a practical, nonthreatening manner.

Schloss and Sedlak (1986) have listed six factors that should be considered when training students in pragmatic skills:

1. Taking turns in conversation
2. Initiating conversations
3. Clarifying a point made in a conversation
4. Following the sequential organization of a conversation
5. Making coherent contributions to a conversation
6. Maintaining a reasonable social distance.

All of these factors must be modeled by the teacher during the daily activities of the class. In addition, the teacher can structure both simulation and independent activities in which students practice these skills. There are several social situations in which older learners must display pragmatic competence, such as using the telephone; making formal and informal introductions; participating in employment interviews; requesting assistance in consumer and employment settings; and sharing personal interests, hobbies, and experiences with peers and authority figures (Mandell & Gold, 1984). As noted earlier, activities that promote pragmatic competence closely resemble those designed to enhance social skills. These activities are described in detail in a subsequent chapter.

Bidialectism

The view that there is an "ideal standard dialect" of American English is no longer accepted. According to Owens (1992), a preference represents only the bias of the listener (p. 429). The issue of dialects and whether the characteristics of nonstandard spoken English should be considered differences, deficiencies, or disorders has been widely debated (e.g., Owens, 1992; Schloss & Sedlak, 1986; Wallace et al., 1987). However, one point on which experts agree is that all speakers tend to shift between a formal and an informal level of language. Therefore some researchers have suggested that speakers of dialects should strive to learn how to shift from informal English to formal English (e.g., Cohen & Plaskon, 1980; Schloss & Sedlak, 1986; Wallace et al., 1987).

Schloss and Sedlak (1986) have suggested the following guidelines for teaching the speaker of informal English:

> 1. *Accept the nonstandard English form, especially in the elementary grades, and build linguistic competence on into high school.*
> 2. *Restate a nonstandard English phrase in standard English, but do not call attention to the nonstandard form. That is, if a student responds with a phrase such as "John be goin' to the store," the teacher should follow with "That's right. John is going to the store."*
> 3. *Teach styles and have students discriminate among different situations in which each style is appropriate.*
> 4. *After the student is able to discriminate style, teach the variant forms and the appropriate situations for each.*
> 5. *Be a good speech model. (p. 232)*

Bilingualism

The issue of bilingual or multicultural secondary education for the student with special needs is a complicated one that is beyond the scope of this chapter. However, by the time a bilingual student reaches a secondary program, he or she may be proficient in one language and exhibit difficulties with the second. In this situation, language use must be evaluated. The following issues must be considered.

1. Is the student proficient in the language of the home and social environment? If so, the student may need to approach the second language through a systematic learning program such as those connected with ESL curriculum.
2. Does the student have trouble with both languages? If so, deficits should be identified and targeted.

In bilingual environments, opportunities exist to stress multicultural education issues for all students in the classroom. Each of the language areas mentioned earlier can be emphasized in both languages. Syntactic differences can be presented together. Semantic differences can be stressed in all class activities and lessons.

Summary

Listening and speaking skills are essential if students with special needs are to succeed in secondary settings. Whether a student is enrolled in a regular or special class, the primary means of receiving directions or content-related instruction is through listening to the teacher. Similarly, the primary means of participating during instruction is speaking. Unfortunately, students with disabilities may be at risk for incomplete development of listening and speaking skills. Therefore, secondary educators must be aware of normal patterns of development and be alert for signs of delay or deviance among secondary learners. This chapter presented an overview of many factors involved in listening and speaking. Five components of language were discussed, including phonology, semantics, syntax, morphology, and pragmatics. Also presented was a brief discussion of the assessment and treatment of speech and language disorders as they affect secondary students. Finally, cultural and linguistic differences were considered. These differences are not considered to be deficits; nonetheless, they have implications for working effectively with secondary students.

While typical professional preparation courses may describe normal and abnormal patterns of development in listening and speaking, it is unlikely that teachers possess the skills necessary to diagnose and remediate problem areas. This task is better left to speech and language pathologists. Nonetheless, regular and special secondary educators are in ideal positions to observe students performance, note any irregularities, and request assistance. This assistance may take many forms, including the provision of therapy in a separate setting or the presence of the speech and language pathologist in the student's classroom during delivery of content-related instruction. Collaboration between speech and language pathologists and regular and special educators can enhance students' listening and speaking skills, thereby increasing the chance for success in secondary settings.

References

Alley, G. R., & Deshler, D. D. (1979). *Teaching the learning disabled adolescent: Strategies and methods.* Denver, CO: Love.

Baker, H., & Leland, B. (1967). *Detroit tests of learning aptitude.* Indianapolis, IN: Bobbs-Merrill.

Bankson, N. W. (1981). *Articulation disorders.* Englewood Cliffs, NJ: Prentice-Hall.

Berry, M. F. (1969). *Language disorders in children.* Englewood Cliffs, NJ: Prentice-Hall.

Bloodstein, O. (1984). *Speech pathology: An introduction.* Boston: Houghton-Mifflin.

Bloom, L., & Lahey, M. (1978). *Language development and language disorders.* New York: Wiley.

Calvert, D. R. (1986). *Descriptive phonetics* (2nd ed.). New York: Thieme.

Cohen, S. B., & Plaskon, S. P. (1980). *Language arts for the mildly handicapped.* Columbus, OH: Merrill.

Cole, M. L., & Cole, J. T. (1989). *Effective intervention with the language impaired child.* Rockville, MD: Aspen Systems.

Crystal, D. (1981). *Clinical linguistics.* New York: Springer-Verlag Wien.

Dunn, L. M., & Dunn, L. M. (1981). *Peabody picture vocabulary test—Revised.* Circle Pines, MN: American Guidance Service.

Fitzgerald, E. (1954). *Straight language for the deaf: A system of instruction for deaf children.* Washington, DC: Volta Bureau.

Fokes, J. (1976). *Fokes sentence builder.* Boston: Teaching Resources.

Locke, J. (1980). The inference of speech perception in the phonologically disordered child. Part II: Some clinically novel procedures, their use, some findings. *Journal of Speech and Hearing Disorders, 45,* 445–468.

Lucas, E. V. (1980). *Semantic and pragmatic language disorders.* Rockville, MD: Aspen Systems.

McReynolds, L., & Elbert, M. (1981). Criteria for phonological process analysis. *Journal of Speech and Hearing Disorders, 46,* 197–204.

Mandell, C. J., & Gold, V. (1984). *Teaching handicapped students.* St. Paul, MN: West.

Marquis, M. A. (1990). *Pragmatic-language trivia for thinking skills.* Tucson, AZ: Communication Skill Builders.

Mowrer, D. E., & Case, J. L. (1982). *Clinical management of speech disorders.* Rockville, MD: Aspen Systems.

Owens, R. E. (1992). *Language development: An introduction* (3rd ed.). Columbus, OH: Merrill.

Reich, P. A. (1986). *Language development.* Englewood Cliffs, NJ: Prentice-Hall.

Schloss, P. J., & Sedlak, R. A. (1986). *Instructional methods for students with learning and behavior problems.* Boston: Allyn and Bacon.

Sedlak, R. A., & Sedlak, D. M. (1985). *Teaching the educable mentally retarded.* Albany: State University of New York Press.

Shames, G. H., & Wiig, E. H. (1982). *Human communication disorders: An introduction.* Columbus, OH: Merrill.

Wallace, G., Cohen, S. B., & Polloway, E. A. (1987). *Language arts: Teaching exceptional students.* Austin, TX: Pro-Ed.

Warren, S. F., & Rogers-Warren, A. K. (1985). *Teaching functional language.* Baltimore, MD: University Park Press.

Weiner, F. F. (1981). Systematic sound preference as a characteristic of phonological disability. *Journal of Speech and Hearing Disorders, 46,* 281–286.

Weiner, F. F. (1986). A phonologic approach to assessment and treatment. In J. M. Costello & A. Holland (Eds.), *Handbook of speech and language disorders* (pp. 75–91). San Diego, CA: College-Hill.

Weiner, F. F., & Wacker, R. (1982). The development of phonology in unintelligible speakers. In N. Lass (Ed.), *Speech and language: Advances in basic research and practice* (Vol. 8). New York: Academic Press.

Weinrauch, J. D., & Swanda, J. R., Jr. (1975). Examining the significance of listening: An exploratory study of contemporary management. *Journal of Business Communication, 13,* 25–32.

Weiss, C., & Lillywhite, H. (1976). *Communicative disorders.* St. Louis, MO: Mosby.

Werner, E. K. (1975). *A study of communication time.* Unpublished master's thesis, University of Maryland, College Park.

Wiig, E. H., & Semel, E. M. (1980a). *Clinical evaluation of language functions.* San Antonio, TX: Psychological Corporation.

Wiig, E. H., & Semel, E. M. (1980b). *Language assessment and intervention for the learning disabled.* Columbus, OH: Merrill.

Chapter 9

Written Language

STEPHEN ISAACSON

Did you know that . . .

- There are three facets to a complete written language curriculum: process, product, and purpose?
- Most descriptions of the writing process include three operations: planning, sentence generation, and revising?
- A student's process can be assessed informally through observation or interview?
- The teacher models the cognitive processes in writing by thinking aloud as he or she demonstrates the task?
- Writing can involve collaboration with peers as well as the teacher?
- The writing process can be prompted through the use of "think sheets"?
- Self-instructional strategies allow the student to use the process independently?
- Word processors are effective only if students have been taught the necessary computer skills and composition strategies?
- The writing product has five components: fluency, content, conventions, syntax, and vocabulary?
- Conventions, the features of a text that reflect mechanical concerns, are the product component that instructors should approach with the greatest caution?
- The writing curriculum should take into account various school-related and job-related *purposes* for writing?

Can you . . .

- State the four principles related to teaching the process of writing?
- Describe one way in which a teacher can model the subprocess of planning for writing?

Stephen Isaacson is program coordinator and associate professor of special education, Department of Special Education, Western Oregon State College, Monmouth, Oregon.

- Describe one way to entice a student to revise and write a second draft?
- State the guidelines you would teach to student response groups?
- Give an example of a self-instructional strategy for writing?
- Distinguish between revising and editing?
- Give an example of how to informally assess each of the five product components?
- Give an example of how to improve a student's skills in each of the five product components?
- State two school writing tasks that students should be taught in order to succeed in content area classes?
- State three job-related writing tasks that students should be taught in order to succeed in the workplace?

Studies consistently have shown that students in special education programs have problems with written expression. On norm-referenced measures of written language, adolescents with learning disabilities are lower in nearly every area of performance (Poplin, Gray, Larsen, Banikowski, & Mehring, 1980). Using measures taken from student writing samples, Moran (1987) reported that junior and senior high school students with learning disabilities were lower in spelling performance, used optional words (e.g., adjectives) less frequently, and made more errors in writing conventions such as capitalization and punctuation than nondisabled students.

When planning writing instruction and assessing writing skills, it is useful to keep in mind the three facets of written language: process, product, and purpose. First, writing is a complex *process* that begins with generating and organizing ideas. The process requires the author to coordinate decisions about mechanical concerns such as spelling and punctuation at the same time that thoughts are being converted into written words. The process ends with editing and producing the final draft.

Second, writing results in a *product*. The process is successful only if the product clearly conveys the author's message. The product is most often judged by the writer's success in meeting the widely accepted standards of spelling, grammar, and punctuation, but other aspects of the product are also important, such as variation and economy in the use of syntax, appropriate word choices, and clear organization of ideas.

Third, people write for different *purposes*. The mode of writing (e.g., persuasive) usually depends on the purpose. The product will be judged according to the degree to which it fulfills its intended purpose. This chapter examines all three facets. Indeed, process, product, and purpose should all be considered when assessing any writing.

Writing as a Complex Process

Studies of adult writers have shown that the composition process consists of coordinating three major operations: planning, sentence generation, and revising (Hayes & Flower, 1987). First, the writer develops an implicit or explicit writing plan, generating ideas and organizing them in some fashion. Then the writer translates the ideas into sentences designed to be read by someone else. In revising, the writer reads what has been written, evaluates it, and attempts to improve it.

Hayes and Flower (1987) emphasized that these processes are *interleaved*; that is, the cycle—planning, generating sentences, revising—may occur repeatedly throughout short sections of the composition. They also may be applied recursively; that is, one operation may interrupt and influence another. For example, a writer may write a sentence or two, plan what he or she is going to say next, write some more, reread, plan, revise, and so forth until the last word is written on the final draft.

The process must be made explicit for inexperienced writers. Students can best be taught how to handle the writing task by dividing the process into specific operations, beginning with prewriting planning activities (Graham & Harris, 1987; Hull, 1987). The resulting plans can then guide the writing of the draft. Throughout the guided composition lesson, the act of generating text is kept separate from that of revising the text, and revising content separate from editing for mechanical errors. Kellogg (1988) made a useful distinction between the recursive operations of the *process* (planning, sentence generation, revising) and the linear *phases* of product development, which include prewriting activities, first draft, and subsequent draft(s).

Assessing the Process

Informal assessment of the student's progress during each step of the writing process can be made through observation or interview. If students are observed as they write in class, a checklist like the one in Action Plan 9.1 can be used. The checklist should include steps from initial choice of topic to final editing. The teacher should keep in mind that progress through all phases of the assignment may take more than one day to accomplish and, therefore, to observe.

One recommended interview format for assignments that might be done outside of class contains 22 questions regarding the selection of the topic, the writer's perception of the intended reader(s), prior knowledge regarding the topic, the writing plan, characteristics of the initial drafts, and self-evaluation of the final product (Wiener, 1986; see also Hayes & Flower, 1980). The purpose of this type of assessment is to determine which corresponding strategies need to be taught to the adolescent with writing problems.

Teaching the Process

Writing instruction cannot focus only on isolated skills, such as sentence grammar, spelling, and punctuation. Students in writing programs that emphasize mechanics and grammar achieve significantly lower qualitative gains in writing than students receiving instruction that emphasizes the organization of ideas and the problem-solving process of writing (Hillocks, 1984). The teacher must introduce the student to the entire process of writing, from initial idea generation to editing of the final draft. A process approach has four characteristics.

1. *The process should be modeled.* The teacher should model planning strategies by leading students in carefully prepared prewriting discussions. Preparing to write is the most essential step in helping students make decisions about content. Planning can begin with the teacher leading the class in a prewriting discussion of the topic. The critical skill

Action Plan 9.1

The following instrument may be used to assist in the students' writing.

Prewriting Phase

1. Is the topic . . .   _____ teacher-selected   _____ student-selected?

   How would you rate in terms of . . . ?   Low   High

	Low			High
Prior knowledge	1	2	3	4
Interest	1	2	3	4

2. Did the student spend time . . .
   - _____ thinking about topic?
   - _____ discussing topic with peer?
   - _____ making an outline, semantic map, or notes?
   - _____ in research outside of class?
   - _____ no observable planning

First Draft

3. Did the student refer to prewriting plan as he/she wrote?   No   Yes

4. The student drafted the text
   - _____ by handwriting
   - _____ on word processor
   - _____ by dictating to another

   How would you rate mechanical demands of transcription in terms of . . . ?   Low   High

	Low			High
Difficulty	1	2	3	4
Fluency	1	2	3	4

5. How frequently did the student seek assistance?

Seldom			Often
1	2	3	4

6. How frequently did the student stop and reread what was written?

Seldom			Often
1	2	3	4

7. Did the rereadings result in changes to the text?

Seldom			Often
1	2	3	4

8. Was the text shared with others as it was being drafted?   No   Yes

9. The student received feedback on finished first draft from . . .
   - _____ a friend
   - _____ peers in the response group
   - _____ teacher
   - _____ no one

Final Draft

10. How many drafts were made before the final product?   0   1   2   3   4

(continued)

Action Plan 9.1 Continued

11. Changes (from first to final draft) reflect . . .

	_____ letter formation correction
Surface	_____ spelling corrections
Concerns	_____ capitalization and punctuation rules

                _____ margins and headings

                _____ grammatical corrections

                _____ word changes

                _____ addition of adjectives, transition phrases

                _____ syntax changes (rearranging sentence)

Content   _____ elaboration (addition of detail sentences)

Revisions   _____ reordering of information

                _____ addition of topic sentences or summary statements

                _____ improvement of style with respect to intended audience

12. The student shared his final product by . . .

                _____ reading orally to a large group

                _____ reading orally to a small response group

                _____ publishing (class anthology, school newspaper, etc.)

---

for the teacher may be knowing when to cut off discussion (Rubin, 1987). If students have spent their ideas in talk, they may no longer experience the dissonance created by an incomplete idea that motivates them to write.

Planning may begin by raising questions of the WH type (Moore, Moore, Cunningham, & Cunningham, 1986): who, what, where, when, and how (*Who* were the first people to explore the territory? *What* dangers did they encounter? *Where* did they first settle?). Questions also can be generated by listing "What We Know" and "What We Don't Know" about the topic. As the students contribute information, everything is written down—accurate or not. Verification of the "What We Know" facts comes as students research the topic.

Some students may not yet have the prerequisite research skills to use references on their own. In this case, the teacher can provide sets of data (e.g., tools used by pioneers, sources of energy) and model ways to organize the data in order to write something about it. Often, the teacher might demonstrate the use of a grid (Figure 9.1), chart, or semantic map (Figure 9.2) as a way of organizing information.

The teacher should also demonstrate how to convert planning notes into written sentences. Expert and average writers construct sentences in much the same way (Hayes & Flower, 1987). Sentences are composed of parts containing about 7 to 12 words in length, with thinking pauses in between. One important teaching function is to model *self-regulatory* thoughts that occur in the thinking pauses and assist in controlling the writing process. The teacher models these by thinking aloud while performing the task, using a verbal style matched to the student's own vocabulary (Harris & Graham, 1992). For example, as the teacher generates sentences, she might think aloud by saying things

Building Stones

	Limestone	Marble
Hardness		
Difficulty of use		
Surface texture		
Color		
Expense		
Where found		

FIGURE 9.1   Compare/Contrast Grid

like, "I'm thinking: what is the best way to introduce this topic to make it interesting to the reader? . . . We should add an example here to make the point more clear. . . . I'm stuck here, but I won't panic. I'm going to look at my notes and let my mind play around with that a little more."

The teacher should model reviewing and revising strategies. The more expert the writer, the greater the proportion of writing time he or she will spend on revision (Hayes & Flower, 1987). Revision can be triggered by: (a) dissonance between intention and text (*Does this actually say what I meant it to say?*), (b) the discovery of better things to say (*Can I find a better example here?*), (c) negative evaluation of the plan (*Is this organized in a clear way?*), and (d) failure to comprehend the text (*Is the reader going to understand this at all?*)

Many times students balk at having to rewrite something they considered finished. This resistance can be overcome by making first drafts obviously different from a completed product. One method of doing this is to use colored paper for first drafts (Raphael, Kirschner, & Englert, 1986). Students can be instructed to write on every other line, leaving a space between lines to make corrections and insertions. Another idea comes from research by Crealock, Sitko, Hutchinson, Sitko, and Martlett (1985) with 10th-grade students with learning disabilities. In their first draft, the students wrote each sentence on a separate slip of paper. After talking with the teacher, who gave them

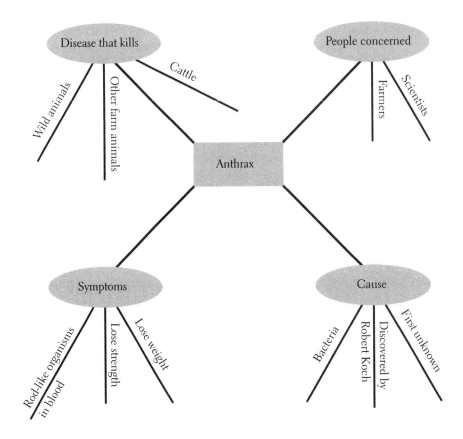

FIGURE 9.2   Semantic Map

feedback regarding the content, the sentence strips were taped to a larger sheet of paper with large spaces between each sentence. The spaces allowed room to rewrite sentences, add detail, and insert transitions. After the teacher made suggestions for technical improvements, the students wrote their final copy. Other teachers have students do their first drafts in writing and then allow final drafts to be typed on the word processor and printed. In each case, first drafts have a much different form than the finished copy, and students realize that the form of the first draft is not adequate for the finished copy.

Hull (1987) drew the distinction between *revision*—reworking the text in such a way as to alter its content or structure—and *editing,* the process of correcting errors in grammar, syntax, punctuation, and spelling. Reading aloud helps some writers correct a few of their grammatical errors, but many others may read their compositions without realizing that their correct oral reading differs from the faulty version in the text. Hull stressed that editing requires a special kind of reading that students must develop.

2. *The process can be collaborative.* Writing can be undertaken in collaboration with either the teacher or peers. Writing with the teacher is sometimes a good starting point

for the student with learning disabilities. The teacher can assist in coordinating the various processes and functions of writing and, when necessary, alleviate the mechanical demands by transcribing the text as the student dictates. Collaboration provides the teacher with an opportunity to model the process and guide the student through its steps.

Collaboration can also involve other students. Students can collaborate in the planning process by jointly brainstorming ideas, contributing needed information, or organizing information into an outline, comparison grid, or semantic map. Students can work in pairs, one transcribing what has been rehearsed first verbally while the other serves as a "scribal auditor" (Zoellner, 1969, p. 299). Students also can work together as teams, listening to each other's first drafts, giving constructive feedback, and editing each other's work for mechanical errors.

Collaboration can occur in the prewriting stage. Crealock and her colleagues (1985) developed an interactive planning procedure for 10th-grade students with learning problems. In group discussion, the students first listed seven components of a good story (setting, hero/heroine, climax, etc.). Then, during group brainstorming, they listed beside each story component 10 words or phrases appropriate for each category, forming a large 7×10 grid. After choosing one word or phrase from each category, they discussed with a peer how they would integrate the seven elements into a story.

Collaboration can occur when planning ideas are first being copied down. Zoellner (1969) proposed a *talk–write* model of composition in which students could work as pairs or teams in front of chalkboards or writing easels with large pads of newsprint. The most important rule for this routine is this: Whatever is written must be spoken first. The intent of the talk–write procedure is to disinhibit students who have good ideas but have a hard time translating them into written form. When confronted with an example of their own unclear writing and asked what they meant, many students often can *say* what they had intended to write. Once the utterance has been made, the student is instructed to write it down exactly as he or she said it. Saying aloud the idea or thought to a teacher or a peer functions as a form of verbal rehearsal that helps students to find their voice as an author.

Collaboration is particularly beneficial during the reviewing and revising stages of the process. Several authors (e.g., Gere, 1987) have recommended interactive writing groups for the purpose of sharing writing and developing ideas. Peer review has several benefits. First, when students know that they will be reading what they have written to an audience of peers, they become aware of the expected audience as they write. Sharing one's writing with others increases student motivation toward writing and particularly toward revising. Participating in writing groups also fosters students' critical capacities (Gere, 1987). As Hayes and Flower (1987) have pointed out, writers' knowledge of their own texts often makes it difficult for them to detect faults in those texts. Feedback from others teaches the writer principles of good writing that can be applied to the next composition.

Gere (1987) also maintained that writing groups could enhance individual self-esteem and create a positive classroom atmosphere. However, in order for this to occur, the teacher must carefully structure and supervise the interaction within groups. Students must understand and demonstrate which type of feedback is appropriate and which type is inappropriate. Appropriate responses to another's writing include paraphrasing the main idea of the piece as it was understood by the listener, asking questions that clarify, and suggesting parts of the piece the reader might like to hear more about. Moore and colleagues (1986) recommended four guidelines for peer response groups: (1) initial reactions must focus on what was done well; (2) all negative reactions should be stated as questions; (3) reactions can be oral or written; and (4) the writer must not respond immediately to the others' reactions (to avoid defensiveness and arguments).

The peer team is also a good arrangement for editing written work. By reading aloud, some inexperienced writers can correct a few of their errors. However, writers may be too close to their texts to detect faults. Indeed, students have been found to detect a larger proportion of faults in another's text than in their own (Hayes & Flower, 1987). One way to make editing more palatable is to teach students to use proofreader's marks when editing one another's work and, later, when editing their own drafts. The proofreading marks recommended by Tompkins and Friend (1988) are shown in Figure 9.3.

3. *The process can be prompted.* Bereiter and Scardamalia (1982) described *procedural facilitation* as any reduction in the executive demands of a task that permits learners to make fuller use of the knowledge and skills they already have. In the case of writing, the teacher can provide facilitative assistance by prompting the steps of the process or helping students with the many decisions that have to be made throughout the complex process. Procedural facilitation can apply to planning, generating sentences, or revising.

Function	*Mark*	*Example*
Delete	ℒ	A pirate ~~who~~ attacks and robs ships.
Insert	∧	Blackbeard was a ∧*famous* pirate.
Capitalize	≡	The pirate flag was known as the jolly Roger.
Change to lower case	/	The flag had a white skull and Crossbones on a black background.
Add period	⊙	People became pirates because they wanted to get rich quickly⊙
Insert comma	∧	A pirate carried a pistol∧ dagger∧ and a long sword in his belt.
Possible misspelling	⬭	Pirates probable didn't make their victims "walk the plank."

FIGURE 9.3   Proofreader's Marks

Source: From "After Your Students Write: What's Next?" by G. E. Tompkins & M. Friend, *TEACHING Exceptional Children,* 20, 1988, 4–9. Copyright 1988 by The Council for Exceptional Children. Reprinted with permission.

An example of a prompt procedure related to planning is to have the students list, before writing on a topic, isolated words related to the topic that might be of use in the composition. Generating a list of words prompts a memory search for topic ideas as well. In the study reported by Bereiter and Scardamalia (1982), listing words first resulted in longer, more substantial content than not listing words first.

Raphael and colleagues (1986) focused students' attention on text structure and content through the use of "think sheets," which prompted questions related to planning and revising. For example, the think sheet for planning a problem/cause essay included the following questions:

- What was the problem?
- What details should you include in your paper to help the reader understand the problem?
- What caused the problem?
- Was there more than one cause of the problem?
- If so, what cause would you talk about first? Second?
- Did one cause lead to another?

In another technique reported by Bereiter and Scardamalia (1982), students were supplied with lists of discourse elements. For example, in an assignment to write an opinion essay, they were given cards with statements such as "give a reason for an opinion," "give a statement that supports the other side," or "tell more about the reason." Students considered each card and decided whether or not to use the discourse element according to their own criteria. The cards prompted ideas for constructing and expanding their opinion paper.

Hull (1987) made three recommendations for making the editing process more manageable for the inexperienced writer. First, as mentioned before, editing should be separated from revision when taught to inexperienced writers. Attention should first be directed to the content of the composition, and editing should be the last step in the process. Second, teachers can structure the search process by pointing out the general location of the errors. The teacher can write in the margin a code for the type of error the student should look for in that same line: *sp* for spelling, *cap* for capitalization, *v* for verb form, and so on. This procedure still leaves to the student the responsibility for finding and correcting the error. Third, the task can be made simpler by focusing the student's search on one category of error at a time. An example of an error-correcting

Case for Action 9.1

A ninth-grade student comes to you for help in writing a social studies report due in a week and a half. What approach would you take to assist the student in the process of writing his report? What are the specific ways in which you would address the three phases of the process?

strategy that guides the search one category at a time is "COPS," a mnemonic for capitals, overall appearance, *p*unctuation, and spelling (Schumaker, Nolan, & Deshler, 1985).

4. *The process should become self-initiated and self-monitored.* Eventually students should be able to instruct themselves successfully in the processes necessary for writing. At this stage of skill development, the teacher gives students specific writing strategies, ideas for self-instruction statements, and explicit instruction in how to employ them. Several writing strategies were developed for secondary students at the Kansas Institute for Research in Learning Disabilities (Schumaker, Deshler, Alley, & Warner, 1983), including the error-correcting procedure mentioned earlier in the chapter ("COPS"). Another strategy from the Kansas Institute is taught through the acronym *TOWER*, which stands for five steps:

T   *Think* about content: the title, major subtopics, and details.
O   *Order* topics and details.
W   *Write* the rough draft.
E   Look for *errors* (use "COPS").
R   *Revise*/rewrite.

A successful procedure for teaching a writing strategy is described in Action Plan 9.2. The procedure has been used to teach students a strategy to increase the vocabulary diversity of their compositions (Harris & Graham, 1985). Action Plan 9.2 illustrates how to encourage students to use more action verbs in their writing. The five steps of the strategy are: (1) look at the picture stimulus and write down good action words; (2) think of a good story to use the words in; (3) write the story while concentrating on making sense and using good action words; (4) read the story, asking yourself "Is this good? Did I use action words?"; and (5) fix the story if it needs changes.

Using Word Processors to Write

Many authors have claimed that word processors can help students improve their writing skills. Word processors are said to have motivational appeal, in part because typing is easier than handwriting for many students, revisions can be made easily, and there is no need for tedious recopying (Ellis & Sabornie, 1986). Although word processors may have these advantages for certain students, research has not yet confirmed that this is the case for most students with learning problems (MacArthur, 1988). MacArthur, Graham, and Skarvold (1986), for example, found no differences on a number of variables between handwritten stories and those composed on a word processor.

Ellis and Sabornie (1986) listed several problems that students with learning problems encounter when using a word processor and for which they need specific instruction. Many students have problems using the cursor, because they move it inefficiently and make erroneous deletions. Many students do not have keyboard skills, and the resulting "hunt and peck" actually takes longer than handwriting. Rather than using computer functions to revise text content and rearrange sentences, students with learning problems still tend to focus on fixing minor errors. Simply providing word processors without teaching students how to use them will not improve the writing of those with

Action Plan 9.2   Teaching a Writing Strategy

Harris and Graham (1992) recommended the following steps for teaching a writing strategy:

Step 1   *Preskill Development*
The teacher instructs the student in any preskills (including new vocabulary and concepts) not yet acquired but necessary for successful use of the strategy.

Step 2   *Initial Conference—Instructional Goals and Significance*
The teacher and student discuss the importance of the strategy, examine the student's current performance level, and set a training goal.

Step 3   *Discussion of the Composition Strategy*
The teacher describes the composition strategy and discusses how and when to use it.

Step 4   *Modeling of the Composition Strategy and Self-Instruction*
The teacher models the strategy while writing an actual composition and thinking aloud self-instructional commands.

Step 5   *Mastery of the Strategy*
The student memorizes and rehearses the strategy steps.

Step 6   *Collaborative Practice*
The student applies the strategy while writing a composition. The teacher encourages, prompts as necessary, and provides feedback.

Step 7   *Independent Performance*
The student applies the strategy independently, using self-instructional commands covertly.

---

learning problems. Composing on a word processor is most effective when paired with strategy instruction (Ellis & Sabornie, 1986; MacArthur, 1988).

Computers can expand opportunities for students to publish their work for real audiences (MacArthur, 1988). Programs such as *Newsroom* (Springboard Software) help students produce school newsletters complete with columns, headlines, and graphics. The Quill system from D. C. Heath (Rubin & Bruce, 1985) includes a program called *The Planner*, which helps students generate ideas by prompting them with questions

---

Case for Action 9.2

A student's IEP stipulates that he do his written work on a microcomputer to help him compensate for poor fine motor skills. What do you need to teach him in order to maximize the benefits of using the computer?

appropriate for selected types of writing. When used for a newspaper article, for example, it might prompt a student with the five WH questions. The student's responses are printed out for use in writing the news article.

In summary, word processors and publishing programs can enhance writing instruction. However, in order to contribute to the development of writing skills, teachers must teach the necessary subskills (e.g., keyboarding) and self-monitoring strategies for writing that take advantage of computers' full capabilities.

Writing as a Successful Product

A writing process is successful only if it results in a good composition. Teachers must consider all aspects of the written product. When various theories of writing are compared (Isaacson, 1984), five principal components emerge: *fluency* (the amount written); *content* (originality of ideas, organization of thought, and maturity of style); *conventions* (the mechanical aspects such as spelling, punctuation, and correct verb endings that teachers expect students to use); *syntax* (construction of the sentences); and *vocabulary* (originality and maturity in the student's choice of words).

Fluency

Fluency usually is assessed by the number of words a student has written. While this may seem to be a superficial measure of a student's writing ability, several studies have revealed a significant correlation between fluency and other measures of writing skill (Anderson, 1982; Daiute, 1986; Grobe, 1981). A student who is able to write more words is likely to be more fluent in generating ideas as well. Although there is no fixed standard for how many words a secondary student should write, the student who always writes relatively few words should be expected to gradually increase composition length with frequent opportunities to write and teacher encouragement and prompting.

Fluency is usually the first writing goal for the beginning writer. The single best method of prompting fluency is prewriting discussion. Connie Ann Nygaard, a high school English teacher in Tucson, Arizona, uses "fire drills" to stimulate ideas and provide opportunities for students to write daily. A "fire drill" is a short (one-minute) writing session in response to a quotation or, sometimes, a single word. The students quickly write any images or ideas generated by the stimulus. The only rule enforced is that during the designated writing time pencils must be moving, if only to write "I can't think of anything to say." After everyone has written one or two sentences, ideas are shared and discussed as a way of generating and organizing additional writing ideas. Students then write paragraphs or short compositions that elaborate the ideas discussed.

Daily writing in an interactive journal can also increase fluency. The teacher responds to the ideas expressed (rather than to mechanical concerns or *conventions*) by writing brief remarks back to the student. Fluency develops as teachers provide frequent opportunities for students to write and share what they have written.

Content

The ideas, style, and organization of student compositions are best assessed with an analytical scale such as the one shown in Figure 9.4. The analytical scale should specify the desirable features of a composition appropriate for its purpose and mode.

Inexperienced writers sometimes are too preoccupied with the mechanics of writing to give much thought to the prospective reader. Several authors (Englert et al., 1988; Gere, 1987; Perl, 1983) have recommended group interaction and feedback for remediating writers' difficulties in making their message clear to their readers. In small groups, students can read their works in progress to their peers and use the feedback to make changes in their composition. Initially, teachers should begin by forming small groups (two or three members only) and directly teaching group processes and rules for interaction. There are four things a teacher must do to establish successful feedback groups:

1. Disallow put-downs. Teach students to replace criticism with questions or "I want to know . . . " statements. For example, a listener might respond by saying, "I would like to know about the *differences* between squash and raquetball." On another theme, a student might respond with the question, "How did your friend manage to write the letter if both of his arms were in a cast?"

2. Reinforce helping behaviors through praise or group points, first in nonacademic tasks that require group cooperation, then in group writing tasks. After the teacher models for the whole class the kind of feedback that is appropriate, a small role-playing group can be selected to demonstrate how the interaction should work while the teacher prompts and reinforces helpful remarks.

3. Model respect. Provide opportunities throughout the week for positive sharing activities in which all feelings and opinions are accepted.

4. Ignore mechanical errors when focusing on content. Misspellings, grammatical errors, and incorrect punctuation can be addressed later, in a final editing activity, but these concerns will interfere with concentration on ideas, organization, and clarity.

The content of student compositions also can be improved by teaching organization strategies. As described on preceding pages, the teacher provides sets of data (e.g., tools used by pioneers) and models ways to organize the data in order to write something about it. Organization strategies are often linked to prescribed text structures appropriate for different writing purposes. For example, a persuasive essay usually follows the following structure: (a) state the problem; (b) state the position you support and summarize the reasons; (c) reason number 1: statement followed by *proof*, *information*, or *examples* support ("Statement-PIE"); (d) reason number 2: Statement-PIE; (e) continue with the same structure for other reasons; (f) conclude by summarizing your position and reasons.

A comparison/contrast text addresses the questions: (a) What is being compared? (b) On what factors or attributes? (c) first factor: How are they alike? How are they different? (d) second factor: How are they alike? How are they different? (e) and so forth (Englert et al., 1988). In addition, the teacher should model the use of key words that signal the important information being addressed. For example, in a comparison/contrast essay, key words such as *similarly, in contrast to,* or *however* are used frequently.

Maximum Points = 32

Introduction (2)
(2) clearly defined purpose for the composition
(1) incomplete attempt to identify the purpose; nearly verbatim restatement of the assignment
(0) no introduction

Suggestions (2 times) $3 \times 2 = (6)$
(3) suggestion related to the topic; feasible suggestion, clearly stated
(2) appropriate statement; vaguely stated
(1) not related to the topic; not complete
(0) no suggestion; restatement of prior statement

Reasons (4 times) $2 \times 4 = (8)$
(2) clear support for suggestion
(1) not clearly related to suggestion
(0) reason not given; reason repeated; incorrect reason

Conclusion (3)
(3) inferencing from or extending suggestions and reasons (e.g., therefore); cohesive
(2) limited attempt to extend or draw conclusion beyond suggestions and reasons given
(1) concluding statement that makes nonspecific references to suggestion
(0) no conclusion

Summary (2)
(2) adequate restatement of main theme of assignment
(1) cursory attempt at ending or closure
(0) no summary

Sense of Audience (3)
(3) excellent clarity; no inferencing required of reader
(2) good clarity; reader required to inference 1–4 times
(1) poor clarity; reader required to inference 5 or more times
(0) unclear to reader who/what is happening

Organization(5)
(5) introduction, suggestions, reason, conclusion/summary are all in clearly logical order
(4) all are in logical order
(3) major parts (i.e., suggestions and reasons) are in logical order
(2) some parts are in logical order
(1) most parts are *not* in logical order
(0) no logical organization

Cohesiveness (3)
(3) clear intersentence relationships
(2) occasionally unclear intersentence relationships
(1) generally unclear intersentence relationships
(0) disjointed, unconnected sentences

FIGURE 9.4   Analytical Scale for Evaluating Content of Persuasive Writing

Source: Reprinted with permission from *The Volta Review*, Vol. 89, No. 3, "Evaluating Hearing-Impaired Students' Writing," by K. Gormley and A. B. Sarachan-Delly. Copyright 1987 by the Alexander Graham Bell Association for the Deaf, 3417 Volta Place, NW, Washington, DC 20007.

Conventions

Writing conventions—spelling, punctuation, correct usage, and handwriting—can be assessed in terms of specific errors that interfere with successful communication of the message. For example, Howell and Morehead (1987) described the problems of poor handwriting under the categories of letter formation, spacing, consistent slant, line quality, alignment, letter size, and fluency (the relative speed at which a person can write). Grammatical errors made by students with learning problems fall in the categories of subject–predicate agreement, tense, plurals, possessive endings, word order, omissions, and incomplete sentences or fragments. Error patterns for spelling, punctuation, and capitalization can be analyzed in a similar manner through the use of error checklists.

Writing conventions are the elements of writing most frequently taught, but they are also the elements that should be approached with the most caution in the context of composition. Students in writing programs that emphasize mechanics and grammar achieve significantly lower gains in writing quality than students receiving instruction in which mechanics and grammar are not stressed (Hillocks, 1984). The teaching of spelling, punctuation, and handwriting should be separated from and not interfere with a beginning writer's composition attempts. There is no evidence that the teaching of grammar rules, at least as it has been traditionally done, has any significant effect on either oral or written language (Glatthorn, 1981; Hillocks, 1984; Straw, 1981). Grammar, it seems, is best learned through practice in expression and exposure to good language models.

Syntax

Although there are quantitative measures of syntactic maturity based on the length of clauses (Isaacson, 1988), teachers can make their own qualitative assessment by examining the types of sentence a student uses most frequently. The following patterns are adapted from Powers and Wilgus (1983):

Level 1   Repetitive use of simple sentence forms (kernel sentences). For example,

I like Burger King.
I like Pizza Hut.
I don't like McDonald's.
I don't like their burgers.

Level 2   Variations in the use of simple sentence patterns. There are five basic types of simple sentences (Phelps-Gunn & Phelps-Terasaki, 1982): (1) Subject + Verb (The man jumped); (2) Subject + Verb + Object (He threw the football); (3) Subject + State of Being or Linking Verb + Adjective (The girl is sunburned); (4) Subject + State of Being or Linking Verb + Predicate Nominative (The girl was a pianist); and (5) Subject + State of Being or Linking Verb + Adverbial Phrase (The queen was in the castle).

Level 3   First expansions: (a) adverbial phrases, infinitives, and object complements may be added to each basic form. For example,

> The baby *always* goes to sleep *after her lunch*.
> The man wants *to live here in the city*.
> Then later the city grew *bigger*.

Or the student may use compound sentences. For example,

> The guy was tall *and* the girl was short.
> Mr. Smith is a nice guy *but* his wife is a witch.

Level 4 Transformations that combine kernel sentences into longer sentences with relative clauses and subordinate clauses. For example,

> He gave a rose to the girl *who kissed him*.
> Mrs. Green trusted him *because he was always nice to her*.

Sentence-combining practice is an effective way to increase a student's syntactic maturity. These three sentences

> Microwaves do not heat the cookware.
> Dishes can get hot.
> Heat is generated by the food.

can be combined into this longer, more complex sentence:

> Microwaves do not heat the cookware, although dishes can get hot from the heat generated by the food.

The purpose of sentence-combining exercises is to make students more conscious of the transformational choices available to them for expressing their ideas (Mellon, 1981).

In his sentence-combining program, Strong (1983) began with just two kernel sentences in each problem, then gradually increased the number into problems that would result in whole paragraphs. If a student favors one type of combination almost exclusively, other transformations can be encouraged through patterned models, such as those proposed by Hunt and O'Donnell (1970):

> Model: The monkey eats bananas.
>   The monkey is in the tree.
>
> Solution: The monkey in the tree eats bananas.

The model was followed by problems that required the same transformation. Mellon (1969) went even further in prompting the combining task. His curriculum consisted of a series of short sentences to be combined in a certain way signaled both by indentation and by symbols. For example,

Mother wondered SOMETHING.
Sally would come home from school sometime. (WHEN)

Solution: Mother wondered *when* Sally would come home from school.

Studies conducted from the mid-1960s until the present consistently have shown the beneficial effects of sentence combining on students of various ages and ability levels (Hillocks, 1984; Mellon, 1979; Stotsky, 1975). Few literacy-teaching methods are better supported by research.

Vocabulary

Vocabulary can be assessed according to the uniqueness or maturity of words used in the composition. In a qualitative analysis the teacher can pick out unusual but appropriate words that suggest a mature vocabulary as well as inappropriate or overused words that suggest a word-finding problem. Quantitative measures of written vocabulary (Isaacson, 1988) usually calculate the proportion of large words used (generally defined as seven or more letters), proportion of mature words (those not found on a list of common, frequently used words), and proportion of unrepeated words.

A direct way to teach vocabulary is to teach synonyms for overused words. Synonym and antonym charts can be hung in the room for reference during writing periods. Mercer and Mercer (1985) recommended giving the student a short passage in which several words are underlined. The teacher then asks the student to substitute for the underlined word a more colorful or interesting word or phrase. After fluency has increased and the student is attending to text structure and other aspects of content, the teacher can use the same underlining routine on drafts of the student's own work.

Varied and colorful word choices can be prompted by word brainstorming in the planning stages of the process as described earlier in the chapter. The Harris and Graham (1985) strategy can be applied to adjectives and adverbs, as well as action verbs used in the previous example.

Writing for Different Purposes

In a functional writing curriculum, students need to learn writing skills required for success in classes and, most importantly, success in future occupations. Writing tasks in

Case for Action 9.3

An 11th-grade student has just moved to your district and has been assigned to your class. You were given no assessment information related to written expression. How would you informally assess the student's writing skills, taking into account process and product factors?

content area classes include taking notes, answering chapter questions, and writing reports or essays. Job-related tasks may include writing business letters, progress reports, requisitions, technical descriptions, résumés, contracts, advertisements, brochures, and project proposals.

Answering Chapter Questions

The most common written assignment given in content area classes is answering chapter questions (Archer & Gleason, 1988). A student with learning problems might have difficulties in completing such an assignment because of failing to read the material before attempting the questions, not reading questions carefully, writing answers that have little relation to the question, and writing incomplete answers. Archer and Gleason (1988) field-tested a strategy that addresses all these concerns. The steps are included in Action Plan 9.3.

As with any strategy, the subtasks that may be difficult for the student should be isolated and taught to the mastery level before the entire strategy is presented. Archer and Gleason (1988) identified two difficult steps in the strategy for chapter questions: turning the question into part of the answer and locating the chapter section that addresses the topic. Therefore, these are preskills that need to be mastered first. Changing the question into part of the answer is critical to the strategy because it forces the student to contemplate the question and write an answer that reflects the question.

Writing Reports

The process of writing a research report consists of four stages (Moore et al., 1986, p. 136): identifying questions to be answered, locating information, organizing the information, and reporting the information. Questions can be generated from the five question words or the lists of "what we know, what we don't know" mentioned earlier in the

---

Action Plan 9.3

The following strategy, proposed by Archer and Gleason (1988), is recommended to assist students in writing in content areas:

1. Read the question carefully. (e.g., What are the three purposes of roots?)
2. Change the question into part of the answer. (Student writes, "The three purposes of roots are_____.")
3. Locate the section of the chapter that talks about the topic. (Student finds subtopic "Roots.")
4. Read the section of the chapter until you find the answer. (Chapter section says: "Roots have three purposes. . . .")
5. Complete the answer. (Student fills in: "The three purposes of roots are *to anchor the plant, to absorb water and minerals*, and *to store food*.")

Source: Copyright 1988 Curriculum Associates®, Inc. Reproduced by permission of the publisher.

chapter (Moore et al., 1986, pp. 138–140). The teacher might assist students by directing them to materials in which they could find relevant information. Organizing the material could be facilitated through comparison grids, think sheets, or self-initiated planning strategies. The first draft of the report is written in paragraph form, to be followed by one or more revised drafts.

Teachers often have unstated expectations for students' written assignments. They expect the work to be legible and reasonably neat in appearance, to be completed according to directions, and to meet a certain standard of accuracy. Many teachers unconsciously judge students by the appearance of their papers. For this reason, Archer and Gleason (1988) also devised a strategy to improve the appearance of a student's written work, using the acronym HOW. HOW your paper should look:

H = Heading, which should include name, date, subject, and page number if needed.
O = Organized, which means started on the front of the paper (holes on the left), includes a left margin and right margin, has at least one blank line on top and on the bottom, and is well spaced.
W = Written neatly, which means words or numbers are on the line, they are neatly formed, and errors are neatly erased or crossed out.

Many students also need a strategy for planning and completing work according to written directions. Common problems are failing to read directions carefully, not getting prepared before they begin, and not completing all the items. Archer and Gleason (1988) recommended a four-step approach for planning and completing written work. This approach is included in Action Plan 9.4.

Writing for Future Vocations

Algozzine, O'Shea, Stoddard, and Crews (1988) surveyed 249 employers from different communities in the state of Florida to determine critical job-related reading and writing skills. The researchers selected corporations and businesses that were most likely to hire recent high school graduates. Writing accurate messages and requests, noting work assignments, and completing forms were the writing tasks employers ranked as most important. Therefore, a curriculum for students with learning problems should include functional writing skills such as writing short messages and completing forms.

The most important form a high school graduate will complete is a job application. The applicant's responses on the job application influence the employer's first impression of the applicant and may influence the decision to proceed with an interview. Schloss, Schloss, and Misra (1985) examined the specific information students were asked to report on job applications. They collected 200 application forms representing four types of businesses: fast food, service, retail, and light industry. They then identified and ranked the 70 questions that appeared most frequently. Application questions referred to personal information, educational background, and employment history. Action Plan 9.5 lists some of the questions that appeared on more than 20% of the forms. Readers interested in the entire list are referred to Schloss, Schloss, and Misra (1985).

Action Plan 9.4

The following approach was recommended by Archer and Gleason (1988) for helping youths with learning problems to complete written work:

Step 1   *Plan it*
Read the directions and circle the words that tell you what to do. Get out the materials you need. Tell yourself what you are going to do.

Step 2   *Complete it*
Do all the items. If you can't do an item, ask for help. Use HOW (the neat-paper strategy).

Step 3   *Check it*
Did you do everything? Did you get the right answer? Did you proofread? (*Note:* Here the student could use Schumaker, Nolan, & Deshler's [1985] "COPS" strategy; the mnemonic reminds the student to look for errors in capitalization, overall appearance, punctuation, and spelling, one at a time.)

Step 4   *Turn it in.*

Source: Copyright 1988 Curriculum Associates®, Inc. Reproduced by permission of the publisher.

As with other writing skills, the process of writing office messages or completing application forms should be modeled. The teacher can model the planning stage of messages through the use of the *Who, What, Where, When,* and *How* questions. The teacher can model the transcription of messages using common abbreviations when appropriate to promote fluent transcription. The teacher should model the reviewing of the message to make sure all necessary information is there, again using the five WH

Action Plan 9.5

The following questions—asked on more than 20% of job application forms surveyed by Schloss, Schloss, and Misra (1985)—can be used as a basis for writing instruction.

Personal Information	*Frequency*
Name	200
Social Security number	196
Phone number	190
Date	175
Age	151
Disability (illness, injury)	145
Address	140
Marital status	125
In emergency notify (address, phone)	110
Citizen of the United States	102

Case for Action 9.4

A student's IEP stipulates that you prepare her for transition from school to life after graduation. She currently has many problems writing reports or producing other extended compositions. What will be the writing skills you will teach her to prepare her for work?

questions. Teaching students how to complete a job application begins with teaching the necessary prerequisite skills, such as accurately reading the questions on the form, knowing the information requested, and being able to spell the words required to answer the questions. As with messages, the teacher should explain and show how to complete the form. Modeling should be followed by guided practice on controlled materials—forms specifically designed to include items found on nearly all application forms. In addition, the students' skills should be checked by giving them real application forms that vary from those used in guided practice to fill in by themselves.

Summary

A writing curriculum should reflect three facets of writing: process, product, and purpose. First, writing is a complex *process* in which the writer coordinates three major operations: planning, sentence generation, and revising. Informal assessment of the student's attention to each step in the writing process can be made through observation or interview. Four principles should be followed when teaching the process to students: (1) the process should be modeled, from the planning stage to final revision and editing tasks; (2) the process can be collaborative, the student receiving assistance either from the teacher or peers; (3) the process can be prompted, through word lists, think sheets, or self-evaluation cards; and (4) the process should become self-initiated and self-monitored, through instruction in self-control strategies. If word processors are used to facilitate the process, attention must be given to teaching the necessary computer skills.

Second, attention should be given to all aspects of the written *product*, not just obvious surface features. When various theories of writing are compared, five principal components emerge: fluency, content, conventions, syntax, and vocabulary. Several methods can be used to assess and teach the skills related to each product component. Conventions—or the mechanical "secretarial" aspects of producing text—are the component that should be approached most cautiously. Content is the aspect of writing that should receive the most emphasis in instruction.

Third, a writing curriculum should take into account the various *purposes* of writing. School writing tasks include answering chapter questions and writing reports or essays. Students can be taught strategies for planning, completing, and checking written work. Job-related writing tasks include writing accurate messages and requests, noting work assignments, and completing forms. The most important form a student will have to complete is a job application.

Teachers have three important functions in providing instruction in written expression. First, teachers must allocate sufficient time for writing in the classroom curriculum. Writing will not improve unless students have an opportunity to write. Second, teachers must actively be involved with students, guiding the process, teaching necessary subskills, and giving specific feedback on first drafts. Third, teachers must work from a complete model of writing that encompasses all stages of the process and skills related to the product. Writing is an important aspect of literacy and therefore deserves careful, systematic instruction.

References

Algozzine, B., O'Shea, D. J., Stoddard, K., & Crews, W. B. (1988). Reading and writing competencies of adolescents with learning disabilities. *Journal of Learning Disabilities, 21*, 154–160.

Anderson, P. L. (1982). A preliminary study of syntax in the written expression of learning disabled children. *Journal of Learning Disabilities, 15*, 359–362.

Archer, A. L., & Gleason, M. M. (1988). *Skills for school success.* Boston: Curriculum Associates.

Bereiter, C., & Scardamalia, M. (1982). From conversation to composition: The role of instruction in a developmental process. In R. Glaser (Ed.), *Advances in instructional psychology* (Vol. 2, pp. 1–64). Hillsdale, NJ: Erlbaum.

Crealock, C. M., Sitko, M. C., Hutchinson, A., Sitko, C., & Marlett, L. (1985, April). Creative writing competency: A comparison of paper and pencil and computer technologies to improve the writing skills of mildly handicapped adolescents. Paper presented at the Annual Meeting of the American Educational Research Association. (ERIC Document Reproduction Service No. ED 259 531)

Daiute, C. A. (1986). Performance limits on writers. In R. Beach & L. S. Bridwell (Eds.), *New directions in composition research* (pp. 205–224). New York: Guilford.

Ellis, E. S., & Sabornie, E. J. (1986). Effective instruction with microcomputers: Promises, practices, and preliminary findings. *Focus on Exceptional Children, 19*(4), 1–16.

Englert, C. S., Raphael, T. E., Anderson, L. M., Anthony, H. M., Fear, K. L., & Gregg, S. L. (1988). A case for writing intervention: Strategies for writing informational text. *Learning Disabilities Focus, 3*, 98–113.

Gere, A. R. (1987). *Writing groups: History, theory, and implications.* Carbondale: Southern Illinois University Press.

Glatthorn, A. A. (1981). *Writing in the schools: Improvement through effective leadership.* Reston, VA: National Association of Secondary School Principals.

Gormley, K., & Sarachan-Deily, A. B. (1987). Evaluating hearing-impaired students' writing: A practical approach. *Volta Review, 89*, 157–169.

Graham, S., & Harris, K. R. (1987). Improving composition skills of inefficient learners with self-instructional strategy training. *Topics in Language Disorders, 7*(4), 66–77.

Grobe, C. (1981). Syntactic maturity, mechanics, and vocabulary as predictors of quality ratings. *Research in the Teaching of English, 15*, 75–85.

Harris, K. R., & Graham, S. (1985). Improving learning disabled students' composition skills: Self-control strategy training. *Learning Disability Quarterly, 8*, 27–36.

Harris, K. R., & Graham, S. (1992). *Helping young writers master the craft: Strategy instruction and self-regulation in the writing process.* Cambridge, MA: Brookline.

Hayes, J. R., & Flower, L. S. (1980). Identifying the organization of writing processes. In L. W. Craig & E. R. Steinberg (Eds.), *Cognitive processes in writing.* Hillsdale, NJ: Erlbaum.

Hayes, J. R., & Flower, L. S. (1987). On the structure of the writing process. *Topics in Language Disorders, 7*(4), 19–30.

Hillocks, G., Jr. (1984). What works in teaching composition: A meta-analysis of experimental treatment studies. *American Journal of Education, 93,* 133–170.

Howell, K. W., & Morehead, M. K. (1987). *Curriculum-based evaluation for special and remedial education.* Columbus, OH: Merrill.

Hull, G. (1987). Current views of error and editing. *Topics in Language Disorders, 7*(4), 55–65.

Hunt, K. W., & O'Donnell, R. C. (1970). *An elementary school curriculum to develop better writing skills* (Cooperative Research Project No. 8–0903). Tallahassee: Florida State University. (ERIC Document Reproduction Service No. ED 050 108)

Isaacson, S. (1984). Evaluating written expression: Issues of reliability, validity, and instructional utility. *Diagnostique, 9,* 96–116.

Isaacson, S. (1988). Assessing the writing product: Qualitative and quantitative measures. *Exceptional Children, 54,* 528–534.

Kellogg, R. T. (1988). Attentional overload and writing performance: Effects of rough draft and outline strategies. *Journal of Experimental Psychology: Learning, Memory, & Cognition, 14,* 355–365.

MacArthur, C. A. (1988). Computers and writing instruction. *Teaching Exceptional Children, 20*(2), 37–39.

MacArthur, C. A., Graham, S., & Skarvold, J. (1986). *Learning disabled students' composing with three methods: Handwriting, dictation, and word processing* (Research Report No. 109). College Park: University of Maryland Institute for the Study of Exceptional Children and Youth.

Mellon, J. C. (1969). *Transformational sentence-combining: A method for enhancing the development of syntactic fluency in English composition* (Research Report No. 10). Urbana, IL: National Council of Teachers of English.

Mellon, J. (1979). Issues in the theory and practice of sentence combining: A twenty year perspective. In D. A. Daiker, A. Kerek, & M. Morenburg (Eds.), *Sentence combining and the teaching of writing* (pp. 1–38). Akron, OH: Brooks.

Mellon, J. (1981). *Sentence-combining skills: Results of the sentence combining exercises in the 1978–79 National Writing Assessment* (Special Paper No. 10-W-65 prepared for the National Assessment of Educational Progress). (ERIC Document Reproduction Service No. ED 210 696)

Mercer, C. D., & Mercer, A. R. (1985). *Teaching students with learning problems* (2nd ed.). Columbus, OH: Merrill.

Moore, D. W., Moore, S. A., Cunningham, P. M., & Cunningham, J. W. (1986). *Developing readers and writers in the content areas.* White Plains, NY: Longman.

Moran, M. R. (1987). Individualized objectives for writing instruction. *Topics in Language Disorders, 7*(4), 42–54.

Perl, S. (1983). How teachers teach the writing process: Overview of an ethnographic research project. *Elementary School Journal, 84,* 19–24.

Phelps-Gunn, T., & Phelps-Terasaki, D. (1982). *Written language instruction: Theory and remediation.* Rockville, MD: Aspen Systems.

Poplin, M., Gray, R., Larsen, S., Banikowski, A., & Mehring, T. (1980). A comparison of components of written expression abilities in learning disabilities and non-learning disabled children at three grade levels. *Learning Disability Quarterly, 3,* 46–53.

Powers, A. R., & Wilgus, S. (1983). Linguistic complexity in the written language of hearing-impaired children. *Volta Review, 85,* 201–210.

Raphael, T. E., Kirschner, B. W., & Englert, C. S. (1986). *Text structure instruction within process-writing classrooms: A manual for instruction* (Occasional Paper No. 104). East Lansing: Michigan State University, Institute for Research on Teaching.

Rubin, A., & Bruce, B. (1985). *Learning with QUILL: Lessons for students, teachers, and software designers* (Reading Report No. 60). Washington, DC: National Institute of Education.

Rubin, D. L. (1987). Divergence and convergence between oral and written communication. *Topics in Language Disorders, 7*(4), 1–18.

Schloss, P. J., Schloss, C. N., & Misra, A. (1985). Analysis of application forms used by special needs youths applying for entry-level jobs. *Career Development for Exceptional Individuals, 8,* 80–89.

Schumaker, J., Deshler, D., Alley, G., & Warner, M. (1983). Toward the development of an intervention model for learning disabled adolescents: The University of Kansas Institute. *Exceptional Education Quarterly, 4,* 45–74.

Schumaker, J. B., Nolan, S., & Deshler, D. D. (1985). *Learning strategies curriculum: The error monitoring strategy.* Lawrence: University of Kansas, Institute for Research in Learning Disabilities.

Stotsky, S. (1975). Sentence combining as a curricular activity: Its effect on written language development and reading comprehension. *Research in the Teaching of English, 9,* 30–71.

Straw, S. B. (1981). Grammar and teaching of writing: Analysis versus synthesis. In V. Froese & S. B. Straw (Eds.), *Research in the language arts: Language and schooling* (pp. 147–161). Baltimore, MD: University Park Press.

Strong, W. (1983). *Sentence combining: A composing book* (2nd ed.). New York: Random House.

Tompkins, G. E., & Friend, M. (1988). After your students write: What's next? *Teaching Exceptional Children, 20,* 4–9.

Wiener, J. (1986). Alternatives in the assessment of the learning disabled adolescent: A learning strategies approach. *Learning Disabilities Focus 1,* 97–107.

Zoellner, R. (1969). Talk-write: A behavioral pedagogy for composition. *College English, 30,* 267–320.

C h a p t e r **10**

Reading Instruction

DEBORAH GARTLAND

Did you know that . . .

- Reading ability can be likened to the performance of a symphony orchestra?
- There are five stages in learning to read?
- Adjusting the rate of reading affects comprehension?
- Teachers should use a combination of formal and informal reading measures?
- Each student has four reading levels?
- Study skills are important reading objectives for secondary students?
- Instructional strategies are linked to the assessment process?
- There are commercially published high interest–low vocabulary reading materials?

Can you . . .

- Describe the two basic processes in reading ability?
- Explain the importance of literacy in today's society?
- Identify and describe the four levels of reading comprehension?
- Explain the cloze procedure used as an informal assessment measure?
- Contrast direct instruction and functional instruction?
- Identify three strategies used in vocabulary instruction?
- Identify the components of a direct reading activity?

Deborah Gartland is coordinator and associate professor of special education at Towson State University in Towson, Maryland.

Of all the academic skills students acquire in U.S. schools, reading ability is the most highly valued. Despite its importance, considerable controversy still shrouds the reading process. Numerous conceptualizations of reading exist. Reading is a highly complex activity in which the individual constructs meaningful interpretations of written symbols. Rather than defining reading as simply reading words and coming to a single, shared idea of what the text said, professionals are talking about multiple literacies that acknowledge personal interpretations and cultural differences (McGill-Franzen, 1993).

The Commission on Reading (Anderson, Hiebert, Scott, & Wilkinson, 1985) has likened reading to the performance of a symphony orchestra. The analogy conveys three points. First, reading is a holistic act that depends on the integrated performance of its various subskills. Second, success in reading comes from life-long endeavor and from practice over extended periods of time. Third, more than one interpretation of a text may be elicited depending upon the purpose of reading, the context in which reading takes place, and the background of the reader.

Reading involves two basic processes: a decoding or word recognition process and a comprehension process. Word recognition skills contribute to the reading comprehension process. Word recognition is the means to comprehension, the all-important end. The skills enable the individual to pronounce the words correctly. Word recognition skills evolve from subskills in the following five areas:

1. *Phonetic analysis.* In phonetic analysis, the student employs specific sound–symbol associations to pronounce each part of the word. To perform this skill, the student must know the phonemes of the language and the rules governing them.

2. *Structural analysis.* In structural analysis, the student uses the meaningful parts of words as an aid to pronouncing and discerning the meaning of the whole word. Structural analysis permits a faster rate of reading than the phonetic analysis of individual sounds.

3. *Sight words.* Sight words are words that the student recognizes without applying phonic skills. Many words with irregular spelling are taught in this whole-word fashion.

4. *Clues.* There are three types of word analysis clues: context clues, picture clues, and configuration clues. The student uses the surrounding words and their meanings, accompanying pictures, and the shape of the unknown word to determine its identity.

5. *Vocabulary.* At the secondary level, three types of vocabulary exist. *General* vocabulary consists of common words with generally accepted word meanings. *Special* vocabulary contains words that have both general and specialized meaning, depending upon the context. *Technical* vocabulary comprises words representing a specific concept applicable to a specified content area.

The comprehension process enables the reader to understand the meaning of the text. Without comprehension, reading is reduced to little more than word calling. Written material cannot be comprehended until word recognition skills are learned. The secondary student who has not mastered word recognition skills faces the insurmountable task of memorizing every word. The skilled reader uses word recognition skills and knowledge about people, places, and things to determine the intended meaning of the passage. Knowledge possessed by the reader and information from the text interact to produce full comprehension. As a student's language experience increases, comprehension of increasingly difficult reading material also increases.

Barrett (1968) formulated a taxonomy of reading comprehension in which there are four levels:

1. *Literal recognition or recall.* Literal comprehension means the reader recognizes or recalls information, ideas, and happenings that are explicitly stated in the reading materials.

2. *Inference.* Inferential comprehension can be defined as the hypotheses or conjectures arrived at from a synthesis of the literal content of a selection and the products of intuition, personal knowledge, and imagination.

3. *Evaluation.* Evaluation refers to the judgments a reader makes about the content of the written material by comparing it with external criteria.

4. *Appreciation.* Appreciation refers to the student's awareness of the forms, styles, literary techniques, and structures employed by authors to stimulate emotional responses in their readers.

Modern society appears to thrive on technological information. Many of its rewards require increasing levels of literacy. The level of literacy deemed satisfactory in 1950 will probably be considered marginal by the year 2000 (Resnick & Resnick, 1977). Although literacy opens doors to communication and enjoyment for many readers, it inspires disinterest, frustration, or alienation for many others (Turner, 1993).

Children begin to receive formal reading instruction in kindergarten. Learning to read in the elementary grades sets the stage for later learning. Excellence in high school and beyond is unattainable without the ability to read (Chall, 1983). Given the assigned importance of reading ability in our society, adults who read well are regarded as intelligent and educated. Conversely, an intelligent adult who is deficient in reading ability may have serious adult adjustment problems. Faced with persistent failure and disapproval from family and peers and subjected to discrimination by employers, poor readers experience less self-satisfaction and a lower opinion of themselves.

Reading Abilities of Adolescents with Disabilities

The National Committee on Reading (Gray, 1925) divided the process of learning to read into five stages: (1) readiness for reading, (2) beginning to read, (3) rapid development of reading skills, (4) wide reading, and (5) refinement of reading. This conceptualization still has merit today, especially in regard to the reading ability of adolescents with disabilities. The first three stages normally occur in kindergarten through grade 3, the wide reading stage in grades 4 through 6, and the refinement at the secondary, college, and adult levels. However, a visit to a local middle or senior high school or a glance through professional journals will paint a very different picture: Secondary students with disabilities are deficient in the attainment of reading skills, cannot effectively gain information from a wide variety of reading materials, and are far from having refined reading ability (e.g., Maring & Furman, 1985; Saski & Carter, 1984; Whorton & Daniel, 1986).

Because the reading process is complex and reading problems can stem from numerous causes, secondary students manifest various types of reading difficulties, depending upon the nature and severity of their disabilities. Along with general learning deficits—such as those related to attention problems, memory disorders, and an inability to transfer information—students may have various specific reading difficulties. They may fail to attain adequate sight vocabulary, a problem compounded by the fact that they are not consistent in applying phonetic or structural analysis, and do not make adequate use of contextual, picture, or configuration clues. In oral reading, these students tend to skip or reverse letters, words, or sentences; omit words or substitute words of similar phonetic characterization; exhibit more hesitations and repetitions; fail to observe, or misinterpret, punctuation; and read with poor phrasing and a lack of expression.

Secondary students with disabilities are also limited in their comprehension abilities. They are more successful with the literal level than with comprehension of an inferential, evaluation, or appreciation level. They do not adequately comprehend content area reading materials, which constitute much of the information presented at the secondary level. In addition, they fail to develop appropriate study skills and fail to adjust their rate of reading according to purpose, both of which affect overall comprehension (Askov & Kamm, 1982; Cottier & Bauman, 1985).

The sections that follow present information designed to give the secondary teacher insight into the demands of reading instruction for students with disabilities. No single approach to the teaching of reading is superior to all other approaches in accommodating all individual differences. Kameenui (1993) argued against a single right method or approach to literacy instruction, asserting that such a search is misguided and takes its greatest toll on students who have diverse learning and curricular needs. The secondary teacher must be knowledgeable about general principles of reading instruction. He or she must also be familiar with the characteristics of poor readers, and be capable in assessing the various reading skills. Furthermore, the teacher must be knowledgeable about the various developmental and functional reading objectives necessary for success in school and independent reading, and skilled in both general principles of reading instruction and classroom-based strategies in vocabulary, comprehension, and study skills instruction.

Assessing Reading Ability

Of all the academic skill areas, reading ability is probably the one most studied as part of special education assessment. Because reading ability is such a complex phenomenon, which is composed of numerous integrated subskills, no single test can encompass all of its aspects. Thus, reading assessment has become a genuine puzzle (Farr, 1992). Confusion and debate continue regarding the goals of reading assessment and the types of tests and other assessments needed to achieve those goals. The bottom line in selecting and using any assessment, however, should be whether it helps the student. According to Afflerbach and Kapinus (1993), meaningful assessment of reading results from a skillful balancing act, the purpose of which is to provide optimal reading instruction and learning for all students. They have offered the following guidelines:

1. There must be a balanced representation of experts in the development and use of assessment.
2. Assessment must be balanced with the effective communication of the nature, purpose, and results of the assessment.
3. There must be a balance of formative and summative assessment.
4. There must be a balance of assessment for the student and from the student.
5. Assessment should include a balance of texts, tasks, and contexts.
6. Confidence in current reading assessments must be balanced with the flexibility that anticipates change in both the way reading and literacy are viewed and the way effective reading assessment is viewed.

Formal Reading Assessment

A variety of formal measures and techniques are available to assess the reading perform-ance of learners with disabilities. The use of standardized reading tests has increased over the past 30 years (Resnick, 1981). These tests differ in many respects, including the skills assessed, task demands, ease of administration, curriculum match, technical qualities, and scoring and interpreting procedures. However, there is a growing recognition of the limitations inherent in formal assessment used to measure student achievement (Na-tional Commission on Testing and Public Policy, 1990).

Although formal reading tests may be superior to general achievement tests in identifying general reading skills, as Sternberg (1991) pointed out, they measure reading in a very narrow range of reading tasks and situations. Professional ethics dictate that before any standardized measure is selected, the test consumer should research the test to arrive at informed judgments about the technical adequacy of the specific test in the given classroom situation. There are numerous guidelines on how to select commercially made assessment instruments, such is *Standards for Educational and Psychological Tests* (American Educational Research Association, American Psychological Association, & National Council on Measurement in Education, 1985). Unfortunately, because the field abounds with technically inadequate reading measures, it is up to consumers to select the most appropriate tests for their purposes.

Informal Reading Assessment

Alternative methods of assessment have surfaced during recent years as a paradigm shift, moving from reliance on standardized testing techniques (Wolf, Bixby, Glenn, & Gardner, 1991). Assessment for planning instructional strategies relies more heavily on informal procedures, including teacher-made tests, checklists, questionnaires, criterion-referenced measures, and clinical reading interviews. Wolf (1993) coined the phrase "informed assessment" to describe the situation when teachers have meaningful goals for instruction and clear purposes for assessment and when they use multiple methods to systematically observe and selectively document their students' performances across diverse contexts and over time. Afflerbach (1993) emphasized the importance of teacher observation and described a system for recording and using classroom observation—System for Teaching and Assessing Interactively and Reflectively (STAIR). Student portfolios (Calfee & Perfumo, 1993; Farr, 1992; Valencia, 1990), a type of performance assessment, rely on a collection of student work samples and are being used to show the student's development and progress in the combined process of reading, thinking, and writing. At the secondary level, three widely used procedures involve the use of informal reading inventories, oral reading error analysis, and the cloze procedure.

The Informal Reading Inventory

The informal reading inventory is a widely used method to determine a student's reading level and to assess the student's specific skills in word recognition and comprehension. At the secondary level, informal reading inventories (IRIs) are helpful in determining what materials in a reading series, as well as in various content areas, a student can read independently and the appropriate level of difficulty for assigned readings used as instructional materials. IRIs consist of a series of passages below, at, and above various grade placements. A student's independent, instructional, frustration, and listening levels are determined on the basis of the number of words recognized and the percentage of correct answers to comprehension questions. Oral reading errors (see the next subsection) can also be tallied. At the secondary level, it may be preferable to use IRIs over standardized measures for learners with disabilities because IRIs provide information about the students' skills in relation to the grade level system of the regular school curriculum. Because IRIs provide only an estimate of reading levels, teachers must use their professional judgment in interpreting the results.

Sedlak and Sedlak (1985) suggested several procedures in constructing an IRI. Their recommendations are included in Action Plan 10.1. They also suggested strategies for administering IRIs. These are included in Action Plan 10.2.

Action Plan 10.1 Constructing an Informal Reading Inventory

Sedlak and Sedlak (1985) have suggested the following procedures for constructing an IRI.

1. Select two passages of approximately 200 words from each level of a series, and type each passage on a separate sheet of paper.
2. Develop five comprehension questions for each passage. Questions should deal with vocabulary, factual information, sequencing, main ideas, and inferences, and should not elicit merely a yes or no response.
3. Construct a list of vocabulary words for each level by selecting every fifth new word, and type the words on a sheet of paper.
4. Develop a scoring sheet. (Often this is just a teacher's copy of the passages and vocabulary words on which errors can be tallied.)

Action Plan 10.2 Administering and Scoring an Informal Reading Inventory

Sedlak and Sedlak (1985) have recommended the following procedures in administering and scoring an IRI:

1. Have the student read the vocabulary words in isolation while the teacher records all errors, tallying them by type (e.g., omission, repetition). Stop the student when 25% of the words on one level are missed. (Note: Self-corrections are not errors.)

2. Allow the student to silently read the first passage at the highest level for which vocabulary recognition was 100%, recording start and finish times. Orally ask the comprehension questions and record responses.

3. Ask the student to read the passage aloud while the teacher records all errors. The second passage may be used as a reliability check when needed. The student should be stopped when comprehension drops to less than 50% and oral reading is characterized by meaningless substitutions, word recognition difficulties, and a lack of rhythm.

4. Orally read the parallel passage for the last completed level and ask the student to respond to the comprehension questions. Continue this process until the comprehension question errors drop below 75%.

5. Use the following criteria as guidelines for establishing a student's independent, instructional, frustration, and listening levels:

    a. *Independent.* The level at which comprehension is at least 90% and the student reads in a natural, rhythmical, conversational tone, free from tension and with few oral recognition errors.

    b. *Instructional.* The level at which comprehension is at least 75% and the student reads with good phrasing and no more than 1 word recognition error per 20 words after silently reading the passage.

    c. *Frustration.* The level at which comprehension is less than 60%, and word recognition is less than 90%. The student shows extreme difficulty in reading, making meaningless word substitution, and reads with a lack of rhythm.

    d. *Listening.* The level at which the student responds correctly to at least 60% of the comprehension questions after listening to the teacher read. The listening level indicates that the student understands the syntactic structure and vocabulary.

Although by their nature IRIs are teacher-made tools, there are several commercially made IRIs. Certainly, constructing teacher-made IRIs requires time and effort, but using locally prepared inventories that reflect the reading materials peculiar to a school is a significant advantage.

Oral Reading Error Analysis

Oral reading error analysis is another frequently used technique in the informal assessment of secondary students with disabilities. The focus of analysis here is the mistakes students make. The student orally reads a text or a passage on the IRI form while the teacher notes the kinds of errors that occur in the student's reading. In addition, the teacher may also note the instructionally important behaviors that typify the student's oral reading. These behaviors might include a lack of intonation or expression, the use of finger guides, word-by-word reading, or other inappropriate phrasing. The teacher should remember that although error analysis is a time-consuming scrutiny of a student's oral reading accuracy, information from this process yields valuable information needed to determine the appropriate direction of instructional interventions.

Prior to the assessment session, the teacher must decide which errors are instructionally important and therefore need to be tallied. The following are 10 categories of errors that may be considered when assessing oral reading accuracy:

1. *Hesitations.* The student pauses for two or more seconds before attempting the word.
2. *Insertions.* The student adds one or more words into the sentence being read.
3. *Inversions.* The student changes the order of the words in the sentences being read.
4. *Mispronunciations.* A *gross* mispronunciation of a word is scored when the student's rendition bears little resemblance to the correct pronunciation. A *partial* mispronunciation of a word is scored when the student omits part of a word, makes errors in syllabication or accent, or phonetically mispronounces part of the word.
5. *Omissions.* The student deletes a word or group of words while reading.
6. *Omissions or disregard of punctuation.* The student does not observe the punctuation marks. For example, the student fails to pause at a comma or stop at a period.
7. *Repetitions.* The student repeats a word, phrase, or sentence while reading.
8. *Self-corrections.* An error is scored if the student fails to correct himself or herself within three seconds.
9. *Substitutions.* The student replaces the printed word with another word. For example, the student reads "house" instead of "home."
10. *Unknown or aided words.* The student does not attempt the word within five seconds and the teacher supplies the word.

The Cloze Procedure

The cloze procedure is both an instructional technique and an informal measure of comprehension used to determine whether content area or reading materials are appropriate for a particular secondary student. As an informal measure, it is relatively easy to construct, administer, and score. The teacher selects a passage of approximately 250 words and retypes the passage on a sheet of paper, keeping the first and last sentences intact. In each of the other sentences, every fifth word is deleted and replaced with a uniform-length blank. In administering the cloze procedure, the student silently reads the entire passage and then rereads it, filling in words for those that have been deleted. The student must rely on context clues within the passage to comprehend the story in order to close each sentence correctly. So the assumption is that if a student can supply the exact word or a synonym or other reasonable substitution, the student must adequately comprehend the sentence and the overall meaning of the passage. Roe, Stoodt, and Burns (1991) recommended that the following criteria be used in determining the secondary student's reading levels:

Reading Level	Accuracy (%)
Independent	57 or greater
Instructional	44–57
Frustration	Below 44

Developmentally Based Reading Objectives

Scope-and-sequence charts provide teachers of elementary school students with a list of reading objectives associated with specific grade levels. However, learners with special needs may not be working within a traditional age- or grade-referenced scheme. For example, as noted earlier, many secondary students are deficient in word recognition skills. These skills are presumed to be mastered by the end of the elementary school years. Presented here is a sequence of developmentally based reading objectives in word recognition, comprehension, and study skills. As with any taxonomy of skills, the secondary teacher will need to adjust the scope according to the organization of skills used in the teacher's school district and according to each reading student's strengths, weaknesses, and needs. Note also that many of these objectives could be further broken down into component subskills. This is particularly true of the objectives of phonetic analysis. More detailed skills are not presented here because it is presumed that students with only disabilities have learned many of these skills in their elementary school years. For more details, the teacher can refer to scope-and-sequence charts in elementary school reading texts or basal series.

Word Recognition Skills

1. *Phonetic Analysis*

   a. The student will identify consonants.
   b. The student will identify vowels.
   c. The student will identify consonant–vowel blends.
   d. The student will identify vowel–consonant blends.
   e. The student will use phonic generalizations.

2. *Structural Analysis*

   a. The student will identify inflectional forms.
   b. The student will identify compound words.
   c. The student will identify root words.
   d. The student will identify affixes.
   e. The student will identify possessives.
   f. The student will identify contractions.
   g. The student will identify antonyms.

h. The student will identify synonyms.
i. The student will identify homonyms.
j. The student will identify accents.
k. The student will identify punctuation.
l. The student will use syllabication generalizations.

3. *Sight Words*
   a. The student will use auditory discrimination skills.
   b. The student will use visual discrimination skills.
   c. The student will use auditory-visual discrimination skills.

4. *Clues*
   a. The student will use context clues.
   b. The student will use picture clues.
   c. The student will use configuration clues.

5. *Vocabulary*
   a. The student will use general vocabulary terms.
   b. The student will use special vocabulary terms.
   c. The student will use technical vocabulary terms.

Comprehension Skills

1. *Literal Recognition or Recall*
   a. The student will recognize details.
   b. The student will recall details.
   c. The student will recognize main ideas.
   d. The student will recall main ideas.
   e. The student will recognize sequences.
   f. The student will recall sequences.
   g. The student will recognize comparisons.
   h. The student will recall comparisons.
   i. The student will recognize cause–effect relationships.
   j. The student will recall cause–effect relationships.
   k. The student will recognize character traits.
   l. The student will recall character traits.
   m. The student will paraphrase.
   n. The student will follow written directions.
   o. The student will understand symbols, abbreviations, and acronyms.
   p. The student will read for stated purpose.

2. *Inference*
   a. The student will infer supporting details.
   b. The student will infer main ideas.
   c. The student will infer sequences.

    d. The student will infer comparisons.

    e. The student will infer cause–effect relationships.

    f. The student will infer character traits.

    g. The student will make inferences about figurative language.

    h. The student will predict outcomes.

    i. The student will summarize information.

    j. The student will perceive relationships (e.g., time and place, analogies).

    k. The student will make generalizations.

    l. The student will draw conclusions.

    m. The student will understand mood and emotional reactions.

    n. The student will synthesize data.

3. *Evaluation*

    a. The student will make judgments of reality or fantasy.

    b. The student will make judgments of fact or opinion.

    c. The student will make judgments of adequacy or validity.

    d. The student will make judgments of appropriateness.

    e. The student will make judgments of worth, desirability, or acceptability.

    f. The student will determine reliability of author.

    g. The student will recognize fallacies of reasoning.

    h. The student will use problem-solving techniques.

    i. The student will interpret propaganda techniques.

4. *Appreciation*

    a. The student will identify literary type (e.g., fable, myth, biography).

    b. The student will appreciate the use of imagery.

    c. The student will react to the author's use of language.

    d. The student will appreciate the emotional response to plot or theme.

    e. The student will identify with characters and incidents.

Study Skills

1. *Reference Materials*

    a. The student will use a dictionary.

    b. The student will use encyclopedias.

    c. The student will use an almanac.

    d. The student will use an atlas.

    e. The student will use library card catalogs.

    f. The student will use a thesaurus.

2. *Organizational Skills*

    a. The student will take notes from readings.

    b. The student will underline key points in readings.

    c. The student will develop outlines from readings.

3. *Specialized Skills*
   a. The student will develop test-taking skills.
   b. The student will use study techniques.
   c. The student will adjust rate of reading according to purpose.
   d. The student will use various parts of a book.
   e. The student will read graphs, charts, diagrams, tables, maps, and other graphic aids.

Reading Objectives Based on Community Demands

At the secondary level, the reading curriculum for students with disabilities includes instructions for developing, maintaining, and applying developmental reading objectives previously taught. However, another important aspect of the curriculum is instruction in the functional reading objectives or reading objectives based on community demands. This functional component ensures that students will acquire the reading skills they need to survive and be independent in the community. Presented here are objectives related to following directions, gaining information, understanding forms, and recreation and leisure-time activity.

Following Directions

1. *Basic*
   a. The student will comply with building signs.
   b. The student will comply with pedestrian and road signs.

2. *Sequential*
   a. The student will follow directions in first aid procedures.
   b. The student will follow directions in emergency procedures.
   c. The student will follow directions in telephone use.
   d. The student will follow directions in "do-it-yourself" assembly kits.
   e. The student will follow directions in playing games.
   f. The student will follow directions in child care.
   g. The student will follow directions in cooking and sewing.
   h. The student will follow directions in operating household appliances.
   i. The student will follow directions in voting machine use.

3. *Location*
   a. The student will use local, state, national, and international maps.
   b. The student will use mass transportation procedures.
   c. The student will follow directions in a work schedule.

4. *Labels and Warnings*
   a. The student will follow directions on food labels.
   b. The student will follow directions on survival signs (e.g., danger, poison, high voltage).

   c. The student will follow directions in car care.
   d. The student will follow directions on the care of clothing.
   e. The student will follow directions on a medicine bottle.
   f. The student will follow directions on household goods.

Gaining Information

1. *At Home*
   a. The student will read newspaper articles and magazines.
   b. The student will read consumer information pamphlets.
   c. The student will read government publications.
   d. The student will read lease agreements.
   e. The student will read sales and rental agreements.
   f. The student will read pamphlets on day care.
   g. The student will read religious bulletins.
   h. The student will read contracts.
   i. The student will read sales policies.
   j. The student will read credit card bills and policies.
   k. The student will read financial agreement policies.
   l. The student will read retail catalogs.
   m. The student will read telephone books.

2. *At Work*
   a. The student will read training manuals.
   b. The student will read office memoranda.
   c. The student will read classified advertisements.
   d. The student will read job and union contracts.
   e. The student will read company policy statements.
   f. The student will read safety and job requirements.

3. *In the Community*
   a. The student will read travel guides.
   b. The student will read public transportation schedules and timetables.
   c. The student will read unit pricing codes.
   d. The student will read chamber of commerce materials.
   e. The student will read emergency procedures.
   f. The student will read public notices.
   g. The student will read political publications.
   h. The student will read legal documents.
   i. The student will read abbreviations.

Understanding Forms

1. The student is able to complete driver's license or learner's permit forms.
2. The student is able to complete W-2 forms.

3. The student is able to complete local, state, and federal tax forms.
4. The student is able to complete Social Security forms.
5. The student is able to complete medical and health forms.
6. The student is able to complete insurance applications.
7. The student is able to complete work permit and job applications.
8. The student is able to complete welfare forms.
9. The student is able to complete subscription order forms.
10. The student is able to complete mail order purchase forms.
11. The student is able to complete credit card applications.
12. The student is able to complete loan applications.

Recreation and Leisure-Time Activity

1. The student will read recreational books, magazines, newspapers, and pamphlets.
2. The student will read television guides.
3. The student will read movie brochures.
4. The student will read music, theater, and sporting event programs.
5. The student will read community events calendars.
6. The student will read as an independent activity.
7. The student will read for personal enjoyment.
8. The student will read to enrich oral and written language.
9. The student will read for better understanding of self and others.
10. The student will read to enrich and expand experiences.
11. The student will read to entertain others.
12. The student will read restaurant guides and menus.

General Principles of Reading Instruction

As is true with any solid educational program, reading instruction for secondary students with disabilities is based on information from the assessment process. General instructional strategies can be planned only after the teacher has identified a student's strengths, weaknesses, and needs in the area of reading skills. Reading instruction then begins from what the student knows, building on strengths and working toward improving weaknesses. The instructional methods and materials selected should be of an appropriate level of difficulty while arousing interest and maintaining effort. General principles of reading instruction are presented in Action Plan 10.3.

The reading curriculum at the secondary level is traditionally organized around "direct" and "functional" instruction (Vacca & Vacca, 1985). Direct instruction focuses on skills arranged according to scope-and-sequence charts and proceeds systematically. Emphasis is on developing these reading skills so they can eventually be applied to various reading situations. In functional instruction, however, reading skills are not taught or practiced in drill, in isolation from their actual use in a real reading situation. Functional instruction centers around the application of skills to real-life tasks. In ele-

Action Plan 10.3 General Principles of Reading Instruction

The secondary teacher should remember the following general principles when planning reading instruction (adapted from Dixon, Carnine, & Kameenui, 1992):

1. Guard against lost instructional time.
2. Intervene and remediate early, strategically, and frequently.
3. Teach less more thoroughly.
4. Communicate reading strategies in an explicit manner, especially during initial phases of instruction.
5. Guide student learning through a sequence of teacher-directed, student-centered activities.
6. Formatively evaluate student progress to examine the effectiveness of instruction and educational tools.

mentary school, reading instruction is mostly of a direct nature. At the secondary level, the teacher integrates the teaching of content with the teaching of skills required to learn the content. Although some reading instruction is direct instruction, the main thrust is on functional instruction.

The Commission on Reading (Anderson et al., 1985) offered five generalizations on the nature of reading flowing from the research of the previous decade. First, reading is a constructive process. It is necessary for the reader to learn to reason about written material using knowledge from disciplined fields of study and everyday life. Second, reading must be fluent. To free attention for the analysis of meaning, the reader must master basic processes to the point where they become automatic. Third, reading must be strategic. Skilled readers learn to direct their reading in relation to their purpose, the nature of the text, and whether they are comprehending. Fourth, reading requires motivation. Skilled readers learn to sustain attention and learn that written text can be informative and interesting. Fifth, reading is a continuously developing skill. Becoming a skilled reader requires development, refinement, and continuous practice. When planning instructional strategies, English and content area teachers of secondary students who have disabilities need to provide their students with opportunities that take these generalizations into consideration.

Classroom-Based Reading Instruction

Vocabulary Instruction

Vocabulary instruction focuses on words and word meanings. Because fluency in word recognition and in understanding words contributes to increased reading comprehension, vocabulary instruction for secondary students with disabilities is an important aspect of the educational program in both English and the content areas. Many teachers make the mistake of assuming that readers will automatically assimilate new words just because they are introduced in the reading materials. Consequently, direct instruction of almost any kind is better than none at all (Petty, Herold, & Stoll, 1968).

Professionals in reading instruction are rethinking several of the components of traditional instruction, including vocabulary instruction (Baumann & Kameenui, 1991; Beck & McKeown, 1991). Blachowicz and Lee (1991) have outlined the following general guidelines for classroom vocabulary instruction that are appropriate for content area subjects as well as English classes:

1. Choose all vocabulary for instruction from contextual reading to be done in the classroom.
2. Use maps or organizers of the reading material to help identify the words for study, in contrast to more frequency-based selection processes.
3. Plan prereading activities so the words are at least seen and heard prior to reading.
4. Involve vocabulary in postreading discussion.
5. Use contextual reinspection and semantic manipulation for words that remain unclear after reading and discussion.
6. Use vocabulary in an integrated way.

Although instruction in general vocabulary and special vocabulary is necessary at the secondary level, a majority of the words encountered in content area reading materials are of a technical nature related to a specific subject. Words and concepts are interrelated, so understanding vocabulary helps to lay the foundation for understanding concepts, especially in the content areas.

There are three major differences between the vocabulary of reading lessons and that of content area lessons (Armbruster & Nagey, 1992). First, in reading lessons knowing the new words may not be necessary for understanding the gist of the story, while content area vocabulary often represents major concepts that are essential for comprehension and learning. Second, learning new vocabulary in reading lessons often involves simply learning a new label for a concept the student already possesses (e.g., learning a synonym). In contrast, new vocabulary in content areas is mostly associated with unfamiliar concepts. As students learn new content area vocabulary, they are also learning whole new concepts. Third, while new vocabulary words associated with reading lessons are typically unrelated to each other, vocabulary words in content areas often are related in meaning. The implication for instruction, therefore, is that it is important to distinguish between *target vocabulary* (i.e., concepts that are introduced and explained in the text) and *prerequisite vocabulary* (i.e., words and concepts needed for understanding the text) and adjust instruction accordingly.

The number of words in printed school English is estimated to be about 88,500 (Nagey & Anderson, 1984). Teachers should focus on teaching key vocabulary words, because it may be impossible to teach every unknown word, given the high proportion of unknown words contained in content materials. The following is a summary of strategies used in vocabulary instruction at the secondary level:

1. Teachers should preview reading materials to identify potentially difficult vocabulary words and introduce those words before students begin to read. The appropriate word recognition skill for a particular word will depend on the given word.

   a. *Phonetic analysis* may be used to help students pronounce unknown words. Teachers can introduce the word along with its phonetic spelling, complete with diacritical markings.

   b. Teachers may use *structural analysis* to emphasize the word's meaningful elements. The procedure may involve examining the root word and various prefixes and suffixes.

   c. Before assigning the reading, the teacher can introduce a core list of *sight words* using chalkboards, charts, overhead projectors, handouts, flashcards, tachistoscopes, or microcomputers. When appropriate, the real object or a reasonable facsimile can be used to introduce the word.

   d. The *cloze procedure*, described earlier as an assessment technique, can also be used as an instructional method.

2. Context clue instruction will improve overall comprehension since it helps students to read between the lines and process text on a deeper level. Teaching vocabulary through syntactic and semantic clues will give students thinking tools necessary to deal with the wide range of reading material they will encounter (Sinatra & Dowd, 1991). Students' ability to use naturally occurring context to learn the meanings of unknown words markedly increases when they work in pairs to problem solve (Buikema & Graves, 1993). Blachowicz (1993) devised C(2)QU, a strategy to model context use:

   C1—Give the word in a broad but meaningful context.
   C2—Provide more explicit context with some definitional information.
   Q—Ask a question that involves semantic interpretation of the word.
   U—Ask the students to use the word in meaningful sentences.

The teacher can go back into the loop as needed.

3. Vocabulary instruction should focus on functional words. Numerous studies of textbooks indicate that they are loaded with unnecessary rare and technical words (Harris & Sipay, 1990). Teachers should teach those words that will be important to the students' future environments or, according to Carr and Wilson (1986), words that will help students figure out related words.

4. Word meanings are best taught in context rather than in isolation. Teachers should provide examples in which the vocabulary word is used correctly as well as provide multiple opportunities for students to apply the word's meaning (Gipe & Arnold, 1979). According to McKeown (1993), simply learning definitions is not a potent route to vocabulary development; instead, teachers might promote their students' learning by transforming definitions into explanations that characterize a word's prototypical use in readily comprehensible language.

5. Teachers must decide to what extent the new vocabulary should be part of students' listening, reading, speaking, or writing vocabulary, and adjust instruction accordingly.

Vocabulary instruction should provide opportunities for students to expand word meanings. After students understand the word in its given context, discussions of synonyms and antonyms for the word can take place.

6. Word meanings are best taught through concept development (Blachowicz, 1985) whereby mere surface understanding is replaced with a deeper level of understanding. Concepts might be developed by providing examples, associations, or relationships and a background of experience.

Schwartz (1988) suggested concept maps, graphic organizers that aid the student by literally mapping out what the student knows about the vocabulary word. Concept maps can be used to aid the student's understanding of a vocabulary word by having the student identify the concept to be defined, a subordinate phrase that helps the student to understand what it is, traits, and examples. Another technique that can be used is semantic mapping, promoting categorical structuring of information in graphic form by displaying known and new words under labeled categories or conceptual subtopics (Johnson, Pittelman, & Heimlich, 1986).

Norton (1993) suggested that webbing, a process similar to semantic mapping, can be used for important vocabulary from a book at any grade level. To develop a webbing activity, the teacher places the title of the book in the center of the web and then extends the vocabulary on spokes drawn from the center of the web.

7. Teachers can make use of sources of information that fall outside the passage in which the new vocabulary word appears. These external references might include dictionaries, encyclopedias, glossaries, and a thesaurus. Captioned television can be used as a supplement to reading instruction (Koskinen, Wilson, Gambrell, & Neuman, 1993). Captions put words in a motivating environment where the audio and video context helps students understand printed words they might not know how to read. Of the many uses of captioned video in the development of literacy skills, vocabulary learning is one of the most valuable. It allows viewers to focus attention on both definitional and contextual information, enhancing word meaning by providing a visual context that includes both printed words and pictorial images.

8. Teachers should help students acquire vocabulary words by being enthusiastic models and by reinforcing their use of newly acquired terms.

Comprehension Instruction

Comprehension is the essence of the reading act. There is no shortage of instructional methods for teaching secondary students to comprehend (Alvermann, 1987). Professional journals and reading texts routinely feature teaching strategies designed to increase students' ability to understand printed matter, although not all strategies are equally effective in promoting all types of comprehension. A number of practices have been proposed for helping secondary students read content materials. These methods help students develop background knowledge, understand unfamiliar text organizational patterns, learn new vocabulary associated with the content, and overcome other challenges associated with content materials (Olson & Gee, 1991).

Readence, Bean, and Baldwin (1989) have emphasized that content reading is the domain of *all* teachers and that subject matter specialists are best qualified to implement strategies. This is not because they will make students better readers in general, but because they will convert students into more efficient learners in science, math, English, and social studies classes and more adept consumers of information in our technological society. Readence and colleagues (1989) have made the following instructional recommendations for when a teacher wants to emphasize content area reading:

1. Present content and processes concurrently, integrated within a total lesson framework, by providing direct instruction in the processes necessary to acquire content in addition to pointing out what content is to be acquired.
2. Provide guidance in all aspects of the instructional lesson—before, during, and after reading. Students need to be prepared to read a text, given guidance in reading for selected ideas, and provided with reinforcement to retain the material learned.
3. Use all language processes, not just reading, to help students learn from text. Although reading will undoubtedly remain the major means of dealing with the text, listening, speaking, and writing become additional tools to teach more content.
4. Use small groups to enhance learning by promoting active learning and emphasizing peer interaction.
5. Be patient in strategy implementation. Do not expect instant results; first attempts are fraught with errors.

The following is a summary of strategies used in comprehension instruction at the secondary level:

1. The directed reading activity (DRA) is an instructional method for guiding secondary students through readings in English and content area materials. Directed reading approaches vary in the number of steps involved, depending on the source, but follow basically the same pattern of (1) developing readiness, (2) guiding reading, (3) skill instruction, and (4) follow-up activities. The DRA is a sound approach used by many teachers to develop reading comprehension skills in students at all levels (Johnston, 1993).
2. Research in reading identifies modeling as an effective way to increase comprehension of text. Dole, Duffy, Roehler, and Pearson (1991) emphasized using modeling to help teachers explain the reasoning involved in performing various reading tasks. Norton (1992a) described a modeling lesson to gain meaning through inferred characterization. It requires readers to go beyond the information provided in the text by using clues from the text to hypothesize about the character's feelings, actions, beliefs, or values and ultimately gain better reading comprehension. The think-aloud technique (Baumann, Jones, & Seifert-Kessell, 1993; Nist & Kirby, 1986) is a teacher-modeling technique in which the teacher reads aloud from the text and verbalizes whatever comes to mind to demonstrate how to reason during reading. Megyeri (1993) found that secondary students' oral reading, writing, and listening skills improved dramatically using modeling of reading aloud as students followed along.

3. Research supports the use of various student discussion groups as a way to increase reading comprehension. Bath (1992) devised a way to actively engage students in cooperative exploration of high-quality literature in which small groups of students organize, develop, and direct a literature unit within a carefully defined social context. A goal of trade-book minigroups was to provide opportunities for students to learn responsibility, leadership, and social skills through literary discussions. Leal (1993) found that peer-group discussions of all types of texts had the potential to be a powerful tool for enriching classroom learning. Such discussions provide teachers with a wealth of information about their students' prior knowledge as well as providing a place for students to negotiate textual meaning through collaboration. Goldberg's (1992/93) model includes the following conversational elements: (a) use of few "known-answer" questions; (b) teacher responsivity to student contributions, (c) connected discourse in which the discussion is interactive and utterances build upon and extend previous ones, (d) a challenging but nonthreatening atmosphere, and (e) general participation, including self-selected turns.

4. Teaching students to self-question (Gillespie, 1990) while reading allows them to take a more active role in their learning. To facilitate comprehension, students can be taught the student-generated questioning technique, a metacognitive strategy from which students with low verbal ability apparently receive the greatest benefit (Groller, Kender, & Honeyman, 1991; Nolan, 1991).

5. Secondary students with disabilities often are frustrated because books geared to their interest level are often beyond their reading ability. High interest–low vocabulary materials provide these adolescents with a relatively easy vocabulary while maintaining an interest level appropriate for the more mature learner. High interest–low vocabulary materials are available from numerous publishers. Teachers can select books on a wide range of topics, estimate the reading level of such books by using various readability formulas, and match up more appropriate materials to these students.

6. Norton (1992b) has suggested that older students benefit from drawing plot diagrams for person-against-person and person-against-self plots and relating the plot diagrams to developing characterizations and themes. Webbing (Norton, 1993) is another method for graphically displaying relationships among ideas and concepts. This technique encourages higher thought processes, stimulates oral interactions, and fosters ideas. Webbing helps students understand important characteristics of story structure, increases their appreciation of literature, and improves their reading competencies. The teacher draws a web on the board with the title of the book in the center. On the spokes are placed setting, characterization, conflicts, and themes. The web can also include names of leading characters and types of conflicts that are found in the book. Thematic units webs are popular in literature-based programs as well as in programs that integrate various content areas. Armbruster, Anderson, and Meyer (1991) have suggested the use of a particular type of instructional graphic called a *frame*. Frames are a visual representation of the organization of important ideas in informational texts intended to help the student focus attention on important information and perceive the organization of that information in content area reading.

7. The technique of teaching children to construct mental images as they read has been helpful in enhancing students' abilities to construct inferences, make predictions,

and remember what has been read (Gambrell & Jawitz, 1993). The construction of mental images encourages use of prior knowledge as part of creating vivid representations of prose (Gambrell, Kapinus, & Wilson, 1987).

8. Use of technology is a pragmatic way of developing emergent literacy skills. Using computers can ensure privacy, individualization, achievement gains, cost effectiveness, control of learning, and flexibility in scheduling, and it is a modern way to learn (Askov & Clark, 1991). Hypermedia is a computer format in which several media can be viewed in an order chosen by the user. Dillner (1993/94) described its success in an American history class in which computer-aided reading lessons were designed by the classroom teacher to increase content area comprehension. Finnegan and Sinatra (1991) have listed sources for software at beginning, intermediate, and advanced levels.

9. The use of writing in journals (Livdahl, 1993) has been successful in increasing reading comprehension of secondary students. Hancock (1993) used character journals and found that when adolescent readers comment on a story repeatedly in the voice of one of the characters, they think more about what they are reading. When they disagree with a character's actions or attitudes, they come away with a better sense of their own identity.

10. It is important for secondary students with disabilities to learn to use a repertoire of learning strategies (Kletzien, 1991). Strategy instruction has been successful with secondary students, especially with content area materials. K-W-L (Ogle, 1989) is a technique that prompts the student's thinking about the relevant background knowledge he or she has brought to the reading task, purposes for reading, and information gleaned from what he or she has just read. It combines new information with prior knowledge to build vocabulary and concepts. The "K" stands for what the student already knows; the "W" stands for what the student wants to learn; and the "L" stands for what the student has learned.

Study Skills Instruction

Study skills instruction is intended to teach basic learning tools that, when developed and appropriately applied, will enable the secondary student to acquire information effectively, efficiently, and independently. Askov and Kamm (1982) pointed out that learning on one's own is particularly important today, given the wealth of media sources that make vast amounts of information easily accessible. It has been reported that students who have not been specifically taught study skills do not pick them up on their own throughout their elementary and secondary school careers (Askov, Kamm, Klumb, & Barnette, 1980). So for secondary students with disabilities who have difficulty in acquiring content area knowledge, instruction in study skills is a particularly important component of their educational program.

There is a lack of agreement among educators concerning which of the more than 100 study systems is most effective in facilitating long-term learning (Brozo & Simpson, 1991). Stress should be on learning the ways of knowing (Hennings, 1993). Successful learning for secondary students often depends on their own planning and organizing (Davey, 1993). Therefore, effective instruction at the secondary level should focus on enhancing students' awareness of the components of their own study style and increasing students' ability to select appropriate strategies for various study tasks (Archambeault, 1992).

Until recently, few investigations have looked into the teaching of study skills in the secondary classroom. Basic study skills pertain to using reference materials, organization skills, and specialized skills. Here we present the specialized skill of using the study techniques SQ3R, EVOKER, and SQRQCQ. An elaboration of these and other study techniques appropriate for secondary students can be found in Roe and colleagues (1991).

SQ3R

SQ3R, developed by Robinson in 1962, is the oldest and most widely used systematic study procedure. It can be applied to English and content area reading materials. This system involves five steps:

1. **Survey.** The student makes a quick overview of the material.
2. **Question.** The student turns each heading and subheading into a question.
3. **Read.** The student reads to find answers to the questions.
4. **Recite.** The student states the answers and evidence found.
5. **Review.** The student reviews the information at appropriate intervals for long-term retention.

PARS (Preview, Ask questions, Read, Summarize) is a modified, simplified strategy developed by Smith and Eliot (1979) appropriate for younger students or students who have limited experience in using study techniques.

EVOKER

EVOKER was developed by Pauk (1963) to assist students in reading prose, poetry, and drama. There is no provision for previewing the material, as in SQ3R, because of the nature of the material to be read. The study technique has six steps:

1. **Explore.** The student reads to develop an idea of the overall message.
2. **Vocabulary.** The student studies key unknown words.
3. **Oral reading.** The student reads aloud with good expression.
4. **Key ideas.** The student locates the key ideas needed to understand the author's message.
5. **Evaluation.** The student evaluates how key ideas and words relate to the central theme.
6. **Recapitulation.** The student rereads the selection.

SQRQCQ

SQRQCQ (Fay, 1965) is a strategy to aid students in reading mathematics word problems. Even skilled readers will sometimes have difficulty in completing word problems. The SQRQCQ consists of six steps:

1. **Survey.** The student previews the word problem to learn its general nature.
2. **Question.** The student decides what is being asked.
3. **Read.** The student carefully reads the question, noting details and relationships.
4. **Question.** The student questions what operations should be used.
5. **Compute.** The student computes the operations.
6. **Question.** The student checks the process and asks whether the answer seems to be logical.

Textbook Instruction

Many secondary students with disabilities have difficulty in reading from content area textbooks. As Readence and colleagues (1989) pointed out, students often lack experiential background and are unfamiliar with the vocabulary and concepts in social studies, science, or any other content areas. Therefore, one of the content area teacher's roles is to facilitate learning from text. This can be accomplished by adapting lessons to match students' abilities and experiential background, helping link prior knowledge to what they are to learn, motivating them to attend to selected pieces of the text, and monitoring comprehension by checking to see whether they understand important parts of a text presentation. The following is a summary of strategies used in textbook instruction at the secondary level.

1. Because textbooks play such an important role in learning in the content areas at the secondary level, the teacher should carefully evaluate the quantitative and qualitative factors before selecting a text for use with secondary students. The following should be considered in the evaluation: readability; quality of writing; use of abstract concepts and technical vocabulary; appropriateness and quantity of graphics; advance organizers; headings/subheadings; introductory and summary statements; glossary; end-of-chapter self-quizzes; and whether the text is nondiscriminatory, accurate, and up to date.

2. The teacher should also consider the use of illustrations. Purnell and Solman (1991) found that technical content that lends itself to presentation as an illustration will be comprehended better as an illustration than as text, and it will be comprehended best of all if presented in both forms.

3. Sammons and Davey (1993/94) described an interview procedure that teachers or reading specialists can use to gain information about how middle or high school students learn from textbooks. This procedure can aid in identifying a student's areas of strength and need when the student undertakes tasks requiring textbook reading.

4. Grant (1993) devised SCROL, a strategy to show students how to use text headings to improve their reading and learning from content area texts:

   (a) **Survey.** The student reads the headings and subheadings in the assigned text selection and asks, "What do I already know about this topic? What information might the writer present?"

   (b) **Connect.** The student asks, "How do the headings relate to one another?" and writes down key words from the headings that might provide connections.

(c) **Read.** The student reads the heading segment, paying particular attention to words and phrases that express important information about the heading.

(d) **Outline.** The student writes the heading and outlines the major ideas and supporting details in the heading segment without looking back to the text.

(e) **Look back.** The student looks back at the heading segment, checking the outline for accuracy and correcting inaccuracies.

5. Because they believe that secondary students must be able to analyze an academic task and plan actions appropriate for completing it, Schumm and Mangrum (1991) devised FLIP, a framework for content area reading. The student asks the following questions, and then decides whether asking for assistance is necessary:

(a) **Friendliness.** How friendly is my reading assignment? (i.e., text features)

(b) **Language.** How difficult is the language in my reading assignment?

(c) **Interest.** How interesting is my reading assignment?

(d) **Prior knowledge.** What do I already know about the material covered in my reading assignment?

6. Graphic displays (Gillespie, 1993) improve comprehension and provide a mnemonic in a way that the narrative text cannot. The dominant types of graphic displays in content area textbooks are maps, which show relationships among areas; charts and tables, which focus on relationships between items; and graphs, which compare things and show quantitative information (Harris & Sipay, 1990). However, many students with disabilities have difficulty in reading and interpreting them. In today's technological world, graphic displays are widely used not only in textbooks but also in newspapers and magazines. Therefore, it is important that content area teachers draw students' attention to the graphic displays found in textbooks and explicitly teach them how to read the displays.

7. Dreher (1992) emphasized the increasingly important literacy task of searching for information in textbooks. The goal is to locate specific information for a specific purpose, using features such as headings and indexes to avoid irrelevant information while targeting critical portions. Because it involves different processes than reading to learn an entire passage, explicit instruction in searching for information is suggested.

Reading Instruction in Simulation and Community Settings

Reading is a basic life skill. Literacy is the cornerstone of an individual's success in school and the foundation of lifelong learning. As is evident from the reading objectives based on community demands presented earlier in this chapter, reading is a valuable means of acquiring knowledge and learning new skills, a source of entertainment, and a means of expanding understanding and fulfilling personal goals. Secondary students with reading difficulties generally tend to read only assigned materials and rarely read supplemental or recreational materials. In the past, they had little or no opportunities to develop reading skills in functional or recreational reading materials. The addition of a functional component to the secondary reading curriculum is intended to help the adolescent make the transition into adulthood. These skills are seldom taught in the community setting for individuals with disabilities. Poor readers shy away from employment requiring reading skills. Thus, it is particularly important to include this functional component in classroom-based reading instruction.

To determine priorities for reading research, the National Reading Research Center (1991) conducted a poll. The results revealed that research on how to enhance student's interest and motivation for reading was the top priority. Studies indicate that a strong relationship exists between reading interest and comprehension (Wigfield & Asher, 1984). Not surprisingly, students comprehend reading material better if it concerns a topic they like. In fact, topic interest makes a substantial contribution to students' comprehension even when prior knowledge of a topic is low (Baldwin, Peleg-Brucker, & McClintock, 1985). As Readence and colleagues (1989) indicated, when students are confronted with expository textbooks that seem to hold little intrinsic appeal, their motivation for reading and learning may ebb. The following is a summary of strategies used to motivate reluctant readers at the secondary level.

1. Sustained Silent Reading (SSR) (Hilbert, 1992/93) requires a regular reading time to provide students with an opportunity to practice their reading skills using pleasurable and self-selected content-related materials silently and without interruption. The purpose of SSR is to promote independent reading and provide opportunities to extend reading skills through practice. Clary (1991) described DEAR, the "drop everything and read" technique.

2. Kletzien and Hushion (1992) and Swift (1993) had success with Reading Workshop, which allows students to choose the books they want to read, gives them time to read in class, and requires them to share their thoughts about the books through dialogue journals. Sanacore (1992) suggested cluttering up the classroom, surrounding students with various reading materials that will tempt them to browse and read.

3. In a survey conducted by Bintz (1993), secondary students reported assigned reading as not meaningful or relevant to their personal lives. They believed that it required little use of sophisticated reading processes or higher-level thinking skills. The students understood the benefits of using shortcut strategies in the short term, but it did not appear that they understood the implications of using these strategies in the long term to become more proficient readers. The survey implies, therefore, that teachers should use relevant material and explicitly teach the relevance of assigned readings. In the same vein, Frager (1993) suggested teaching students to monitor and express their affective responses to the content text along with their cognitive responses.

4. Hudley (1992) used successful Hispanic or African-American women as role models to help motivate high school girls to stay in school, use school and community resources, and develop an interest in recreational reading.

5. Sentence collecting (Speaker & Speaker, 1991) is planned discussion based on the sentences displayed on charts. Learner excitement mounts as students discuss where they found their sentences and the merits of each.

Summary

Reading ability is the most highly valued academic skill that students acquire in U.S. schools today. Despite its importance, considerable controversy shrouds the reading process. We do know that reading is a highly complex activity in which the individual constructs meaningful interpretations of written symbols. Reading involves two basic purposes: a decoding or word recognition process and a comprehension process. Word recognition skills enable the individual to pronounce the words correctly. These skills include phonetic analysis; structural analysis; sight words; context, picture, and configuration clues; and general, special, and technical vocabulary. The comprehension process enables the individual to understand the meaning of the text. Comprehension becomes possible only after word recognition skills are learned. Barrett (1968) formulated a taxonomy of comprehension having four levels: literal recognition or recall, inference, evaluation, and appreciation.

Success in secondary school programs and beyond is contingent upon the ability to read. Unfortunately, many middle and senior high school students with disabilities are deficient in reading skills. However, aids are available for the secondary teacher attempting to instruct students with disabilities in reading. Formal and informal reading assessment procedures can be used in combination to identify and remedy reading deficits in learners with disabilities. Because these learners may not be working within a traditional age- or grade-referenced scheme, teachers should follow a sequence of developmentally based reading objectives in word recognition, comprehension, and study skills. They should also introduce reading objectives based on community demands, particularly those related to following directions, gaining information, understanding forms, and recreation and leisure-time activity. This functional component of the reading curriculum ensures that students will acquire the reading skill necessary for survival and independence in the community.

References

Afflerbach, P. (1993). STAIR: A system for recording and using what we observe and know about our students. *The Reading Teacher, 47*, 260–263.

Afflerbach, P., & Kapinus, B. (1993). The balancing act. *The Reading Teacher, 47*, 62–64.

Alvermann, D. E. (1987). Comprehension/thinking skills. In D. E. Alvermann, D. W Moore, & M. W. Conley (Eds.), *Research within reach: Secondary school reading* (pp. 52–63). Newark, DE: International Reading Association.

American Educational Research Association, American Psychological Association, & National Council on Measurement in Education. (1985). *Standards for educational and psychological testing*. Washington, DC: American Psychological Association.

Anderson, R. C., Hiebert, E. H., Scott, J. A., & Wilkinson, I. A. G. (1985). *Becoming a nation of readers: The report of the Commission on Reading*. Washington, DC: National Institute of Education.

Archambeault, B. (1992). Personalizing study skills in secondary students. *Journal of Reading, 35*, 468–472.

Armbruster, B. B., Anderson, T. H., & Meyer, J. L. (1991). Improving content-area reading using instructional graphics. *Reading Research Quarterly, 26*, 393–416.

Ambruster, B. B., & Nagey, W. E. (1992). Vocabulary in content area lessons. *The Reading Teacher, 45,* 550–551.

Askov, E. N., & Clark, C. J. (1991). Using computers in adult literacy instruction. *Journal of Reading, 34,* 434–448.

Askov, E. N., & Kamm, K. (1982). *Study skills in the content areas.* Boston: Allyn and Bacon.

Askov, E. N., Kamm, K., Klumb, R., & Barnette, J. J. (1980). Study skill mastery: Comparisons between teachers and students on selected skills. In M. L. Kamil & A. J. Moe (Eds.), *Perspectives in reading research and instruction* (pp. 207–212). Washington, DC: National Reading Conference.

Baldwin, R. S., Peleg-Brucker, Z., & McClintock, A. (1985). Effects of topic interest on children's reading comprehension. *Reading Research Quarterly, 20,* 497–504.

Barrett, T. C. (1968). Taxonomy of cognitive and affective dimensions of reading comprehension. In T. Clymer (Ed.), *Innovation and change in reading instruction.* Chicago: University of Chicago Press.

Bath, S. R. (1992). Trade-book minigroups: A cooperative approach to literature. *The Reading Teacher, 46,* 272–275.

Baumann, J. F., Jones L. A., & Seifert-Kessell, N. (1993). Using think alouds to enhance children's comprehension monitoring abilities. *The Reading Teacher, 47,* 182–193.

Baumann, J. F., & Kameenui, E. J. (1991). Research on vocabulary instruction: Ode to Voltaire. In J. Flood, J. M. Jensen, D. Lapp, & J. R. Squire (Eds.), *Handbook on teaching the English language arts* (pp. 604–632). New York: Macmillan.

Beck, I., & McKeown, M. (1991). Conditions of vocabulary acquisition. In R. Barr, M. Kamil, P. Mosenthal, & P. D. Pearson (Eds.), *Handbook of reading research (Vol. 2,* pp. 789–814). White Plains, NY: Longman.

Bintz, W. P. (1993). Resistent readers in secondary education: Some insights and implications. *Journal of Reading, 36,* 604–615.

Blachowicz, C. L. Z. (1985). Vocabulary development and reading: From research to instruction. *Reading Teacher, 38,* 876–881.

Blachowicz, C. L. Z. (1993). C(2)QU: Modeling context use in the classroom. *The Reading Teacher, 47,* 268–269.

Blachowicz, C. L. Z., & Lee, J. J. (1991). Vocabulary development in the whole literacy classroom. *The Reading Teacher, 45,* 188–195.

Brozo, W. G., & Simpson, M. L. (1991). *Readers, teachers, learners: Expanding literacy in secondary schools.* Columbus, OH: Merrill.

Buikema, J. L., & Graves, M. F. (1993). Teaching students to use context cues to infer word meanings. *Journal of Reading, 36,* 450–457.

Calfee, R. C., & Perfumo, P. (1993). Student portfolios: Opportunities for a revolution in assessment. *Journal of Reading, 36,* 532–537.

Carr, E., & Wilson, K. K. (1986). Guidelines for evaluating vocabulary instruction. *Journal of Reading, 29,* 588–595.

Chall, J. S. (1983). Literacy: Trends and explanations. *Educational Researcher, 12,* 3–8.

Clary, L. M. (1991). Getting adolescents to read. *Journal of Reading, 34,* 340–345.

Cottier, S. J., & Bauman, S. K. (1985). A study skills unit for junior high students. In W. J. Harker (Ed.) *Classroom strategies for secondary reading* (2nd ed., pp. 123–127). Newark, DE: International Reading Association.

Davey, B. (1993). Helping middle school learners succeed with reading assignments: A focus on time planning. *Journal of Reading, 37,* 170–173.

Dillner, M. (1993/94). Using hypermedia to enhance content area instruction. *Journal of Reading, 37,* 260–270.

Dixon, R., Carnine, D. W., & Kameenui, E. J. (1992). *Curriculum guidelines for diverse learners.* [Monograph for National Center to Improve the Tools of Educators]. Eugene: University of Oregon.

Dole, J., Duffy, G., Roehler, L., & Pearson, P. D. (1991). Moving from the old to the new: Research on reading comprehension. *Review of Educational Research, 61,* 239–264.

Dreher, M. J. (1992). Searching for information in textbooks. *Journal of Reading, 35,* 364–371.

Farr, R. (1992). Putting it all together: Solving the reading assessment puzzle. *The Reading Teacher, 46,* 26–37.

Fay, L. (1965). Reading study skills: Math and science. In J. A. Figurel (Ed.), *Reading and inquiry* (pp. 93–94). Newark, DE: International Reading Association.

Finnegan, R., & Sinatra, R. (1991). Interactive computer-assisted instruction with adults. *Journal of Reading, 35,* 108–119.

Frager, A. M. (1993). Affective dimensions of content area reading. *Journal of Reading, 36,* 615–622.

Gambrell, L., & Jawitz, P. B. (1993). Mental imagery, text illustrations, and children's story comprehension and recall. *Reading Research Quarterly, 28,* 265–273.

Gambrell, L., Kapinus, B. A., & Wilson, R. M. (1987). Using mental imagery and summarization to achieve independence in comprehension. *Journal of Reading, 30,* 638–642.

Gillespie, C. (1990). Questions about student-generated questions. *Journal of Reading, 34,* 250–257.

Gillespie, C. S. (1993). Reading graphic displays: What teachers should know. *Journal of Reading, 36,* 350–354.

Gipe, J., & Arnold, R. (1979). Teaching vocabulary through familiar associations and contexts. *Journal of Reading Behavior, 11*(3), 281–285.

Goldberg, C. (1992/93). Instructional conversations: Promoting comprehension through discussion. *The Reading Teacher, 46,* 316–326.

Grant, R. (1993). Strategic training for using text headings to improve students' processing of content. *Journal of Reading, 36,* 482–488.

Gray, W. S. (1925). A modern program of reading instruction for the grades and high school. In G. M. Whipple (Ed.), *Report of the National Committee on Reading* (pp. 21–74). Bloomington, IL: Public School Publishing.

Groller, K. L., Kender, J. P., & Honeyman, D. S. (1991). Does instruction on metacognitive strategies help high school students use advance organizers? *Journal of Reading, 34,* 470–475.

Hancock, M. R. (1993). Character journals: Initiating involvement and identification through literature. *Journal of Reading, 37,* 42–50.

Harris, A., & Sipay, E. (1990). *How to increase reading ability* (9th ed.). White Plains, NY: Longman.

Hennings, D. G. (1993). On knowing and reading history. *Journal of Reading, 36,* 362–370.

Hilbert, S. B. (1992/93). Sustained, silent reading revisited. *The Reading Teacher, 46,* 354–356.

Hudley, C. A. (1992). Using role models to improve the reading attitudes of ethnic minority high school girls. *Journal of Reading, 36,* 182–188.

Johnson, D. D., Pittelman, S. D., & Heimlich, J. E. (1986). Semantic mapping. *The Reading Teacher, 39,* 779–782.

Johnston, F. R. (1993). Improving student response in DR-TAs and DL-TAs. *The Reading Teacher, 46,* 448–449.

Kameenui, E. J. (1993). Diverse learners and the tyranny of time: Don't fix the blame; fix the leaky roof. *The Reading Teacher, 46,* 376–383.

Kletzien, S. B. (1991). Strategy use by good and poor comprehenders reading expository text of differing levels. *Reading Research Quarterly, 26,* 67–86.

Kletzien, S. B., & Hushion, B. C. (1992). Reading Workshop: Reading, writing, thinking. *Journal of Reading, 35,* 444–451.

Koskinen, P. S., Wilson, R., Gambrell, L. B., & Neuman, S. B. (1993). Captioned video and vocabulary learning: An innovative practice in literary instruction. *The Reading Teacher, 47,* 36–43.

Leal, D. J. (1993). The power of literary peer group discussions: How children collaboratively negotiate meaning. *The Reading Teacher, 47,* 114–120.

Livdahl, B. S. (1993). "To read it is to live it, different from just knowing it." *Journal of Reading, 37,* 192–200.

Maring, G. H., & Furman, G. (1985). Seven "whole class" strategies to help mainstreamed young people read and listen better in content area classes. *Journal of Reading, 28,* 694–700.

McGill-Franzen, A. (1993). "I can read the words!": Selecting good books for inexperienced readers. *The Reading Teacher, 46,* 424–426.

McKeown, M. G. (1993). Creating effective definitions for young word learners. *Reading Research Quarterly, 28,* 17–31.

Megyeri, K. A. (1993). The reading aloud of ninth-grade writing. *Journal of Reading, 37,* 184–190.

Nagey, W. E., & Anderson, R. C. (1984). How many words are there in printed school English? *Reading Research Quarterly, 19,* 304–330.

National Commission on Testing and Public Policy. (1990). *From gatekeeper to gateway: Transforming testing in America.* Chestnut Hill, MA: Boston College.

National Reading Research Center. (1991). Conceptual framework: The engagement perspective. In *National Reading Research Center: A proposal from the University of Maryland and the University of Georgia.* Athens, GA, & College Park, MD: Author.

Nist, S. L., & Kirby, K. (1986). Teaching comprehension and strategies through modeling and think aloud. *Reading Research Quarterly, 25,* 254–264.

Nolan, T. E. (1991). Self-questioning and prediction: Combining metacognitive strategies. *Journal of Reading, 35,* 132–138.

Norton, D. E. (1992a). Modeling inferencing of characterization. *The Reading Teacher, 46,* 64–67.

Norton, D. E. (1992b). Understanding plot structures. *The Reading Teacher, 46,* 254–258.

Norton, D. E. (1993). Webbing and historical fiction. *The Reading Teacher, 46,* 432–436.

Ogle, D. M. (1989). The know, want to know, learn strategy. In K. D. Muth (Ed.), *Children's comprehension of text* (pp. 205–223). Newark, DE: International Reading Association.

Olson, M. W., & Gee, T. C. (1991). Content reading instruction in the primary grades: Perceptions and strategies. *The Reading Teacher, 45,* 298–307.

Pauk, W. (1963). On scholarship: Advice to high school students. *Reading Teacher, 17,* 73–78.

Petty, W. T., Herold, C. P., & Stoll, E. (1968). *The state of knowledge about the teaching of vocabulary.* Champaign, IL: National Council of Teachers of English.

Purnell, K. N., & Solman, R. T. (1991). The influence of technical illustrations on students' comprehension in geography. *Reading Research Quarterly, 26,* 277–299.

Readence, J. E., Bean, T. W., & Baldwin, R. S. (1989). *Content area reading: An integrated approach.* (3rd ed.). Dubuque, IA: Kendall/Hunt.

Resnick, D. P. (1981). Testing in America: A supportive environment. *Phi Delta Kappan, 62,* 625–628.

Resnick, D. P., & Resnick, L. B. (1977). The nature of literacy: An historical exploration. *Harvard Educational Review, 47,* 370–385.

Robinson, F. P. (1962). *Effective reading.* New York: Harper & Row.

Roe, B. D., Stoodt, B. D., & Burns, P. C. (1991). *Secondary school reading instruction: The content areas* (4th ed.). Boston: Houghton-Mifflin.

Sammons, R. B., & Davey, B. (1993/94). Assessing students' skills in using textbooks: The Textbook Awareness and Performance Profile (TAPP). *Journal of Reading, 37,* 280–286.

Sanacore, J. (1992). Encouraging the lifetime reading habit. *Journal of Reading, 35,* 474–477.

Saski, J., & Carter, J. (1984). Effective reading instruction for mildly handicapped adolescents. *Teaching Exceptional Children, 16,* 177–182.

Schums, J. S., & Mangrus, C. T., II. (1991). FLIP: A framework for content area reading. *Journal of Reading, 35,* 120–124.

Schwartz, R. M. (1988). Learning to learn vocabulary in content area textbooks. *Journal of Reading, 32,* 108–118.

Sedlak, R. A., & Sedlak, D. M. (1985). *Teaching the educable mentally retarded.* Albany: State University of New York Press.

Sinatra, R., & Dowd, C. A. (1991). Using syntactic and semantic clues to learn vocabulary. *Journal of Reading, 35,* 224–229.

Smith, C. B., & Eliot, P. G. (1979). *Reading activities for middle and secondary schools.* New York: Holt, Rinehart, & Winston.

Speaker, R. B., Jr., & Speaker, P. R. (1991). Sentence collecting: Authentic literacy events in the classroom. *Journal of Reading, 35,* 92–96.

Sternberg, R. J. (1991). Are we reading too much into reading comprehension tests? *Journal of Reading, 34,* 540–545.

Swift, K. (1993). Try Reading Workshop in your classroom. *The Reading Teacher, 46,* 366–371.

Turner, J. C. (1993). Situated motivation in literacy instruction. *Reading Research Quarterly, 28,* 288–290.

Vacca, R. T., & Vacca, J. L. (1985). Functional reading in competency programs. In W. J. Harker (Ed.), *Classroom strategies for secondary reading* (2nd ed., pp. 138–141). Newark, DE: International Reading Association.

Valencia, S. (1990). A portfolio approach to classroom reading assessment: The whys, whats, and hows. *The Reading Teacher, 43,* 338–339.

Whorton, J. E., & Daniel, D. N. (1986). A psychometric comparison of learning disabled and educable mentally retarded children. *Reading Improvement, 23,* 63–67.

Wigfield, A., & Asher, S. R. (1984). Social and motivational influences on reading. In P. D. Pearson (Ed.), *Handbook of reading research* (pp. 423–452). White Plains, NY: Longman.

Wolf, D., Bixby, J., Glenn, J., III, & Gardner, H. (1991). To use their minds well: Investigating new forms of student assessment. In G. Grant (Ed.), *Review of research in education (vol. 17).* Washington, DC: American Educational Research Association.

Wolf, K. P. (1993). From informal to informed assessment: Recognizing the role of the classroom teacher. *Journal of Reading, 36,* 518–523.

$$C \ h \ a \ p \ t \ e \ r \quad \textbf{\textit{11}}$$

Mathematics Instruction

RICH WILSON, DAVID MAJSTEREK, AND ERIC D. JONES

Did you know that . . .

- Students who have failed to learn by traditional means can often learn to compensate for their weaknesses?
- Students with disabilities learn skills best when they are taught directly?
- Increases in teacher-led instruction are associated with higher student achievement?
- Many students with disabilities will receive math instruction in the regular classroom?
- Most students with learning disabilities are served in resource rooms?
- Several types of learning must be taught?
- Fluency involves both speed and accuracy?
- Students may not be able to use in the community the skills that they exhibit in the classroom?

Can you . . .

- Construct a criterion-referenced test in fractions?
- Identify a student's optimal instructional level?
- Set overall mastery goals for learning?
- Create an instructional file system?
- Model and demonstrate as you teach?

Rich Wilson is an associate professor and Eric Jones is a professor of special education in the Department of Special Education, Bowling Green University, Bowling Green, Ohio. David Majsterek is an associate professor of education in the Department of Education, Central Washington University, Ellensburg, Washington.

- Test for student acquisition?
- Deliver effective prompts?
- Develop effective drill and practice lessons?
- Deliver appropriate feedback to students?
- Motivate your students?
- Decide when to modify an instructional program?
- Determine whether your program has been successful?

Teachers of students with learning disabilities are faced with a difficult task. Whether their students are identified for services in regular classrooms, resource rooms, or special classes, they have all been referred for services because they have failed to make average-level academic achievement. They frequently also have negative attitudes toward themselves and their abilities (Morgan & Jenson, 1988). Typically, these reduced student self-perceptions are developed following many years of below-average achievement. The presence of both low self-efficacy and below-average achievement often destroys the motivation to learn (Dyer, 1978) and leads students to think that they are no longer capable of mastering grade-level material as well as their nondisabled peers. The net effect is that teachers of students with learning disabilities must not only focus on remediating both significant academic failure, they must also frequently expend great energies to motivate and improve the self-confidence of their students.

Teachers who lower their expectations to match student perceptions can make matters worse. The fact that students with disabilities have not performed as well as their nondisabled peers can cause teachers to water down the curriculum because they expect their students to continue learning at below-average rates. There is evidence that teachers adjust instruction on the basis of the "effort, ability, and personal-social characteristics" of their students (Shavelson & Stern, 1981, p. 467). If the academic level and demand of instruction are reduced because of affective variables rather than prior academic achievement or cognitive abilities, students' opportunities to make maximum academic gains will be reduced. Sustaining high expectations for the academic growth of students with disabilities may cause some frustrations for teachers, but in order to halt and reverse the trends toward greater failure and loss of self-efficacy, students with disabilities must not only learn as much as the average student (in which case achievement deficits would stabilize at below-average levels), but also learn at an above-average rate in order to reach age- or grade-level performance.

As difficult as it sounds, students with mild disabilities can often master regular class material if they are provided with an extra allotment of intensive learning strategies by effective teachers using empirically validated techniques (Deshler, Schumaker, Lenz, & Ellis, 1984), and they can become well established in the mainstream (Larrivee, 1986). Students with more moderate or severe disabilities for whom average performance is a more distant goal can greatly improve their performance on many of the complex tasks required for success in regular education classrooms (Brown, Campione, & Day 1981; Horton, 1985). Thus, there are hopeful indications and compelling reasons for teachers to use well-designed methods and materials with students with disabilities. This chapter describes instructional practices in math that have, for the most part, been empirically supported for use with secondary students experiencing learning and behavior problems.

Principles of Effective Secondary Math Instruction

To be truly effective, instruction must be adapted to meet the constantly evolving needs of the learner. This educational process can be most successful if it is founded on a sound theoretical basis. In addition, teachers who develop and articulate a theoretical foundation will find that the resulting principles will help them select more wisely from among currently available methods and materials, and enable them to adapt teaching techniques and instructional programs for students for whom existing methods or materials are inappropriate. The tenets presented below are offered in the belief that programs designed from this set of principles are most likely to assist students with disabilities in reaching their potential in academic, personal, and social activities in secondary schools and in making a successful transition to the after-school world.

1. *Ensure that the student experiences success.* "Education" implies that all students deserve an opportunity to develop both competence and confidence in their abilities. One of the best ways teachers can enhance self-competence is to provide a program designed to ensure success and increase attainment (Whelan, Mendez, deSaman, & Fortmeyer, 1984). The fact that math achievement and self-concept are interrelated provides additional support for this assertion (Kruger & Wandle, 1992).

2. *Provide functional academic instruction.* Instructional objectives taught in the school setting should be directly tied to the skills necessary to succeed in life and career activities (Langone, 1981; Polloway & Epstein, 1985; Schwartz & Budd, 1981). There are many things that are presented in school curricula that would be fine to learn, but students with disabilities gain very little from brief instructional exposures. Instead they learn more and make better adaptations with the mastery of skills and knowledge that have the greatest potential for later application. Since secondary-level students will shortly be leaving school, it is important that the teacher be careful to select the skills that will have the greatest value in adapting to life outside of school. Thus, basic math fact drill, an activity that consumes considerable instructional time in elementary school, needs to be supplanted with relevant consumer math. Teachers should continually be asking themselves whether the tasks they are teaching will be important once their students leave the classroom.

3. *Provide age-appropriate instruction.* Teachers must help students with disabilities master as many age- and grade-appropriate tasks as possible (Farey, 1986). This requires a sensitivity to social, academic, and career needs. Achieving age-appropriate objectives is often difficult because commercial materials are written for students whose achievement levels match their age levels. For example, driver's manuals and health texts for adolescents often have ninth-grade or higher readability levels. Since students with disabilities need to master the content in these areas, it is up to the teacher either to adapt the commercial materials or to locate instructional materials that are relevant to an adolescent's interests and have the appropriate level of readability.

4. *Offer compensatory instruction.* If instructional time is limited and students are failing to master traditional academic tasks (e.g., telling time or computing sums of money), teach students to compensate by using a digital timepiece, calculator (Horton, 1985), typewriter (Calhoun, 1985), and even a small alarm clock. If teachers fail to permit their students to use compensatory learning methods, valuable instructional time will be used up that could have been better spent teaching advanced skills.

5. *Teach skills directly.* Once skills have been sequenced and students assessed, the teacher must take the most efficient and direct path to instruct the student and not depend on incidental learning, discovery learning, or divergent questioning techniques (Bigler, 1984). Generically, this can be described as a three-step procedure: demonstrate, prompt or lead, and test (Silbert, Carnine, & Stein, 1990; Rosenshine, 1983). Direct skill instruction has proven to be the most effective format to teach knowledge and skills to students with disabilities.

6. *Increase teacher-led, active student responding.* Teacher–student interactions should be maximized and independent math seatwork closely controlled and limited, because if seatwork consumes more than 80% of instructional time, student achievement decreases (Fisher et al., 1980). In addition, the teacher should ensure a high rate of active student responding since the combination of many minutes of teacher-led instructional time, numerous teacher questions, and active student responses creates a powerful means of enhancing achievement (Bennett, 1987).

7. *Begin with and then fade teacher control of the program.* The teacher is in large part responsible for selecting the instructional objectives, methods, and materials. Very little instruction should be left to chance. Instead, the teacher should assume the role of program manager and control the setting, method, materials, reinforcement, and other instructional variables. Of course, one of the responsibilities of a good teacher/manager is knowing when to teach self-monitoring, self-correction, and independent student work habits and how to increase student responsibility for and control of learning. Secondary school teachers need to create a mathematics program that prepares students to function independently in the after-school world.

8. *Provide structure and rigorous scheduling.* Students learn best when the learning environment is designed for efficient and effective delivery of instruction. This includes classroom design, material selection, teacher talk, and very importantly, expression of a "We're here to work hard and learn" attitude. In addition, the teacher-controlled variable most associated with student achievement is the amount of time students spend learning. Teachers can maximize learning time by adhering to a tight schedule, eliminating unneeded transitions, reducing disruptions, and increasing academic learning time (Fisher et al., 1980; Wilson & Wesson, 1986). The key to maximizing instructional time is planning ahead. The more the teacher is prepared; the more the students will learn.

9. *Use empirically supported instructional practices.* Teachers should make every effort to use strategies that research has shown to be effective. Teachers should always use the best way to teach a concept or operation. Students will also learn best when teachers control the task difficulty level of assigned activities. Tasks on which students are working must be neither too easy (if they are already mastered, there is no point in teaching them) nor too difficult (if they are too hard, frustration and resignation are likely to occur). Methods to control and maximize task difficulty are presented later in this chapter.

10. *Refrain from criticism.* The temptation when working with adolescent learners who are having academic problems may be to attribute their failure to home conditions or lack of effort. However, refraining from making critical comments is a teacher characteristic associated with effective mainstreaming practices (Larrivee, 1986).

Process of Effective Transition-Oriented Math Instruction

This section presents a generic model for planning, delivering, and evaluating effective transition-oriented math instruction for secondary students with disabilities. This model does not contain the exact components of any particular commercial program; rather, it incorporates features from numerous sources and is based on the principles previously described. The process of providing effective transition-oriented math instruction can be divided into the following four categories:

1. Assessing instructional demands as they relate to the learner, task, setting, and program goals
2. Planning specific math instructional activities
3. Implementing math instruction
4. Measuring student performance in a math course of study.

Step 1: Assessing Instructional Demands

Assessment of Program Goals.   All special education teachers are required by Public Law 94-142 to develop long-term or *annual goals* for their students. Typically, annual goals are developed within an instructional area (e.g., students with learning disabilities may exhibit performance deficits in listening comprehension, basic reading, reading comprehension, oral expression, written expression, math reasoning, or math computation). During this process, teachers must select which skills they will and will not teach to their students. Because there is always a limited amount of instructional time available, some skill areas will either not be taught at all or given only cursory coverage. The math areas listed below often represent skill-deficit areas for students with disabilities:

time	basic computations	calculus
money	decimals	trigonometry
geometry	fractions	business math
algebra	measurement	consumer math

Special education teachers who teach transition-oriented math to students with disabilities must make decisions about what and how much to teach from within each of these categories. By applying the principles described earlier (especially those involving relevance, compensation, and student success), teachers can match student needs to curriculum goals by making individual decisions for every student in a math program. For some students, all of the regular math curriculum goals may be taught, although there may be variations in pace, materials, testing, group size, or instructional time. For most students with disabilities, teachers need to select the most important skills from within a math area, providing added instruction on these objectives while deleting other objectives from the course of study. Case for Action 11.1 is designed to approximate this decision-making process in the area of fractions.

Assessment of the Learner's Entry-Level Skills. Once teachers know what is to be taught, they must determine exactly which instructional objectives each student has already mastered. Entry skills cannot be assessed effectively in transition-oriented programs unless all activities are focused on relevant, practical instructional goals (Cobb & Larkin, 1985; Forness, Horton, & Horton, 1981).

Typically, math skills are assessed by constructing, administering, and interpreting criterion-referenced (CR) informal tests (Frank & McFarland, 1980). Examples of several tests are presented in the appendix to this chapter. Commercial versions of CR tests are also available (e.g., Brigance Diagnostic Inventory of Essential Skills, Brigance, 1980). With practice, teachers can construct CR tests that are more specific to the objectives and content of their instructional programs. If they are carefully constructed, teacher-made CR tests can be more valid and useful than commercially published tests. Action Plan 11.1 presents seven steps for constructing and using CR tests.

The process outlined in Action Plan 11.1 provides a structure for identifying the most appropriate instructional task (i.e., the student's *optimal instruction level*)—in other words, the task that is neither too easy nor too difficult and, therefore, should be taught next. The process begins with a review of instructional goals. For example, the teacher may want students to learn the math skills that are necessary for using checkbooks. Once the instructional area has been identified, the functional tasks that must be taught within that area must be listed and arranged sequentially from easiest to hardest. Since the number of possible applications for secondary math programs is potentially very broad, teachers will have to perform at least the initial stages of the task analyses that are part of Step 2 themselves. Silbert, Carnine, and Stein (1990) presented a set of hierarchies for basic math skills. These hierarchies are useful because they provide well-articulated sequences of tasks. The examples that accompany each step in the hierarchies can be directly used as test items. Two or three items will usually be a sufficient sample of test items for deciding which skills the student needs to begin with. In some cases the teacher may decide that the steps in the hierarchy are too finely cut and may decide to skip steps. However, since the hierarchies are already laid out, the teacher will know clearly which steps are being skipped. If a mistake is made in estimating the student's level of proficiency, it will be possible to slice back to more appropriate tasks. When the test is administered, the assessment should be be consistent with the actual performance conditions. For example, in checkbook math, students will align quantities and perform computations with paper and pencil. The test should provide for that mode of response. Similarly, speeded responding is not apt to be important in checkbook math, but it may be appropriate for some students to use a calculator.

Finally, after the test has been scored and proficiencies and weaknesses have been identified, the teacher must construct and present instructional activities at the students' optimal level of instruction. In functional skill domains, it will be necessary for teachers to give close attention to their individual students' levels of proficiency across a variety of

Action Plan 11.1   Constructing Criterion-Referenced Tests

We recommend the following procedures for constructing a criterion-referenced test:

1. Determine the instructional area (e.g., checkbook math).
2. Select the tasks to be taught from within that area.
3. Arrange the tasks sequentially from easiest to hardest.
4. Develop test items for each task.
5. Administer the test.
6. Score and interpret the test.
7. Begin instruction at the student's optimal instructional level.

Case for Action 11.1

Listed below are 10 skills from a criterion-referenced instructional hierarchy in fractions. You are a secondary special education teacher of students with mild mental retardation and developmental disabilities. Examine the instructional hierarchy and rate each task according to the relevance and importance it has had in your post-high school life on a scale where 3 is very important, 2 is somewhat important, 1 is barely important, and 0 is not important.

Of course, when teachers make decisions on what to teach, some other factors must also be considered. List and discuss the questions you would want answered before you would plan to include or exclude objectives from instruction. Would you want to know, for example, what career your student is considering or how much time you can devote to teaching fractions?

Fraction Hierarchy

1. Drawing diagrams to represent fractional parts
2. Adding fractions with like denominators
3. Reducing fractions to lowest terms
4. Changing improper fractions to mixed numbers
5. Subtracting fractions with like denominators
6. Subtracting fractions with mixed numbers
7. Multiplying fractions
8. Multiplying two mixed numbers
9. Dividing fractions
10. Working story problems involving the division of fractions.

skills that are interrelated in their functional application. To interpret test results, the teacher compares obtained student scores (e.g., 100% correct on adding two numbers with a calculator) to the standard educational guidelines in Table 11.1 and rates student performance at the mastery, instructional, or frustration levels for each task assessed. The results of such a comparison and rating are depicted in Table 11.2 for calculator usage.

TABLE 11.1   Student Performance Guidelines

Level	Percent
Mastery or independent	90 or more correct
Instructional	70–90 correct
Frustration	Less than 70 correct

In this example, Task 5 (adding more than two numbers) represents this student's optimal instructional level task.

Assessment of Relevant Student Characteristics. In addition to program and task demands, relevant student characteristics should be determined prior to instruction. Over the duration of a transition-oriented secondary school program, students will be expected to learn numerous math-related skills that have physical task demands. Thus, physical disabilities and the necessary adaptations to materials and programs will be important considerations when teaching cooking, writing, typing, and operating a cash register or calculator.

Step 2: Planning Specific Instruction

Setting Mastery Goals. After teachers have determined the student's optimal instructional level by identifying the task that will be taught, they need to determine the level of student proficiency to be achieved before the task can be said to be mastered. This process must be done for each individual and involves predicting the complex interaction between two factors: the instructional time needed for a student to master a task and the

TABLE 11.2   Calculator Task-Hierarchy Segment

Task	Description	Percentage Correct	Rating
1	Add two whole numbers	100	M
2	Subtract two whole numbers	100	M
3	Multiply two whole numbers	100	M
4	Divide two whole numbers	100	M
5	Add more than two whole numbers	80	I
6	Subtract more than two whole numbers	80	I
7	Multiply more than two whole numbers	70	I
8	Divide more than two whole numbers	50	F
9	Add two decimal numbers	30	F
10	Subtract two decimal numbers	0	F

Key: M = mastery level; I = instructional level; F = frustration level.

level of correct performance that defines mastery. Although research in this area is lacking, there are a number of guidelines available to help teachers set mastery levels.

1. *Standard educational guidelines.* Teachers can apply the widely accepted guidelines developed for special education (Stevens, 1977) that set mastery level at approximately 90% for most academic tasks. Not all tasks, however, should be assigned the same mastery-level criterion. Basic skills (e.g., measuring by inches) that are prerequisites for higher-order tasks (e.g., measuring by eighths of an inch) often need to be mastered at 100% correct before instruction begins on the next task. For other skills (e.g., dividing fractions) teachers can set mastery performance closer to 90% correct. Thus, teachers need to apply the standard educational guidelines in Table 11.1 with a measure of common sense.

2. *Functional rate.* Setting mastery goals using the principle of functional rate is probably the best strategy to use in transition-oriented math programs (Haring, Lovitt, Eaton, & Hansen, 1978). In this method the mastery goal is set at the level of math performance that a student needs to achieve to be successful either in subsequently taught, higher-order tasks or in real-life activities (e.g., the amount of school-based training needed to run a cash register successfully in a supermarket or the amount of calculator training needed to balance a checkbook). Unfortunately, empirically validated functional rate standards have not been determined for the vast majority of math tasks, and much work remains to be done in this area.

3. *Social validation.* Kazdin (1977) introduced the concept of social validation in order to help teachers and therapists set goals for successful behavior management programs. A socially valid goal is attained if, after treatment, the student's behavior approximates the average performance of normally functioning peers. The social validation principle can be used to set numerous math instructional goals, such as the writing rate needed to complete a math competency exam on time; the on-task rate needed for satisfactory math assignment performance; the attention span needed to complete complex tasks such as reading story problems or setting a digital watch; or the average math skills of successful practicing mechanics, carpenters, or technicians who use math in their occupation. Teachers can apply the principle of social validation to set math goals by following the steps in Action Plan 11.2.

One of the side benefits of using social validation data is that, after instruction proves successful, the special education teacher can use the results to demonstrate empirically that the students can perform as well as persons considered to be doing well. These findings can be used to enhance placement in both mainstream classes and the workforce.

4. *Normative data.* Normative data are gathered by testing large numbers of students and employing descriptive statistics to determine the mean, standard deviation, percentile rank, and other indices of the group. School districts that have incorporated a curriculum-based methodology (Deno, 1985) routinely assess student math skills in order to determine how every student is performing on the tasks in the math curriculum. Normative data have already been gathered in many instructional and behavior manage-

Action Plan 11.2   Determining Socially Valid Math Performance Standards

We recommend the following four-step process for establishing socially valid math performance standards:

Generic Steps	Specific Example
1. Gather data in order to measure the average performance level of mainstream peers or employees who are doing well.	Test the linear measurement skills of 10 practicing woodworkers at local cabinet-making shops.
2. Measure the performance of a target student on the same task.	Test the linear measurement skills of a class of secondary students with developmental disabilities.
3. Compare the results to determine the instructional need.	Determine which skills the woodworkers have mastered (e.g., using a Vernier caliper) and how the students perform on these tasks.
4. Begin instruction and continue until goal is attained.	Begin instruction on the easiest task not mastered by the students (e.g., measuring accurately to within $\frac{1}{32}$ of an inch).

ment areas, including spelling, reading fluency, reading comprehension, math computation, story problems, writing, success rates, and on-task rates (Fisher et al., 1980; Starlin & Starlin, 1973).

Perhaps the easiest way to use normative data to set instructional goals is to determine the average range of student performance in a specific task and to use the lower limit of the average range as the goal for students with disabilities. Consider the following example. Assume that regular education students who succeed in a two-year technical school after high school can solve higher-order computational problems (e.g., addition with regrouping or long division) at an average rate of 90% correct with a standard deviation of 5%. This means that the average range (i.e., the mean plus and minus one standard deviation, representing the performance of 68% of those students) is from 85% to 95% correct. Students with disabilities who wish to attend and succeed at a technical school could work toward becoming as proficient in computation (i.e., at least 85% correct) as students at the lower end of the average range.

Selecting Instructional Materials and Settings.   Teacher management of the instructional setting is a critical consideration (Englemann, Carnine, & Steely, 1991; Hanley-Maxwell, Wilcox, & Heal, 1982), and selecting materials for students with disabilities is an important and time-consuming teacher task. It is important because the type of materials used has an impact on student achievement. It is time-consuming because appropriate commercially made materials are difficult to locate, especially materials needed to teach functional or compensatory tasks (Lambie, 1980). Even when appropriate math materials are available, teachers must supplement commercial programs since students with disabilities often require additional instruction to attain task mastery.

Teachers will find that they often have to make their own or locate materials from several sources in order to provide high-quality instruction. Teachers who wish to select and store materials in a highly organized fashion can follow the steps in Action Plan 11.3.

Although developing this system may appear burdensome, teachers will find that once initial materials are gathered, instruction can be delivered efficiently and the materials can be reused or adapted for any future student who needs to master the same tasks.

Selection of the instructional setting is another important variable to consider. Several key setting variables along with suggestions for practitioners are contained in Action Plan 11.4.

Selecting Instructional Techniques and Format. Teachers must select instructional strategies and teaching formats that will maximize student achievement. There is empirical evidence that both teaching strategies and lesson format are related to student performance (Fisher et al., 1980; Sindelar, Rosenberg, Wilson, & Bursuck, 1984). The strategies that follow are especially relevant for teaching math skills to secondary students in a transition-oriented program.

1. *Demonstrating or modeling the correct task solutions.*   A teaching method that has received much research support was developed by those who employ a "generic direct instruction" approach (Rosenshine, 1983). The basic instructional sequence is made up of three steps: demonstrate, prompt, and test. Since it is important for students to make few errors during skill acquisition, new instruction should begin with a teacher demonstration of correct task performance. Instead of asking Bill, "What key on the computer do you press if you want to multiply two numbers?" begin by telling and showing him the correct behavior. If Bill knows the correct key, he probably should not be part of the acquisition lesson. Instead, provide him with fluency-building, drill and practice, or generalization lessons. If Bill does not know the correct key, he is likely to guess, perhaps using a faulty problem-solving strategy that will need to be displaced later during the teaching of the correct strategy. The purpose of a demonstration step is to show a student how to complete an instructional objective successfully.

Action Plan 11.3   Creating Instructional File Systems

We recommend the following procedures for creating instructional file systems:

1. Begin with the task hierarchy that defines the relevant instructional area.
2. Label file folders, drawers, or boxes with tags for each task in the hierarchy.
3. Visit a curriculum library, special education resource center, or other site where large numbers of activities can be found.
4. Duplicate worksheets, activity descriptions, units, computer programs, and other materials for each task.
5. File a permanent, not-to-be-used original that can be copied for use by individual students.

Action Plan 11.4   Setting Variables

We offer the following recommendations based on setting variables:

Variable	Recommendation
1. Group size (Sindelar, Rosenberg, Wilson, & Bursuck, 1984)	Three to eight students
2. Seating (Silbert et al., 1990)	Close proximity to and eye contact with teacher
3. Furniture management (Wilson & Wesson, 1986)	Control of traffic patterns to minimize disruptions

A demonstration step typically consists of two components: teacher behaviors and the necessary stimulus materials. If the instructional objective is to teach a student how to multiply using a computer, the stimulus material is the computer and the teacher behaviors include stating the directions: "To multiply 3 times 2 on the computer first press the 3 key, then the * key, then the 2 key, and finally the = key." During a demonstration step, a teacher should model all the steps a student will perform to complete the task, repeat the demonstration as needed, and provide as little superfluous verbal information as possible.

2. *Testing for student acquisition.*   If students acquired instructional tasks immediately, then the sequence of instructional events would only be two steps: demonstrate and test. Teachers would demonstrate the correct way to measure in centimeters and students would use a metric ruler correctly when asked to do so. Teaching, however, is seldom this simple, and for many tasks teachers can expect mastery to occur only after multiple learning trials and practice sessions over many days. Still, testing student performance is an important component of effective teaching that provides a teacher with information about how well a student has mastered an instructional objective.

As important as testing is, it can be overemphasized—to the detriment of student achievement. Duffy and McIntyre (1982) found that many teachers engaged in very little actual teaching, instead spending most of their time monitoring student work and asking students to recite answers, as if their students already knew the skill before the lesson began. Instead, teachers should use a thoughtful blend and sequence of instructional events known to be positively related to achievement. They should begin with teacher demonstration (Rosenshine, 1983), maximize teacher-led instructional time (Fisher et al., 1980), and follow with numerous, relevant teacher questions (Sindelar, Smith, Harriman, Hale, & Wilson, 1986). Testing student performance should be accomplished in a variety of ways in addition to the standard paper-and-pencil assessment. Tests can be group or individual, oral or written, formal or informal, prompted or unprompted, and administered in the classroom or in the workplace. In all cases, however, the purpose (to assess the degree of student mastery) and the process (systematically presenting teacher questions and monitoring student performance) remain the same. Several guidelines for good testing procedures are listed in Action Plan 11.5.

Action Plan 11.5   Guidelines for Effective Testing during Lessons

We recommend the following activities for ensuring effective testing:

1. Test after instruction has occurred.
2. Match the testing method to the teaching method.
3. Ensure a maximum overlap between tasks taught and tasks tested.
4. Test in the classroom for acquisition.
5. Test in the applied setting for generalization.
6. Provide for numerous, active student responses during testing.
7. Conduct direct and frequent measurements.

---

3. *Prompting correct student responses.*   Many teachers deliver prompts (i.e., temporary instructional hints that lead to accurate student responding) as part of their everyday teaching. In practice, however, prompting occurs infrequently and unsystematically. Nonetheless, all teachers should be trained and prepared to deliver a variety of prompts in order to ensure high student success rates (Schloss, 1986).

During transition-oriented math instruction for students with disabilities, teachers are most likely to deliver three types of prompts: verbal, visual, and manual. Verbal prompts are the least intrusive and can be delivered easily during instruction. Teachers should be prepared to deliver verbal prompts during two phases of instruction—after a demonstration step has been modeled and after a student responds incorrectly. In the first instance a prompt acts as an intervening instructional technique between a teacher demonstration and an unassisted student response. Action Plan 11.6 depicts this sequence of events.

Action Plan 11.6   Providing Verbal Prompts after Teacher Demonstration

The following table illustrates our recommended prompting procedure.

Instructional objective: After being shown from one to four dollar bills, a student will write the symbols and numerals with 100% accuracy on five consecutive trials for two consecutive days.

Teacher Behavior	Student Response	Feedback
Trial 1 (demonstration): One dollar is written $1.00; teacher writes $1.00 on board. Prompt: "Remember that the dollar sign looks like an "S" with a line through it." Test: "Now you write the symbols for one dollar on your paper."	Student writes $1.00 on paper.	"That's right, the dollar sign followed by a 1, a decimal point, and two zeroes."

Teachers also will employ visual prompts during instruction. Visual prompts can be gestures that cue correct student responding. If the instructional objective involves using the keys on a calculator or typewriter, a teacher might point toward a group of keys, encouraging a student to select a single key from within the group. Most visual prompts, however, are graphic or pictorial in nature. The examples in Action Plan 11.7 illustrate ways that a teacher can use visual prompts to increase the likelihood of student success.

A teacher uses a manual prompt when physically guiding a student through a task. At this prompting level, the teacher assumes primary responsibility for completion of a task. Examples include guiding a student through the writing stages of a division problem, moving a body into a correct working position, or leading a student through the steps required to access a computer program.

4. *Practicing task solution.*   Teachers must provide students with numerous opportunities to practice assigned tasks. There are two types of practice lessons (controlled and independent), and each is defined by the degree of teacher involvement. In a typical controlled practice lesson (the type that occurs immediately after a demonstration les-

---

Action Plan 11.7   Pictorial and Written Prompts

We suggest the following procedures for providing written prompts:

1. Tape a copy of the daily schedule on a student's desk.
2. Provide students with one correctly solved math problem on the top of a drill and practice worksheet.
3. Use arrows (McLeskey, 1982) or other symbols to remind students, for example, to add from right to left.

$$\leftarrow$$
$$387$$
$$\underline{+659}$$

4. Provide students with reading problems with a deck of picture cards that illustrate successful task completion. For example, the correct sequence of computer keys needed to access math software could be photographed and posted at the CAI (computer-assisted instruction) learning center.
5. Post in the classroom, in either written or picture format, the following instructions for students who need teacher assistance after encountering task failure:
   a. Relax; take a deep breath.
   b. Reread, review, or rethink the problem.
   c. Try again.
   d. Indicate that you need help—perhaps by raising your hand, taking a number (as in a bakery), raising a red flag attached to your desk, or signing up for assistance.
   e. Get back to work until help arrives (perhaps on the next problem or on a different assignment, or, at the very least, read a book reserved for such occasions).

son), a teacher might write problems on a chalkboard or overhead transparency and check student responses periodically. In a typical independent practice lesson, students work on their own, perhaps on a worksheet or computer-assisted instruction (CAI) program, and teacher feedback is less immediate and less frequent. Teachers who implement the guidelines in Action Plan 11.8 will find that their students will benefit from drill and practice activities. Research on the effective use of practice has revealed two points that should be remembered about the relationship between practice and the effectiveness of instructional programs. First, with systematic, well-designed instructional programs, students require less practice to master complex math skills than with less efficiently designed programs (Darch, Carnine, & Gersten, 1984). Second, Fisher and colleagues (1980) found too much practice and too little teaching to be associated with lower levels of student achievement.

  5. *Providing feedback.* One of the most important instructional variables is teacher feedback. Feedback includes error correction, additional information, and praise. Each of these factors is related to student achievement. Error correction lets students know whether they performed correctly or incorrectly. Additional information is provided either to tell a student how to perform correctly or to elaborate on an instructional objective. Praise serves two functions: It lets a student know that a response was correct and it can provide positive reinforcement for accurate responding.

  Providing feedback to adolescents with learning difficulties can be a complicated process. Providing praise for some students, for example, will not be reinforcing, so teachers must be able to measure the effect of praise and to alter the content of their feedback, if necessary. Some students will be oversensitive to error correction, and their teachers must be able to recognize and avoid this occurrence. The guidelines in Action Plan 11.9 are designed to help teachers deliver effective feedback to youths with disabilities.

Action Plan 11.8   Guidelines for Drill and Practice Activities

The following drill and practice activities are recommended for use with youths with disabilities:

1. Match the practice activity to the instructional objective.
2. Require no new learning.
3. Control task difficulty carefully.
4. Provide for numerous *active* student responses.
5. Provide efficient error correction.
6. Program sufficient practice to ensure mastery.
7. Program for the development of fluency.
8. Maximize teacher questions during controlled practice (Sindelar et al., 1986).
9. Limit independent practice to less than 80% of total instructional time (Fisher et al., 1980).

Action Plan 11.9   Feedback Guidelines

We suggest the following guidelines for delivering feedback:

1. Generic praise, "Nice work" is good; content-related praise containing task-specific information, "That's right, the final check balance is $34.35," is better.
2. Avoid extended error correction for one student when the rest of the class is ready to move on. Class achievement suffers. Instead, schedule a later individual help session.
3. Avoid terse "No, that's wrong" responses that do not provide a student with constructive information leading to correct responding.
4. Avoid labeling a student's response as totally incorrect when part or most of an answer is correct. If a student missed only one of the 11 steps in a long division problem, sure, the answer is wrong, but consider how much more effective your teaching would be if you acknowledged the accuracy of the 10 correct steps and provided the prompts necessary for the student to correct the error.

6. *Building periodic review into teaching.* Every instructional lesson should contain some review. As important as this feature is for all learners, it is even more important for youths with disabilities, who seem to forget faster than their nondisabled peers. Teachers should program for at least four types of review:

   a. *Review before beginning a math lesson.* Typically, this consists of reviewing the rules for appropriate behavior (Rosenberg, 1986) and providing advance organizers for upcoming instruction (Lenz, Alley, & Schumaker, 1987). These two practices are associated with better student behavior and higher student achievement.
   b. *Review homework.* Math teachers who assign but do not review or correct homework are taking the chance that their students will be practicing error patterns that may become quite difficult to overcome.
   c. *Review within every lesson.* Teachers should plan to include periodic reviews of important information while conducting a lesson. This is especially important when there are rules that define accurate responding. Teachers should intersperse and require their students to repeat rules in the division of fractions (invert and multiply), multiplication of bases with like exponents (add the exponents), and general computation (multiply and divide before you add or subtract).
   d. *Review across lessons.* Teachers can never assume that students, even those who have attained mastery of an instructional objective, will maintain mastery over time. Periodic, distributed review, in which past instructional objectives are practiced for a few minutes, will enhance maintenance and let the teacher know whether reteaching is necessary.

In summary, teachers who want to maximize student achievement should strive to structure their lessons carefully, including as many of the instructional techniques pre-

Action Plan 11.10   A Six-Pack of Teaching Variables That Should Occur within Lessons

The following variables should occur in a lesson:

1. Demonstrate — Model correct performance.
2. Test — Evaluate student performance.
3. Prompt — Provide a temporary cue to ensure correct responding.
4. Provide feedback — Provide error correction or positive information about student responses.
5. Provide practice — Provide numerous opportunities to repeat task performance until mastery is achieved.
6. Review — Reteach periodically to ensure maintenance and understanding.

viously described as possible. Action Plans 11.10 and 11.11 contain abbreviated lists of 12 techniques known to increase the achievement of students with mild and moderate learning disabilities.

Selecting Motivational Strategies.   In addition to the instructional content and format, teachers of youth with disabilities must consider which, if any, motivational strategies will be employed to enhance student achievement. The general rule is to use the minimum motivational techniques required to achieve the objective. If students are internally motivated, then teachers should not implement external reinforcement techniques. However, many secondary students who have experienced failure will require supplemental motivation, at least initially. Teachers can enhance student achievement by applying the guidelines in Action Plan 11.12.

Step 3: Implementing Math Instruction

Teachers of students with mild and moderate disabilities will find that, in general, comprehensive commercial math programs cannot be used in their entirety when transition-oriented instruction is being planned (Fine, Welch-Burke, & Fondario, 1985).

Action Plan 11.11   A Six-Pack of Teaching Variables to Consider When Planning Instruction

The following variables should be considered when planning instruction:

1. Academic time and focus — Maximize the minutes of academic instruction and project a "We're here to work and learn" atmosphere.
2. Task difficulty — Assign activities that maintain a high student success rate.
3. On-task rate — Maintain a high level of attention-to-task behavior.
4. Mastery instruction — Teach until students perform tasks correctly and fluently.
5. Data-based decision making — Gather performance data and use these data to determine how and what to teach.
6. Research-validated techniques — Use teaching methods that have been empirically validated in the professional literature.

Action Plan 11.12   Guidelines for Implementing Motivational Strategies

We suggest the following guidelines for motivating youths:

1. Consult and negotiate reinforcement with students and, if appropriate, with parents.
2. Engage students in charting their own progress.
3. Prepare ahead of time to fade all external rewards.
4. Deliver reinforcement immediately after correct responding.
5. Consider individual behavioral contracting for older students.
6. Use content-related praise to supplement generic praise.
7. Monitor the effects of all reinforcement procedures.
8. Be consistent.
9. Locate reinforcement present in the generalization setting and use these in the classroom.

Instead, teachers should develop their own and obtain materials from a wide variety of sources. Armed with appropriate materials, teachers must be prepared to bring their students up to mastery-level performance in each of the three major stages of learning: acquisition, fluency, and generalization.

Acquisition.   The first major learning stage involves student mastery of newly taught instructional objectives. Typically, all students, including those with learning disabilities, are exposed to a large number of concepts and operations during secondary math instruction. The concepts to be learned include vocabulary words associated with consumer purchasing, banking, and measurement (to name a few) and the facts and information objectives associated with the same instructional areas. A large number of operations are also introduced in the secondary curriculum, including all the algorithms that define the correct solution of arithmetic problems (e.g., the steps needed to calculate successfully when subtracting fractions); the steps to balance a checking account, calculate interest, and similar formulas; and many others. Teachers can apply the guidelines in Action Plan 11.13 to enhance mastery of newly introduced tasks.

Fluency.   After students have mastered the math concepts and operations, teachers must ensure that their students can perform with both speed and accuracy. Thus, during fluency teaching, they must retain the high accuracy component of acquisition instruction (e.g., 95% correct) and add criteria that specify the completion of a certain number of tasks within a stated time interval (e.g., 40 digits per minute). By adding speeded task completion criteria, teachers can help students prepare for competency and standardized tests, for jobs that require rapid math responding (e.g., supermarket cashier), and for any activity that requires both speed and accuracy. In many cases successful competitive employment requires more than accurate-but-slow responding.

Following acquisition instruction, the emphasis should be on enhancing fluency. Students who are not able to solve problems accurately during untimed assessment

Action Plan 11.13   Acquisition Guidelines

The following guidelines are suggested for enhancing acquisition:

1. Use concrete materials when introducing abstract concepts (e.g., angles, area, money, volume, and measurement).
2. Maximize use of specific teacher questions (Alper, 1985).
3. Ensure that students are responding actively and frequently.
4. Maximize teacher-directed instructional time (Fisher et al. 1980).
5. Limit lengthy, abstract explanations.
6. Teach tasks directly to students instead of relying on discovery, vicarious, or spontaneous learning to occur.
7. Use teacher prompts to ensure that students respond correctly and make as few errors as possible (Schloss, 1986).
8. Control the context when introducing new math vocabulary words (e.g., use the same key words in all story problems involving division [How many in each . . . ?] or subtraction [How many are left over?]).
9. Use mnemonic instructional aids to help students remember concepts, vocabulary, algorithm steps, and formulas (Farb & Throne, 1978; Scruggs & Laufenberg, 1986).
10. If reading is included in the math lesson, use advance organizers to cue students to remember important information.
11. Employ compensatory teaching methods for students who have specific long-standing weaknesses. For example, teach students who have failed to master arithmetic skills to use a calculator (Horton, 1985).

should not be required to work toward fluency (Hasselbring & Goin, 1988). Typically, most fluency-building lessons are drill and practice activities designed to provide students both with additional exposure to an instructional objective and a means to increase the rate of responding. The guidelines in Action Plan 11.14 will help teachers design and implement effective practice activities.

Generalization.   After students have attained fluency in problem solving, teachers must ensure that they can use these skills in applied settings. This type of generalization typically does not occur unless specific planning and instruction are implemented (Mascari & Forgnone, 1982). For special education teachers serving secondary students with disabilities, three generalization concerns are paramount: (1) Will students retain skill mastery after instruction has concluded? (2) Will students use the skills acquired in the special education setting in mainstream classrooms? (3) Will students use acquired skills in community and career settings? To enhance maintenance and generalization, teachers should apply the guidelines described in Action Plan 11.15.

Decision Making During Teaching.   As students progress through material and assigned tasks, their teachers must be prepared to answer several instructional questions

Action Plan 11.14   Fluency-Building Guidelines

We recommend the following fluency-building strategies:

1. Since the major shortcoming of commercial math programs is inadequate provision of practice (Silbert et al., 1991), teachers must ensure that sufficient opportunities are provided.
2. Gradually shift from concrete (e.g., real money) to semiconcrete (e.g., pictures of real money) to abstract symbols (e.g., $ or ¢).
3. Use peer tutors during practice sessions (Maheady, Sacca, & Harper, 1988).
4. Use appropriate educational games (Beattie & Algozzine, 1982; Wesson, Wilson, & Mandlebaum, 1988).
5. Increase the amount of self-checking required of students.
6. Teach students to self-monitor their work as they solve problems. Math self-monitoring strategies include estimation, self-questioning, and periodic rechecking.
7. Follow lessons where students practice large numbers of problems (massed practice) with lessons that provide review spaced over many lessons (distributed practice).
8. Always control the difficulty level of drill and practice problems. High student success rates, approaching 100% correct, should be the rule for review exercises.

(Colozzi et al., 1986). Has a task been mastered? Has a particular teaching, motivational, or prompting practice been effective? As students progress (or fail to progress) through instructional lessons, the answers to these questions lead teachers to make one of three decisions related to the effectiveness of instruction—EXIT (if a task has been mastered), CONTINUE (if student progress is at the expected level), or CHANGE (if a student is not making satisfactory progress). Objective decision making is accomplished by following the steps in Action Plan 11.16.

Teachers who directly and frequently measure student performance and make data-based instructional decisions have at least two types of evaluative methodology available. First are the data-reactive single-subject designs. Although single-subject designs are typically used by researchers who publish in the professional literature, several designs (e.g., alternating-treatments design, changing-conditions design, and changing-criteria design) can be used appropriately by teachers as decision-making aids. Single-subject designs, like the alternating-treatments design in Figure 11.1, can be used to identify more effective instructional methods. Teachers interested in acquiring more information on single-subject designs should consult Alberto and Troutman (1990) or Hersen and Barlow (1976).

Another data-based decision-making method is to apply one of two models described in the professional literature: Precision Teaching (Lovitt & Haring, 1979) or Data-Based Program Modification (Deno & Mirkin, 1977). Both decision-making programs provide highly structured techniques and rules that enable teachers to decide to EXIT, CONTINUE, or CHANGE instruction in an objective way. Since proficiency in these decision-making methods requires substantial teacher training, interested readers should

Action Plan 11.15   Guidelines to Enhance Maintenance and Generalization

The following guidelines are recommended for enhancing maintenance and generalization:

1. Build lots of review into daily instruction.
2. Periodically retest students to determine whether mastery has been retained. If not, reteach essential skills.
3. Teach in the most relevant applied setting. For example, take students to an auto shop, grocery store, or bowling alley (Ellis, Lenz, & Sabornie, 1987).
4. Use materials and lessons in the classroom that approximate those used in mainstream classes or job sites (Smith & Schloss, 1986).
5. Develop cue cards and other prompting devices (e.g., graphic depictions of appropriate behaviors) to enhance student performance after they have left the special education classroom (Wilson & Wesson, 1986).
6. Incorporate procedures into teaching that fade teacher control and increase student responsibility. For example, replace teacher evaluation with student evaluation or eliminate tangible reinforcement (Santogrossi, O'Leary, Romanczyk, & Kaufman, 1973; Turkewitz, O'Leary, & Ironsmith, 1975).

consult the training manuals (Deno & Mirkin, 1977; Haring et al., 1978; White & Haring, 1976). An interesting footnote in the area of data-based decision making is that even though the technology is present and we know that conducting direct and frequent measurement is related to increased student achievement, many, if not most, teachers fail to monitor student progress systematically (Wesson, King, & Deno, 1984; Wesson, Skiba, Sevcik, King, & Deno, 1984).

Action Plan 11.16   Generic Data-Based Decision-Making Steps

We suggest the following general decision-making steps:

1. Pretest to measure entry skill levels.
2. Set an instructional goal (e.g., 95% correct on a given task).
3. Conduct direct and frequent measurement of student performance.
4. Record and graph data from the first few lessons (this is base-rate performance).
5. Decide how long it should take to progress from base-rate performance to an instructional goal.
6. Record and graph more student data points.
7. Decide whether your student is making satisfactory progress toward the instructional goal.
8. Make one of the three decisions defined in the text (EXIT, CONTINUE, or CHANGE).

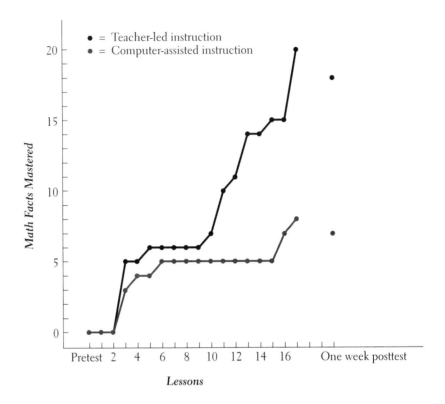

FIGURE 11.1   An Alternating-Treatments Design Depicting the Results of Two Programs

Making Instructional CHANGES.   Of the three instructional decisions, deciding to CHANGE a student's program is the most complex. If a teacher decides to EXIT, a task has been mastered and the student is ready to begin the next skill in the task hierarchy. If a teacher decides to CONTINUE, everything is going well and the student should remain in the current program. The CHANGE decision, however, is made only after an instructional program has failed to work as predicted. Many believe that a teacher's ability to modify programming once the CHANGE decision has been made is one of the most critical elements in effective teaching of students with disabilities (Lambie, 1980).

Making and implementing effective CHANGE decisions depends largely on two teacher abilities: determining the most likely element of the program that is deficient and implementing new, improved techniques. To determine program weaknesses, one must reexamine the instructional planning steps described earlier in this chapter. The ability to implement new techniques depends largely on the size of a teacher's "bag of tricks." Action Plan 11.17 contains a sample of some of the techniques that teachers can try if their students with disabilities are not making satisfactory progress through a math program of study.

Step 4: Measuring Program Success

The final step in the instructional process is to determine how well a teacher's program has produced the desired results. Since the desired result of math programs for secondary students with disabilities involves successful job, community, and leisure performance (rather than the more limited goal of successful classroom performance), effective teachers must design programs that are related to after-school life and follow up on students who finish their programs (Nietupski, Welch, & Wacker, 1983). Teachers must not assume that skills learned in the classroom, such as a unit on fractions (Perkins & Cullinan, 1985), will automatically be performed in a real-life setting (Bourdeau, Close, & Sowers, 1986).

Assessment of generalization should be a straightforward process. Rather than relying on commercial tests that purport to measure job readiness, teachers should observe and evaluate student performance in several real-life settings. Computational, computer, or cash register skills can be assessed directly by observing students performing in a cooperating grocery and dry goods store. Leisure math skills can be measured by observing students at bowling, Bingo, or card parties. Community math skills can be evaluated during either simulated or actual bus or car trips (map skills), major appliance purchases (consumer math), bank transactions (checking and savings account skills), and a wide variety of additional "in situ" experiences. The use of curriculum-based measurement (CBM) techniques with problems selected from functional settings is an excellent choice for program evaluation (Fuchs & Fuchs, 1991).

Teachers should assess student performance on at least three occasions after the initial instruction has brought the student to the mastery level: one or two weeks after the

---

Action Plan 11.17 Selected Program CHANGE Alternatives

The following program change alternatives are suggested:

1. Increase the amount of instructional time.
2. Increase or change the type of reinforcement.
3. Maximize on-task rates by training students to monitor their own behavior (Morrow, Burke, & Buell, 1985).
4. Teach more and test less (i.e., increase teacher-led instruction).
5. Provide more frequent corrective feedback.
6. Try peer tutoring.
7. Try a new teaching technique (e.g., computer-assisted instruction).
8. Adapt the instructional materials (e.g., rewrite a training manual to a level that a student can read independently).
9. Increase the emphasis on independent learning by training students to self-check, self-monitor, and self-record their performance.
10. Institute more intrusive prompts to ensure that students respond accurately.
11. Reassess and reteach prerequisite skills if necessary.
12. Use a cooperative learning method (Johnson & Johnson, 1986).

program ends to measure short-term maintenance, several months later to assess long-term maintenance, and in the applied setting to determine generalization. If it is determined that mastery-level performance has been lost, it is often necessary to reteach the skills. At the very least teachers will know that some aspect of their instructional program needs to be altered so that future students will have a greater chance of achieving success.

Summary

Effective instruction is based on teacher belief in the tenets of effective instruction, knowledge of relevant student and school program characteristics, and, most important, the implementation of empirically supported teaching methods.

The principles of effective instruction can be summarized as follows:

1. Ensure success experiences.
2. Provide functional academic instruction.
3. Provide age-appropriate instruction.
4. Offer compensatory instruction.
5. Teach skills directly.
6. Increase teacher-led, active student responding.
7. Begin with and then fade teacher control of the program.
8. Provide structure and rigorous scheduling.
9. Use empirically supported instructional practices.
10. Refrain from criticism.

Students with mild disabilities can be divided into three groups: students with learning disabilities, mild mental retardation, and behavior disorders. All bring a wide variety of traits, skills, and behaviors into the instructional setting. Teachers who are aware of these factors can design programs that build on strengths and compensate for weaknesses. Youths with disabilities sometimes receive math instruction in special education placements. These students may be found in regular education classes, resource rooms, self-contained programs, and vocational programs. To some extent, the nature and demands of these settings will shape secondary math programs.

The practice of effective instruction begins with the assessment of several types of instructional demands. Teachers must set or plan to meet program goals, determine the learner's entry skill level, and assess relevant student characteristics. Second, teachers must be able to plan to deliver high-rate instruction by setting mastery goals, selecting materials and settings, selecting techniques and lesson formats, and choosing appropriate motivational strategies. Third, teachers must implement effective instructional procedures by (a) delivering empirically supported teaching methods designed to ensure that students acquire, become fluent in, and generalize skills; (b) monitoring student performance, and (c) changing instructional methods when needed. Finally, teachers must conduct postinstructional assessment to determine whether the desired results have been achieved in real-life student performance.

If teachers follow the guidelines and instructional suggestions described in this chapter, they will be able to design and implement effective math programs for adolescents with mild disabilities. Perhaps the greatest danger for secondary special education teachers is to assume that classroom instruction is an end in itself. It is all too easy for teachers to neglect planning instruction that is designed to enhance student performance in real-life experiences. Rather, teachers should frequently ask themselves if what they are teaching to youths with disabilities will be important and relevant long after secondary school has ended. Students of teachers who answer affirmatively will have received the most effective instructional program.

References

Alberto, P., & Troutman, A. (1990). *Applied behavior analysis for teachers* (3rd ed.). Columbus, OH: Merrill.

Alper, S. (1985). The use of teacher questioning to increase independent problem solving in mentally retarded adolescents. *Education and Training of the Mentally Retarded, 20*(1), 83–88.

Beattie, J., & Algozzine, B. (1982). Improving basic academic skills of educable mentally retarded adolescents. *Education and Training of the Mentally Retarded, 17*(3), 255–258.

Bennett, W. J. (1987). *What works: Research about teaching and learning* (2nd ed.). Washington, DC: U.S. Department of Education.

Bigler, J. K. (1984). Increasing inferential comprehension scores of intermediate-age mildly retarded students using two direct teaching procedures. *Education and Training of the Mentally Retarded, 19*(2), 132–140.

Bourdeau, P. E., Close, D. W., & Sowers, J. (1986). An experimental analysis of generalization of banking skills from classroom to bank settings in the community. *Education and Training of the Mentally Retarded, 21*(2), 98–107.

Brigance, A. (1980). *Brigance Diagnostic Inventory of Essential Skills*. North Billerica, MA: Curriculum Associates.

Brown, A. L., Campione, J. C., & Day, J. D. (1981). Learning to learn: On training students to learn from texts. *Educational Researcher, 10*(2), 14–21.

Calhoun, M. L. (1985). Typing contrasted with handwriting in language arts instruction for moderately mentally retarded students. *Education and Training of the Mentally Retarded, 20*(1), 48–52.

Cobb, R. G., & Larkin, D. (1985). Assessment and placement of handicapped pupils into secondary vocational education. In N. S. Bley, & C. A. Thornton (Eds.), *Teaching mathematics to the learning disabled*. Rockville, MD: Aspen Systems.

Colozzi, G. A., Coleman-Kennedy, M., Fay, R., Hurley, W., Magliozzi, M., Shackle, K., & Walsh, P. (1986). Data-based integration of a student with moderate special needs. *Education and Training of the Mentally Retarded, 21*(3), 192–199.

Darch, C., Carnine, D., & Gersten, R. (1984). Explicit instruction in mathematics problem solving. *Journal of Educational Research, 77*, 351–359.

Deno, S. (1985). Curriculum-based assessment: The emerging alternative. *Exceptional Children, 52*, 219–232.

Deno, S., & Mirkin, P. (1977). *Data-based program modification: A manual*. Minneapolis: University of Minnesota, Leadership Training Institute.

Deshler, D., Schumaker, J., Lenz, B., & Ellis, E. (1984). Academic and cognitive interventions for LD adolescents. *Journal of Learning Disabilities, 17*, 170–179.

Duffy, G., & McIntyre, L. (1982). A naturalistic study of instructional assistance in primary grade reading. *Elementary School Journal, 83*(1), 15–23.

Dyer, W. (1978). Implications of the helping relationship between learning disabled students and their teachers. *Learning Disability Quarterly, 2*, 55–61.

Ellis, E., Lenz, B., & Sabornie, E. (1987). Generalization and adaptation of learning strategies to natural environments: Part I: Critical agents. *Remedial and Special Education, 8,* 6–20.

Engelmann, S., Carnine, D., & Steely, D. (1991). Making connections in mathematics. *Journal of Learning Disabilities, 24,* 292–303.

Farb, J., & Throne, J. M. (1978). Improving the generalized mnemonic performance of a Down's syndrome child. *Journal of Applied Behavior Analysis, 11*(3), 413–419.

Farey, J. W. (1986). An analysis of written dialogue of educable mentally retarded writers. *Education and Training of the Mentally Retarded, 21*(3), 181–191.

Fine, A. H., Welch-Burke, C. S., & Fondario, L. J. (1985). A developmental model for the integration of leisure programming in the education of individuals with mental retardation. *Mental Retardation, 23*(6), 289–296.

Fisher, C., Berliner, D., Filby, N., Marliave, R., Cahen, L., & Dishaw, M. (1980). Teaching behaviors, academic learning time, and student achievement: An overview. In C. Denham & A. Liberman (Eds.), *Time to learn.* Washington, DC: National Institute of Education.

Forness, S. R., Horton, R. L., & Horton, A. A. (1981). Assessment of applied academic and social skills. *Education and Training of the Mentally Retarded, 16*(2), 104–109.

Frank, A. R., & McFarland, T. D. (1980). Teaching coin skills to EMR children: A curriculum study. *Education and Training of the Mentally Retarded, 15*(4), 270–277.

Fuchs, L., & Fuchs, D. (1991). Curriculum-based measurements: Current applications and future directions. *Preventing School Failure, 35*(3), 6–11.

Hanley-Maxwell, C., Wilcox, B., & Heal, L. W. (1982). A comparison of vocabulary learning by moderately retarded students under direct instruction and incidental presentation. *Education and Training of the Mentally Retarded, 17*(3), 214–221.

Haring, N., Lovitt, T., Eaton, M., & Hansen, C. (1978). *The fourth R: Research in the classroom.* Columbus, OH: Merrill.

Hasselbring, T. S., & Goin, L. I. (1988). *Effective practices for computer use with mildly handicapped learners.* Paper presented at the 66th Annual Convention of The Council for Exceptional Children, Washington, DC.

Hersen, M., & Barlow, D. H. (1976). *Single case experimental designs: Strategies for studying behavior change.* New York: Pergamon.

Horton, S. (1985). Computational rules of educable mentally retarded adolescents with and without calculators in comparison to normals. *Education and Training of the Mentally Retarded, 20*(1), 14–24.

Johnson, D., & Johnson, R., (1986). Mainstreaming and cooperative learning strategies. *Exceptional Children, 52,* 553–561.

Kazdin, A. (1977). Assessing the clinical or applied significance of behavior change through social validation. *Behavior Modification, 1,* 427–452.

Kruger, L., & Wandle, C. (1992). A preliminary investigation of special needs students' global and mathematics self-concepts. *Psychology in the Schools, 29,* 281–289.

Lambie, R. A. (1980). A systematic approach for changing materials instruction and assignments to meet individual needs. *Focus on Exceptional Children, 13*(1), 1–16.

Langone, J. (1981). Curriculum for the trainable mentally retarded . . . Or "What do I do when the ditto machine dies!" *Education and Training of the Mentally Retarded, 16*(2), 150–154.

Larrivee, B. (1986). Effective teaching for mainstreamed students is effective teaching for all students. *Teacher Education and Special Education, 9,* 173–179.

Lenz, B., Alley, G., & Schumaker, J. (1987). Activating the inactive learner: Advance organizers in the secondary content classroom. *Learning Disability Quarterly, 10,* 53–67.

Lovitt, T., & Haring, N. (1979). *Classroom application of precision teaching.* Seattle, WA: Special Child Publications.

McLeskey, J. (1982). Procedures for ameliorating attentional deficits of retarded children through instructional medial design. *Education and Training of the Mentally Retarded, 17*(3), 227–233.

Maheady, L., Sacca, M., & Harper, G. (1988). Classwide peer tutoring with mildly handicapped high school students. *Exceptional Children*, 55, 52–59.

Mascari, B. G., & Forgnone, C. (1982). A follow-up study of EMR students four years after dismissal from the program. *Education and Training of the Mentally Retarded*, 17(4), 288–292.

Morgan, D. P., & Jenson, W. R. (1988). *Teaching behaviorally disordered students: Preferred practices*. Columbus, OH: Merrill.

Morrow, L. W., Burke, J. G., & Buell, B. J. (1985). Effects of a self-recording procedure on the attending to task behavior and academic productivity of adolescents with multiple handicaps. *Mental Retardation*, 23(3), 137–141.

Nietupski, J., Welch, J., & Wacker, D. (1983). Acquisition, maintenance, and transfer of grocery item purchasing skills by moderately and severely handicapped students. *Education and Training of the Mentally Retarded*, 18(4), 279–286.

Perkins, V., & Cullinan, D. (1985). Effects of direct instruction intervention for fraction skills. *Education and Treatment of Children*, 8, 41–50.

Polloway, E. A., & Epstein, M. H. (1985). Current research issues in mild mental retardation: A survey of the field. *Education and Training of the Mentally Retarded*, 20(3), 171–174.

Rosenberg, M. (1986). Maximizing the effectiveness of structured classroom management programs: Implementing rule-review procedures with disruptive and distractible students. *Behavioral Disorders*, 11, 239–248.

Rosenshine, B. (1983). Teaching functions in elementary school programs. *Elementary School Journal*, 83, 335–352.

Santogrossi, D., O'Leary, K., Romanczyk, R., & Kaufman, K. (1973). Self-evaluation by adolescents in a psychiatric hospital school program. *Journal of Applied Behavior Analysis*, 6, 227–287.

Schloss, P. J. (1986). Sequential prompt instruction for mildly handicapped learners. *Teaching Exceptional Children*, 18, 181–184.

Schwartz, S. E., & Budd, D. (1981). Mathematics for handicapped learners: A functional approach for adolescents. *Focus on Exceptional Children*, 13(7), 1–12.

Scruggs, T. E., & Laufenberg, R. (1986). Transformational mnemonic strategies for retarded learners.

Education and Training of the Mentally Retarded, 21(3), 165–173.

Shavelson, R. J., & Stern, P. (1981). Research on teachers' pedagogical thoughts, judgements, decisions, and behavior. *Review of Educational Research*, 51(4), 455–498.

Silbert, J., Carnine, D., & Stein, M. (1990). *Direct instruction mathematics*. (2nd ed.). Columbus, OH: Merrill.

Sindelar, P., Rosenberg, M., Wilson, R., & Bursuck, W. (1984). The effects of group size and instruction method on the acquisition of mathematical concepts by fourth-grade students. *Journal of Educational Research*, 77, 178–183.

Sindelar, P., Smith, M., Harriman, N., Hale, R., & Wilson, R. (1986). Teacher effectiveness in special education programs. *Journal of Special Education*, 20, 195–207.

Smith, M., & Schloss, P. (1986). A "superform" for enhancing competence in completing employment applications. *Teaching Exceptional Children*, 18, 277–280.

Starlin, C., & Starlin, A. (1973). *Guides for continuous decision making*. Bemidji, MN: Unique Curriculums.

Stevens, T. (1977). *Teaching skills to children with learning and behavior disorders*. Columbus, OH: Merrill.

Turkewitz, H., O'Leary, K., & Ironsmith, M. (1975). Generalization and maintenance of appropriate behavior through self-control. *Journal of Consulting and Clinical Psychology*, 43, 577–583.

Wesson, C., King, R., & Deno, S. (1984). Direct and frequent measurement of student performance: If it's so good for us, why don't we do it? *Learning Disability Quarterly*, 7, 45–48.

Wesson, C., Skiba, R., Sevcik, B., King, R. P., & Deno, S. (1984). The effects of technically adequate instructional data on achievement. *Remedial and Special Education*, 5(5), 17–22.

Wesson, C., Wilson, R., & Mandlebaum, L. (1988). Learning games for active student responding. *Teaching Exceptional Children*, 20, 12–14.

Whelan, R. J., Mendez, D., deSaman, L., & Fortmeyer D. J. (1984). Oh! Those wonderful feelings (The relationship between pupil affect and achievement). *Focus on Exceptional Children,* 16(8), 1–8.

White, O., & Haring, N. (1976). *Exceptional teaching.* Columbus, OH: Merrill.

Wilson, R. (1989). *Criterion referenced assessment and instruction.* Unpublished manuscript.

Wilson, R., & Wesson, C. (1986). Making every minute count: Academic learning time in LD classrooms. *Learning Disabilities Focus, 2,* 13–19.

Appendix: Instructional Hierarchies in Math

The six instructional hierarchies in math are (1) fractions, (2) decimals, (3) calculator tasks, (4) geometry, (5) algebra, and (6) money.

Fraction Hierarchy

1. Identifying fractional parts from diagrams.
2. Drawing diagrams to represent fractional parts.
3. Determining how many fractional parts equal a whole.
4. Representing whole numbers as fractions.
5. Writing numbers as fractions.
6. Determining whether a fraction is greater than, equal to, or less than 1.
7. Adding fractions with like denominators.
8. Determining all the factors of a given number.
9. Reducing fractions to their lowest terms.
10. Recognizing equivalent fractions.
11. Changing improper fractions to mixed numbers.
12. Writing fractions as mixed numbers.
13. Adding fractions with unlike denominators.
14. Adding fractions containing mixed numbers.
15. Working story problems involving the addition of fractions.
16. Subtracting fractions with like denominators.
17. Subtracting fractions with unlike denominators.
18. Subtracting fractions with mixed numbers.
19. Subtracting mixed numbers from a whole number.
20. Subtracting fractions containing mixed numbers when the fraction must borrow from the whole number.
21. Working story problems involving the subtraction of fractions.
22. Multiplying fractions.
23. Multiplying a whole number by a fraction.
24. Multiplying two mixed numbers.
25. Working story problems involving the multiplication of fractions.
26. Dividing fractions.
27. Dividing a whole number by a fraction.

From *Criterion referenced assessment and instruction* by R. Wilson, 1989, unpublished manuscript. Reprinted by permission of the author.

28. Dividing a fraction by a whole number.
29. Working story problems involving the division of fractions.

Skill Hierarchy—Decimals

1. Reading tenths and hundredths.
2. Writing tenths and hundredths.
3. Reading mixed decimals; tenths and hundredths.
4. Writing mixed decimals: tenths and hundredths.
5. Adding like decimals: tenths to tenths and hundredths to hundredths.
6. Column alignment: adding tenths, hundredths, and whole numbers.
7. Working story problems involving the addition of decimals.
8. Subtracting like decimals: tenths from tenths and hundredths from hundredths.
9. Subtracting tenths and hundredths from whole numbers.
10. Working story problems involving the subtraction of decimals.
11. Ordering mixed decimals.
12. Reading thousandths.
13. Writing thousandths.
14. Multiplying decimals: one digit factor times three digit factor.
15. Multiplying decimals: zero to be placed after decimal points.
16. Working story problems involving the multiplication of decimals.
17. Rounding off decimals.
18. Dividing decimals: whole number divisor, no remainder.
19. Dividing by whole number: quotient begins with zero.
20. Rounding off where there is a 9 or a 99 after the decimal.
21. Dividing: whole number divisor, zeros must be added to dividend after decimal point.
22. Dividing: whole number divisor, rounding off.
23. Working story problems involving the division of decimals.
24. Converting proper fractions to decimals, no rounding off required.
25. Converting proper fractions to decimals, rounding off required.
26. Multiplying mixed decimal by 10 or 100, no zeros added.
27. Multiplying mixed decimal by 10 or 100, zeros added.
28. Dividing: divisor is decimal, no adding zeros in dividend necessary.
29. Dividing: divisor is decimal, adding zero in dividend required.
30. Converting decimals to fractions.
31. Converting mixed fractions to mixed decimals.
32. Solving story problems involving the addition, subtraction, multiplication, and division of decimals, with conversion of fractions to decimals and rounding off of answers required.

Calculator Task Hierarchy

1. Add two whole numbers.
2. Subtract two whole numbers.
3. Multiply two whole numbers.

4. Divide two whole numbers.
5. Add more than two whole numbers.
6. Subtract more than two whole numbers.
7. Multiply more than two whole numbers.
8. Divide more than two whole numbers.
9. Add two decimal numbers.
10. Subtract two decimal numbers.
11. Multiply two decimal numbers.
12. Divide two decimal numbers.
13. Add more than two decimal numbers.
14. Subtract more than two decimal numbers.
15. Multiply more than two decimal numbers.
16. Divide more than two decimal numbers.
17. Add and subtract in the same problem.
18. Multiply and divide in the same problem.
19. Combine any/all operations in the same problem.
20. Solve a one-step word problem.
21. Solve a multiple-step word problem.

Geometry Hierarchy

1. Identify circles, triangles, squares, and rectangles.
2. Match geometric shapes (same shapes).
3. Identify points inside, outside, and on a figure.
4. Sketch triangles, circle, square, and rectangles.
5. Draw a line of symmetry to determine halves.
6. Recognize a line, line segment, a ray, and a point.
7. Measure the sides of triangles, rectangles, and squares.
8. Recognize angles and right angles.
9. Determine when two segments are congruent.
10. Recognize polygons and quadrilaterals.
11. Find the perimeter of a polygon.
12. Draw a circle and find its parts (radius and diameter).
13. Find the area of a region by counting unit squares.
14. Recognize spheres, cubes, cylinders, and cones.
15. Find volume by counting unit cubes.
16. Identify intersecting, perpendicular, and parallel lines.
17. Identify congruent angles.
18. Identify acute and obtuse angles.
19. Recognize parallelograms (opposite angles are congruent).
20. Measure angles using a protractor.
21. Use a compass to bisect a segment.
22. Identify scalene, isosceles, and equilateral triangles.
23. Identify pentagon, hexagon, and octagon.

24. Classify triangles by their angles.
25. Find the perimeter, using a formula.
26. Find the area, using a formula.
27. Use a compass to bisect an angle.
28. Construct a perpendicular line.
29. Construct isosceles and equilateral triangles.
30. Find the volume using a formula.
31. Identify the interior and exterior of angles.
32. Construct congruent angles, using a protractor.
33. Identify simple closed curves as concave or convex.
34. Find unknown measures of an angle of a triangle.
35. Find the area of a circular region.
36. Find the surface area of a triangular prism.
37. Find the volume of a triangular prism.
38. Use the Pythagorean rule.
39. Identify angle formed by intersecting or parallel lines.

Algebra Hierarchy

1. USING VARIABLES: To simplify numerical expressions and evaluate variable expressions.
2. TRANSLATING AND SOLVING WORD PROBLEMS: To represent problem situations by mathematical expressions or equations.
3. SUBTRACTING POLYNOMIALS.
4. MULTIPLYING A MONOMIAL AND A POLYNOMIAL.
5. SOLVING COST, WAGE, MONEY, DISTANCE-RATE-TIME PROBLEMS: To solve some problems involving money and uniform motion.
6. FACTORING INTEGERS.
7. DIVIDING MONOMIALS: To divide and factor monomials and polynomials.
8. MULTIPLYING BINOMIALS: To find the product of two binomials.
9. FINDING DIFFERENCE OF SQUARES.
10. FINDING SQUARES OF BINOMIALS: To find squares of binomials and to factor trinomial squares.
11. FACTORING PATTERNS: To factor quadratic trinomials.
12. FACTORING BY GROUPING: To factor polynomials using the distributive axiom.
13. SOLVING EQUATIONS AND PROBLEMS IN FACTORED FORM: To solve equations when one side is in factored form and the other side is zero.
14. SIMPLIFYING FRACTIONS: To simplify algebraic fractions.
15. MULTIPLYING FRACTIONS.
16. DIVIDING FRACTIONS.
17. FINDING LEAST COMMON DENOMINATOR: To express fractions with their least common denominator.
18. WRITING MIXED EXPRESSIONS: To write mixed expressions as fractions in simplest form.

Secondary Money Skill Hierarchy

1. Reads values to $1.00.
2. Writes values to $1.00.
3. States value of mixed groups of coins to $1.00.
4. Determines equivalents among coins.
5. Determines the total cost of a multiple item purchase to $1.00.
6. Determines if amount of money is sufficient for a purchase to $1.00.
7. Makes change to amounts of $1.00.
8. Reads values to $5.00.
9. Writes values to $5.00.
10. States values of coins and bills to $5.00.
11. Determines the total cost of a multiple item purchase to $5.00.
12. Makes change for purchases up to $5.00.
13. Reads values to $10.00.
14. Writes values to $10.00.
15. States values of coins and bills to $10.00.
16. Determines the total cost of a multiple item purchase to $10.00.
17. Makes change for purchases up to $10.00.
18. Reads values to $20.00.
19. Writes values to $20.00.
20. States values of coins and bills to $20.00.
21. Determines the total cost of a multiple item purchase to $20.00.
22. Makes change for purchases up to $20.00.
23. Reads values to $100.00.
24. Writes values to $100.00.
25. States values of coins and bills to $100.00.
26. Determines the total cost of a multiple item purchase to $100.00.
27. Makes change for purchases up to $100.00.
28. Determines the purchase price from a price list.
29. Determines the sale price of an item using "dollars (or cents) off" language.
30. Determines the sale price of an item using "fraction off" language.
31. Determines the sale price of an item using "percentage off" language.
32. Determines the price of an item when using a manufacturer's coupon.
33. Determines the "best buy."

$C\ h\ a\ p\ t\ e\ r$ *12*

Vocational Instruction

Did you know that . . .

- Despite participation in special education programs, students have experienced major difficulties in their transition from school to work?
- A vocational program's success is determined by the placement and advancement of students in occupations related to their training?
- Aptitude tests are used to determine the likelihood of an individual's success in a given occupation?
- Curriculum-based vocational assessment uses informal procedures based on the individual student's learning needs?
- Career education aids in the vocational instruction process by providing a foundation for specific skills training?
- Vocational goals and objectives should be developed to maximize an individual's potential for independence?
- A student's employment value has become increasingly important to society?
- Vocational programs that are based on business and industry's needs are likely to ensure future success in employment?
- Vocational education should encompass all aspects of successful performance in an occupation?
- Individual vocational goals and objectives should be based on the characteristics and needs of the student?

Can you . . .

- Identify the relationship between vocational education and business and industry?
- Identify the two most important skill areas noted by employers?
- Differentiate between vocational skill tests and vocational aptitude tests?
- Observe appropriate safeguards when using or interpreting vocational aptitude tests?

- Conduct a curriculum-based vocational assessment?
- Identify the essential features of Life-Centered Career Education?
- Include career education competencies in the educational program of students who have disabilities?
- Establish a vocational curriculum on the basis of the characteristics of a student and his or her community?
- Identify employment opportunities for high school graduates who have disabilities?
- Establish a vocational program that meets the unique needs of a student and his or her community?

Numerous authors have expressed concern about the postsecondary experiences of students with disabilities, particularly the poor employment rates and the lack of functional educational and vocational experiences. These are viewed as major detriments to the success of youth with disabilities (Schloss, Hughes, & Smith, 1988). One is therefore led to ask whether there is life after school, and whether individuals with disabilities can be productive citizens.

This chapter is concerned with the manner in which vocational and special educators can provide meaningful experiences leading to successful postsecondary adjustment. Emphasis is placed on strategies that ensure that youths with disabilities will become productive adult citizens.

The need for preparatory programs for secondary-aged students is evident from a survey of local education agencies (LEAs) nationwide (Fairweather, 1988). This survey investigated the availability of programs, extent of transition assistance, and demographic features of the school districts. More than 50% of the schools responding reported that vocationally oriented programs are offered to school-aged persons with disabilities. Smaller LEAs reported that they were less likely than larger ones to provide services. Furthermore, less than 50% of those responding stated that they provide transition programs. Smaller LEAs were more likely than larger ones to provide transition-assistance services.

Although many students participate in special education programs, they experience great difficulty in making the transition from school to work (Benz & Halpern, 1987; Edgar, 1987; Hasazi, Gordon, & Roe, 1985; McAfee 1988a, 1988b; Mithaug, Horiuchi, & Fanning, 1985). Most youths with disabilities (a) are unemployed or underemployed, (b) obtain jobs through family-friend connections as opposed to vocational training and placement services, (c) earn only slightly above minimum wage in unskilled or service related positions, and (d) are unlikely to advance above the entry-level position.

In a study conducted by the U.S. Departments of Labor, Education, and Commerce (1988), 134 business representatives were asked to assess their needs, goals, and expectations of the education process when hiring today's youth. Their conclusions can be summarized as follows:

1. *The economy and the workplace are changing rapidly, and the pace of change is accelerating.*
2. *The content and skill requirements of the jobs themselves are changing, regardless of type or size of business.*
3. *The "basic skills gap" between what business needs and the qualifications of the entry-level worker is widening.*
4. *Employers are practically unanimous in their concern about being able to employ well-trained entry-level workers.*
5. *Skill deficiencies in the workplace are costing American employers a great deal as a result of waste, lost productivity, increased remediation costs, reduced product quality, and ultimately a loss in competitiveness.*
6. *Educators and business leaders agree about the overall goals of education, and about the skills needed in the workplace.*
7. *Educators may not be translating their understanding of business needs into what happens in the classroom.*
8. *Business must do a better job of anticipating future work force needs, and communicating these needs to educators, parents, students, and other community resources.*
9. *Although progress has been made in education reform efforts, many experts conclude that the student who is not bound for college and who drops out has been least affected.*
10. *Aggressive action may be needed by business and education. These groups must learn from each other if the nation is to have a high-quality and productive work force.*

Businesses continue to cite difficulties in finding qualified applicants. The gap between the skills needed by business and industry and those available is widening. This situation is also creating a need for vocational preparation among school-aged individuals with disabilities (Johnson, 1988). The following examples illustrate just how important this training is:

1. The New York Telephone Company reports that 20% of those taking an operator's test pass.
2. Only 1 out of 20 applicants for secretarial jobs qualify for employment at Campbell-Mithun Advertising in Minneapolis.
3. Only 20% of applicants to Motorola can pass seventh-grade English or fifth-grade math tests.
4. The number of bank teller applicants who passed a basic math test at Chemical Bank in New York dropped from 70% in 1983 to 55% percent in 1987.
5. Three out of five 20 year olds cannot get from point A to point B on a map, according to the National Assessment of Educational Progress (NAEP). Three out of five cannot add their lunch bill.
6. Nearly half of 17 year olds cannot perform math problems normally taught in junior high school.

When employers were asked what entry-level skills they expect youths to perform, responses focused on their employability and academic skills (Johnson, 1988). Employability is defined by the following competencies:

1. Ability to learn, be flexible, and respond to change quickly
2. Ability to deal with complexity
3. Ability to identify problems, perceive alternative approaches, and select the best approach
4. Ability to operate independently after a brief but intensive orientation period or after an initial training period
5. Ability to work cooperatively with people of different personalities, race, and sex across different authority levels and organizational divisions
6. Ability to be punctual and dependable as well as show pride in and enthusiasm for performing well.

Academic competencies include the following items:

1. Read and comprehend policy and instruction manuals as well as technical material
2. Write sentences with correct sentence form, spelling, and punctuation
3. Identify errors in writing and edit draft copies

Action Plan 12.1   Transition Plan

We recommend the following steps in developing a transition plan:

1. Infuse a life-centered career education program into the school's academic program, grades K–12.
2. Promote a functional curriculum throughout the student's educational program.
3. Conduct an individual assessment of the student. Include vocational interests, vocational aptitudes, occupational skills, employability skills, and special services.
4. Develop individual goals and objectives to maximize the student's potential in a vocational program.
5. Place the student in a vocational skill-training program appropriate for the student's goals and objectives.
6. Provide the student support services to ensure success in the vocational skill-training program.
7. Place the student in a vocational setting appropriate to the training received.
8. Provide support services at the location of placement (i.e., emphasize interagency collaboration).
9. Conduct activities that will make the individual aware of alternative programs, if appropriate (i.e., technical school, military, community college).
10. Promote other services appropriate to the individual's needs (i.e., medical, independent living, recreation, mobility, residential living).

4. Speak and explain ideas clearly
5. Answer and ask questions and follow verbal directions
6. Perform basic mathematical operations and work with fractions and decimals
7. Measure and comprehend spatial relationships and use metric measurements
8. Type with accuracy and speed
9. Use modern technology, including microcomputers and word processors.

The preceding data point to the national need for and the value of vocational education. The type of education required at the local level, however, must be established through continual evaluation of the effectiveness of local programs. Educators should collect follow-up data asking program graduates whether the vocational instruction provided was adequate. Educators should determine whether their past students are employed, where they are employed, and whether their employment is related to the training received. Data may also be collected on the problems students are experiencing in seeking, keeping, and advancing in jobs. The information gathered will help educators develop and provide future vocational programs and a transition plan, as recommended in Action Plan 12.1. Current students also need to be studied to ensure that individual programs are designed appropriately. Information should be obtained on (a) career interests, (b) individual skills and abilities, (c) community and industrial needs, and (d) potential intervention strategies. Several strategies and instruments may be used to collect this information.

Assessing Interests and Skills

Vocational evaluation is an ongoing process that provides information practitioners can use to design and implement vocational instruction for each student. This information may relate to vocational aptitudes, work interests, work habits, social skills, personal care skills, and attitudes.

Vocational Aptitude Tests

Vocational aptitude tests are designed to determine whether an individual has the potential to succeed in a given occupation. A high aptitude score in a quantity foods occupation suggests that the student has the ability to learn the competencies necessary to become a chef, restaurant manager, or owner. A low aptitude score might suggest that the student will have difficulty in acquiring these complex skills. Careful matching of capability to level of potential is important to ensure interest and success in employment.

Some authors have questioned the validity of vocational aptitude tests when used with special populations (Schloss & Sedlak, 1986). Because reading and writing are prerequisite to performance on many of these measures, the performance of students with disabilities may not reflect their actual vocational ability. Even when actual performance items are used that do not require reading and writing, it is questionable whether the standardized testing conditions adequately mirror actual work conditions. Furthermore, aptitude tests provide a static indication of current ability. Vocational instruction may alter a person's aptitude. Unfortunately, data from an aptitude test may be used unwisely to deny a student the necessary vocational education.

Schloss and Sedlak (1986) have suggested the following guidelines for applying information from vocational aptitude tests.

1. Ensure that the student has been previously exposed to the test.
2. Ensure that the student is motivated to perform well on the test.
3. Ensure that the student possesses the necessary test-taking abilities (e.g., reading and writing).
4. Ensure that the test format and expected student response accurately reflect work demands in the actual vocational setting.
5. Corroborate results of the test with other measures.

Curriculum-Based Vocational Assessment

Special educators and vocational educators have long recognized the importance of individual assessment services. Congress has confirmed this need by prescribing a full range of services in the Carl D. Perkins Vocational Education Act of 1985 (PL 98-524). Specifically, students with disabilities who enroll in a secondary vocational education program must receive an "assessment of the interest, abilities, and special needs of such student[s] with respect to completing successfully the vocational education program." Vocational assessment practices must be organized to provide such services. Many commercial products are available, but over time may not fulfill the assessment services needed by students with disabilities (Albright & Cobb, 1988).

Curriculum-based vocational assessment is an alternative approach to commercial assessments. This approach is characterized by the use of informal assessment procedures, developed and used by local vocational and special service personnel, based on each student's learning needs. Curriculum-based vocational assessment has four distinct characteristics. First, it responds to the information needs of personnel during the beginning stage in planning a student's vocational program. Second, it views assessment as an integral part of a student's vocational educational program. Third, it ensures that personnel conducting curriculum-based vocational assessment activities are also responsible for the student's vocational instruction. Fourth, it uses informal and direct methods to determine student achievement in the vocational education program.

Case for Action 12.1

Students in your classroom have just completed vocational aptitude tests. One student interested in veterinary science has scores that suggest an occupation with limited science and math competence. In talking with the student, you discover that the student's aunt is a veterinarian.

What guidance might you give this student in determining an appropriate career choice? How might you intervene in providing an occupational experience?

Curriculum-based vocational assessment is used to conduct formative and summative evaluation. Information can be gathered when determining placement, during participation in the program, and when exiting the program. This approach provides both ongoing information about students as they progress through their current vocational education programs and the information necessary to make decisions about future placements.

Career Awareness Process

Career development is a continuous process, beginning at birth and continuing until death. The development of this lifelong process is crucial to students with disabilities. Students may have severe deficits in academic areas and not be able to understand how these deficits might affect their lives when they leave school. Career education is defined as the process of systematically coordinating all school, family, and community components to facilitate each individual's potential for economic, social, and personal fulfillment (Brolin, 1993). Career education not only provides vocational preparation but also promotes awareness, exploration, decision making, entry, and advancement. Career education experiences should be integrated into regular education programs to provide a foundation for specific skills.

Career education makes a unique contribution to the educational system (Brolin, 1993):

1. Education and work interface in career education work.
2. All levels of education and all school personnel are affected by career education.
3. Career education and traditional subject matter coexist.
4. Career education and development occur in stages through carefully planned experiences.
5. Life skills, affective skills, and employability skills are the focus of career education.
6. Schools work more closely with families and community resources through career education

Career education should also be a significant and integral part of the curriculum for school-aged youths with disabilities (Brolin, 1995). It focuses on the total life plan of an individual. It facilitates growth and development in all life roles and settings. This total life plan is best represented in the *Life-Centered Career Education Curriculum* (Brolin, in press), which organizes 22 (see Figure 12.1) competencies into three primary curriculum areas: daily living skills, personal-social skills, and occupational guidance and preparation. Life-centered career education is designed to enhance and promote transition skills. Instruction for academic competencies in a student's program would support each of these three skill areas. For example, if the academic area to be taught is math and the skill area is daily living skills, the competency might be managing personal finances. Action Plan 12.2 notes six key points to be reviewed when considering such a curriculum.

Curriculum Area	Competency	Subcompetency: The student will be able to:	
Daily Living Skills	1. Managing Personal Finances	1. Count money & make correct change	2. Make responsible expenditures
	2. Selecting & Managing a Household	7. Maintain home exterior/interior	8. Use basic appliances and tools
	3. Caring for Personal Needs	12. Demonstrate knowledge of physical fitness, nutrition & weight	13. Exhibit proper grooming & hygiene
	4. Raising Children & Meeting Marriage Responsibilities	17. Demonstrate physical care for raising children	18. Know psychological aspects of raising children
	5. Buying, Preparing & Consuming Food	20. Purchase food	21. Clean food preparation areas
	6. Buying & Caring for Clothing	26. Wash clean clothing	27. Purchase clothing
	7. Exhibiting Responsible Citizenship	29. Demonstrate knowledge of civil rights & responsibilities	30. Know nature of local, state & federal governments
	8. Utilizing Recreational Facilities & Engaging in Leisure	33. Demonstrate knowledge of available community resources	34. Choose & plan activities
	9. Getting Around the Community	38. Demonstrate knowledge of traffic rules & safety	39. Demonstrate knowledge & use of various means of transportation
Personal Social Skills	10. Achieving Self-Awareness	42. Identify physical & psychological needs	43. Identify interests & abilities
	11. Acquiring Self-Confidence	46. Express feelings of self-worth	47. Describe others' perception of self
	12. Achieving Socially Responsible Behavior	51. Develop respect for the rights & properties of others	52. Recognize authority & follow instructions
	13. Maintaining Good Interpersonal Skills	56. Demonstrate listening & responding skills	57. Establish & maintain close relationships
	14. Achieving Independence	59. Strive toward self-actualization	60. Demonstrate self-organization
	15. Making Adequate Decisions	62. Locate & utilize sources of assistance	63. Anticipate consequences
	16. Communicating with Others	67. Recognize & respond to emergency situations	68. Communicate with understanding
Occupational Guidance and Preparation	17. Knowing & Exploring Occupational Possibilities	70. Identify remunerative aspects of work	71. Locate sources of occupational & training information
	18. Selecting & Planning Occupational Choices	76. Make realistic occupational choices	77. Identify requirements of appropriate & available jobs
	19. Exhibiting Appropriate Work Habits & Behavior	81. Follow directions & observe regulations	82. Recognize importance of attendance & punctuality
	20. Seeking, Securing & Maintaining Employment	88. Search for a job	89. Apply for a job
	21. Exhibiting Sufficient Physical-Manual Skills	94. Demonstrate stamina & endurance	95. Demonstrate satisfactory balance & coordination
	22. Obtaining Specific Occupational Skills		

FIGURE 12.1   Life Centered Career Education (LCCE) Curriculum (Revised 1/87)

3. Keep basic financial records	4. Calculate & pay taxes	5. Use credit responsibly	6. Use banking services	
9. Select adequate housing	10. Set up household	11. Maintain home grounds		
14. Dress appropriately	15. Demonstrate knowledge of common illness, prevention & treatment	16. Practice personal safety		
19. Demonstrate marriage responsibilities				
22. Store food	23. Prepare meals	24. Demonstrate appropriate eating habits	25. Plan/eat balanced meals	
28. Iron, mend & store clothing				
31. Demonstrate knowledge of the law & ability to follow the law	32. Demonstrate knowledge of citizen rights & responsibilities			
35. Demonstrate knowledge of the value of recreation	36. Engage in group & individual activities	37. Plan vacation time		
40. Find way around the community	41. Drive a car			
44. Identify emotions	45. Demonstrate knowledge of physical self			
48. Accept & give praise	49. Accept & give criticism	50. Develop confidence in oneself		
53. Demonstrate appropriate behavior in public places	54. Know important character traits	55. Recognize personal roles		
58. Make & maintain friendships				
61. Demonstrate awareness of how one's behavior affects others				
64. Develop & evaluate alternatives	65. Recognize nature of a problem	66. Develop goal seeking behavior		
69. Know subtleties of communication				
72. Identify personal values met through work	73. Identify societal values met through work	74. Classify jobs into occupational categories	75. Investigate local occupational & training opportunities	
78. Identify occupational aptitudes	79. Identify major occupational interests	80. Identify major occupational needs		
83. Recognize importance of supervision	84. Demonstrate knowledge of occupational safety	85. Work with others	86. Meet demands for quality work	87. Work at a satisfactory rate
90. Interview for a job	91. Know how to maintain post-school occupational adjustments	92. Demonstrate knowledge of competitive standards	93. Know how to adjust to changes in employment	
96. Demonstrate manual dexterity	97. Demonstrate sensory discrimination			
There are no specific subcompetencies as they depend on skill being taught				

Source: From *Life Centered Career Education: A Competency Based Approach* (4th ed.). Ed. Donn E. Brolin. Copyright 1993 by The Council for Exceptional Children. Reprinted with permission.

Action Plan 12.2   Life-Centered Career Education

When infusing a life-centered career education model in your program, keep in mind that the model is

1. Community based
2. Competency based
3. Individualized to the student's needs
4. Cost effective
5. Practical
6. Manageable.

Each of the 22 competencies and individual subcompetencies can be classified into one of the three curriculum skill areas. This classification can guide the teacher in developing educational objectives for each individual's program.

Extensive assessment materials and instructional units are now available to assist educators in teaching students at all educational levels these 22 important competencies (Brolin, 1992).

Vocational Objectives

The development of goals and objectives that will lead to employment should be a concern of all educators. They should begin to focus on developing vocational competence in the preschool years and continue to do so through postsecondary levels, regardless of whether an individual is in an academic or technical program. Goals should be specific to each individual. They should be based on an assessment of what skills the learner needs in order to become an independent citizen. The instructional strategies used to teach the necessary skills should be taught not only in a classroom, but in the natural environment as well. Training in natural environments may enhance the transfer of learning.

A functional curriculum is one in which students learn community-referenced skills in the most appropriate setting for specific skill acquisition (Fredricks & Evans, 1987). It is considered the conceptual framework for developing learning activities and experi-

Case for Action 12.2

Your school superintendent recently charged all faculty to develop a warranty program on the quality of its graduates. The superintendent stated that "Contractors give warranties on their homes. Car manufacturers give a warranty on their cars. Now, schools must give warranties on their products too." How does this responsibility affect your program and teaching? What action will you take?

ences appropriate to adolescents and adults who are experiencing learning problems (Bender & Valetutti, 1982; Polloway & Patton, 1993). A functional curriculum prepares students for vocational competence and an independent life because it is based on real-life experiences of individuals. Action Plan 12.3 includes the steps suggested by Schloss, Smith, Goldsmith, and Selinger (1984).

The functional curriculum approach outlined in Action Plan 12.3 prepares students to function directly in the natural vocational settings in which they may be employed. This curriculum model serves as a basis for Project PROGRESS, a model demonstration project for developing vocational skills in youths with mild and moderate disabilities (Schloss, McEwen, Lang, & Schwab, 1986). The first step is to identify future vocational settings in which the youth may be employed. This step may be accomplished through the use of Brolin's (1993) *Life Centered Career Education* approach. Emphasis should be placed on the assessment of the student's career interests and aptitudes as well as the vocational opportunities available in the community.

The second step is to observe others in the specific vocational setting to determine the specific skills the student will need to succeed in the placement. In this step, all subenvironments of the vocational placement should be considered. For example, observations may reveal that successful workers are able to perform math, utilize social skills, and read the menu while at the customer order station. They are also able to exhibit assertiveness skills while in the employer's office and display specific social and personal skills while on lunch break in the employee's lounge.

Action Plan 12.3

We recommend that the following steps be completed when developing a functional curriculum:

1. Identify current and/or future environments in which the learner is expected to participate.
2. Observe others in these settings to determine what skills are needed for successful participation.
3. Develop a skill checklist that assesses learner competence in using the skills required by the setting.
4. Apply the checklist to determine what skills the student possesses and what skills are lacking.
5. Determine what skills may be accommodated through prosthetics (e.g., calculators, charts, color codes, amplification).
6. Delineate developmentally sound task sequences to improve skill deficits not covered by prosthetics.
7. Provide educational experiences that promote the acquisition of the skill sequences.
8. Assess the learner using the skill checklist to determine the effectiveness of instruction and the degree to which the learner is prepared to participate in the target environment.

The third step is to develop a checklist that can be used to evaluate performance of skills identified in the preceding step. This checklist indicates all skills necessary for success on the job. The skills should be listed in chronological order referenced to each subsetting (e.g., work floor, commissary, employer's office, washroom) in the vocational placement. The skills in the checklist should be based on the capabilities of the learner. Advanced students may benefit from a few more general entries such as "cleans the rest room," "arranges chairs in the seating area," or "takes orders." Less capable students may require a larger number of more precise entries such as "mops the floor," "cleans the stool," or "replaces the tissue paper."

The fourth step is to identify skills that can be developed through assistive devices. As a general rule, a prosthetic should be used any time that the cost of training (i.e., time, effort, or actual expense) outweighs the disadvantages of relying on the artificial assistive device.

The fifth step is to establish developmentally sound task sequences. In this step, the educator determines the skills to be taught and the order of instruction. Instruction should be sequenced logically (Schloss et al., 1986). For example, it could be forward-chained from the first task to the last, or backward-chained from the last to the first used on the actual job. Again, the size of the chain should be matched to the capabilities of the student.

The sixth step is to provide instruction. We recommend using concrete materials, multiple modalities, distributed drill and practice, and frequent feedback. In many cases, the most direct and efficient form of instruction may be workstation simulation or actual on-the-job training. In other cases, basic skill instruction in traditional academic classes may be advisable.

The last step in the functional curricula sequence is to assess learner competence using the checklist developed in Step 3. Success in each area of the checklist should indicate that the student is fully prepared to participate in the vocational setting.

As should be apparent from the preceding curriculum process, basic academic and interpersonal skills are likely to be among the skills required for a majority of positions.

Basic Skills

Academic Skills. Vocational competence cannot be achieved without some basic academic skills. At primary school levels, academic subjects are usually taught using worksheet and textbook exercises outside of a vocational context. Once the student advances to the secondary level, activities are directed to everyday living and vocational situations. Math activities may include budgeting and ordering; tallying while reading might focus on occupational manuals and directions. These activities can then be implemented in a community setting by performing them in a bank, grocery store, or auto shop.

Social Skills. Social skills have been identified as a key factor contributing to the success of individuals with disabilities (Greenan & Browning, 1989). Authors have reported that a lack of social skills is a major reason for the termination of employment (Greenspan & Shoultz, 1981; Schloss & Schloss, 1987; Shafer, Banks, & Kregel, 1991; Wehman, Kregel, & Banks, 1989). Along with basic academic skills, social skills should be taught in the primary grades by a functional approach. Basic skill building is taught in the primary grades, and the skills are implemented in vocational contexts in the secondary grades. Actual guided practice should take place in community and vocational settings.

Personal Care Skills.   Employment success also depends on skills related to grooming, hygiene, and dress. If individuals are to live independently, they must be able to care for themselves. Dressing, toileting, personal hygiene, and general nutrition are typical personal care components taught to primary-level students. In the secondary years, students may learn to purchase and care for items. For example, youngsters have their clothing selected for them and they are told when and where to wear it. As adults, they learn (a) how to plan and budget their wardrobe; (b) what size, color, and style are appropriate; (c) when and where to wear specific clothes; and (d) how to care for clothing. Instruction geared to developing personal care skills should eventually take place in natural community settings. In the case of clothing, instruction could begin in the classroom, continuing at a shopping center, laundry room, apartment, or employment setting.

Motor Skills.   Motor skills will contribute to vocational competencies that rely on strength, speed, dexterity, coordination, and balance. The performance of motor skills will become increasingly refined with age. At the primary levels, fine and gross motor skills are developed through academic and recreational activities. Motor development is then directed to vocational activities in the secondary grades by the use of tools, keyboarding, and the manipulation of large objects. For example, students interested in quantity food production may develop motor skills by learning the proper use of cutlery and the use of large paddles and spoons.

Specific Goal Selection

As already mentioned, the functional curriculum approach takes into account student and community or industry needs. Thus, the skills taught are based on those the student will need in real-life situations (Cartwright, Cartwright, & Ward, 1989).

After studying the needs of employers in light industry, Rusch, Schutz, Mithaug, Steward, and Mar (1982) developed an empirically based assessment and curriculum guide for individuals with learning disabilities. This assessment, the Vocational Assessment and Curriculum Guide (VACG), reviews eight performance categories important for employment success: attendance and endurance, independence, production, learning, behavior, communication skills, social skills, and grooming and eating. The results of an individual's performance on the assessment are interpreted on the basis of employers' expectations for each. Areas in which students scored less than expected by employers are suggested as student objectives. The VACG is one example of how community and industrial needs may be incorporated into the curriculum.

A student's success in society is often determined by his or her employment value. The employment value of individuals with disabilities has been stressed by their parents and advocates, as well as local education agencies (Renzaglia & Hutchins, 1988). Vocational education programs must continue to evaluate the services offered and ensure that individuals with disabilities will acquire the vocational skills they need to adjust to community life. According to Renzaglia and Hutchins (1988), service providers must be able to perform five basic functions:

1. Identify potential employment opportunities
2. Functionally assess the student or client
3. Design an individualized vocational curriculum
4. Select the appropriate training experiences and placements with respect to the abilities and needs of the individual and the prospective employer
5. Using sound methodological procedures, effectively instruct persons with disabilities to successfully perform all necessary job requirements.

Performing functions 1 and 2 will aid in identifying the vocational programs needed to be taught. Specific skills can then be determined.

Historically, follow-up studies have been conducted in regular and vocational education programs. As noted earlier, these studies aid in measuring the effectiveness of education programs. They also serve to produce a demographic record of educational outcomes. Follow-up studies focus on students' educational needs as well as their in-school experiences. Information received from these studies is an excellent resource for determining current employment trends of graduates and nongraduates, vocational/career awareness information received while enrolled in school, and vocational/career awareness information they might need to be successful in their present occupations.

A number of other resources may be used to determine employment trends and make educators aware of employment opportunities. Two excellent resources for projecting employment trends are publications printed by the U.S. Department of Labor and individual state employment commissions (Shafer, Parent, & Everson, 1988). These publications provide information regarding labor growth and opportunity.

This information may not always be applicable to an individual's location and may be inappropriate, owing to regional and economic differences. In this case, local and regional employers should be surveyed regarding projected labor growth, industry concern, turnover data, and identified areas of growth and opportunity. Suggested contacts are the Chamber of Commerce, employment offices, clubs and organizations, local employers, newspapers, telephone book, private industry councils, and school advisory councils. This information should then be reviewed and analyzed, and appropriate vocational programs for the location in question should be identified. Action Plan 12.4 presents some possible resources for various types of educational programs.

Once vocational programs have been identified, the practitioner should select the specific skills to be taught. These should include specific occupational and vocational competencies (e.g., interview skills), which can be identified by conducting on-site job analyses; employer interviews; and reviews of published research, curricula, and job-skill catalogs. Vocational education providers can thus obtain validated information that can help them define appropriate goals and objectives. Individuals with disabilities can then be evaluated to determine their level of competence, and appropriate individualized goals and objectives can be determined.

Action Plan 12.4　Developing Vocational Programs

The following resources are useful when developing a vocational program:

School

Follow-up studies
Employer studies
Vocational placements
Advisory board members

Community

Employers
Private industry council
Chamber of Commerce
Small business association
Employment office
Telephone book
Newspaper
Radio/television

State/Nationwide

U.S. Department of Labor
U.S. Department of Commerce
U.S. Employment Service
Labor/apprenticeship programs
Dictionary of Occupational Titles (DOT)
Specific occupational references
Newspapers
Periodicals
Reference books
Radio/television

General Principles of Vocational Instruction

Vocational education is defined as an organized educational effort that directly prepares individuals for paid or unpaid employment requiring other than a baccalaureate or advanced degree (Sarkees & Scott, 1985). Vocational education encompasses all aspects of an occupation, including theory, occupational skill components, and nonoccupational skill components. In the teaching of vocational education theory and occupational skill-building components, it is usually assumed that nonoccupational skills are "givens," or are present. In teaching learners with disabilities, it is not appropriate to assume any "givens." All vocational components should be taught.

Students in vocational programs are expected to be employable after completing a program. To ensure employability, they must meet certain proficiency and employability

Case for Action 12.3

Two of your students want to participate in your school's vocational printing program. You discussed their request with the vocational director and were told that you must vouch for their competence after training. The director stated students cannot be enrolled unless capable of success in their trained area.

You realize that this may be possible for one of the students. How would you pursue this conversation? What direction would you take?

standards or competencies. Vocational programs should be competency based, with the curriculum and instruction focusing on the specific competencies necessary to successfully perform a position.

Program competencies that ensure success in an occupation should be adjusted only as a last resort. Alternative intervention strategies should be considered when traditional strategies are not effective. Each student's goals and objectives should reflect his or her particular capabilities. This method enables the vocational teacher to match an individual student's abilities with realistic employment opportunities.

Specialized and integrated transitional services should be provided throughout the vocational program to help students experience a smooth transition from school to work. Special attention should be paid to ensuring that skills acquired in the vocational program are carried over to employment settings. The development of a transition plan by the special educator, vocational rehabilitation personnel, employers, parents, and others may serve this end.

Summary

Vocational education should be designed to provide a meaningful and practical experience for all learners with disabilities. The ultimate goal of vocational education is the successful integration of a student into the workforce. To meet this goal, educators may have to teach both specific occupational skills and basic academic skills.

The vocational evaluation process provides data that can be used to design and monitor the key components of vocational instruction. Aptitude tests are used to determine an individual's prospects for success in a given occupation. Curriculum-based vocational assessment uses informal procedures based on the student's individual learning needs. These assessment techniques will provide data for determining placement, evaluating a student's progress during placement, and planning future goals.

Career education is a life-long practice that enhances vocational instruction by providing a foundation for specific skills training. Life-centered career education is a useful approach in this regard as it organizes instruction into three curriculum areas: daily living skills, personal-social skills, and occupational guidance and preparation. Academic competencies serve as a support to each of these curriculum areas.

Vocational goals and objectives should be based on an individual's strengths and weaknesses. The goals and objectives should maximize the individual's potential for independence in society. This process begins in primary levels and continues up to placement. It focuses on functional skills curricula leading to employment. These include academic, social, motor, and specific goal selection. A student's employment value has become increasingly important to society. Vocational programs need to continue evaluating their services in order to ensure that the skills acquired contribute to employment success.

Realistic program goals and objectives should be included in all vocational instruction programs. Investigating local and regional needs of employers and communities, follow-up studies of previous students, and literature reviews are examples of the resources that can help educators plan appropriate vocational programs. Programs based on business and industry's needs in your local or regional area will improve students' chances of success in employment placement.

Students with disabilities need to be taught all vocational skills, particularly nonoccupational skills. Individual vocational goals and objectives will vary, but they should be flexible enough so that students can exit at any appropriate point.

References

Albright, L., & Cobb, R. B. (1988). Curriculum based vocational assessment: A concept whose time has come. *Journal for Vocational Special Needs Education, 10*(2), 13–16.

Bender, M., & Valetutti, P. J. (1982). *Teaching functional academics: A curriculum guide for adolescents and adults with learning problems.* Baltimore, MD: University Park Press.

Benz, M. R., & Halpern, A. S. (1987). Transition services for secondary students with mild disabilities: A statewide perspective. *Exceptional Children, 53,* 507–514.

Brolin, D. (1992). *Life centered career education assessment batteries and competency units.* Reston, VA: The Council for Exceptional Children.

Brolin, D. (1993). *Life centered career education: A competency based approach* (4th ed.). Reston, VA: The Council for Exceptional Children.

Cartwright, G. P., Cartwright, C. A., & Ward, M. E. (1989) . *Educating special learners* (3rd ed.). Belmont, CA: Wadsworth.

Edgar, E. (1987). Secondary programs in special education: Are many of them justifiable? *Exceptional Children, 53,* 555–561.

Fairweather, J. S. (1988). Preparing secondary-level handicapped students for work and life after school: Traditional vs. nontraditional approaches. *Journal for Vocational Special Needs Education, 10*(2), 23–27.

Fredricks, M., & Evans, V. (1987). Functional curriculum. In C. M. Nelson, R. B. Rutherford, Jr., & B. I. Wolford (Eds.), *Special education in the criminal justice system.* Columbus, OH: Merrill.

Greenan J., & Browning, D. A. (1989). Generalizable interpersonal action skills for students with handicapping conditions. *Journal for Vocational Special Needs Education, 11*(2), 23–29.

Greenspan, S., & Shoultz, B. (1981). Why mentally retarded adults lose their jobs: Social competence as a factor in work adjustments. *Applied Research in Mental Retardation, 2,* 23–38.

Hasazi, S. B., Gordon, L. R., & Roe, L. A. (1985). Factors associated with the employment status of handicapping youth exiting high school from 1979 to 1983. *Exceptional Children, 51,* 455–469.

Johnson, C. (1988, October). *Reauthorization of the Carl D. Perkins Vocational Education Act.* Paper presented at the Missouri LINC: Vocational Special Needs Fall Conference.

McAfee, J. (1988a). Adult adjustment of individuals with mental retardation. In P. J. Schloss, C. A. Hughes, & M. A. Smith (Eds.), *Mental retardation: Community transition* (pp. 115–162). Boston: College-Hill.

McAfee, J. M. (1988b). Retardation: Occupational, economic, and community living issues. In P. J. Schloss, C. A. Hughes, & M. A. Smith (Eds.), *Mental retardation: Community transition* (pp. 163–205). Boston: College-Hill.

Mithaug, D. E., Horiuchi, C. N., & Fanning, P. N. (1985). A report on the Colorado statewide follow-up survey of special education students. *Exceptional Children, 51,* 397–404.

Polloway, E. A., & Patton, J. R. (1993). *Strategies for teaching learners with special needs* (5th ed.). New York: Merrill/Macmillan.

Renzaglia, A., & Hutchins, M. (1988). A community referenced approach to preparing persons with disabilities for employment. In P. Wehman & M. S. Moon (Eds.), *Vocational rehabilitation and supported employment* (pp. 91–110). Baltimore, MD: Paul H. Brookes.

Rusch, R., Schutz, R., Mithaug, D., Steward, J., & Mar, D. (1982). *The vocational assessment and curriculum guide.* Seattle, WA: Exceptional Children.

Sarkees, M., & Scott, J. (1985). *Vocational special needs.* Homewood, IL: American Technical Publishers.

Schloss, P. J., Hughes, C. A., & Smith, M. A. (1988). *Mental retardation: Community transition.* Boston: College-Hill.

Schloss, P. J., McEwen, D., Lang, E., & Schwab, J. (1986). PROGRESS: A model program for pro-

moting school to work transition. *Career Development for Exceptional Individuals, 9,* 16–23.

Schloss, P. J., & Schloss, C. N. (1987). A critical review of social skills research in mental retardation. In R. P. Barrett, & J. L. Matson (Eds.), *Advances in developmental disorders* (pp. 107–151). Greenwich, CT: JAI.

Schloss, P. J., & Sedlak, R. A. (1986). *Instructional methods for students with learning and behavior problems.* Boston, MA: Allyn and Bacon.

Schloss, P. J., Smith, M. A., Goldsmith, L., & Selinger, J. (1984). Identifying current and relevant curricula sequences for multiply involved hearing impaired youth. *American Annals of the Deaf, 129,* 417–423.

Shafer, M. S., Banks, P. D., & Kregel, J. (1991). Employment retention and career movement among individuals with mental retardation working in supported employment. *Mental Retardation, 11*(2), 103–110.

Shafer, M. S., Parent, W. S., & Everson, J. M. (1988). Responsive marketing by supported employment programs. In P. Wehman & M. S. Moon (Eds.), *Vocational rehabilitation and supported employment* (pp. 235–250). Baltimore, MD: Paul H. Brookes.

Wehman, P., Kregel, J., & Banks, P. D. (1989). Competitive employment for persons with mental retardation. In P. Wehman & J. Kregel (Eds.), *Supported employment for persons with disabilities: Focus on excellence* (pp. 97–113). New York: Human Sciences.

U.S. Department of Labor, Department of Education, & Department of Commerce (1988). *Building a quality workforce.* Washington, DC: U.S. Government Printing Office.

Leisure Education for Positive Leisure Life-Styles

DIANE LEA RYNDAK, BARBARA P. SIRVIS,
AND DEBBIE S. ALCOULOUMRE

Did you know that . . .

- Leisure and a positive leisure life-style make a significant contribution to our overall mental health and life satisfaction?
- The vast majority of nondisabled adults have not developed a positive leisure life-style?
- Leisure education is a much broader concept than the activity-oriented view familiar to most educators?
- Central to the concept of leisure are freedom of choice and control over your own actions?
- Opportunities for leisure occur in every environment?
- It is critical to include both traditional and nontraditional aspects of adult leisure life-styles in leisure education programs for adolescents with disabilities?
- Leisure education must be individualized for adolescents with disabilities?
- For adolescents with disabilities, leisure education must be a distinctive component of the curriculum with specific objectives for each learner?

Diane Lea Ryndak is associate professor of special education in the Exceptional Education Department at Buffalo State College. Barbara Sirvis is vice president for Academic Affairs at the State University of New York, Brockport. Debbie S. Alcouloumre is a doctoral candidate in the Department of Special Education, Teachers College, Columbia University.

Can you . . .

- Identify traditional and nontraditional leisure activities at work, at home, or in the community?
- Identify the general principles of leisure instruction?
- Obtain information about leisure options available and appropriate in a learner's environment?
- Access and develop opportunities for leisure?
- Assess a learner's ability to participate in specific leisure options outside the school environment?
- Conduct a family inventory to identify leisure options important to teach a learner?
- Obtain information from a learner's nondisabled chronological age peers and co-workers about leisure options available and appropriate for them?
- Obtain information from the learner about leisure preferences?
- Identify the most important leisure options to include in a learner's leisure education program?
- Incorporate content from other curricular areas into leisure instruction?

Leisure is freedom to experience what is personally rewarding. The leisure experience reaches to the center of our development; it encourages self actualization. (Carter & Nelson, 1992, p. 25)

Play is a word that is generally applied to the enjoyable activities of children. In adolescence and adulthood, the same concept is more often referred to as *leisure*—activities during unobligated time that bring a level of personal satisfaction. Many individuals do not understand the role and function of leisure in their daily lives and frequently see leisure simply as a reward for surviving the stresses of life at work or at home. However, leisure fulfills a more important role in our lives. Beyond rewards, leisure encompasses choice, freedom, and control of our individual environments. Leisure enhances involvement, challenge, and friendships. Imagine that someone you know was unable to utilize and enjoy their leisure opportunities. Imagine their boredom, their loneliness, and their frustration. Commonly, the more severe a person's disability, the more time the individual has to devote to leisure and the less likely it is that he or she will possess the skills and resources to plan for and use leisure opportunities.

Leisure-related problems are particularly significant for today's adolescents. Often unsure about their emerging self-image, increasing numbers of children, adolescents, and working adults are using their unobligated time by turning to nonconstructive activities such as substance abuse, vandalism, or gang activities to bolster their egos. This may be particularly true for learners with disabilities. For example, it is easy for a learner with disabilities to use drugs to become an accepted member of a social group. Why? Is it possible there are no barriers related to disability for participation in the drug culture?

Is it possible that substances become a bridge into the nondisabled world? Is it possible that learners with disabilities do not (a) know how to find meaningful and enjoyable leisure activities, interesting events, or appropriate resources or (b) have the skills to make such choices? Do they feel that substance use is their only leisure option?

Newfound freedoms associated with adolescence include driving, less supervised time, and more options for personal choices. In addition, adolescents often feel forced to experiment with sexual intimacy before they are ready. Many adolescents with disabilities are excluded from dating, which is an important teenage ritual in learning to develop lifetime partners. Their choices of leisure activities and the development of a positive leisure life-style are influenced by peers, media images, and personal insecurity. All of these situations can be either productive or dangerous, depending on the extent to which each adolescent is prepared for leisure options and independence.

All adolescent learners, and especially those with disabilities, need to have access to leisure choices while learning to make leisure-related decisions. This is especially true because learners with disabilities increasingly are in inclusive settings with nondisabled peers, both at school and in the community. For this chapter, inclusion at school refers to the provision of special education and related services for a learner with disabilities within the general education settings and general education activities, along with non-disabled classmates of the same chronological age (Ryndak & Alper, in press). To be effective, an inclusive educational program provides the learner both the support and the adaptations required to successfully meet his or her individualized goals within those settings and activities (Ryndak & Alper, in press). Inclusion also encompasses the learner's belonging, in every way, to the community of learners in the school. The feeling of belonging to that community emanates from the learner with disabilities, the nondis-abled classmates, and each teacher involved in providing services to the learner.

Learners with disabilities, therefore, need to learn to identify and plan for unobli-gated time in inclusive settings, while acquiring the skills to implement each aspect of a leisure option (e.g., locating resources; paying for supplies; developing activity skills.) They need to learn to become accepted members of appropriate social groups in inclu-sive settings by making and maintaining friendships. Most of all, learners with disabilities need to discover and build their own leisure identity through practicing these skills and incorporating them into their daily lives. Action Plan 13.1 lists ways that teachers can use the individualized education program (IEP) to enhance the development of leisure skills by students with disabilities.

Few teachers have considered that learners with disabilities require a formal leisure education program to learn to implement a positive leisure life-style, or that leisure can be an educational bridge to the inclusion of learners with disabilities in society. This chapter presents a framework for understanding the importance of leisure across the life span and for incorporating effective leisure education into the educational curriculum for adolescents who have disabilities. It emphasizes the use of information relevant to an individual adolescent to determine the most important and relevant leisure education curriculum content for that learner. There is a more traditional model of leisure educa-tion, but it often leaves many learners with mild disabilities with the ability to participate in recreational activities, yet without the necessary social and leisure skills to construc-

Action Plan 13.1   Leisure Education Programs and Individualized Education Programs (IEPs)

Educational plans must reflect the support many learners need to engage in meaningful leisure lives both during and beyond the school years. Considerations might include one or more of the following:

1. Learners may need practice in cognitive skills (e.g., deciding, organizing, sequencing, and planning an activity).
2. Learners may experience problems with money or time management.
3. Social dilemmas may require skill development in (a) identifying and inviting friends to participate; (b) using social etiquette and appropriate interpersonal skills; (c) maintaining personal hygiene; (d) participating in social conversations; and/or (e) reacting appropriately to various situations.
4. Learners may experience physical difficulties with mobility, architectural barriers, fine or gross motor problems, and fatigue.
5. Learners may require assistance with (a) adapted leisure equipment; (b) rules; (c) methods of participation; or (d) emotional support and strategies to weather disappointments, loneliness, and rejection.

tively fill and enjoy their free time. The purpose of this framework is to ensure that each adolescent is provided the opportunity to learn the social and leisure skills necessary to participate successfully, both immediately and in the future, in leisure options of their choice with nondisabled peers, coworkers, neighbors, and community members.

Concepts of Leisure and Leisure Education

Leisure is a much broader concept than the activity-oriented view familiar to most educators. Most people do not realize the significant contribution of leisure and a positive leisure life-style to overall mental health and life satisfaction (Carter & Nelson, 1992). The fact that the vast majority of adults have not yet learned to develop and express a positive leisure life-style suggests that adolescents with disabilities may well have similar, if not greater, difficulties with leisure.

Leisure is generally considered to be synonymous with recreational activities and "free time." However, as highlighted in Action Plan 13.2, leisure is a complex concept that incorporates opportunity, time, control and choice, activity, and personal satisfaction. It is a personalized process in which an individual makes choices to determine his or her own leisure life-style, which results in personal satisfaction.

Confusion and a lack of understanding about leisure often result from the inability to recognize the difference between *real* leisure and *enforced* leisure. Real leisure is never imposed on an individual (Brightbill, 1966). Rather, it is an activity freely chosen at a specific time because it brings personal satisfaction (Kelly, 1982). The freedom of choice and control over individual action are central to the real issue.

Action Plan 13.2   Concept of Leisure

Leisure is a personalized process in which an individual makes choices to determine his or her own leisure life-style, which will result in personal satisfaction. As such, it includes

1. Opportunity
2. Time
3. Choice
4. Activity
5. Personal satisfaction.

Leisure education is the development of various leisure-related skills, attitudes, and knowledge that are fundamental to personal leisure life-style (Peterson, in press). Leisure education facilitates a learner's growth in a number of ways. Brannan, Chinn, and Verhoven (1981) have suggested that leisure education can serve the following functions:

1. It enables individuals with disabilities to participate in a variety of settings with their nondisabled peers.
2. It teaches knowledge, skills, and attitudes that are related to leisure.
3. It allows for a variety and choice of pursuits.
4. It aids in the development of a positive self-concept.
5. It increases the development of social skills.
6. It increases the use of techniques that facilitate generalization and transfer.
7. It develops self-initiation.
8. It enhances community learning.
9. It provides a meaningful outlet for the skills taught throughout the educational curriculum.

Thus, leisure education can provide the means for learning and using a number of applicable skills, while also meeting its primary function of assisting learners in the development of concepts of choice that are critical to successful leisure.

For adolescents without disabilities, recreational activities may be used as a means to teach academic curriculum content. For adolescents with disabilities, however, leisure education should be an end in itself. Although many of the skills learned through leisure education have potential impact across a learner's life, leisure education is critical for adolescents with disabilities primarily in developing both leisure skills and positive leisure life-styles.

Peterson (in press) has presented a clear model for the components of leisure education, including leisure awareness, social interaction skills, leisure activity skills, and identification and use of leisure resources. This model provides the framework for the instructional applications that follow.

Leisure awareness means knowing and understanding the concept of leisure as well as the relevance of a positive leisure life-style to overall life satisfaction. Leisure life-style develops as an individual learns to assume responsibility for his or her personal behavior. Self-awareness is also an aspect of leisure awareness since individuals must understand their abilities and disabilities, both actual and perceived, in order to engage in successful choices of activities to meet their leisure goals. Recognition of one's personal attitudes toward activities, as well as the societal attitudes toward certain events, will shape options and choices. Personal selection, choice of leisure options, and related participation and decision-making skills are critical variables of this component.

Social interactions are critical for learners with disabilities to access the nondisabled world and, therefore, must be incorporated into leisure education. Appropriate social skills are necessary to form and maintain relationships, which require social interactions. Learners need to know how to converse, share, listen, and be a friend, as well as respond during leisure options to (a) the social milieu; (b) the social culture; and (c) the age, number, and relationship of participants. Specific social skills can be taught, but since some learners experience difficulty in generalizing their use to appropriate inclusive situations, social skill instruction must permeate every aspect of life. These learners must be taught not only basic social skills (e.g., eye contact, body spacing, etiquette), but also subtle social responses critical to success in inclusive settings (e.g., how to observe others within social situations to identify how their own behavior should be modified). In addition, learners practicing social interactions must demonstrate (a) the flexibility that is intrinsic to relationships and (b) negotiation skills required to develop and maintain reciprocal friendships. For successful social interactions, learners must communicate, interact, and behave appropriately within the contexts of activities.

Leisure activity skills are important to the overall leisure education program and a positive individual leisure life-style. For learners to develop a sense of competence, leisure skills must be taught, practiced, and developed, emphasizing the importance of an individual's fully experiencing a leisure activity prior to deciding whether or not he or she likes it. This will be helpful when the component of choice is introduced in conjunction with instruction on the skills required to perform a leisure activity. In addition, activities should represent a broad range of leisure options from inclusive settings, not just the activities favored by the teacher. To accomplish this, the teacher may have to seek instructional assistance from others with skills relevant to different leisure options. When selecting leisure activities to be taught, the teacher must consider and incorporate the needs and resources of the learner (e.g., transportation, financial resources), since each learner eventually will plan and initiate various leisure options based on his or her available resources. Although interactive activities may be emphasized, solitary leisure activities also should be included as typical adult forms of leisure that are especially useful during transitions (e.g., riding a bus) or during activities that require waiting (e.g., doing laundry).

Leisure resources comprise the fourth area of the leisure education model. If individuals are to have maximum choice and satisfaction, they need to know what leisure options are available to them. Learners should understand their own personal resources, including skills, finances, educational level, and experience. They need to be able to identify resources that are available in their home and in their immediate community. Are their leisure resources limited, or are there opportunities for leisure satisfaction at home (e.g., cooperative games with household members, cooking, gardening, reading materials,

Case for Action 13.1

Because it is outdated, your school district is revising its curriculum for learners with disabilities. As a member of the curriculum revision committee, you are responsible for developing the written narrative describing physical education and leisure education. How do you describe leisure education? How is it different from physical education and recreation?

etc.)? Who is available to provide transportation if necessary? What local resources exist (e.g., YM/YWCA programs, community leisure service agencies, fitness centers)? A knowledge of the available resources will facilitate the learner's acceptance of responsibility for his or her own leisure life-style.

General Principles of Leisure Instruction

The ability, right, and responsibility to choose one's own leisure life-style require active participation and practice. To facilitate choice making, teachers should allow each learner to make choices across the entire program. For instance, a learner should be involved in the gathering of information to plan the leisure education program (i.e., conducting surveys of family and friends; collecting information on personal and recreational resources; conducting assessments of skills for identifying, selecting, and participating in a leisure activity). The more actively involved the learner is during this development phase, the more likely the learner will be to participate fully in the program.

To feel competent in participating in leisure choices, the learner needs to participate actively and master specific skills that are systematically taught, reinforced, and practiced. Since leisure skills are best learned through real experiences in the learners's own home and community, they should be practiced in the actual places in which the learner will engage in recreational activities in the future. For example, the learner's program may include instruction in the neighborhood, shopping in local stores, or playing in local parks.

As a learner practices leisure activities, instruction should incorporate planning, initiating, and implementing those activities, including steps such as making telephone calls, arranging for transportation, inviting a friend, and getting directions. To accomplish this, it is critical that the learner develop the skills to make and maintain reciprocal friendships. Teachers can provide practice opportunities by assigning the learner to invite a friend over to participate in an interactive leisure activity. Learners should also be taught about dating and prepared for interactions that may occur during a date. While role playing may provide opportunities to develop cursory skills, double dates with responsible and supportive friends can be effective in providing age-appropriate models of dating behavior. It is important that the learner become his or her own leisure advocate. These principles are summarized in Action Plan 13.3.

Action Plan 13.3   General Principles of Leisure Instruction

To ensure effective leisure instruction, teachers should do the following:

1. Facilitate the learner's active participation in all aspects of leisure and developing the leisure education plan
2. Provide the learner opportunities to choose leisure activities and determine the degree to which he or she will participate in that activity
3. Provide systematic opportunities for practice and role playing
4. Develop the learner's competence in leisure activity and associated social skills
5. Promote the learner's responsibility for self and personal decisions
6. Facilitate the learner's participation in planning, initiating, and implementing leisure activities
7. Provide the support needed from the teacher, family, peers, and social coach
8. Provide instruction in real leisure activities of the learner's choice in his or her own environments
9. Encourage the involvement of persons who are important to the learner
10. Facilitate the learner's becoming his or her own leisure advocate.

Leisure Opportunities

The broad concept of leisure education takes into account the need for all of the components of the model proposed by Peterson (in press). In the development of programs, it is also important to consider an adolescent's preferences and the nature of the activities that may be part of the leisure life-style of an individual, as well as the contexts and environments in which the leisure will occur.

Opportunities for leisure occur in virtually any environment—at home, in school, in the community, and at work. This is often difficult to understand if we accept only the traditional definitions of leisure, such as

Sports and games	Dance
Aquatics and water-related activities	Drama
Arts and crafts	Mental games and activities
Outdoor activities	Hobbies
Music	

Peterson (in press), however, has suggested that some nontraditional leisure activities can also represent the *adult* contexts for leisure. These nontraditional leisure activities include, but are not limited to, the following:

Social interaction	Maintenance of living things (pets and
Spectating and appreciating	plants)
Leadership and community service	Self-development

Fitness	Education
Relaxation and meditation	Self-care
Cognitive and mental activities	Travel
Eating	Fantasy and daydreaming
Food preparation	
Shopping	

These lists are presented to provide examples of a broad definition of leisure that includes many traditional activities that are enjoyed by, and are appropriate for, adolescents who have disabilities. However, this broad definition of leisure also recognizes that leisure extends far beyond traditional activities and encompasses activities that are seldom consciously thought of as leisure options. A life span curriculum will prepare adolescents who have disabilities for satisfying adult lives. The preparation for a mature leisure life-style must be less structured than the life-style of childhood, adaptable to adult environments, and less time specific. It is critical, therefore, to consider both the traditional and nontraditional aspects of adult leisure life-styles in the development of leisure education programs for adolescents who have disabilities.

In addition to recognizing the diverse nature of the choices that are available for leisure, educators must recognize the numerous contexts and environments in which leisure might occur. If we accept the more diverse definition of leisure, then it becomes easier to understand how leisure choice and satisfaction might occur in the home, at school, in the community, and at work. For example, a break for coffee or lunch at work can become an opportunity for social interaction while eating. Clearly, this experience can provide leisure satisfaction if the individual has the appropriate social and mealtime skills. It Is also a good example of a leisure skill that can be developed during lunchtime at school.

Leisure is an important aspect of the total educational curriculum for students who have disabilities. The attitudes, knowledge, and skills developed through direct and indirect leisure education can be applied in numerous settings and throughout a learner's life span. The remainder of this chapter focuses on the development of a leisure education program for adolescents who have disabilities.

The reader is reminded that the ultimate goal is that the learner develop a positive leisure life-style and personal satisfaction through the expression of free choice. The model presented has a community-based focus that integrates leisure education into existing curricula. The intent is that the content be incorporated into curricular programs in the way that a positive leisure life-style is incorporated into an individual's life. Leisure education may be found in all areas of the curriculum, from the decision making and mathematics needed to select and pay for a movie to more traditional activities taught in physical education.

Traditional physical education curricula expose students to activities that are typically not part of an adult leisure life-style; however, with a leisure-education focus, physical education may also be an opportunity for skill development related to fitness and wellness (Sirvis, Musante, & Bigge, 1991). A few lifetime leisure activities appropriate for physical education might include bike riding, walking, hiking, jogging, swimming, bowling, dancing, weight lifting, aerobics, yoga, golf, bocce, tennis, or cross country skiing.

Clearly, leisure education is not solely the domain of physical education; it extends across numerous curricular areas. Reading can include newspapers and telephone books to identify community resources. Mathematics can apply budget management to include money for leisure options. Social studies can explore community structures including leisure opportunities. Art and music should include participation and appreciation activities that provide potential leisure pursuits. Home economics can provide food preparation skills while industrial arts/technology education introduces other skills. The ultimate goal is preparation for a positive leisure life-style based on individual choices after developing a positive attitude, becoming aware of activity opportunities, and developing appropriate social interaction skills.

Mechanisms for Developing Leisure Opportunities

The best way to build a social network and create leisure opportunities is by participating in an ongoing, organized leisure group. Such groups usually meet one to five times a month around a similar interest. For children groups such as the Boy Scouts, Girl Scouts, and 4-H Clubs provide a structured social environment. For adolescents there are clubs that meet for folk dancing, aerobics, canoeing, bike riding, birdwatching, dog shows, computers, crafts, exercise, and team sports. Learners can join religious social groups, book clubs, bible study groups, and political action groups. Leisure opportunities can also be developed while volunteering for various community service groups, hospital auxiliaries, or school or church activities. In addition, many high schools have developed social clubs designed to facilitate social interactions, and potentially friendships, between learners with disabilities and their nondisabled peers. These groups provide adolescents with opportunities to meet peers with similar interests, and learners may develop friendships beyond these special interests.

Friendships may also develop as learners participate in inclusive leisure opportunities with a designated peer who acts as a "social coach." This peer helps the learner with disabilities (a) become aware of how his or her behavior impacts others, (b) learn to

Action Plan 13.4   Leisure Options

A leisure option is an activity that is appropriate for a specific time and place in which an individual can choose to participate during his or her free time, in order to bring some level of personal satisfaction. To choose a leisure option, an individual must

1. Recognize free time
2. Know the leisure options that are appropriate and available during that free time
3. Have attitudes or preferences about the leisure options
4. Know how to manage and budget necessary resources to participate in a chosen leisure activity
5. Have the skills to access and participate in the leisure activity
6. Engage in appropriate social behavior related to that activity.

interpret others' body language, and (c) learn to accept feedback about social behaviors. If the learner does not understand social mores or conduct, the social coach answers questions, models appropriate behavior, and provides relevant feedback. The social coach provides opportunities for the learner to practice behaviors and role play prior to the actual social event and provides emotional support as the learner navigates the social scene.

Identifying Appropriate Leisure Options

A leisure option is defined as an activity that is appropriate for a specific time and place in which individuals can choose to participate during their free time, in order to bring some level of personal satisfaction. As highlighted in Action Plan 13.4, in order to choose a leisure option, an individual must

1. Recognize free time
2. Know the leisure options that are appropriate and available during that free time
3. Have the skills to participate in the leisure options
4. Have formed attitudes or preferences about the leisure options.

The initial step in providing effective leisure education for adolescents with disabilities, therefore, is to determine the specific leisure options that are available and appropriate for each individual learner in an average week. Once the leisure options are identified, each adolescent can be taught the skills required to participate successfully in those options.

Inventories

One effective method of determining available and appropriate leisure options and resources for an adolescent with disabilities is to use inventories of relevant people and places in that adolescent's life (Ryndak & Alper, in press). As highlighted in Action Plan 13.5, inventories may be completed for

1. The environments in which the adolescent currently lives or will live in the near future, including the home, school, workplace, and community settings

Action Plan 13.5 Use of Inventories to Identify Potential Leisure Education Content

To determine leisure options from which each learner's leisure education content should be chosen, we suggest the use of three types of inventories:

1. Inventories of environments
2. Family inventories
3. Inventories of coworkers and nondisabled chronological age peers.

2. The adolescent's family members
3. The adolescent's peers at school, in the community, and at work.

Figure 13.1 displays a schema incorporating the procedures required when using numerous inventories to determine potentially appropriate leisure education program content for an adolescent. Such inventories allow the teacher to change the focus of a program from predetermined content to content based on an individual adolescent's needs and choices (Ryndak & Alper, in press).

Inventories of Environments. Inventories of environments are concerned with the settings in which an adolescent currently spends time or will spend time in the near future (Schloss & Sedlak, 1986). As discussed in previous chapters, it is particularly important to identify both the current and future environments for each adolescent in order to ensure that the learner has all the skills necessary to succeed both now and upon leaving the education program. This information can then be used to build a leisure education program for each learner.

Inventories of environments are compiled in four steps. In step one, all of the environments that are or will be used by an adolescent are identified. These should include the adolescent's home, school, workplace, and community settings. Additional community settings may be identified through sources such as the Yellow Pages, local recreation department, community agencies, or youth organizations. In step two, the environments are divided into subenvironments representing each of the areas of the main environment that the learner comes into contact with. In step three the teacher identifies the leisure options that are available and appropriate in each of the subenvironments. Step four consists of identifying how the learner can participate independently in each of the leisure options.

In the following example inventories are used to prepare an adolescent to use leisure effectively at home. First, identify both where the adolescent currently resides and the most probable options for homes after leaving the educational program (e.g., independent or sheltered living in an apartment or home). Second, in each of those home settings, identify the subenvironments with which the adolescent will come into contact (e.g., bedroom, laundry area, balcony, entryway). Third, identify the leisure options that naturally occur in those subenvironments (e.g., listening to music, reading, barbecuing, conversing). Fourth, for each of those leisure options, list the steps that the adolescent must complete in order to participate successfully in that leisure option. This is frequently referred to as a *task analysis*. Although it is critical at this point to have a general idea of the skills required for each leisure option, it may not be necessary to complete a detailed task analysis at this time. Rather, it might be more appropriate to do so after identifying the priority leisure options for each student.

To be effective, the procedure should be carried out for one subenvironment at a time. In this way, all of the leisure options that exist in those subenvironments will be identified, along with the regularly occurring opportunities and times to participate in those options. Once all of the leisure options have been identified, it is easy to move systematically through the list and determine whether each of the leisure options has already been taught to an adolescent. If it has already been taught, verify that the student

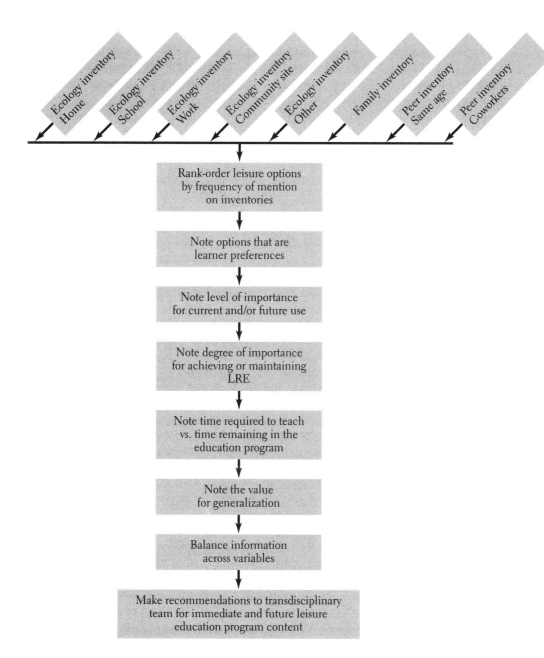

FIGURE 13.1   Identifying Leisure Options Appropriate to Teach a Learner

can participate effectively in that leisure option at the appropriate time in those settings. If a leisure option has not been taught to the adolescent, consciously choose either to teach that leisure option or not to teach it. The main reason to decide not to teach that leisure option would be that the adolescent has a greater need or desire to learn another leisure option.

How could one leisure option be more important to learn than another, when both are appropriate and available in an environment? Here's an example. Adolescents are almost always taught traditional recreation activities such as those found in almost every recreation curriculum. Frequently, however, we neglect to teach adolescents how to use their time in situations that are not specifically leisure centered. A commonly neglected leisure opportunity that occurs in a subenvironment in the home is the time spent waiting for the wash cycle to end while doing laundry. Although this leisure opportunity occurs in most home environments, adolescents are seldom taught appropriate leisure options for this time. It might be important for an adolescent to learn a leisure option to fill this time in a positive manner to deter him or her from either wasting time or using the time in a destructive or trouble-making manner. This situation and its leisure options would then be considered more important than teaching the adolescent another leisure option in the home setting.

Similar examples can be cited at school, in the community, and at work. For example, consider the leisure opportunities available when

1. Going between classes in the hallway
2. Waiting for a school bus or public bus
3. Riding the bus
4. Eating lunch at a shopping mall
5. Standing in a long line at the bank
6. Leaving a concluded church service
7. Walking with a coworker through several corridors
8. Waiting for some supplies or materials required for work
9. Leaving at the end of the workday, before catching transportation home.

Each of these is a commonly occurring situation in which appropriate leisure behaviors are required for successful inclusion in the environment. Each of these is also frequently overlooked in the leisure education content for individual adolescents. When inventories of environments are used, the situations that are experienced by each individual adolescent become obvious. Appropriate leisure options can then be identified for the leisure education curriculum content for that adolescent. In this way, we ensure that each adolescent is prepared to succeed in the leisure opportunities he or she encounters.

Family Inventories.   Numerous authors have described the use of a family inventory to determine the most appropriate curriculum content for learners with disabilities (Ryndak & Alper, in press). Completing a family inventory for an adolescent with disabilities requires the teacher to meet with the adolescent and his or her family members (or other primary caregivers). During this meeting, a set of structured questions might be asked regarding the leisure options in which both the adolescent and the family members participate and the leisure life-style already established by the adolescent. Through this set of questions, the teacher should be able to determine

1. Leisure opportunities that occur throughout the adolescent's average week
2. Leisure options in which the adolescent already participates, with or without the family
3. The adolescent's level of performance in each of those leisure options
4. Leisure options in which the family participates, with or without the adolescent
5. Reasons for the adolescent's lack of participation in any of those family leisure options
6. Leisure option(s) that, once learned, would greatly increase the adolescent's participation in the family's leisure
7. The family's preferences regarding the content of the adolescent's leisure education program
8. Leisure plans for future participation.

This information can then be used to determine the most important and relevant leisure education curriculum content for the adolescent, in accordance with individual and family leisure life-styles.

Because the adolescent will soon be transitioning out of educational services, consider not only the family with whom the adolescent currently resides, but also the new significant people with whom the adolescent may reside in the future. For instance, if an adolescent is exiting an education program and transitioning to an apartment-living program, obtain information on the following:

1. Leisure opportunities that occur in that apartment
2. Leisure options that are enjoyed by and important to the individuals with whom the adolescent will most probably be sharing the apartment
3. Leisure opportunities in the neighborhood of the apartment.

If the specific individuals with whom the adolescent will be residing are not known, comparable information should be obtained from other individuals who participate in the apartment-living program. Either way, this information is useful when determining the leisure life-style for which the adolescent must be prepared.

It is through the use of a family inventory that meaningful content can be determined for an adolescent's leisure education program. This program should prepare the adolescent to participate as independently as possible in the leisure opportunities that (a) are available in the home setting and (b) will ensure that the adolescent participates in leisure options with family members.

Peer Inventories. The category set of information that might assist in determining an adolescent's leisure education curriculum content involves identifying the leisure options encountered by nondisabled peers of the same chronological age and coworkers (Joswiak, 1975; Ryndak & Alper, in press). This information can be most easily obtained by asking the adolescent's current and future peers about their weekly leisure options. For peers of the same chronological age, the questions included in this inventory should relate to the leisure options available at specific times at home, at school, in the community, and at work and the specified times these options are available. For coworkers in similar positions, the questions should relate to the leisure options and the specific times available before, during, and after work hours. Through the use of information from inventories of peers and coworkers of the same age, adolescents can be prepared to participate in leisure activities with their nondisabled peers.

Prioritizing Leisure Options from Inventories

After information is gathered from inventories of environments, family inventories, and inventories of a learner's peers, a summary can be developed. The goal of this process is to identify the leisure options that should be recommended to the transdisciplinary team for immediate and future inclusion in the learner's IEP.

Leisure Options from Inventories.   The first step is to determine which leisure options appear on the inventories and how many times each leisure option is considered to be both available and appropriate across environments. It is possible that a leisure option is included in any combination of inventories of environments, family, or the learner's peers. When a leisure option is included on more than one inventory, it can be inferred that the learner will be able to participate in that leisure option in more than one environment once it is learned. In addition, the learner will be able to participate in that leisure option with the various people in those environments.

To determine whether a leisure option is a high priority, simply list each leisure option as it is included in the inventories, tally the number of times it appears on different inventories, and rank those options by the number of times they were identified. The more inventories on which a leisure option is included, the higher it will appear on the rank-ordered list. It will therefore be considered a higher priority for inclusion in an individual learner's leisure education program.

Figure 13.2 illustrates this process with an adolescent learner named Emily. In reviewing the information on inventories across her environments, family, and peers, six leisure options were mentioned most frequently. These options were listed in order of the frequency with which they were mentioned.

Learner Preference.   The second step is to determine which of the identified leisure options are high-preference options for the learner. This step requires the learner to make decisions about his or her leisure preferences, which enhances the potential for leisure satisfaction. The goal is to encourage learners to choose new options that interest them, and not necessarily activities with which they are already familiar. Teachers may need to encourage learners to choose activities in which they need to develop the skills for participation. Learners need to be asked if they want, and are willing, to learn the skills necessary for participation in the identified leisure options. For every identified leisure option, complete information about learner preferences, necessary skills, and resources should be included.

Rank Order	Leisure Option	Learner Preference	Use		Importance to LRE	Time (months)		Generalization	Prioritized Order
			Current	Future		To Teach	Left		
1	Reading or other leisure option while waiting	2	////	//// ///	Required	3	9	High	1
2	Window-shop alone	1	////	//// //	Required	6	9	High	2
3	Plant care	3	/	/	No effect	6	9	Low	6
4	Use of VCR	3	/	/	Helpful	1	9	Medium	5
5	Going to a movie alone	2	/	/	Helpful	5	9	High	3 or 4
6	Day at beach with friends	1	/	/	Required	4	9	High	3 or 4

FIGURE 13.2 Worksheet Example: Identifying Leisure Options Appropriate to Teach Emily

List the leisure options selected by the learner from most to least desirable, and include this information on the worksheet. Indicate the leisure options that were independently selected by the learner as preferred choices with the number one. Rank leisure options that were noted by the learner as ones he or she would like to learn as number two. Finally, rank the leisure options the learner did not want to learn as number three.

In reviewing our example for Emily in Figure 13.2, note that the preferred choices she selected independently were ranked second and sixth in the frequency with which they appeared on the inventories. With encouragement, Emily indicated that she would also like to learn the options ranked first and fifth. However, she did not show an interest in learning the options ranked third and fourth.

Use in Current and Future Situations.   The third step is to identify the number of current and future situations in which the learner could most likely participate in each of the leisure options. Initially, this is done by counting the number of settings listed for each leisure option across the inventories. This information may be incomplete, however, if inventories were not completed across every environment and set of people with which the learner currently comes into contact, or will come into contact in the near future. However, it is important to make predictions about other situations, people, and environments that may be relevant to the learner and to decide which of the listed leisure options will be both available and appropriate. Add these predictions to the tally of current and future situations for each leisure option.

In Emily's case, the options ranked first and second are verified or anticipated as relevant for 12 settings each. The remaining options cannot compare with these options for the number of current and future environments in which they can be used.

Relevance for Inclusion.   The fourth step is to identify the degree to which each of the leisure options is required for the learner to achieve or to remain successful in the least restrictive environment (LRE). LRE for learners with disabilities is still an important issue because it is easy for those exiting an education program to revert to unnecessarily overprotective environments. In the case of learners who are exiting from the education program, the least restrictive environments should include (a) competitive jobs that are either supported or not supported, (b) the most independent home setting available in the learner's community that allows maximum interaction with nondisabled peers, and (c) a self-selected leisure life-style incorporating interactions with peers, neighbors, family members, and coworkers. To prioritize the leisure options according to this variable, determine the extent to which each leisure option

1. Is REQUIRED for achieving or maintaining LRE in at least one environment (e.g., home or work setting)
2. Would be HELPFUL in achieving or maintaining LRE in at least one environment
3. Would have NO EFFECT on achieving or maintaining LRE in any environment.

Add this information to the worksheet.

In reviewing the information in the example for Emily, note that three of the options are required for her to either achieve or maintain access to inclusive settings. Two of the options are considered to be helpful, while one option would have no effect on her inclusion. There are numerous possible explanations for these rankings. For example, Emily may be required to wait calmly for short periods of time and keep herself constructively occupied. At other times, Emily may have free time all day and will need many leisure options to fill her day. The ranking of each option should match the situation in which Emily will be participating.

Instructional Time. The fifth step is to determine the amount of time that will be required to teach each leisure option to the learner. Consider both the complexity of each leisure option and the learning rate demonstrated by the learner in the past on other tasks of similar complexity. Remember that the ultimate goal includes the learner's personal choice and independent participation in the leisure option. Therefore, when considering the complexity of each leisure option, include the following:

1. Learning to recognize the appropriate free time
2. Learning the leisure options that are appropriate and available during the free time
3. Learning the skills required to prepare for the leisure option, including skills such as transportation, preparation of materials, and organizing other participants in the leisure option
4. Learning the skills required to prepare for the next life activity, including skills such as ending the leisure option on time, getting transportation from the leisure option to the next scheduled life activity, and returning or replacing the materials used in the leisure option
5. Developing attitudes or preferences about the leisure option
6. Acquiring appropriate social, interactional and behavioral skills for the activity.

With this information, estimate the amount of time required for the learner to develop the skills for that leisure option with enough proficiency to participate successfully in the option in its natural environments. Record this time estimate on the worksheet under Time-to-Teach.

The best estimate of the time required for a learner to learn a leisure option must then be compared with the amount of time left in the learner's education program.

Do not initiate instruction on a leisure option unless the learner will benefit by mastering the skills needed to participate successfully or has the support and resources to continue learning beyond the school experience. Additional instruction may be provided by the learner's job coach, family, adult service provider, or other available sources in the community. If additional instruction cannot be provided, however, weigh the limited benefits of beginning to learn a high-priority leisure option against completely learning one or more lower-priority options.

Emily has nine months left for educational services. Because of her past learning rates and the amount of instructional time available for leisure education in her school day, it was estimated that between one and six months would be required to teach each of these leisure options.

Generalization. The final step on the worksheet is to determine whether or not the leisure option will generalize to other inclusive environments, since it is possible that a leisure option for one inclusive environment might also be appropriate and available in others. For example, the learner could participate in solitary activities such as reading, needlepoint, or letter writing while at home, on break at work, or riding the bus. Besides activities, the skills needed to participate in one leisure option may also be needed for other leisure options. For instance, learners will require appropriate interaction and social skills, ability to take turns, appropriate behavior, transportation skills, and money management skills when participating in many activities.

Whenever overlap occurs, those leisure options should be considered higher priorities than the leisure options that will neither be usable in other environments nor teach skills that are needed for other activities. To complete the worksheet in this area, simply determine whether each leisure option has a high, medium, or low probability of generalizing to other environments or activities. This information can then be added to the worksheet.

In reviewing the example for Emily, four options are noted to have a high probability of generalizing to other environments or activities. Only the third option, plant care, is considered to have a low probability of generalizing for Emily.

Identifying High-Priority Leisure Options. Once the worksheet is completed, the next task is to review all of the information collected. Pay particular attention to the leisure options that were ranked as the highest priorities across the columns. If those leisure

---

Action Plan 13.6 Variables for Prioritizing Leisure Options

Several variables must be considered when prioritizing leisure options for inclusion in a learner's leisure education program:

1. The number of inventories on which a leisure option is included
2. The extent to which the learner demonstrates preference for a leisure option
3. The number of current and future environments in which the leisure option can appropriately occur
4. The importance of the leisure option for achieving or maintaining access to the learner's least restrictive environments
5. The estimated amount of time required to successfully teach the leisure option to the learner, compared with the amount of educational time remaining for the learner
6. The degree to which the skills learned to enable the learner to participate in the leisure option will generalize to other environments or activities.

options match, it is easy to select them as recommendations to the transdisciplinary team. If those options do not match, however, weigh the importance of the areas on the worksheet. Decide which of the areas is most critical for the learner's successful participation in current and future environments. Action Plan 13.6 lists variables that teachers should consider when prioritizing leisure options.

Careful consideration should be given to the learner's stated preferences. Learner preference provides the motivation for learning all the necessary skills and increases the probability of future participation. Other issues, however, may take priority. For instance, if particular leisure skills are important for the learner to remain employed in an inclusive setting, those leisure skills may become critical to teach even if the associated leisure option ranked low in generalization and learner preference.

When reviewing the options selected as the highest priorities for Emily, note that the first priority is a leisure option in which she can participate while waiting for short times, such as reading. This option is one that is acceptable to Emily, is relevant to the largest number of inclusive settings, can be taught within her remaining educational time, and has a high probability of generalizing to other environments and activities. In contrast, the third option, plant care, has the lowest priority. Although it can be taught in the time remaining in her educational program, it is an option that Emily does not want to learn, is not relevant to many of her environments, will have no effect on her inclusion, and has a low probability of generalizing to other inclusive environments or activities.

The difficult decision for Emily's leisure education program comes when selecting the third-priority option. In this case careful consideration must be given to the amount of time required to teach the first two options. If three months are required to teach the first prioritized option (i.e., a leisure option while waiting) and six months are required to teach the second prioritized option (i.e., window shopping alone), Emily's remaining educational time has already been allocated. There is a possibility, however, that Emily will learn these two leisure options more quickly than projected. If this occurs and there is a month of educational time remaining at the end of the school year, which leisure option should then be taught to Emily? Since the second-priority option (i.e., window shopping) will take about six months, a decision about the third option can wait. This gives Emily's teacher the opportunity to see how quickly and how well Emily can learn the skills required for both reading during short periods and window shopping. Based on this new information, Emily's teacher can re-estimate the amount of educational time required to teach the other two options and make a better-informed choice.

Case for Action 13.2

Your new classroom assignment is in a high school with learners who have mild disabilities. In developing IEPs, you want to be certain to address each learner's leisure educational needs. What steps will you complete to determine the most important leisure education for each learner?

Cross-Curriculum Instructional Content
Addressed through Leisure Education

Leisure education automatically creates opportunities for a learner to practice skills traditionally taught in other curricular areas. It is important to consider each of the curriculum areas that are relevant for an adolescent with disabilities, and to incorporate those areas whenever possible into the leisure education program.

For example, money use and management are traditionally taught within the math curriculum. The contents of the math curriculum are traditionally taught during a specific period of the instructional day. When including leisure education in the curriculum, it is possible to incorporate instruction of money use and management skills within leisure instruction. Money skills are needed when learners (a) must determine whether or not they have the resources to participate in a leisure option, (b) actually participate in a leisure option that costs money (e.g., admission to a movie), or (c) purchase the items required for the leisure option (e.g., audio cassette tapes).

Similar examples may be cited for almost every curriculum area traditionally included in the education program for adolescents with disabilities. Figure 13.3 lists several of these curriculum areas in a worksheet format, including

1. Transportation to, during, or from a leisure option
2. Social behaviors and interaction
3. Self-care and hygiene
4. Functional or leisure reading
5. Money use and management
6. Written communication
7. Time use and management
8. Leisure option participation.

When using this worksheet, list the priority leisure options identified for a learner across the top. For each leisure option, delineate the ways in which various curriculum areas can be addressed throughout the leisure education program. In addition, the worksheet provides a place to identify exactly what situations will be used for instruction in the classroom, school, and community. In each of those locations, identify which of the delineated curriculum areas will be incorporated into the instruction. In this way, you can maximize the time and situations in which a learner is able to use the skills addressed throughout the curriculum.

Case for Action 13.3

In order to maximize the effectiveness of your instructional efforts throughout the year, you want to integrate your instruction for each curricular area into the other areas. How will you determine what other curricular content you can integrate throughout your leisure education program?

Learner: _____

	Priority Activity 1	*Priority Activity 2*	*Priority Activity 3*
Transportation or mobility to, during, or from leisure option			
Social behaviors and interaction			
Self-care and hygiene			
Functional or leisure reading			
Money use and management			
Written communication			
Time use and management			
Leisure option participation			

Time & place for instruction of cross-curriculum content

In classroom (1) (2)	Cross-curriculum content (a) (b)	Cross-curriculum content (a) (b)	Cross-curriculum content (a) (b)

In school (1) (2)	Cross-curriculum content (a) (b)	Cross-curriculum content (a) (b)	Cross-curriculum content (a) (b)

In community (1) (2)	Cross-curriculum content (a) (b)	Cross-curriculum content (a) (b)	Cross-curriculum content (a) (b)

FIGURE 13.3   Worksheet: Cross-Curriculum Content within Identified Priority Leisure Options

Other curriculum areas can easily be added to or substituted on this list, such as self-esteem, personal responsibility, and ability to make choices. Each of these is critical to the development of a positive leisure life-style for any adolescent with disabilities. Determine the curriculum areas for a learner on the basis of his or her particular weaknesses. In this way, you can provide that learner with the most opportunities to learn and practice the skills required for success in his or her environments.

Summary

Leisure education should be an important aspect of the curriculum for all adolescent learners, but especially for those with disabilities. Leisure provides opportunities for self-satisfaction and individual choice that are important elements of human development. The establishment of a positive leisure life-style will have lifetime benefits in all settings. If left to chance, it is likely that learners will develop traditional television-watching activities, or become involved in substance abuse or other inappropriate activities as the basis for their leisure. Such inappropriate activities could further isolate learners with disabilities.

A teacher initially needs to make a commitment to include appropriate leisure education in the curriculum. When doing so, remember that leisure should provide a level of satisfaction for all involved, including the teacher. Consider your own leisure life-style, as well as that of the learners in your classroom. Adults often do not know what to do with their free time to establish a leisure life-style that brings personal satisfaction. How, then, can adults guide students?

Take a moment to consider your own attitudes toward leisure. When was the last time you allowed yourself to "do nothing"? Beyond your job satisfaction, what aspects of your life-style feel good and what aspects need development? Is your leisure life-style satisfactory, or is it in need of development? Given the broad definition of leisure and the diverse leisure options provided in this chapter, can you make choices that reflect a positive leisure life-style for yourself? Can you then teach those same decision-making skills to your students?

Leisure education should be incorporated into all aspects of curricula for adolescents with disabilities. The skills for decision making, social interaction, and community resource utilization essential to leisure education are part of the larger life-preparation aspects of education. Although it is important for all adolescents to learn to manage peer pressure and to select appropriate activities for participation, these skills are even more important for adolescents with disabilities. Unless their leisure education curriculum content is tailor made to cover the social and leisure skills necessary in their specific life situations, adolescents with disabilities will be at risk. They will never have the opportunity to develop the necessary skills unless educators take the time to identify and provide direct instruction on those skills. For adolescents with disabilities, leisure can be the "make or break" aspect of life satisfaction and transition to a successful adulthood.

References

Brannan, S. A., Chinn, K. B., & Verhoven, P. J. (1981). *What is leisure education? A primer for persons working with handicapped children and youth.* Washington, DC: Hawkins & Associates.

Brightbill, C. K. (1966). *Educating for leisure-centered living.* Harrisburg, PA: Stackpole.

Carter, M. J., & Nelson, D. A. (1992). Leisure today: Leisure awareness in society. The *Journal of Physical Education, Recreation and Dance,* 63(8), 25, 55.

Joswiak, K. F. (1975). *Leisure counseling program materials for the developmentally disabled.* Washington, DC: Hawkins & Associates.

Kelly, J. B. (1982). *Leisure.* Englewood Cliffs, NJ: Prentice-Hall.

Peterson, C. A. (in press). *Therapeutic recreation program design: Principles and procedures (3rd ed.).* Englewood Cliffs, NJ: Prentice-Hall.

Ryndak, D. L. & Alper, S. (in press). *Curriculum content for students with moderate and severe disabilities in inclusive settings.* Boston: Allyn and Bacon.

Schloss, P., & Sedlak, R. (1986). *Instructional methods for students with learning and behavior problems.* Boston, MA: Allyn and Bacon.

Sirvis, B., Musante, P., & Bigge, J. L. (1991). Leisure education and adapted physical education. In J. L. Bigge (Ed.), *Teaching individuals with physical and multiple disabilities (3rd ed.),* pp. 428–459). Columbus, OH: Merrill.

Social Skill Instruction

Did you know that . . .

- Social competence is a major factor contributing to the success of community integration for individuals who have disabilities?
- Social skill deficits are frequently the cause of terminations from employment for individuals with disabilities?
- Information gained from social skill assessments can be used to identify goals and objectives for individuals who have disabilities?
- Teacher-developed instruments can be used to assess social skills?
- When developing social skill goals and objectives, one should attempt to look at the overall level of social competence and investigate how target behaviors relate to this total picture?
- A functional social skills program will aid in the acquisition of appropriate skills?
- Training procedures can be evaluated to determine their appropriateness for a given individual?
- Teachers can determine when a specific social skill should be taught?

Can you . . .

- Define social skills?
- Explain why the level of social competence may indicate the least restrictive environment appropriate for youth?
- Describe six assessment procedures that are used to determine social skill deficits?
- Describe the difference between in vivo and analogue observations?
- Explain how social competence and adaptive behaviors relate?
- Explain how prosocial responses will affect an individual's behavior in society?
- Describe a social skills training package?
- Differentiate between affect, cognition, and specific skills training programs?
- Explain why deficits in social skills might promote low self-esteem?

Social competence is gaining increasing attention from professionals seeking to integrate students with disabilities into the mainstream of education and society. A lack of social skills has been reported to relate directly to depressed academic achievement (Bender, 1987; Gresham, 1982; Gresham & Elliott, 1989; Hallahan & Kauffman, 1991). This deficit might be attributed to the importance of student-to-student interactions during instruction and the fact that teachers react more favorably to students who are socially skillful (Shinn, Ramsey, Walker, Steiber, & O'Neill, 1987; Polloway & Patton, 1993).

In addition, a lack of social skills has been found to affect teacher willingness to mainstream students (Kauffman, Lloyd, & McGee, 1989). One study found that teachers and professionals ranked social skills as being the most important curricular area for students with learning disabilities and moderate disabilities (Baumgart, Filler, & Askvig, 1991).

Intelligence, specific disabling condition, and academic achievement have not appeared to be the primary factors contributing to the success of school and community integration (Kelly, 1982; Schloss, 1984; Schloss & Schloss, 1987). Instead, personal characteristics—including personal adjustment, initiative, self-esteem, and social competence—have been reported to directly affect success in the mainstream of society (Bender, 1987; Goldstein, Sprafkin, Gershaw, & Klein, 1980; Schloss, 1984; Schloss & Schloss, 1987).

Social competence greatly affects the placement of students in the least restrictive environment. A student who is deficient in social skills may find placement in a regular education classroom unbearable and restrictive. Deficits in social competence may lead to aggression, withdrawal, and inappropriate adaptive behaviors (Bender & Golden, 1988; Carter & Sugai, 1988; Heavy, Adelman, Nelson, & Smith, 1989) and thus may promote low self-esteem for the individual. An individual student's social skill deficits may also be a principal source of conflict with peers, teachers, and school and community authorities. Authors continue to report the importance of interpersonal skills in school and community adjustment (Lovett & Harris, 1987; Schloss & Schloss, 1987; Schloss, Schloss, & Harris, 1984; Schloss & Sedlak, 1986).

Current legislation in the fields of special education, vocational education, and rehabilitation has encouraged people to support the placement of individuals with disabilities in functional community situations. This trend promotes integrated opportunities for individuals with disabilities, allowing them to profit from socially competent models (Blackbourn, 1989; Gresham, 1981). Even so, individuals who have disabilities do not automatically interact with peers, disabled or nondisabled, and may not acquire social competence vicariously through observation of these individuals (Cartwright, Cartwright, & Ward, 1989; Schloss, 1984). Establishing a social skills program has proven to be effective in promoting the acquisition of social competence (Schloss & Sedlak, 1986; Polloway & Patton, 1993; Hallahan & Kauffman, 1991).

Outside of school, the specific disabling condition and achievement do not appear to be influential variables in the employment success of individuals with disabilities. Those components that do intervene and promote occupational success include personal adjustment, self-assurance, self-esteem, initiative, and social competence (Goldstein et al., 1980; Martin, Rusch, Lagomarcino, & Chadsey-Rusch, 1986; Schloss & Schloss, 1985; Schloss & Sedlak, 1986).

Greenspan and Shoultz (1981) conducted a study to determine why individuals with mental retardation were terminated from competitive employment. Results showed that the inability to interact effectively with other people often causes termination. Occupational skill level was not a major factor. Extending this finding, Schloss and Schloss (1985) have argued that adjustment problems in employment settings often result from an inability to integrate socially in the work setting. The employee with disabilities is often viewed negatively because he or she fails to interact effectively with supervisors, coworkers, and customers. Deficiencies in social functioning are often overgeneralized to correlate with deficiencies in overall performance.

Social skill training programs have made a positive impact on students with disabilities and highlight the importance of integrating social skill objectives into a school's curriculum (Blackbourn, 1989; Carter & Sugai, 1988; Nelson, 1988; Schloss & Sedlak, 1986). Social skill programs should incorporate a positive approach, emphasizing skill building in deficit areas, and maximizing the potential of an individual with disabilities for success in school and the community.

Definition of Social Skills

Social skills are complex abilities a person needs to adjust to changing social demands. They depend on the specific social context (Masters & Mori, 1986). Individuals must develop flexible social response mechanisms that will allow behavior to change as each situation demands. The inability to change behavior or responses usually results in rejection or failure.

Repeatedly, the term *social skill* has been defined using two different conceptual approaches: (1) a global reference to the domain of social competence and (2) an emphasis on situation-specific responses. Exemplifying the global approach, Hersen and Bellack (1986) defined social competence as the effectiveness of an individual to state positive and negative feelings without producing negative feelings in others. Other researchers have supported this definition, emphasizing that social competence will produce satisfying consequences from the environment (Gresham & Elliott, 1989; Schloss & Schloss, 1987; Polloway & Patton, 1993).

The specific approach emphasizes the idiosyncratic nature of social skills. Differing social responses may be demonstrated in various environmental contexts. Appropriate social skill responses during vocational activities will vary from those in consumer or recreational activities. For example, it is desirable to interact freely during leisure skill pursuits. However, frequent interactions may be a cause for terminating employment.

For instructional purposes, the situation-specific approach has greater utility because it allows educators to target and assess specific skills (Schloss & Schloss, 1987; Stowitschek, McConaughy, Peatross, Salzberg, & Lignugaris-Kraft, 1988; Polloway & Patton, 1993). For example, social/vocational survival skills would include those behaviors that "increase the likelihood of successful competitive employment in any vocational setting"

(Rusch, 1979, p. 143). Social/consumer survival skills might include those behaviors that promote the likelihood of successful consumer actions (i.e., purchasing groceries at a grocery store). Instruction can be directed precisely at this objective.

Even greater specificity can be achieved by considering the exact nature of expected responses. Some may include eye gazing, conversational skills, question asking, self-disclosures, and compliments (Downing, 1987; Schloss & Schloss, 1985). A specific skill approach can help improve the management of a general skills approach. First, students are aware of associations with specific interpersonal contexts. Second, responses are available in reliable observations. Third, skills may be matched to the student's chronological age. Fourth, specific social skills are constructive in nature, leading directly to the formulation of goals and objectives.

Establishing Objectives

Specific definitions of social competence must be integrated into a larger conceptual system or curriculum. This curriculum should reflect the complexity of the learner as well as his or her social environment. Of specific concern is the interrelationship between variables, including the student's skill deficits, developmentally appropriate skills displayed by the student's cohorts, and social skills expected by significant individuals in the school and community (Schloss & Sedlak, 1986). Students with mental disabilities (Matson & DiLorenzo, 1986; Sargeant, 1988) tend to require more sharply focused training in role taking; decision making; discriminating decisions; and understanding what others are perceiving, thinking, and feeling. Vaughn, Ridley, and Cox (1983) have identified several skills necessary for an individual to be socially competent. An instructional program was designed around these skills and includes the following components: (a) fundamental language concepts, (b) cue sensitivity, (c) goal identification, (d) empathy, (e) alternative thinking, (f) consequential thinking, (g) procedural thinking, and (h) integrating skills.

Social competence must be taught to youth in the schools to ensure that they will adjust to the community after school. Specific objectives to be taught should be related to the characteristics of each student. Of specific concern are the student's age and cognitive abilities (Browning & White, 1986; Carlson, 1987). Sargeant (1988, p. 10) developed six questions to aid teachers in determining when a specific social skill should be taught:

1. *Is the social skill deficient or inadequate?*
2. *Does the student have the cognitive ability to learn the skill?*
3. *Will the student have sufficient opportunity to practice the skill?*
4. *Will changing the student's behavior affect significant others in the student's life?*
5. *Is the skill needed in current or anticipated environments?*
6. *Is acquisition of the skill essential to the individual's ability to remain in their current environment?*

Consistent with this view, Smith and Schloss (1990) have suggested the following considerations for identifying social skill objectives:

1. *Partner.* The relationship of the student to those with whom he or she is interacting is a critical variable. A student may be taught to be informal, brief, irreverent, and so on, when interacting with peers. When talking to an employment supervisor or school administrator, he or she may be instructed to be more formal, respectful, elaborate, and so on.

2. *Setting.* The environment in which the social interactions are occurring is another variable in determining the specific social skills to be taught. As with the partner, more informal interactions may be appropriate in home and leisure settings. Conversely, more elaborate and "proper" interpersonal behavior may be expected in school, work, and consumer settings.

3. *Major skill area.* Another consideration, and possibly the most important, the actual purpose for the interaction will have a major influence on the actual skill. Questioning, complimenting, engaging in small talk, and criticizing are all potentially discrete skills. Each may involve different interpersonal responses.

4. *Role (to vs. from).* The role of the student is the last element in arriving at final objectives. Asking whether the student is principally receiving the compliment or criticism, or delivering the interaction will aid the teacher in determining the role he or she should be trained to perform.

Smith and Schloss (1990) have provided the table in Figure 14.1 to illustrate the manner in which these considerations are interdependent. Two hundred and eighty cells are constructed using the preceding variables. The first cell, indicating one potential objective, is teaching how to ask questions in order to obtain information from an adult at home. The final cell is teaching how to criticize a peer for damaging property in a leisure setting.

Social Validation of Goals and Objectives

A question that constantly arises when developing social skills programs is that of social validation: To what extent does this program affect one's social behavior in society? Will this new behavior promote positive reinforcers? Validation of a social skills program will help students with disabilities gain prosocial responses (Matson & DiLorenzo, 1986; Schloss & Schloss, 1987; Wildman, Wildman, & Kelly, 1986). These responses will (a) enlarge the number of people with whom they interact; (b) increase the number of positive social reinforcers they receive; (c) decrease the number of aversive events; and (d) promote self-control when they are confronted by environmental situations. Socially validated criteria must be developed before a skills program is implemented.

Implementing a social skills program depends on three measures of social validity (Wolf, 1978): (1) the significance of the goals; (2) the importance of the effects of the program; and (3) the appropriateness of the procedures used to implement the program. Measuring the significance of a program's goals is to ask: Is this the prosocial response

Setting	Partner	Home				School				Work				Consumer				Leisure			
Major Skill Area / **Subareas**		from adult	from peer	to adult	to peer	from adult	from peer	to adult	to peer	from adult	from peer	to adult	to peer	from adult	from peer	to adult	to peer	from adult	from peer	to adult	to peer
Questions — Requesting information																					
Questions — Favor																					
Questions — Assistance																					
Questions — Invitation																					
Compliments — Global																					
Compliments — Appearance																					
Compliments — Skill level																					
Compliments — Possession																					
Small Talk — Initiating																					
Small Talk — Terminating																					
Criticisms — Appearance																					
Criticisms — Violating rules																					
Criticisms — Skill level																					
Criticisms — Damaging property																					

FIGURE 14.1   Table Showing Interdependence of Social Skills

Source: Reprinted with permission from: *Teaching Social Skills to Hearing-Impaired Students* by P. J. Schloss and M. A. Smith. Copyright 1990, by the Alexander Graham Bell Association for the Deaf, 3417 Volta Place, NW, Washington, DC 20007.

Case for Action 14.1

Your students continue to show deficits in social competence and you would like to implement a structured program into your curriculum. To do this, you first must write a rationale and submit it to your principal. Describe your rationale.

---

society wants? To find the answer it is important to socially compare responses (Kazdin & Matson, 1981; Matson & DiLorenzo, 1986; Maag, 1989) by observing a group of normal-functioning individuals under a range of natural conditions. For example, when determining criteria for complimenting a person of the opposite sex, several normal-functioning individuals (of both sexes) are observed complimenting individuals of the opposite sex in work, school, and social settings. Another strategy would be to ask individuals for feedback specific to a setting. For example, interview a teacher when observing in a school setting. This strategy, although subjective, will help to establish the social importance of the program's effect.

Measuring the appropriateness of training procedures can be accomplished by answering one of three questions: (1) Is the intensity of each training procedure justified by the program's final outcome? (2) Are the training procedures the most appropriate means to achieve the final outcome? and (3) Is the program cost effective? These questions can be answered easily and will provide socially validating information for a social skills program before implementing it. Justifying the intensity of objectives can be done by collecting relevant information pertaining to the students' reaction to the impact of the program. This can also be completed for other concerned individuals (e.g., parents, school principal). When determining what training procedures would be most appropriate to accomplish a specific goal, it is important to select the ones to be used with great care. Various research studies (Hollin & Trower, 1986a; Schloss & Schloss, 1987) have reported noting specific procedures as significantly effective when training students in social skills. A review of the literature will aid the reader in selecting appropriate procedures.

Measuring the cost effectiveness of a program will determine whether the program is worth the allocation of resources. This is conducted by establishing the actual cost of the program and then determining the cost of each objective achieved by the program. The relative value of the program can then be determined by those individuals concerned.

Assessing Social Competence

Consistent with the instructional model described in Chapter 4 of this text, social skill assessment serves three major purposes. First, assessment is conducted to describe the characteristics of the learner accurately and objectively. This information is subsequently used to establish annual goals and short-term objectives. Second, social skill assessment is conducted to determine the extent to which the goals and objectives are being achieved through instruction. Finally, social skill assessment is conducted to identify deficiencies in the instructional process. Assessment data may indicate to the teacher specific approaches that are ineffective and objectives that require more intensive intervention.

Hammill (1987) has recommended several general principles for assessing social skills. First, review all information currently available that relates to the student's characteristics. School records provide a historical perspective to any potential problems. They may be used to assess the origin of the difficulties as well as to suggest potentially effective intervention strategies.

Second, use existing information and your own observations to determine that the potential problem is of sufficient magnitude to warrant intervention. Many times what an individual teacher perceives to be a problem is not offensive to the student, his or her peers, and other teachers. If this is the case, the teacher's own attitudes or expectations may need to be altered as opposed to the student's behavior.

Third, conduct assessments under conditions as close to natural ones as possible. This guideline will ensure that results are not influenced by contrivances of the assessment situation. For example, a student may perform better under the one-to-one direction of an examiner when contrasted to a group performance situation.

Fourth, go beyond the evaluation of a student by evaluating the environment. It is widely recognized that responses do not occur in isolation. They are all motivated in part by attributes of the environment. In some cases the learner may behave appropriately and the environment may be defective. For example, a teacher may note, on the basis of subjective reports, that a student fights with others often. A close observation of the environment may reveal that he spends a substantial amount of time with aggressive youths in unstructured competitive situations. One may conclude that it is wrong for these situations to occur frequently through the school day and that remediation should be directed at this aspect of the environment.

Fifth, assess the learner and environment continuously. It is important to recognize that social performance is not static. Just as students' academic skills improve or regress, so does their social functioning. Equally important, social skill performance for any individual is highly variable. A student may be highly glib one day and very sedate the next. Isolated observations may not be sensitive to these changes.

Sixth, collect multiple measures to ensure that intervention is effective. Simply noting a reduction in a target response may not indicate that an intervention was truly effective. Was the student pleased with the change to the extent that the improvement will be sustained following schooling? Were others pleased with the change to the extent that they are more willing to interact with the student?

Seventh, we should all be aware that our observations and conclusions are filtered through our own values, biases, and preferences. Again, we must do more than substantiate that we are satisfied with the goals, objectives, and the subsequent extent of the change. The learner, his or her parents, employers, and other significant individuals must contribute to the conclusion that the student is improving.

Five methods are commonly used to assess social skills: (1) self-reports, (2) self-monitoring, (3) reports and ratings by others, (4) direct observation, and (5) commercial instruments.

Self-Reports

Self-report techniques may be the most commonly used procedure in the assessment of social skills (Hollin & Trower, 1986b; Schloss & Schloss, 1987). Glassi and Glassi (1979), for example, have identified a dozen self-report measures of interpersonal functioning. These instruments are generally used to identify goals and objectives for a training program. They may also be used to determine whether the student is satisfied with the outcome of the training program.

Figure 14.2 illustrates a sample self-report instrument. The inventory is used by asking students to record the perception of their individual ability in each of the areas. The instructor may read items to less capable students. The inventory is scored by considering each response and looking for patterns of strengths and weaknesses as perceived by the student. These patterns should be corroborated through direct observation and reports of others. This approach aids the teacher in identifying specific

---

Your response on this inventory will be used to identify possible objectives to be included in a social skills training program. Review each item and circle the number that best describes your ability.

1. Small talk: Initiating and terminating conversations with

Peers at school

1	2	3	4	5
Poor	Below average	Average	Above average	Excellent

Authority at school

1	2	3	4	5
Poor	Below average	Average	Above average	Excellent

Peers at work

1	2	3	4	5
Poor	Below average	Average	Above average	Excellent

Authorities at work

1	2	3	4	5
Poor	Below average	Average	Above average	Excellent

Peers at community sites

1	2	3	4	5
Poor	Below average	Average	Above average	Excellent

Authorities at community sites

1	2	3	4	5
Poor	Below average	Average	Above average	Excellent

FIGURE 14.2   Self-Report Inventory

intervention targets as opposed to looking for a total score indicative of generally low social performance.

Limited abstract thinking skills, memory deficits, time boundedness, and poor social perception problems of many youths with disabilities may reduce the usefulness of self-reports. Because of the complexity of social interactions, a student's self-appraisal may not be an accurate reflection of reality. Also, teachers' and students' expectations may alter their views of social performance. Moreover, questions and response options used on an inventory may not have the same meaning to all respondents.

Self-Monitoring

Self-monitoring is another frequently used procedure. Students are encouraged to monitor their activity of a specific target behavior and report their findings to the teacher (Hollin & Trower, 1986b; Schloss & Schloss, 1987). This procedure may not be appropriate for evaluating a training program because of its subjectivity and the possibly limited reliability of individuals recording their own performance. It is a useful method, however, for use as an adjunct data collection procedure.

Figure 14.3 illustrates a page from a standard daily calendar carried by many business executives. In this example, the calendar is marked as an interval recording device. Every half hour, the youth may indicate whether or not specific interpersonal skills were exhibited. The teacher may meet daily with the youth to discuss the self-monitoring log. He or she should initially reinforce the student for recording accurately. Later the teacher may reinforce the student for correct recording and a desirable rate of the target behavior.

An obvious advantage of this format is its age appropriateness. The daily calendar is a device carried by a large number of "high status" adults. Consequently, the student is unlikely to suffer pejorative reactions for the use of the recording device.

Aside from recording responses in school, self-monitoring can be used to assess a student's behavior in the community, at work, or at home. Once the behavior has been identified, the student can be asked to record his or her responses in other settings and to report back to the teacher. An adult daily calendar can again be used for this purpose. This procedure may allow the teacher to gain insight on the generalization of the skill or transfer of learning outside the school setting to community environments.

Reports and Ratings by Others

This procedure is similar to the self-report procedure. Instead of obtaining a student's self-perception, the professional obtains the perceptions of others (Schloss & Sedlak, 1986). For example, a teacher may ask the parent to complete the self-report inventory presented in Figure 14.2. Or, a less structured interview may be conducted with individuals who are in a position to evaluate the student's behavior (e.g., parents, siblings, peers).

Reports and ratings by others are subjective and based on individual perceptions. Information received should not be used as a basis for evaluating the effectiveness of a training program. Instead, this procedure can be used to gain additional insight into the

March 23, 1990

8:00 _____ *Talked with friend on bus* _____

8:30 _____ *Greeted teacher* _____

9:00 _____ *Etc.* _____

9:30 _____

10:00 _____

10:30 _____

11:00 _____

11:30 _____

12:00 _____

12:30 _____

1:00 _____

1:30 _____

2:00 _____

2:30 _____

3:00 _____

3:30 _____

4:00 _____

FIGURE 14.3   Self-Monitoring

appropriateness of training priorities and the general value to the individual and society of the training outcomes.

Direct Observation

Direct observation has been used frequently in applied skill training programs. High reliability and validity of behavior recordings can be achieved, and data can be used to evaluate the effectiveness of a training program. Chapter 5 describes observational methods that may be appropriate for this purpose.

One advantage of the procedure is that behavioral data can be recorded in an objective manner (Schloss & Sedlak, 1986). Two common observations used for data collection are in vivo and analogue. In vivo observations are those conducted during a specific period of time in the natural setting (e.g., conversation in the cafeteria during lunch). Analogue observations are those not conducted in a natural setting (e.g., conversation in a simulated cafeteria setting during class time), but through situation performance tests in a simulated setting.

Techniques used to record observations include (a) narrative recording, (b) event recording, (c) duration recording, (d) interval recording, and (e) time sampling. A description of each is found in Action Plan 14.1.

Commercial Instruments

Commercial publishing houses have marketed a number of instruments that may be useful in assessing social skills of youths who have disabilities. Many of these instruments can provide objective information to teachers (Masters & Mori, 1986). Unfortunately, they may have the same limitations that teacher-made instruments possess. First, they require either an accurate self-appraisal or an accurate appraisal by others. As noted earlier, students' self-appraisals may be limited by their cognitive abilities. The appraisal of others may be limited by their frame of reference. Parents may provide glowing reports not shared by teachers. Benevolent work supervisors may be highly positive while the actual employer, concerned about the bottom line, may be more critical.

The principal limitation of these instruments is that they are marketed for a mass audience across the country. The questions and potential responses are not referenced to the demands of individual communities. For example, what may be described as being aggressive in Boone County, Missouri, may be assertive behavior in New York City. Commercial instruments are not sensitive to these regional and community differences. Furthermore, they solicit very general information that may not be sufficiently specific to suggest intervention priorities or to assess the effects of intervention. The Cain-Levine Social Competency Scale (Cain, Levine, & Elzey, 1963), for example, includes only ten items used to measure interpersonal skills.

One feature recommending these scales is that a substantial amount of research and development work has gone into their construction. Many have extensive national norms providing reliable comparisons between a student's performance and that of a national

Action Plan 14.1   Recording Techniques

We recommend the following techniques when recording direct observations:

1. *Narrative recording.* Written record of student behaviors, time and duration of observation, environmental conditions, and actions of others present.
2. *Event recording.* A tally of each occurrence for a specific target behavior.
3. *Duration recording.* A recording of the length of time that a target behavior occurs.
4. *Interval recording.* A method used to record one or more behaviors in a given specified time period.
5. *Time sampling.* A recording of behavior that is exhibited after a predetermined time period lapses.

sample. The Adaptive Behavior Inventory (ABI; Brown & Leigh, 1986), for example, provides detailed information for two separate normative groups (Normal Intelligence and Mentally Retarded) with over 1,000 individuals in each group. The ABI reports characteristics of these samples not only in terms of the usual demographic information such as age, sex, and geographic location, but also describes such categories as type of classroom placement, presence of other disabling conditions, urban/rural residential status, parent education and occupation, ethnicity, and language spoken in the home. Data extracted from the *Statistical Abstract of the United States* (U.S. Department of Commerce, 1980) are also published in the ABI manual to permit the reader to ascertain the representativeness of the sample. The percentages reported for the normative samples are very similar to those reported for the population at large, and thus provide credence to the claim for national representativeness.

With these strengths and limitations in mind, we encourage the reader to use commercial instruments as general screening devices. More highly focused teacher-made instruments are recommended for evaluating intervention effects. The commercial instruments commonly used are described in Action Plan 14.2.

Action Plan 14.2   Commercial Instruments

When considering the use of commercial instruments for assessment, you may wish to review one or more of the following for examples. These are just five of many available for your use.

1. Behavior Rating Profile (Brown & Hammill, 1983) provides an ecological assessment of social skill behaviors. Developed for use with children and youth in the age range of 6.6 to 18.6 years. Administered in a minimum amount of time.
2. Vineland Adaptive Behavior Scale (Sparrow, Balla, & Cicchetti, 1984) assesses social competence in four areas of adaptive behavior and one area of maladaptive behavior. Developed for use with individuals from birth to age 19. Designed to be completed by interviewing a knowledgeable informant such as the parent or teacher in approximately one hour.
3. AAMD Adaptive Behavior Scale: School Edition (Lambert, Windmiller, Tharinger, & Cole, 1993) assesses the extent the student meets the social expectations in a school setting. Developed for use with students in the age range of 3.3 to 17.2 years. Observation of specific skills is recorded and scored in approximately 15 to 30 minutes.
4. Devereux Adolescent Behavior Rating Scale (Spivack, Spotts, & Haimes, 1967) assesses the social-affective skill development of youth 13 to 18 years of age. A behavior checklist is completed by an attendant or teacher in 10 to 15 minutes.

Case for Action 14.2

One of your students will not converse with peers in a community setting. How would you assess this social skill to get further information?

General Principles of Social Skill Instruction

Social skill instruction is an approach aimed at increasing interpersonal skills in critical life situations (Hudson, 1986; Lovett & Harris, 1987; Martin et al., 1986). It emphasizes the positive educational aspects of treatment rather than the elimination of maladaptive behaviors (McGinnis, Goldstein, Sprafkin, & Gershaw, 1984). Social skill training follows the assumption that individuals perform select responses and choose the most effective ones in their repertoire when faced with demanding social situations. Owing to cognitive limitations and/or deficient learning histories, the best available response may be viewed by others as being maladaptive. The specific maladaptive behavior can be overcome or compensated for through appropriate training. This training is expected to lead the individual to replace the offensive behaviors with prosocial behaviors.

Training generally consists of a variety of specific procedures, such as social reinforcement, modeling, behavior rehearsal, feedback, and homework.

Social Reinforcement

Social reinforcement is defined as the use of interpersonal interactions to influence the future strength of an individual's behavior (McGinnis et al., 1984; Schloss & Sedlak, 1986). Social reinforcement is advocated in social skill programs because social interactions are motivators for prosocial behavior in natural settings. Parents, peers, and authority figures tend to rely on social reinforcement, which emphasizes its importance to the student. Verbal praise, gestures, and physical contact are the primary social reinforcers used in social skill development. Schloss (1984) has suggested the guidelines presented in Action Plan 14.3 for increasing the effectiveness of social reinforcement.

Modeling

Modeling is defined as learning by imitation (Carter & Sugai, 1988; Herbert, 1986). Modeling is an effective and reliable technique for teaching new behaviors and strengthening deficit behaviors. Learning through modeling occurs by observing an individual's appropriate behavior and imitating the exact behavior. Depending on an individual's competence and ability to discriminate, preplanned observations may be necessary to promote social skill acquisition. Both prosocial and disruptive behaviors can be learned through modeling. A youth learns to be aggressive by observing others being reinforced for aggressive behavior. Conversely, a youth acquires assertive skills by observing others gain satisfaction from socially skillful interactions. Action Plan 14.4, adapted from Schloss (1984), suggests strategies for enhancing the value of peer models.

Behavior Rehearsal

Behavior rehearsal is defined as a situation in which an individual or group of individuals is asked to take a role, to enact a specific situation. By acting out a situation, the students gain insight into specific social skill approaches. Behavior rehearsals are an ideal way of developing behaviors to replace the disruptive responses targeted by punishment

Action Plan 14.3 Social Reinforcement

The following guidelines are suggested for use when incorporating social reinforcement principles:

1. Define target behaviors.
2. In developing a new behavior, follow every occurrence of the behavior by social reinforcement. As the behavior occurs more consistently, social reinforcement should be reduced.
3. Verbally state the behavior likely to result in social reinforcement, using the youth's name when possible.
4. Verbally label process and product behaviors. For example, "Mark, I like the way you wrote your name (process). It is easy to read (product)."
5. Deliver social reinforcers enthusiastically.
6. Any time unnatural incentives are used, pair them with social praise. This will develop the reinforcement value of social praise.
7. Avoid socially reinforcing maladaptive responses.
8. Encourage significant others to socially reinforce the desired behavior(s) in a range of settings.

Action Plan 14.4 Modeling

The following strategies are suggested for use when implementing modeling principles:

1. Specify the behaviors to be influenced through modeling.
2. Arrange situations so that the individual is likely to observe others engaging in the specified (target) behaviors.
3. When another individual engages in the target behaviors, label it verbally, using the person's name (e.g., "You're dressed quite neatly today, Joan").
4. When the youth engages in an approximation of the target behavior, label it verbally, using his or her name (e.g., "You dressed nicely also, Matt").
5. Expose the youth to a variety of models and settings to increase the likelihood that the behavior change will generalize to other settings.
6. Use high-status models when possible, because they will have a stronger influence on the observer's behavior.
7. Avoid situations in which the youth observes maladaptive behavior produce satisfying consequences.

Remember, youths who are easily influenced are more likely to learn through observation.

programs. For example, the youth can be asked to demonstrate a "better way" to act once a disruptive behavior has occurred. Action Plan 14.5 lists nine strategies for implementing behavior rehearsal principles.

Feedback

Feedback is defined as providing the student information on how well he or she performed (Maguire, 1986) during training. Providing students with frequent and clear feedback during training will reinforce their behavior and encourage them to attend future training sessions. Feedback may be offered by the teacher/trainer or by other peers participating in the training. If it is implemented by the teacher/trainer, the student receives immediate social reinforcement after a specific activity and/or behavior by the teacher/trainer. During a training session, peers might provide spontaneous reinforcement (e.g., cue cards, flashing lights) when a specific behavior is exhibited. If this did not occur or was not arranged, peers could then provide reinforcement following the behavior/activity. Action Plan 14.6 provides a list of examples that can be used for feedback by peers and teachers/trainers.

Homework

Homework provides students frequent opportunities to practice social skills (McGinnis et al., 1984; Smith, Schloss, & Schloss, 1984) outside of the training program. This technique may be structured, in that students are told the exact skill or procedure to practice and then asked to report back to the instructor. Homework may also be unstructured, in that students are asked to practice what they have learned and then to report

---

Action Plan 14.5   Behavior Rehearsal

The following guidelines are suggested for use when implementing behavior rehearsal principles:

1. Determine the behavior to be developed.
2. Identify the natural antecedents or signals for the behavior.
3. Identify the natural consequences of the behavior.
4. Decide when to practice the desired response under the natural antecedent and consequent conditions.
5. Develop a plan for rehearsing the desired behaviors.
6. Verbally label the desired response, its antecedents, and its consequences.
7. Use other social learning techniques (e.g., modeling, shaping, and social reinforcement) with behavior rehearsal procedures when necessary.
8. Rehearse the desired behavior under a variety of conditions to enhance generalization (the extent to which the behavior will occur in other settings).
9. Socially reinforce the rehearsed behavior as it occurs naturally.

Action Plan 14.6   Feedback

The following examples are suggested feedback behaviors that can be used by teachers and peers during social skill training programs:

1. Social reinforcement—verbal praise, gestures, physical contact
2. Progress charts and graphs—noting behavior
3. Material reinforcers—awards, points to earn awards, certificate of accomplishment
4. Lights and buzzers—signaling when appropriate or inappropriate behaviors are exhibited
5. Cue cards—identifying the response expected.

back to the class. Action Plan 14.7 presents a sample structured homework assignment. Action Plan 14.8 provides a general unstructured recording form.

Additional Instructional Considerations

Numerous approaches can be used to teach social skills. They depend on a wide range of variables, from age and cognitive ability to communication skills. Improving social competence is a longitudinal process and should be conducted over a student's entire

Action Plan 14.7   Structured Homework

Structured homework assignments may be designed somewhat like this example:

HOMEWORK FORM

Accepting Praise

Name: _____   Date: _____

Directions: After someone praises you, answer these questions:

1. Who praised you?
2. What did they say?
3. Did you smile?
4. Did you say thank you?
5. What else did you say?
6. How did you do? _____ Super _____ OK _____ Poor

Action Plan 14.8   Homework Recording

An example of a general unstructured homework recording is illustrated below:

HOMEWORK

Name: _____   Date: _____

A. Assignment:

   Steps to Follow:

   1. _____
   2. _____
   3. _____
   4. _____
   5. _____
   6. _____
   7. _____
   8. _____
   9. _____
   10. _____

B. Did you do all of the assignment steps?
C. Circle those that you did not complete.
D. How did you do? _____ Super _____ OK _____ Poor

---

school career. Students must attain sufficient social affect and adequate social skills and exercise social cognition to become socially competent (Goldstein et al., 1980; Sargeant, 1988).

Students who think better about themselves will tend to have a better social affect than those who do not. Affect is part of all social behavior and is best taught when integrated into all instructional areas, including academics, self-care, and vocational preparation. Mainstreaming alone is unlikely to improve social affect (Jenkins, Speltz, & Odom, 1986). It can improve a student's disposition if specific socially enhancing activities are structured by the teacher. Cooperative learning, for example, has been shown to be effective in improving peer relations and affect (Johnson & Johnson, 1983). This

Case for Action 14.3

You have a 12-year-old boy in your classroom who is high functioning although considered educationally disabled. He exhibits inappropriate social behaviors in the classroom, which annoys his peers. These include vocalizations when he wants the teacher's attention, tongue clicking when he is reading silently, and staring at peers when he wants to initiate a conversation. Are these behaviors deficient? What behaviors should be taught? What instructional procedures would you follow?

instructional procedure has been reported to provide students who have disabilities with twice as much interaction as in competitive learning situations.

Cognitive behavior modification is another useful strategy (Sargeant, 1988). Students are taught specific skills that alter the way they analyze and respond to a social problem. The teacher may provide a problem and the student may then be asked to verbalize an approach to solving the problem. Strategies are rehearsed and applied when needed. Various programs with a modified version of cognitive behavior modification have been found to have a significant effect on an individual's social affect (Browning & White, 1986; Goldstein et al., 1980; McGinnis et al., 1984; Polloway & Patton, 1993).

Teaching specific social skills to individuals has consistently been reported in the literature (Clement-Heist, Seigel, & Gaylord-Ross, 1992; Foxx, McMorrow, & Schloss, 1983; Mace & Murphy, 1991; McGinnis et al., 1984; Mesibov & LaGreco, 1981; Misra, 1992; Schloss & Schloss, 1984; Schloss, Smith, & Schloss, 1988; Schloss, Thompson, Gajar, & Schloss, 1985; Smith, Schloss, & Schloss, 1984; Wheeler, Bates, Marshall, & Miller, 1988). Direct instruction is used for teaching specific social skills and relies heavily on social reinforcement, modeling, role playing, feedback, and homework techniques.

Summary

Social skills continue to gain increasing attention among the teachers of students with disabilities. When these students are integrated into the community, intelligence, disability, and academic achievement are not as great a concern as social competence. Social skill deficits do appear to make a significant impact on the vocational success of individuals with disabilities. Students without such skills tend to be viewed negatively because they do not interact much with others. Instead, deficiencies become overgeneralized to unrelated competencies.

Deficits in social competence are defined as the discrepancy between the student's achieved skill level and what is expected. This discrepancy can be measured by teacher-made and commercial assessment instruments. Once deficits are identified, objectives are prepared that reflect all information known about the student's learning and behavioral characteristics.

Social skill training is typically composed of a package of techniques most appropriate for the social skill to be taught. Social skills should be taught throughout a student's educational program and integrated into all areas of instruction, including academics, self-care, and vocational preparation.

References

Baumgart, D., Filler, J., & Askvig B. A. (1991). Perceived importance of social skills: A survey of teachers, parents, and other professionals. *The Journal of Special Education, 25,* 236–251.

Bender, W. N. (1987). Secondary personality and behavioral problems in adolescents with learning disabilities. *Journal of Learning Disabilities, 20,* 280–285.

Bender, W. N., & Golden, L. B. (1988). Adaptive behavior of learning disabled and non-learning disabled children. *Learning Disability Quarterly, 11,* 55–61.

Blackbourn, J. M. (1989). Acquisition and generalization of social skills in elementary-aged children with learning disabilities. *Journal of Learning Disabilities, 22,* 28–34.

Brown, L. L., & Hammill, D. D. (1983). *Behavior Rating Profile.* Austin, TX: Pro-Ed.

Brown, L., & Leigh, J. E. (1986). *Adaptive Behavior Inventory.* Austin, TX: Pro-Ed.

Browning, P., & White, W. (1986). Teaching life enhancement skills with interactive video-based curricula. *Education and Training of the Mentally Retarded, 21,* 236–244.

Cain, L., Levine, S., & Elzey, F. (1963). *Manual for the Cain-Levine School Competency Scale.* Palo Alto, CA: Consulting Psychologists Press.

Carlson, C. I. (1987). Social interaction goals and strategies of children with learning disabilities. *Journal of Learning Disabilities, 20,* 306–311.

Carter, J., & Sugai, G. (1988). Teaching social skills. *Teaching Exceptional Children, 54,* 68–71.

Cartwright, G. P., Cartwright, C. A., & Ward, M. E. (1989). *Educating special learners* (3rd ed.). Belmont, CA: Wadsworth.

Clement-Heist, K., Seigel, S., & Gaylord-Ross, R. (1992). Simulated and in situ vocational social skills training for youths with learning disabilities. *Exceptional Children, 58,* 336–345.

Downing, J. (1987). Conversational skills training: Teaching adolescents with mental retardation to be verbally assertive. *Mental Retardation, 25,* 147–155.

Foxx, R. M., McMorrow, M. J., & Schloss, C. N. (1983). Stacking the deck: Teaching social skills to retarded adults with a modified table game. *Journal of Applied Behavior Analysis, 16,* 157–170.

Glassi, J. P., & Glassi, M. D. (1979). Modification of heterosocial skill deficits. In A. S. Bellack & M. Hersen (Eds.), *Research and practice in social skills training* (pp. 131–187). New York: Plenum.

Goldstein, A. P., Sprafkin, R. P., Gershaw, N. J., & Klein, P. (1980). *Skill-streaming the adolescent: A structured learning approach to teaching prosocial skills.* Champaign, IL: Research Press.

Greenspan, S., & Schoultz, B. (1981). Why mentally retarded adults lose their jobs: Social competence as a factor in work adjustment. *Applied Research in Mental Retardation, 2,* 23–38.

Gresham, F. M. (1981). Social skills training with handicapped children: A review. *Review of Educational Research, 51,* 139–176.

Gresham, F. M. (1982). Misguided mainstreaming: The case for social skills training with handicapped children. *Exceptional Children, 48,* 422–433.

Gresham, F., & Elliott, S. N. (1989). Social skills deficits as a primary learning disability. *Journal of Learning Disabilities, 22,* 120–124.

Hallahan, D. P., & Kauffman, J. M. (1991). *Exceptional children: Introduction to special education* (5th ed.). Englewood Cliffs, NJ: Prentice Hall.

Hammill, D. D. (1987). *Assessing the abilities and instructional needs of students.* Austin, TX: Pro-Ed.

Heavy, C. L., Adelman, H. S., Nelson, P., & Smith, D. C. (1989). Learning problems, anger, perceived control, and misbehavior. *Journal of Learning Disabilities, 22,* 46–50, 59.

Herbert, M. (1986). Social skills training with children. In C. R. Hollin & P. Trower (Eds.), *Handbook of social skills training* (Vol. 1, pp. 11–32). Elmsford, NY: Pergamon.

Hersen, M., & Bellack, A. (1986). Assessment of social skills. In A. R. Ciminero, K. S. Calhoun, & H. E. Adams (Eds.), *Handbook of behavioral assessment* (2nd ed., pp. 189–207). New York: Wiley.

Hollin, C. R., & Trower, P. (1986a). Social skills training: A retrospective analysis and summary of applications. In C. R. Hollin & P. Trower (Eds.), *Handbook of social skills training* (Vol. 1, pp. 1–10). Elmsford, NY: Pergamon.

Hollin, C. R., & Trower, P. (1986b). Social skills training: Critique and future development. In C. R. Hollin & P. Trower (Eds.), *Handbook of social skills training* (Vol. II, pp. 237–259). Elmsford, NY: Pergamon.

Hudson, B. L. (1986). Community applications of social skills training. In C. R. Hollin & P. Trower (Eds.), *Handbook of social skills training* (Vol. II, pp. 239–266). Elmsford, NY: Pergamon.

Jenkins, J., Speltz, M., & Odom, S. (1986). Integrating normal and handicapped preschoolers: Effects on child development and social interaction. *Exceptional Children, 52,* 7–17.

Johnson, R., & Johnson, D. (1983). Effects of cooperative, competitive and individualistic learning experiences on social development. *Exceptional Children, 49,* 323–329.

Kauffman, J., Lloyd, J., & McGee, K. (1989) . Adaptive and maladaptive behavior: Teacher attitudes and their technical assistance needs. *The Journal of Special Education, 23,* 185–200.

Kazdin, A. E., & Matson, J. L. (1981). Social validation in mental retardation. *Applied Research in Mental Retardation, 2,* 39–53.

Kelly, J. A. (1982). *Social skills training: A practical guide to intervention.* New York: Springer.

Lambert, N., Windmiller, M., Tharinger, D., & Cole, L. (1993). *Manual for AAMD Adaptive Behavior Scale: School edition* (2nd ed.). Washington, DC: American Association on Mental Deficiency.

Lovett, D. L., & Harris, M. B. (1987). Important skills for adults with mental retardation: The client's point of view. *Mental Retardation, 25,* 351–356.

Maag, J. W. (1989). Assessment in social skills training: Methodological and conceptual issues for research and practice. *Remedial and Special Education, 10*(4), 6–15.

Mace, F. C., & Murphy, D. M. (1991). Training interactional behaviors of adults with developmental disabilities: A systematic replication and extension. *Journal of Applied Behavior Analysis, 24,* 167–174.

Maguire, P. (1986). Social skills training for health professionals. In C. R. Hollin & P. Trower (Eds.), *Handbook of social skills training* (Vol. II, pp. 143–166). Elmsford, NY: Pergamon.

Martin, J. E., Rusch, F. R., Lagomarcino, T., & Chadsey-Rusch, J. (1986). Comparison between nonhandicapped and mentally retarded workers: Why they lose their jobs. *Applied Research in Mental Retardation, 7,* 467–474.

Masters, L. F., & Mori, A. A. (1986). *Teaching secondary students with mild learning and behavior problems: Methods, materials, strategies.* Rockville, MD: Aspen Systems.

Matson, J. L., & DiLorenzo, T. M. (1986). Social skills training and mental handicap and organic impairment. In C. R. Hollin & P. Trower (Eds.), *Handbook of social skills training* (Vol. II, pp. 67–90). Elmsford, NY: Pergamon.

McGinnis, E., Goldstein, A., Sprafkin, R. P., & Gershaw, N. J. (1984). *Skill-streaming the elementary child.* Champaign, IL: Research Press.

Mesibov, G. B., & LaGreco, A. M. (1981). A social skills instructional module. *Directive Teacher, 3,* 6–7.

Misra, A. (1992). Generalization of social skills through self-monitoring by adults with mild mental retardation. *Exceptional Children, 58,* 495–507.

Nelson, C. M. (1988). Social skills training for handicapped students. *Teaching Exceptional Children, 20*(4), 19–23.

Polloway, E. A., & Patton, J. R. (1993). *Strategies for teaching learners with special needs* (5th ed.). New York: Merrill/Macmillan.

Rusch, F. R. (1979). Toward the validation of social vocational survival skills. *Mental Retardation, 17,* 143–145.

Sargeant, L. R. (1988). *Systematic instruction of social skills* (Project SISS) (2nd ed.). Des Moines: Iowa Department of Education.

Schloss, C. N., & Schloss, P. J. (1984). Evaluation of table game designed to promote the acquisition of vocationally oriented social skills with mildly and moderately retarded adults. *Journal of Industrial Teacher Education, 21*(2), 12–25.

Schloss, P. J. (1984). *Social development of handicapped children and adolescents.* Rockville, MD: Aspen Systems.

Schloss, P. J., & Schloss, C. N. (1985). Contemporary issues in social skills research with mentally retarded people. *Journal of Special Education, 19,* 269–282.

Schloss, P. J., & Schloss, C. N. (1987). A critical review of social skills research in mental retardation. In R. P. Barrett & J. L. Matson (Eds.), *Advances in developmental disorders.* Greenwich, CT: JAI Press.

Schloss, P. J., Schloss, C. N., & Harris, L. (1984). A multiple baseline analysis of an interpersonal skills training program for depressed youth. *Behavior Disorders, 9,* 182–188.

Schloss, P. J., & Sedlak, R. A. (1986). *Instructional methods for students with learning and behavior problems.* Boston: Allyn and Bacon.

Schloss, P. J., Smith, M. A., & Schloss, C. N. (1988). Analysis of the relative efficacy of self-monitoring and feedback in the development of emotion adjectives with hearing impaired persons. *Behavior Modification, 12,* 82–89.

Schloss, P. J., Thompson, C., Gajar, A., & Schloss, C. N. (1985). Influence of self-recording on heterosexual conversational behaviors of head trauma youth. *Applied Research in Mental Retardation, 6,* 269–281.

Shinn, M. R., Ramsey, E., Walker, H. M., Stieber, S., & O'Neill, R. E. (1987). Antisocial behavior in school settings: Initial differences in an at risk and normal population. *Journal of Special Education, 21,* 69–84.

Smith, M. A., & Schloss, P. J. (1990). *Social skills development of hearing impaired youth.* Washington, DC: Alexander Graham Bell Association for the Deaf.

Smith, M. A., Schloss, P. J., & Schloss, C. N. (1984). Social skills perspectives in the education and treatment of deaf persons. *Journal of the British Association of Teachers of the Deaf, 8*(6), 157–163.

Sparrow, S. S., Balla, D. A., & Cicchetti, D. V. (1984). *Vineland Adaptive Behavior Scales.* Circle Pines, MN: American Guidance Service.

Spivack, G., Spotts, J., & Haimes, P. E. (1967). *Devereux Adolescent Behavior Rating Scale Manual.* Devon, PA: Devereux Foundation.

Stowitschek, J. J., McConaughy, E. K., Peatross, D., Salzberg, C. L., & Lignugaris-Kraft, B. (1988). Effects of group incidental training on the use of social amenities by adults with mental retardation in work settings. *Education and Training in Mental Retardation, 23,* 202–212.

U.S. Department of Commerce. (1980). *Statistical abstract of the United States.* Washington, DC: Department of Commerce, Bureau of the Census.

Vaughn, S., Ridley, C., & Cox, J. (1983). Evaluating the efficacy of an interpersonal skills training program with children who are mentally retarded. *Education and Training of the Mentally Retarded, 18,* 191–196.

Wheeler, J. J., Bates, P., Marshall, K. J., & Miller, S. R. (1988). Teaching appropriate social behaviors to a young man with moderate mental retardation in a supported competitive employment setting. *Education and Training in Mental Retardation, 23,* 105–106.

Wildman, B. G., Wildman, H. E., & Kelly, W. J. (1986). Group conversational skills training and social validation with mentally retarded adults. *Applied Research in Mental Retardation, 7,* 443–458.

Wolf, M. M. (1978). Social validity: The case for subjective measurement—or how applied behavior analysis is finding its heart. *Journal of Applied Behavior Analysis, 11,* 203–214.

Chapter *15*

Teaching in the Content Areas

Did you know that . . .

- The majority of secondary students with special needs will be educated in regular high school classrooms?
- The majority of secondary special educators have no specific training in the content areas?
- There are two major approaches to teaching science?
- No recent work has been completed involving teaching social studies to secondary students with disabilities?
- There are three components to an effective teaching approach that will benefit all students, not just those with disabilities?
- Peer-mediated strategies enhance academic and social interaction skills?

Can You . . .

- Differentiate between a content approach and a skills approach to secondary special education?
- Identify how the science curriculum is organized in your state?
- Identify how the social studies curriculum is organized in your state?
- Identify content enhancement techniques?
- Develop an advanced organizer?
- Develop a graphic organizer?
- Develop a study guide that uses short-answer questions?
- Develop a study guide that uses a framed outline?
- Develop a study guide that uses matching items?
- Develop a mnemonic device?

As described in Chapter 1 and mentioned periodically throughout this text, the Regular Education Initiative has had a major impact on the delivery of services to students with special needs. This includes those students with disabilities who are in high school. No longer is it automatically assumed that they would be served more appropriately in separate, self-contained classrooms. Rather, the majority of secondary students with special needs will receive their education in traditional classroom alongside their nondisabled peers. Undoubtedly, some students will receive the assistance of resource specialists in separate classrooms; nonetheless, secondary teachers should expect and be prepared to meet the educational needs of students with disabilities for all or part of the school day. Chapter 4 presented instructional methods, including learning strategies and direct instruction, that secondary teachers can use to assist students with disabilities in mastering essential information. Subsequent chapters described specific applications of this information to enhance reading, mathematics, written language, listening and speaking, and social skill development. Suggestions for written language, listening and speaking, and social skills should be useful to all secondary educators, regardless of the content area. Recommendations offered in Chapters 10 and 11 should be useful to secondary educators whose content areas are related to reading and mathematics. In this chapter, we turn our attention to other content areas addressed in typical high school programs, specifically social studies and science.

McKenzie (1991) differentiated between two methods for providing secondary special education services: a content approach and a skills approach. A special educator using a content approach provides instruction in English, language, science, social studies, and other areas to students who it is believed will not profit from inclusion in secondary settings. The skills approach enhances basic reading, writing, computation, and social skills so that secondary students with disabilities can perform better in mainstream classes. McKenzie (1991) reported that the content approach was used by 79% of the teachers surveyed; the skills approach was used by 19%. Nolet and Tindal (1993) suggested that special educators have been more concerned with reducing basic skill deficits of secondary students than with what students are expected to do with these skills. They advised special educators to shift their instructional focus toward the acquisition and use of content knowledge. This shift will not be easy. The special educator is more likely to have an undergraduate or graduate degree in special education, certification to teach special education, and no specific training in a content area. Patton, Polloway, and Cronin (1987) surveyed special educators who taught social studies and reported that 43% of the respondents had no training in social studies education. Because their teachers probably lack background in a content area, special education students probably do not receive instruction comparable to that of peers enrolled in mainstream content area classes (Nolet & Tindal, 1993). Secondary teachers generally have expertise and teacher certification in a content area. Thus, it is more likely that secondary educators will possess a better understanding of the content they are supposed to teach.

Mastery of the content area, existing teaching expertise, the effectiveness of instructional strategies for all students (regardless of the presence of disabilities), and the availability of resource specialists and consulting teachers combine to make the secondary classroom an appropriate placement for many students with disabilities. In this chapter, we discuss science and social studies in more detail and offer suggestions to both regular and special educators that will enhance the success experienced by secondary students with disabilities in typical high school classrooms.

Science Education

There is a heightened awareness that students in the United States do not compare favorably to students from other countries in their knowledge of science and technology (Blough & Schwartz, 1990). As a result, a great deal of national attention has focused on the quality of science education programs (Rutherford & Ahlgren, 1990). Although not specifically mentioned in national report cards, students with disabilities are greatly affected by the quality of science education available in U.S. schools. The U.S. Office of Special Education reported that more than half of all students with disabilities receive instruction in science and mathematics in regular classes (U.S. Department of Education, 1991). Thus, problems associated with the either the content or the methodology of science education programs and the measures developed to address them will affect students with disabilities.

The Science Curriculum

In the secondary school, science may be divided into several separate areas. In New York, for example, the high school science curriculum is divided into five major areas: earth science, environment, biology, chemistry, and physics. As illustrated in Action Plans 15.1 and 15.2, each of these areas is further divided into units, then subdivided into categories

---

Action Plan 15.1   Units Covered by Major Areas in Science

All educators dealing with secondary students with disabilities should understand how the topics in the science curriculum are arranged. In New York, the following units are studied in chemistry (Bureau of Curriculum Development, 1984):

1. Matter and energy
2. Atomic structure
3. Bonding
4. Periodic table
5. Mathematics of chemistry
6. Kinetics and equilibrium
7. Acids and bases
8. Redox and electrochemistry
9. Organic chemistry
10. Application of chemistry principles
11. Nuclear chemistry.

Action Plan 15.2 Subcategories of the Science Curriculum

In New York, each unit within a major heading is subdivided further. For example, chemistry begins with the study of matter and energy. Matter and energy include the following subdivisions (Bureau of Curriculum Development, 1984):

1. Definition of chemistry
2. Matter
   a. Substances
   b. Mixtures
3. Energy
   a. Forms
   b. Energy and chemical change
   c. Measuring energy
4. Phases of matter
   a. Gases
   b. Liquids
   c. Solids.

of study. Science may be organized differently in other states; therefore, regular and secondary educators are encouraged to obtain copies of the curriculum for any content areas for which they assume teaching responsibilities.

Approaches to Teaching Science

The diversity of curricula, the implications that a well-structured curriculum can have for the development of higher-order thinking skills, and the applicability of content to daily living make science a particularly useful content area for students with disabilities. Despite its importance, very little specific information is available regarding the appropriateness of the science instruction provided to students in either regular or special education settings (Parmar & Cawley, 1993). If student grades can be used as indicators, however, then the picture is dismal. Cawley, Kahn, and Tedesco (1989) reported that between 50% and 70% of secondary students with disabilities received grades of "D" or lower.

Scruggs and Mastropieri (1993) classified approaches currently available for teaching science into two general categories: content-oriented approaches and activities-oriented approaches. Each approach is discussed separately.

The Content-Oriented Approach

The content-oriented approach is the most commonly used approach in regular education settings. It relies heavily on the textbook as a primary medium of instruction. In addition, the content-oriented approach requires verbal communication skills. Specifically, students must be able to listen to a lecture, comprehend extensive vocabulary, discuss information, read the text, study, and complete written assignments. These activities are occasionally supplemented with films, filmstrips, or videos. Many topics are covered in the content-oriented approach; however, few are addressed in detail. Progress is measured on the basis of responses to written test items that emphasize basic facts over in-depth mastery of material.

Scruggs and Mastropieri (1993) identified the major disadvantage of the content-oriented approach for students with disabilities. Specifically, language deficits typically experienced by these students seriously undermine their abilities to listen, discuss, and read and write independently. In the absence of modifications or adaptation, secondary students with disabilities will perform poorly in science education classes dominated by the content-oriented approach.

The Activities-Oriented Approach

The activities-oriented approach has also been referred to as the *discovery, inquiry,* or *constructivist* perspective (Roth, 1989) and is based on the work of development theorists such as Piaget. While there are occasional teacher presentations, the activities-oriented approach highlights the use of small groups so that students can explore concepts. These explorations require students to observe, classify, measure, predict, and infer. Because explorations require more time to conduct, fewer topics are covered; however, they are studied in greater detail. In addition, students can develop their independent-thinking and problem-solving skills. The activities-oriented approach deemphasizes reading, vocabulary, and terminology. Progress is measured through performance-based assessment rather than traditional paper-and-pencil formats.

Many benefits are associated with the activities-oriented approach for students with disabilities. Tripp (1991) reported that science becomes more meaningful for students. They learn skills essential for mastery of *all* content areas, not just science. For example, students learn to observe, investigate, gather data, and report. Another benefit is that hypothesizing, creating new problems, and inventing and synthesizing new ideas all contribute to the development of creativity. Scruggs and Mastropieri (1993) noted that the deemphasis on reading and vocabulary may relieve students with disabilities of many frustrating task demands. The use of performance-based assessment also allows students to show what they know about science rather than write about it.

Social Studies Education

The Social Studies Curriculum

Just as science is broken down into major sections, so too is the secondary social studies curriculum divided into major areas. In New York, ninth and tenth graders typically study global studies; eleventh graders study U.S. history and government, and twelfth graders study economics and economic decision making (Bureau of Curriculum Development, 1987a, 1987b, 1987c). Action Plan 15.3 illustrates how these major areas are divided into units. Action Plan 15.4 illustrates the subdivisions included in a unit on U.S. history and government.

Action Plan 15.3   Organizing the Secondary Social Studies Curriculum

Teachers should be aware of the units of study included in major areas of the social studies curriculum. New York State includes the following units:

Global Studies
(Ninth and Tenth Grades)
1. Africa
2. South and Southeast Asia
3. East Asia
4. Latin America
5. The Middle East
6. Western Europe
7. Eastern Europe
8. The World Today

U.S. History and Government
(Eleventh Grade)
1. Constitutional Foundations
2. Industrialization
3. Progressive Movements
4. At Home and Abroad
5. U S. in the Age of Global Crisis
6. A World in Uncertain Times

Economics and Economic Decision Making (Twelfth Grade)
1. Introduction to Economics and Economic Systems
2. Microeconomics
3. Macroeconomics
4. The U.S. and the World Economy

Approaches to Teaching Social Studies

If very little information is available regarding effective science instruction for secondary students with disabilities, even less is known about teaching social studies to these students. A review of the professional literature published since 1988 failed to produce any empirically based methods or techniques for teaching social studies to secondary students with disabilities. Techniques appropriate for use by secondary educators working with normally achieving students include reading, role playing, discussion, debate, and problem solving. Readers interested in detailed discussions of these methods are referred to Dobkin, Fischer, Ludwig, and Koblinger (1985); Gross, McPhie, and Fraenkel (1969); and Wesley and Wronski (1973).

Content Enhancements

It has been noted that very few instructional methods have been documented as effective for secondary students with special needs. As a result, regular and special educators working with secondary students with disabilities must assume responsibility for developing, implementing, and evaluating instructional methods. Adding to the problem is that many secondary teachers must complete this task while meeting the needs of *all* students enrolled in the class, not just those with special needs.

Action Plan 15.4   Units of Study in Major Social Studies Areas

Teachers should familiarize themselves with units addressed by major areas of the social studies curriculum. In New York State, Constitutional Foundations is organized into the following units:

1. The Constitution
   A. Foundations
   B. The Constitutional Convention
   C. The Bill Of rights
   D. Basic Constitutional Principles
   E. Basic Structure and Function
   F. Implementing the New Constitutional Principles
2. The Constitution Is Tested
   A. Constitutional Stress and Crisis
   B. The Civil War.

Hudson, Lignugaris-Kraft, and Miller (1993) identified three components of an effective and efficient teaching approach that can benefit all secondary students, not just those with disabilities. They are listed in Action Plan 15.5. First, they recommend use of an instructional cycle that sequences planning, implementing, and evaluating instruction. Steps in this sequence include a daily review, a homework check, the presentation of new information, guided then independent practice, and weekly and monthly reviews. These steps were described in detail in Chapter 4. The second component is the integration of effective teaching practices into each phase of the instructional cycle. For example, a teacher may begin a lesson by reviewing homework or previously learned material, providing a rationale for learning the new material, or stating the objectives of the lesson. During the presentation of new information, a teacher should give a demonstration, use several examples, allow students with several opportunities to practice the skill and ask questions, and provide feedback regarding performance. This information was also discussed in detail in Chapter 4. The third component is the use of content enhancements, that is, adaptations or techniques to help students identify, organize, understand, and remember important information. Although professionals have not taken a united stand on the nature of these adaptations in content areas such as science (Parmar & Cawley, 1993), secondary teachers in both regular and special education settings should be aware of them and how they can be used to assist learners with disabilities. Careful use of these enhancements and thorough evaluations of their effects can contribute to professional resources.

Hudson and colleagues (1993) and Ellis and Sabornie (1990) identified several content enhancement techniques that have been used successfully with secondary students with disabilities. They are listed in Action Plan 15.6 and include advanced organizers, visual displays, study guides, mnemonic devices, audio recordings, and peer-mediated strategies. Although we discuss these techniques separately, teachers may

---

Action Plan 15.5 Components of Effective Teaching for Secondary Students

Hudson and colleagues (1993) recommended three components of a teaching approach that will benefit all students, not just those with disabilities. They include the following:

1. Use an instructional cycle that sequences planning, implementing, and evaluating instruction.
2. Integrate effective teaching practices into each phase of the instructional cycle.
3. Use content enhancement techniques.

---

opt to combine several within a single lesson. Again, we advise careful evaluation of their effects on student performance.

Advanced Organizers

A teacher uses an advanced organizer at the beginning of a lesson to provide the secondary student with information about what is to be covered. This information can include the tasks that will be performed; topics or subtopics to be presented; background information; new vocabulary; or anticipated student outcomes. An advanced organizer can be written on the blackboard, an overhead transparency, or a handout distributed to the class. The teacher may opt to use a verbal format, either by describing this information or by using questions to elicit it from the students. Figure 15.1 is a sample advanced organizer for a social studies lesson.

Visual Displays

Secondary teachers can use visual displays to illustrate the relationship between two or more pieces of information contained in a content area lesson. Visual displays or graphic organizers (GOs) were discussed in Chapter 4. They can be used during all phases of

---

Action Plan 15.6 Content Enhancement Techniques

Hudson and colleagues (1993) and Ellis and Sabornie (1990) described several content enhancement techniques, including the following:

1. Advanced organizers
2. Visual displays
3. Study guides
4. Mnemonic devices
5. Audio recordings
6. Peer-mediated instruction.

The Civilizations of Africa

  I. Influence of Geography
     A. Rivers
        1. Limited navigatability
     B. Savannahs
     C. Mountains and plateaus
     D. Lakes
 II. Languages
     A. The role of linguists
     B. Bantu
     C. Nilotes
III. Oral Traditions
     A. Examples
     B. Importance to African clans, villages, and dynasties
 IV. Music and Archeology

**FIGURE 15.1   Advanced Organizer for a Social
Studies Lesson in Global Studies**

instruction to highlight and organize essential information into a meaningful whole. Thus, students do not appear to be learning a series of unrelated terms, facts, or concepts.

Horton and Lovitt (1989) described a four-step procedure for constructing GOs. These steps are presented in Action Plan 15.7. First, the teacher chooses a chapter that has proven difficult for students to master or that is, in the teacher's opinion, poorly written. The teacher breaks this chapter into passages of approximately 1,500 words. The text and the resulting GO can be completed by most students within a typical lesson. Next, the teacher outlines the main ideas contained in the passage. Third, the teacher

---

Action Plan 15.7   Graphic Organizers

Secondary teachers can help students see relationships among terms, facts, or concepts by using graphic organizers (GOs). Horton and Lovitt (1989) identified four steps necessary to construct a GO:

1. Select and divide text chapters into passages of about 1,500 words.
2. Make an outline of the main ideas of the passage.
3. Choose the appropriate GO format. A hierarchical format arranges major and minor categories into an outline format. A compare-contrast format is appropriate for text that involves similarities and differences.
4. Prepare teacher and student versions of the GO.

selects an appropriate GO format. Two options include a hierarchical format and a compare-contrast format. A hierarchical format resembles an outline in that it presents major and minor points. A compare-contrast format illustrates similarities and differences. Completed sample graphic organizers are presented in Figures 15.2. and 15.3. Finally, the teacher prepares teacher and student versions of the GO. Ideally, the GO is clear and simple and can be presented on a single page. The teacher's version contains all the necessary information. The student's version has specific information deleted from it.

To use the GO in a lesson, the teacher first has the students mark the beginning and end of the relevant passage, then read it silently for 15 minutes. Books are then closed and student copies of the GO are distributed. The teacher presents his or her copy for 30 seconds (perhaps using a transparency on an overhead projector) and discusses the relationships among the items included on the GO. Items are then covered with pieces of paper. The teacher asks questions regarding the information that goes in each box, and students write correct answers on their copies of the GO.

Study Guides

A study guide is a set of statements or questions that relate directly to printed materials in textbooks (Horton, Lovitt, Givens, & Nelson, 1989). Reviewing a study guide prior to a

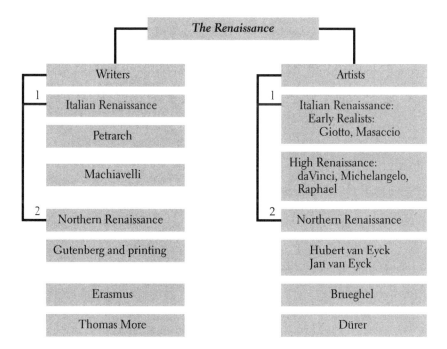

FIGURE 15.2   Sample Graphic Organizer in a Hierarchical Format for a Global Studies Lesson

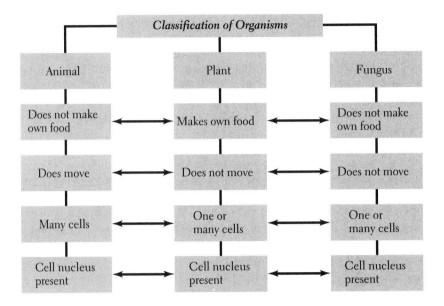

FIGURE 15.3   Sample Graphic Organizer in a Compare-Contrast Format for Life Science

lesson heightens a student's awareness of the key information that is about to be presented. Hudson and colleagues identified many study guide formats described in the professional literature, including short-answer questions, framed outlines, and matching items. Figures 15.4, 15.5, and 15.6 illustrate these formats.

Mnemonic Devices

Mastropieri and Scruggs (1988) have advocated the use of mnemonic devices with secondary students with disabilities. These devices are verbal or pictorial techniques that facilitate the recall of content area information by making it easier to remember. You may already be familiar with the use of mnemonics. Perhaps when studying for a test involving a sequence of steps, you used the first letter of each step to create a word. During the test, you wrote the word in the margin of your booklet then wrote a complete answer. This is a *first-word mnemonic.* Secondary teachers can use this technique to help students remember information. For example, Nagel, Schumaker, and Deshler (1986) used TEENS to help students remember the sensory organs (tongue, ears, eyes, nose, and skin). HOMES can help students remember the names of the five Great Lakes (Huron, Ontario, Michigan, Erie, and Superior). Other mnemonic devices involve pictures. For example, a student may be given a picture of a familiar object that is phonetically similar to a novel term. Mastropieri, Scruggs, and Levin (1986) used a picture of a box to help students remember a mineral called *bauxite.*

Answer these questions.

What are the properties of nonmetals? _____

_____

_____

Identify three nonmetals. _____

_____

How are nonmetals different from metals? _____

_____

_____

**FIGURE 15.4   Study Guide Format Using Short-Answer Questions for
Physical Science**

Audio Recordings

Much of the information that secondary students are expected to master is gained by independently reading their textbooks. Obviously, a student with limited reading abilities is at a disadvantage. In Chapter 4, we suggested that secondary teachers tape record

---

1. Copernicus argued against the _____ theory. He believed the

   _____ was the center of the universe (p. 137).

2. _____ was a great mathematician who proved Copernicus's

   _____ theory (p. 138).

3. Galileo used a _____ to study the planet _____ and prove

   that Copernicus was correct. (p. 139).

FIGURE 15.5   Study Guide Using a Framed Outline for a Global Studies Lesson

Rocks	Characteristics
1. Igneous rocks	Fine-grained
2. Intrusive rocks	Form as a result of temperature and pressure changes
3. Extrusive rocks	The most common rocks on earth
4. Metamorphic rocks	Coarse-grained

FIGURE 15.6   Study Guide Using Matching Items

sections from textbooks that students with disabilities find difficult to read. Students can listen to these recordings as they follow along in their textbooks. We are familiar with a teacher who has taught a normally achieving student to make recordings of chapters from textbooks for a peer with disabilities who is included in the regular class. The two students have developed their own schedule for making and exchanging recordings, leaving their teacher free to concentrate on other tasks.

Peer-Mediated Strategies

Peer-mediated strategies require that peers act as instructional agents for their fellow students. One example of a peer-mediated strategy is peer tutoring. Older students can tutor younger students, or students in the same class can tutor each other. The student who is acting as a tutor asks questions involving basic facts or details. The other student, the *tutee*, responds orally or in writing. If the tutee's answer is correct, the tutor provides reinforcement and proceeds to the next question. If the tutee is incorrect, the tutor provides the right answer and requires that it be written several times. Students who need extra motivation can earn points for their answers and can compete with other tutoring teams to see who has earned the most points.

Peer tutoring has been used successfully with secondary students with disabilities (Maheady, Sacca, & Harper, 1988); however, it requires careful teacher planning to maximize its effectiveness. All students will need to be taught how to ask questions, judge the accuracy of a response, record, praise, provide corrective feedback, and display materials.

Another peer-mediated strategy is cooperative learning. Cooperative learning is an organizational structure in which a small group of students collaborate to complete academic assignments and achieve academic goals. Action Plan 15.8 lists the steps involved in using cooperative learning. First, the teacher needs to develop a task or a project for the students. This task needs to be clearly explained, with any necessary directions made explicit. Second, the students need to be assigned to groups of three to five individuals. Groups should be heterogeneous; that is, teachers should mix males and females and ensure that the group represents diverse ability levels and ethnic backgrounds. Third, students may need to be taught social skills prior to implementation of

Action Plan 15.8. Cooperative Learning

To use cooperative learning in the secondary classroom, teachers should follow these steps:

1. Select a task.
2. Assign students to groups.
3. Preteach essential social skills.
4. Monitor groups while they are working.
5. Allow students to evaluate their performance.

cooperative learning. Important social skills include listening, taking turns, complimenting, and giving and receiving constructive criticism. Fourth, the teacher should monitor the group to make sure everyone is participating and working cooperatively. Finally, the teacher should provide time for students to evaluate their work.

Ellis and Sabornie (1990) suggested that cooperative learning procedures can also include the use of a pause procedure. The teacher presents content area instruction for approximately eight minutes, then cues preestablished cooperative learning groups to engage in specific discussions. For example, the teacher may tell students to talk with other group members and identify the main idea and two important details in what was just taught. The teacher allows group discussion for two minutes, then selects a student to present the group's response.

Peer-mediated strategies do more than just increase the academic skill levels of secondary students with disabilities. They also increase the frequency of interactions between students with disabilities and their normally achieving peers. These interactions provide students with more opportunities to get to know each other better and to increase their appreciation for diversity. In addition, students with disabilities are provided with more direct models of appropriate interaction skills.

Hudson and colleagues (1993) identified numerous studies supporting the efficacy of content enhancement techniques for secondary students with disabilities. However, they also discussed some concerns associated with their use. For example, they pointed out that content enhancements have been used primarily to increase student mastery of factual information rather than higher-order skills. Secondary teachers are encouraged to provide students with disabilities with the opportunity to analyze, synthesize, and apply content area information. In addition, Hudson and colleagues (1993) pointed out that some content enhancement techniques may require substantial investments of valuable teacher time. Teachers are encouraged to assess the effectiveness of the techniques they

Case for Action 15.1

You are preparing a series of lessons focusing on the Civil War. Develop several content enhancement techniques to assist your students.

use, to work cooperatively to develop these techniques, to work jointly with resource specialists and consulting teachers, and to share their efforts with other. Finally, teachers are reminded that *all* students, not just those with disabilities, can benefit from the use of content enhancement techniques.

Summary

It is likely that more secondary students with special needs will be receiving the majority of their instruction in the regular class alongside their normally achieving peers. Such inclusive placements offer students the opportunity to work with teachers who have mastered important content areas. They also allow all students, disabled and normally achieving alike, to learn to work together effectively and productively. These benefits will not be realized without careful planning of all aspects of instruction. Unfortunately, secondary educators, whether primarily involved in regular or special settings, will find only a limited number of professional resources to assist them in developing and implementing appropriate instructional practices. Resources currently available emphasize how to adapt existing practices and materials to facilitate mastery of content materials by students with disabilities. Secondary teachers are encouraged to work together to solve instructional problems and maximize student success. They are also strongly encouraged to carefully document their work and share it with their colleagues and the professional community.

References

Blough, G. O., & Schwartz, J. (1990). *Elementary school science and how to teach it* (8th ed.). Fort Worth, TX: Holt, Rinehart, & Winston.

Bureau of Curriculum Development. (1984). *Regents chemistry syllabus*. Albany, New York: State Education Department.

Bureau of Curriculum Development. (1987a). *Social studies 9 and 10: Global studies*. Albany, New York: State Education Department.

Bureau of Curriculum Development. (1987b). *Social studies 11: U.S. history and government*. Albany, New York: State Education Department.

Bureau of Curriculum Development. (1987c). *Social studies 12: Economics and economic decision making*. Albany, New York: State Education Department.

Cawley, J. F., Kahn, H., & Tedesco, A. (1989). Vocational education and students with learning disabilities. *Journal of Learning Disabilities, 22,* 630–634.

Dobkin, W. S., Fischer, J., Ludwig, B., & Koblinger, R. (1985). *A handbook for the teaching of social studies* (2nd ed.). Boston: Allyn and Bacon.

Ellis, E. S., & Sabornie, E. J. (1990). Strategy-based adaptive instruction in content-area classes: Social validity of six options. *Teacher Education and Special Education, 13,* 133–144.

Gross, R. E. , McPhie, W. E., & Fraenkel, J. R. (1969). *Teaching the social studies: What, why, and how.* Scranton, PA: International Textbook.

Horton, S. V., & Lovitt, T. C. (1989). Construction and implementation of graphic organizers for academically handicapped and regular secondary students. *Academic Therapy, 24,* 625–640.

Horton, S. V., Lovitt, T. C., Givens, A., & Nelson, R. (1989). Teaching social studies to high school students with academic handicaps in a mainstreamed setting: Effects of a computerized study guide. *Journal of Learning Disabilities, 22,* 102–107.

Hudson, P., Lignugaris Kraft, B., & Miller, T. (1993). Using content enhancements to improve the performance of adolescents with learning disabilities in content classes. *Learning Disabilities Research and Practice, 8,* 106–126.

Maheady, L., Sacca, K. C., & Harper, G. F. (1988). Classwide peer tutoring with mildly handicapped high school students. *Exceptional Children, 55,* 52–59.

Mastropieri, M. A., & Scruggs, T. E. (1988). Increasing content area learning of learning disabled students: Research implementation. *Learning Disabilities Research, 4,* 17–25.

Mastropieri, M. A., Scruggs, T. E., & Levin, J. R. (1985). Mnemonic strategy instruction with learning disabled adolescents. *Journal of Learning Disabilities, 18,* 94–100.

McKenzie, R. G. (1991). Content area instruction delivered by secondary learning disabilities teachers: A national survey. *Learning Disabilities Quarterly, 14,* 467–470.

Nagel, D. R., Schumaker, J. B., & Deshler, D. D. (1986). *The first-letter mnemonic strategy.* Lawrence, KS: Excel.

Nolet, V., & Tindal, G. (1993). Special education in content area classes: Development of a model and practical procedures. *Remedial and Special Education, 14*(1), 36–48.

Parmar, R. S., & Cawley, J. F. (1993). Analysis of science textbook recommendations provided for students with disabilities. *Exceptional Children, 59,* 518–531.

Patton, J. R., Polloway, E. A., & Cronin, M. E. (1987, May/June). Social studies instruction for handicapped students: A review of current practices. *The Social Studies,* pp. 131–135.

Roth, K. J. (1989). Science education: It's not enough to "do" or "relate." *American Educator, 13,* 16–48.

Rutherford, F. J., & Ahlgren, A. (1990). *Science for all Americans.* New York: Oxford.

Scruggs, T. E., & Mastropieri, M. A. (1993). Current approaches to science education: Implications for mainstream instruction of students with disabilities. *Remedial and Special Education, 14*(1), 15–24.

Tripp, A. (1991). The scientific method: It works. *Teaching Exceptional Children, 23*(2), 16–20.

U.S. Department of Education. (1991). *Thirteenth annual report to Congress on the implementation of the Education of Handicapped Act.* Washington, DC: U.S. Government Printing Office.

Wesley, E. B., & Wronski, S. P. (1973). *Teaching secondary social studies in a world society* (6th ed.). Lexington, MA: D. C. Heath.

Author Index

Subject Index